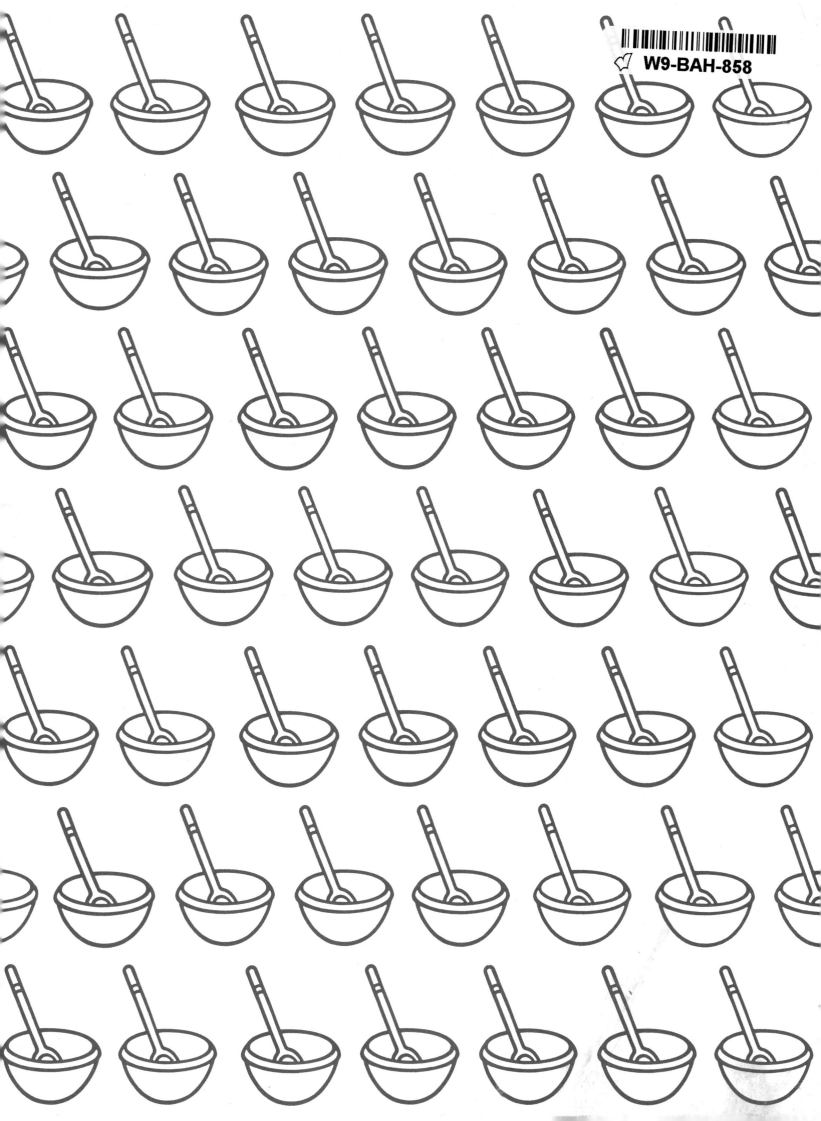

—500—
ALL-TIME
GREAT
RECIPES

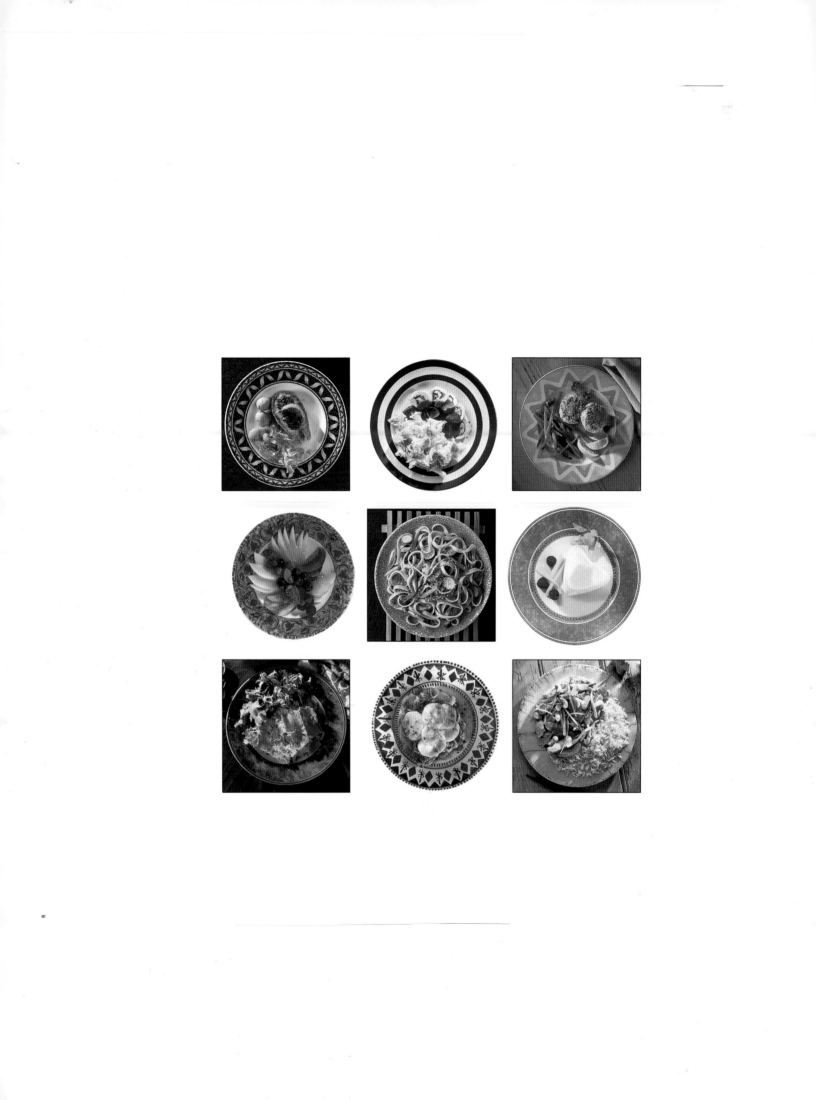

500
ALL-TIME
GREAT
RECIPES

SMITHMARK

© Anness Publishing Limited 1996

This edition published in 1996
by SMITHMARK Publishers, a division of US Media Holdings, Inc.
16 East 32nd Street
New York
NY 10016

SMITHMARK Books are available for bulk purchase
for sales promotion and for premium use. For details write or call the
Manager of Special Sales, SMITHMARK Publishers,
16 East 32nd Street, New York, NY 10016; (212) 532-6600

Produced by Anness Publishing Limited
1 Boundary Row
London SE1 8HP

ISBN 0 7651-9954-8

Publisher: Joanna Lorenz
Managing Editor: Linda Fraser
Designer: Siân Keogh
Photographers: Karl Adamson, Edward Allwright, Steve Baxter, James
Duncan, Michelle Garrett, Amanda Heywood, Don Last, Patrick
McLeavy, Michael Michaels
Additional photography: Sopexa UK
Recipes: Carla Capalbo, Maxine Clark, Frances Cleary, Carole Clements,
Roz Denny, Christine France, Sarah Gates, Shirley Gill, Rosamund Grant,
Sue Maggs, Annie Nichols, Jenny Stacey, Liz Trigg, Hilaire Walden,
Laura Washburn, Steven Wheeler, Elizabeth Wolf-Cohen
Food for Photography: Joanne Craig, Wendy Lee, Jenny Shapter, Jane
Stevenson, Elizabeth Wolf-Cohen
Home Economists: Carla Capalbo, Jenny Shapter
Stylists: Madeleine Brehaut, Carla Capalbo, Michelle Garrett, Hilary Guy,
Amanda Heywood, Blake Minton, Kirsty Rawlings, Rebecca Sturrock,
Fiona Tillett

Printed and bound in China

CONTENTS

Soups *8*

Appetizers *24*

Fish and Seafood *40*

Poultry and Game *70*

Meat *98*

Vegetarian Dishes *126*

Pasta, Pizza and Grains *146*

Vegetables and Salads *178*

Hot Desserts *210*

Cold Desserts *230*

Index *254*

Introduction

In the modern world's quest for innovation and new taste sensations, it's often easy to forget just how delicious and fulfilling a classic recipe can be. This volume contains a definitive selection of best-ever recipes which will serve as an essential reference point for beginners and as a timely reminder to the experienced cook when planning the perfect meal.

These cosmopolitan creations have gained world-wide status through their harmonious balance of fresh ingredients, herbs and spices. Stemming from justified popularity in their homelands, they have attained universal appeal as part of the international chef's repertoire. Even more appealing is the fact that many traditional recipes are based on a natural nutritional equilibrium which was taken for granted before the days of "fast food" and a high intake of saturated fats. Many of these dishes excel when analyzed in the light of today's vogue for healthy eating. Others are unashamedly sinful (chocoholics, beware!).

The dishes presented in this book are tailored to every season and every event: you can mix and match cooking styles and influences to suit the mood and the occasion, not to mention your pocket. There is a fine selection of hearty soups such as Red Pepper Soup with Lime, which are satisfying enough for a light meal yet attractive enough to serve as an impressive dinner party appetizer. Sophisticated appetizers include Smoked Salmon and Dill Blinis or Chicken Liver Pâté with Marsala, Avocados with Tangy Topping or Pears and Stilton.

Fish and shellfish are increasingly popular in today's health-conscious society. Flavorful taste sensations such as Smoked Trout with Cucumber or Grilled Fresh Sardines are classic dishes

that will always provide a light, fresh main course to tantalize your tastebuds.

Present directions in menu planning may point away from a truly carnivorous way of life, yet there are many occasions when a mouth-watering meat course will win the day. This volume will arm you with the confidence and conviction needed to present a perfect Roast Beef with Yorkshire Pudding or a melting Cottage Pie. Also included is a variety of more unusual dishes such as Duck with Chestnut Sauce, a simple yet impressive dinner party presentation, and economical yet nutritious main courses that will appeal to adults and children alike, such as Sausage and Bean Ragoût. Whether we choose western fare such as Tuna Fishcake Bites or an exotic Kashmir Coconut Fish Curry, these recipes are characterized by a distinctive depth of flavor created by a judicious blend of herbs and spices.

The vegetable dishes in this book are mouth-watering concoctions that can be prepared at short notice for an accompaniment or for a complete, well-balanced meal. Some are long-standing favorites of vegetarian fare, such as Chick-pea Stew; others are innovative versions of world-famous dishes, such as a Chunky Vegetable Paella which combines a colorful appearance with satisfying texture and harmonious flavors.

To finish, the moment that many have been waiting for: the dessert course. These dishes range from light, fluffy mousses and cool, super-smooth sherbets to the richest trifles, and dream puddings made from fruit, cream and chocolate.

This collection of recipes has been drawn together from the combined talents of some of the world's most respected cooks and food writers. With the help of this authoritative guide, your cooking will not only withstand the scrutiny of your most demanding critic – be it yourself or a fierce rival – but will win them over in style.

Carrot and Cilantro Soup

Use a good homemade stock for this soup – it adds a far greater depth of flavor than stock made from cubes.

Serves 4

4 tablespoons butter
2 leeks, sliced
1 pound carrots, sliced
1 tablespoon ground coriander
5 cups chicken stock

⅔ cup strained plain yogurt
salt and ground black pepper
2–3 tablespoons chopped fresh cilantro, to garnish

1 Melt the butter in a large saucepan. Add the leeks and carrots and stir well, coating the vegetables with the butter. Cover with a tight-fitting lid and cook for about 10 minutes, until the vegetables are beginning to soften but not color.

2 Stir in the ground coriander and cook for about 1 minute. Pour in the stock and season to taste with salt and pepper. Bring to a boil, cover and simmer for about 20 minutes, until the leeks and carrots are tender.

3 Leave to cool slightly, then purée the soup in a blender until smooth. Return the soup to the pan and add about 2 tablespoons of the yogurt, then taste the soup and adjust the seasoning again to taste. Reheat gently but do not boil.

4 Ladle the soup into bowls and put a spoonful of the remaining yogurt in the center of each. Scatter over the cilantro and serve immediately.

Leek, Potato and Arugula Soup

Arugula, with its distinctive peppery taste, is wonderful in this filling soup. Serve it hot with ciabatta croûtons.

Serves 4–6

4 tablespoons butter
1 onion, chopped
3 leeks, chopped
2 potatoes, diced
3¾ cups light chicken stock

2 large handfuls arugula, coarsely chopped
⅔ cup heavy cream
salt and ground black pepper
garlic-flavored ciabatta croûtons, to serve

1 Melt the butter in a large heavy-based saucepan, add the onion, leeks and potatoes and stir until all the vegetable pieces are coated in butter.

2 Cover with a tight-fitting lid and leave the vegetables to sweat for about 15 minutes. Pour in the stock, cover once again with the lid, then simmer for another 20 minutes, until the vegetables are tender.

3 Press the soup through a strainer and return to the rinsed-out pan. (When puréeing the soup, don't use a blender or food processor, as these will give the soup a gluey texture.) Add the chopped arugula, stir in and cook gently for about 5 minutes.

4 Stir in the cream, then season to taste with salt and pepper. Reheat gently. Ladle the soup into warmed soup bowls, then serve with a few ciabatta croûtons in each.

Cook's Tip
To make the croûtons, cut the bread into ½ inch cubes, without the crust if you wish, and either fry or bake in a roasting pan in oil until golden and crunchy.

Tomato and Basil Soup

In the summer, when tomatoes are both plentiful and cheap to buy, this is a lovely soup to make.

Serves 4

2 tablespoons olive oil	1 oregano sprig
1 onion, chopped	4 fresh basil leaves,
½ teaspoon sugar	coarsely torn
1 carrot, finely chopped	1¼ cups light chicken or
1 potato, finely chopped	vegetable stock
1 garlic clove, crushed	2–3 pieces sun-dried
1½ pounds ripe tomatoes,	tomatoes in oil
coarsely chopped	2 tablespoons shredded
1 teaspoon tomato paste	fresh basil leaves
1 bay leaf	salt and ground black
1 thyme sprig	pepper

1 Heat the oil in a large saucepan, add the onion and sprinkle with the sugar. Cook gently for 5 minutes.

2 Add the chopped carrot and potato, cover the pan and cook over a low heat for another 10 minutes, without browning the vegetables.

3 Stir in the garlic, tomatoes, tomato paste, herbs and stock, and season to taste with salt and pepper. Cover the pan with a tight-fitting lid and cook gently for about 25–30 minutes, or until the vegetables are tender.

4 Remove the pan from the heat and press the soup through a strainer to extract all the skins and pits. Season again with salt and pepper to taste.

5 Reheat the soup gently, then ladle into four warmed soup bowls. Finely chop the sun-dried tomatoes and mix with a little oil from the jar. Add a spoonful to each serving, then scatter the shredded basil over the top.

Corn and Shellfish Chowder

Chowder comes from the French word *chaudron*, meaning a large pot in which the soup is cooked.

Serves 4

2 tablespoons butter	6-ounce can white
1 small onion, chopped	crabmeat, drained and
12-ounce can corn,	flaked
drained	⅔ cup light cream
2½ cups milk	pinch of cayenne pepper
2 scallions, finely	salt and ground black
chopped	pepper
1 cup peeled, cooked	4 whole shrimp in the
shrimp	shell, to garnish

1 Melt the butter in a large saucepan and gently fry the onion for 4–5 minutes, until softened.

2 Reserve 2 tablespoons of the corn for the garnish and add the rest to the pan, along with the milk. Bring the soup to a boil, then reduce the heat, cover the pan with a tight-fitting lid and simmer over a low heat for 5 minutes.

3 Pour the soup, in batches if necessary, into a blender or food processor. Process until smooth.

4 Return the soup to the pan and stir in the scallions, crabmeat, shrimp, cream and cayenne pepper. Reheat gently over a low heat.

5 Meanwhile, place the reserved corn kernels in a small frying pan without oil and dry-fry over a moderate heat until golden and toasted.

6 Season to taste with salt and pepper and serve each bowl of soup garnished with a few of the toasted corn kernels and a whole shrimp.

Spiced Parsnip Soup

This pale, creamy-textured soup is given a special touch with an aromatic garlic and mustard seed garnish.

Serves 4–6

3 tablespoons butter
1 onion, chopped
1½ pounds parsnips, diced
1 teaspoon ground coriander
½ teaspoon ground cumin
½ teaspoon ground turmeric
¼ teaspoon chili powder
5 cups chicken stock
⅔ cup light cream
1 tablespoon sunflower oil
1 garlic clove, cut into julienne strips
2 teaspoons yellow mustard seeds
salt and ground black pepper

1 Melt the butter in a large saucepan and fry the onion and parsnips gently for about 3 minutes.

2 Stir in the spices and cook for 1 minute more. Add the stock, season to taste with salt and pepper and bring to a boil, then reduce the heat. Cover with a tight-fitting lid and simmer for about 45 minutes, until the parsnips are tender.

3 Cool slightly, then place in a blender and purée until smooth. Return the soup to the pan, add the cream and heat through gently over a low heat.

4 Heat the oil in a small pan, add the julienne strips of garlic and yellow mustard seeds and fry quickly until the garlic is beginning to brown and the mustard seeds start to pop and splutter. Remove the pan from the heat.

5 Ladle the soup into warmed soup bowls and pour a little of the hot spice mixture over each. Serve immediately.

Cook's Tip
Crushed coriander seeds may be substituted for the mustard seeds in the garnish.

Pumpkin Soup

The flavor of this soup will develop and improve if it is made a day in advance.

Serves 4–6

2-pound pumpkin
3 tablespoons olive oil
2 onions, chopped
2 celery stalks, chopped
1 pound tomatoes, chopped
6¼ cups vegetable stock
2 tablespoons tomato paste
1 bouquet garni
2–3 strips lean bacon, crisply fried and crumbled
2 tablespoons chopped fresh parsley
salt and ground black pepper

1 With a sharp knife cut the pumpkin into thin slices, discarding the skin and seeds.

2 Heat the oil in a large saucepan and fry the onions and celery for about 5 minutes. Add the pumpkin and tomatoes and cook for another 5 minutes.

3 Add the vegetable stock, tomato paste and bouquet garni to the pan. Season with salt and pepper. Bring the soup to a boil, then reduce the heat, cover and simmer for 45 minutes.

4 Allow the soup to cool slightly, remove the bouquet garni, then purée (in two batches, if necessary) in a food processor or blender.

5 Press the soup through a strainer, then return it to the pan. Reheat gently and season again. Ladle the soup into warmed soup bowls. Sprinkle with the crispy bacon and parsley and serve immediately.

Jerusalem Artichoke Soup

Topped with saffron cream, this soup is wonderful to serve on a chilly winter's day.

Serves 4

4 tablespoons butter
1 onion, chopped
1 pound Jerusalem artichokes, peeled and cut into chunks
3¾ cups chicken stock
⅔ cup milk

⅔ cup heavy cream
large pinch of saffron powder
salt and ground black pepper
chopped fresh chives, to garnish

1 Melt the butter in a large heavy-based saucepan and cook the onion for 5–8 minutes, until soft but not browned, stirring occasionally.

2 Add the artichokes to the pan and stir until coated in the butter. Cover with a tight-fitting lid and cook gently for 10–15 minutes; do not allow the artichokes to brown. Pour in the stock and milk, then cover again and simmer for about 15 minutes. Cool slightly, then process in a food processor or blender until smooth.

3 Strain the soup back into the pan. Add half the cream, season to taste with salt and pepper, and reheat gently. Lightly whip the remaining cream and saffron powder. Ladle the soup into warmed soup bowls and put a spoonful of saffron cream in the center of each. Scatter over the chopped chives and serve immediately.

Broccoli and Stilton Soup

A really easy, but rich, soup – choose something simple to follow, such as plainly broiled meat, poultry or fish.

Serves 4

3 cups broccoli florets
2 tablespoons butter
1 onion, chopped
1 leek, white part only, chopped
1 small potato, diced
2½ cups hot chicken stock
1¼ cups milk

3 tablespoons heavy cream
4 ounces Stilton cheese, rind removed, crumbled
salt and ground black pepper

1 Discard any tough stems from the broccoli florets. Set aside two small florets for the garnish.

2 Melt the butter in a large saucepan and cook the onion and leek until soft but not colored. Add the broccoli and potato, then pour in the stock. Cover with a tight-fitting lid and simmer for 15–20 minutes, until the vegetables are tender.

3 Cool slightly, then purée in a food processor or blender. Strain through a sieve back into the pan.

4 Add the milk, cream and seasoning to the pan and reheat gently. At the last minute add the cheese, stirring until it just melts. Do not boil.

5 Meanwhile, blanch the reserved broccoli florets and cut them vertically into thin slices. Ladle the soup into warmed bowls and garnish with the broccoli florets and a generous grinding of black pepper.

Cook's Tip
Be very careful not to boil the soup once the cheese has been added.

Minestrone with Pesto

This hearty, Italian mixed vegetable soup is a great way to use up any leftover vegetables you may have.

Serves 4

2 tablespoons olive oil
2 garlic cloves, crushed
1 onion, sliced
2 cups diced lean bacon
2 small zucchini, quartered and sliced
1½ cups green beans, chopped
2 small carrots, diced
2 celery stalks, finely chopped
bouquet garni
½ cup short cut macaroni
½ cup frozen peas
7-ounce can red kidney beans, drained and rinsed

1 cup shredded green cabbage
4 tomatoes, skinned and seeded
salt and ground black pepper

For the toasts

8 slices French bread
1 tablespoon ready-made pesto sauce
1 tablespoons grated Parmesan cheese

1 Heat the oil in a large saucepan and gently fry the garlic and onions for 5 minutes, until just softened. Add the bacon, zucchini, green beans, carrots and celery to the pan and stir-fry for another 3 minutes.

2 Pour 5 cups of cold water over the vegetables and add the bouquet garni. Cover the pan with a tight-fitting lid and simmer for 25 minutes.

3 Add the macaroni, peas and kidney beans and cook for 8 minutes more. Then add the cabbage and tomatoes and cook for an additional 5 minutes.

4 To make the toasts, spread the bread slices with the pesto, sprinkle a little Parmesan over each one and gently brown under a hot broiler. Remove the bouquet garni from the soup, season to taste and serve with the toasts.

French Onion Soup

Onion soup comes in many different guises, from smooth and creamy to this – the absolute classic from France.

Serves 4

2 tablespoons butter
1 tablespoon oil
3 large onions, thinly sliced
1 teaspoon brown sugar
1 tablespoon all-purpose flour
2 x 10-ounce cans condensed beef consommé
2 tablespoons medium sherry
2 teaspoons

Worcestershire sauce
8 slices French bread
1 tablespoon French coarse-grained mustard
1 cup grated Gruyère cheese
salt and ground black pepper
1 tablespoon chopped fresh parsley, to garnish

1 Heat the butter and oil in a large saucepan and cook the onions and brown sugar gently for about 20 minutes, stirring occasionally until the onions start to turn golden brown.

2 Stir in the flour and cook for another 2 minutes. Pour in the consommé plus two cans of water, then add the sherry and Worcestershire sauce. Season with salt and pepper, cover and simmer gently for another 25–30 minutes.

3 Preheat the broiler and just before serving, toast the bread lightly on both sides. Spread one side of each slice with the mustard and top with the grated cheese. Broil the toasts until bubbling and golden.

4 Ladle the soup into bowls. Pop two croutons on top of each bowl of soup and garnish with chopped fresh parsley. Serve immediately.

Curried Parsnip Soup

The mixture of spices in this soup impart a delicious, mild flavor to the parsnips.

Serves 4

2 tablespoons butter
1 garlic clove, crushed
1 onion, chopped
1 teaspoon ground cumin
1 teaspoon ground cilantro
1 pound (about 4) parsnips, sliced
2 teaspoons medium curry paste
scant 2 cups chicken or vegetable stock

scant 2 cups milk
4 tablespoons sour cream
good squeeze of lemon juice
salt and ground black pepper
fresh cilantro sprigs, to garnish
ready-made garlic and cilantro nan bread, to serve

1 Heat the butter in a large saucepan and fry the garlic and onion for 4–5 minutes, until lightly golden. Stir in the spices and cook for another 1–2 minutes.

2 Add the parsnips and stir until well coated with the butter, then stir in the curry paste, followed by the stock. Cover the pan with a tight-fitting lid and simmer for 15 minutes, until the parsnips are tender.

3 Ladle the soup into a blender or food processor and blend until smooth. Return to the pan and stir in the milk. Heat gently for 2–3 minutes, then add 2 tablespoons of the sour cream and the lemon juice. Season well with salt and pepper.

4 Serve in bowls topped with spoonfuls of the remaining sour cream and the fresh cilantro accompanied by the warmed, spicy nan bread.

Cook's Tip
For the best flavor, use homemade chicken or vegetable stock in this soup.

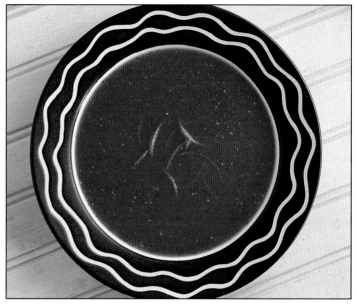

Red Pepper Soup with Lime

The beautiful rich red color of this soup makes it a very attractive appetizer or light lunch.

Serves 4–6

4 fresh red bell peppers, seeded and chopped
1 large onion, chopped
1 teaspoon olive oil
1 garlic clove, crushed
1 small red chili, sliced
3 tablespoons tomato paste

juice and finely grated rind of 1 lime
3¼ cups chicken stock
salt and ground black pepper
shreds of lime rind, to garnish

1 Cook the onion and peppers gently in the oil in a saucepan covered with a tight-fitting lid for about 5 minutes, shaking the pan occasionally, until softened.

2 Stir in the garlic, then add the chili with the tomato paste. Stir in half the stock, then bring to the boil. Cover the pan and simmer for 10 minutes.

3 Cool slightly, then purée in a food processor or blender. Return to the pan, then add the remaining stock, the lime rind and juice and seasoning.

4 Bring the soup back to a boil, then serve immediately with a few shreds of lime rind scattered into each bowl.

Thai-style Corn Soup

This is a very quick and easy soup. If you are using frozen shrimp, defrost them before adding to the soup.

Serves 4

½ teaspoon sesame or
   sunflower oil
2 scallions, thinly sliced
1 garlic clove, crushed
2½ cups chicken stock
15-ounce can cream-style
   corn
2 cups peeled, cooked
   shrimp

1 teaspoon green chili
   paste or chili sauce
   (optional)
salt and ground black
   pepper
fresh cilantro leaves, to
   garnish

Heat the oil in a large heavy-based saucepan and sauté the onions and garlic over a moderate heat for 1 minute, until softened but not browned. Stir in the chicken stock, cream-style corn, shrimp and chili paste or sauce, if using. Bring the soup to a boil, stirring occasionally. Season to taste with salt and pepper, then serve immediately, sprinkled with fresh cilantro leaves to garnish.

Haddock and Broccoli Chowder

This hearty soup makes a meal in itself when served with crusty, country-style bread.

Serves 4

4 scallions, sliced
1 pound new potatoes,
   diced
1¼ cups homemade fish
   stock, or water
1¼ cups skim milk
1 bay leaf
2 cups broccoli florets,
   sliced

1 pound smoked haddock
   fillets, skinned
7-ounce can corn,
   drained
ground black pepper
chopped scallions, to
   garnish

Place the scallions and potatoes in a pan and add the stock, milk and bay leaf. Bring to a boil, reduce the heat, cover and simmer for 10 minutes. Add the broccoli. Cut the fish into bite-size chunks; add to the pan with the corn. Season well with black pepper, then cover again and simmer until the fish is cooked through. Remove the bay leaf, scatter over the chopped scallions and serve immediately.

Cock-a-leekie Soup

This hearty main course soup is given a sweet touch by the inclusion of prunes.

Serves 4–6

Gently cook 2 chicken portions, 5 cups chicken stock and a bouquet garni for 40 minutes. Cut 4 leeks into 1 inch slices, add to the pan along with 8–12 soaked prunes and cook gently for 20 minutes. Discard the bouquet garni. Remove the chicken, discard the skin and bones and chop the flesh. Return the chicken to the pan and season to taste. Heat the soup, then serve with soft, buttered rolls.

Green Pea and Mint Soup

This soup is equally delicious lightly chilled. Stir in the swirl of cream just before serving.

Serves 4

4 tablespoons butter	2½ cups milk
4 scallions, chopped	pinch of sugar (optional)
4 cups fresh or frozen peas	salt and ground black pepper
2½ cups chicken or vegetable stock	light cream, to serve small fresh mint sprigs, to garnish
2 large fresh mint sprigs	

1 Heat the butter in a large saucepan and gently fry the scallions until just softened but not colored.

2 Stir the peas into the pan, add the stock and mint and bring to a boil. Cover and simmer very gently for about 30 minutes for fresh peas or 15 minutes if you are using frozen peas, until the peas are very tender. Remove about 3 tablespoons of the peas using a slotted spoon, and reserve for the garnish.

3 Pour the soup into a food processor or blender, add the milk and purée until smooth. Then return the soup to the pan and reheat gently. Season to taste with salt and pepper, adding a pinch of sugar if you wish.

4 Pour the soup into bowls. Swirl a little cream into each, then garnish with mint and the reserved peas.

Cook's Tip
Fresh peas are increasingly available during the summer months from grocers and supermarkets. The effort of podding them is well worthwhile, as they impart a unique flavor to this delicious, vibrant soup.

Beet and Apricot Swirl

This soup is most attractive if you swirl together the two colored purées, but mix them together if you prefer.

Serves 4

4 large cooked beets, coarsely chopped	⁷⁄₈ cup ready-to-eat dried apricots
1 small onion, coarsely chopped	1 cup orange juice salt and ground black pepper
2½ cups chicken stock	

1 Place the beets and half of the onion in a saucepan with the stock. Bring to a boil, then reduce the heat, cover with a tight-fitting lid and simmer for about 10 minutes. Purée in a food processor or blender.

2 Place the rest of the onion in a pan with the apricots and orange juice, cover and simmer gently for about 15 minutes until tender. Purée in a food processor or blender.

3 Return the two mixtures to the saucepans and reheat. Season to taste with salt and pepper, then swirl the mixtures together in individual soup bowls to create a marbled effect.

Cook's Tip
Beets are available ready cooked. To cook your own, simply place in a saucepan with enough water to cover, bring to a boil, then cover and cook for 1 hour. Drain, then peel the beets with your fingers when cool enough to handle.

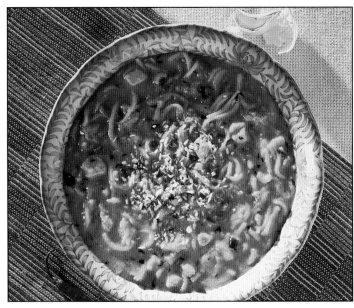

Thai-style Chicken Soup

Omit the red chili from the garnish if you prefer a milder flavor in this soup.

Serves 4

1 tablespoon vegetable oil	peanut butter
1 garlic clove, finely chopped	1 cup thread egg noodles, broken into small pieces
2 x 6-ounce boned chicken breasts, skinned and chopped	1 tablespoon scallions, finely chopped
½ teaspoon ground turmeric	1 tablespoon chopped fresh cilantro
¼ teaspoon hot chili powder	salt and ground black pepper
3 ounces creamed coconut	2 tablespoons dried coconut and ½ red chili, seeded and finely chopped, to garnish
3¾ cups hot chicken stock	
2 tablespoons lemon or lime juice	
2 tablespoons crunchy	

1 Heat the oil in a large saucepan and fry the garlic for 1 minute until lightly golden. Add the chicken and spices and stir-fry for another 3–4 minutes. Crumble the creamed coconut into the stock and stir until dissolved. Pour onto the chicken and add the lemon juice, peanut butter and egg noodles. Cover and simmer for 15 minutes. Add the scallions and cilantro, season to taste with salt and pepper and cook for another 5 minutes.

2 Fry the coconut and chili for 2–3 minutes, stirring until the coconut is lightly browned. Use as a garnish for the soup.

New England Pumpkin Soup

For a smooth-textured soup, process all the mixture in a food processor or blender.

Serves 4

2 tablespoons butter	1 teaspoon brown sugar
1 onion, finely chopped	
1 garlic clove, crushed	**For the croutons**
1 tablespoon all-purpose flour	1 tablespoon vegetable oil
pinch of grated nutmeg	2 slices granary bread, without the crusts
½ teaspoon ground cinnamon	2 tablespoons sunflower seeds
2¼ cups pumpkin, seeded, peeled and diced	salt and ground black pepper
2½ cups chicken stock	
⅔ cup orange juice	

1 Melt the butter in a large saucepan and gently fry the onions and garlic for 4–5 minutes, until softened.

2 Stir in the flour, spices and pumpkin, then cover and cook gently for 6 minutes, stirring occasionally.

3 Add the chicken stock, orange juice and brown sugar. Cover again, and bring to a boil, then simmer for 20 minutes until the pumpkin has softened.

4 Process half the mixture in a blender or food processor. Return the soup to the pan with the remaining chunky mixture, stirring constantly. Season to taste and heat through.

5 To make the croutons, heat the oil in a frying pan, cut the bread into cubes and gently fry until just beginning to brown. Add the sunflower seeds and fry for 1–2 minutes. Drain the croutons on paper towels. Serve the soup hot, garnished with a few of the croutons scattered over the top, and serve the remaining croutons separately.

Split Pea and Zucchini Soup

Rich and satisfying, this tasty and nutritious soup is ideal to serve on a chilly winter's day.

Serves 4
1 cup yellow split peas
1 teaspoon sunflower oil
1 large onion, finely
   chopped
2 zucchini, finely diced
3¾ cups chicken stock
½ teaspoon ground
   turmeric
salt and ground black
   pepper

1 Place the split peas in a bowl, cover with cold water and let soak for several hours or overnight. Drain, rinse in cold water and drain again.

2 Heat the oil in a saucepan. Add the onion, cover with a tight-fitting lid and cook until soft. Reserve a handful of diced zucchini and add the rest to the pan. Cook, stirring constantly, for 2–3 minutes.

3 Add the stock and turmeric to the pan and bring to a boil. Reduce the heat, then cover and simmer for about 30–40 minutes, or until the split peas are tender. Add seasoning to taste.

4 When the soup is almost ready, bring a large saucepan of water to a boil, add the reserved diced zucchini and cook for 1 minute, then drain and add to the soup before serving hot with warm crusty bread.

Cook's Tip
For a quicker alternative, use split red lentils for this soup. They do not require presoaking and cook very quickly. Adjust the amount of chicken stock used, if you need to.

Mediterranean Tomato Soup

Children will love this soup – especially if you use fancy pasta such as alphabet or animal shapes.

Serves 4
1½ pounds ripe plum
   tomatoes
1 onion, quartered
1 celery stalk
1 garlic clove
1 tablespoon olive oil
scant 2 cups chicken
   stock
2 tablespoons tomato
   paste
½ cup small pasta shapes
salt and ground black
   pepper
fresh cilantro or parsley
   sprigs, to garnish

1 Place the tomatoes, onion, celery and garlic in a saucepan with the oil. Cover with a tight-fitting lid and cook over a gentle heat for 40–45 minutes, shaking the pan occasionally, until the vegetables become very soft.

2 Spoon the vegetables into a food processor or blender and process until smooth. Press through a sieve to remove the tomato seeds, then return to the pan.

3 Stir in the stock and tomato paste and bring to a boil. Add the pasta and simmer gently for about 8 minutes, or until the pasta is tender. Add salt and pepper to taste, then sprinkle with cilantro or parsley to garnish and serve hot.

White Bean Soup

Small white lima beans or pinto beans work well in this soup, or try great northern beans for a change.

Serves 6

1½ cups dried navy or
    other white beans
1 bay leaf
5 tablespoons olive oil
1 onion, finely chopped
1 carrot, finely chopped
1 celery stalk, finely
    chopped
3 tomatoes, peeled and
    finely chopped

2 garlic cloves, finely
    chopped
1 teaspoon fresh thyme
    leaves or ½ teaspoon
    dried thyme
3⅔ cups boiling water
salt and ground black
    pepper
extra virgin olive oil, to
    serve

1 Pick over the beans carefully, discarding any stones or other particles. Soak the beans in a large bowl of cold water overnight. Drain. Place the beans in a large saucepan of water, bring to a boil, and cook for 20 minutes. Drain. Return the beans to the pan, cover with cold water, and bring to a boil again. Add the bay leaf, and cook 1–2 hours until the beans are tender. Drain again. Remove the bay leaf.

2 Purée about three-quarters of the beans in a food processor or blender. Alternatively, pass through a strainer, adding a little water if needed.

3 Heat the oil in a large saucepan and cook the onion until softened but not browned. Add the carrot and celery, and cook for another 5 minutes.

4 Stir in the tomatoes, garlic and fresh or dried thyme. Cook for 6–8 minutes more, stirring often.

5 Pour in the boiling water. Stir in the beans and the bean purée. Season to taste with salt and pepper. Simmer for about 10–15 minutes. Serve in individual soup bowls, sprinkled with a little extra virgin olive oil.

Fish Soup

For extra flavor use some smoked fish in this soup and rub the bread with a garlic clove before toasting.

Serves 6

2¼ pounds mixed fish
    fillets such as dogfish,
    whiting, red mullet or
    cod
6 tablespoons olive oil,
    plus extra to serve
1 onion, finely chopped
1 celery stalk, chopped
1 carrot, chopped
4 tablespoons chopped
    fresh parsley

¾ cup dry white wine
3 tomatoes, peeled and
    chopped
2 garlic cloves, finely
    chopped
6¼ cups boiling water
salt and ground black
    pepper
French bread, to serve

1 Cut all the fish fillets into large pieces. Rinse well in cool water.

2 Heat the oil in a large saucepan and cook the onion over a low to moderate heat until just softened. Stir in the celery and carrot and cook for 5 minutes more. Add the parsley.

3 Pour in the wine, raise the heat and cook until it reduces by about half. Stir in the tomatoes and garlic. Cook for 3–4 minutes, stirring occasionally. Pour in the boiling water and bring back to a boil. Cook for 15 minutes.

4 Stir in the fish and simmer for 10–15 minutes, or until the fish is tender. Season to taste with salt and pepper.

5 Remove the fish from the soup with a slotted spoon. Discard any bones. Place in a food processor and purée until smooth. Taste again for seasoning. If the soup is too thick, add a little more water.

6 To serve, heat the soup to simmering. Toast the rounds of bread and sprinkle with olive oil. Place two or three in each soup plate before pouring over the soup.

Barley and Vegetable Soup

This soup comes from the Alto Adige region, in Italy's mountainous north. It is thick, nourishing and warming.

Serves 6–8

1 cup pot barley, or peas	1 bay leaf
9 cups meat stock or water, or a combination of both	3 tablespoons chopped fresh parsley
3 tablespoons olive oil	1 small fresh rosemary sprig
2 carrots, finely chopped	salt and ground black pepper
2 celery stalks, finely chopped	freshly grated Parmesan cheese, to serve (optional)
1 leek, thinly sliced	
1 large potato, finely chopped	
½ cup diced ham	

1 Pick over the barley and discard any stones or other particles. Wash the barley in cold water and soak it in cold water for at least 3 hours.

2 Drain the barley and place it in a large saucepan with the stock or water. Bring to a boil, lower the heat and simmer for 1 hour. Skim off any scum.

3 Stir in the oil, all the vegetables and the ham. Add the herbs. If necessary add more water; the ingredients should be covered by at least 1 inch. Simmer for 1–1½ hours, or until the vegetables and barley are very tender.

4 Season to taste with salt and pepper. Serve hot with grated Parmesan cheese, if desired.

Pasta and Dried Bean Soup

In Italy this soup is made with dried or fresh beans and served hot or at room temperature.

Serves 4–6

1¼ cups dried borlotti or navy beans	3½ cups water
14-ounce can plum tomatoes, chopped, with their juice	2 teaspoons salt
	scant 2 cups ditalini or other small pasta
3 garlic cloves, crushed	3 tablespoons chopped fresh parsley
2 bay leaves	freshly grated Parmesan cheese, to serve
coarsely ground black pepper	
6 tablespoons olive oil, plus extra to serve	

1 Soak the beans in water overnight. Rinse and drain well. Place them in a large saucepan and cover with water. Bring to a boil and cook for 10 minutes. Rinse and drain again.

2 Return the beans to the pan. Add enough water to cover them by 1 inch. Stir in the coarsely chopped tomatoes with their juice, the garlic, bay leaves, black pepper and the oil. Simmer for 1½–2 hours, or until the beans are tender. Add more water if necessary.

3 Remove the bay leaves. Pass about half of the bean mixture through a strainer, or purée in a food processor. Stir into the pan with the remaining bean mixture. Add the water and bring the soup to a boil.

4 Add the salt and the pasta. Stir, then cook until the pasta is just done. Stir in the parsley. Allow the dish to stand for at least 10 minutes, then serve with extra olive oil and grated Parmesan cheese.

Pasta and Lentil Soup

Small brown lentils are usually used in this wholesome soup, but green lentils may be substituted.

Serves 4–6

1 cup dried green or brown lentils
6 tablespoons olive oil
¼ cup ham or salt pork, finely diced
1 onion, finely chopped
1 celery stalk, finely chopped
1 carrot, finely chopped

9 cups chicken stock or water
1 fresh sage leaf
1 fresh thyme sprig or ¼ tsp dried thyme
salt and ground black pepper
2½ cups ditalini or other small soup pasta

1 Carefully check the lentils for small stones. Place them in a bowl, cover with cold water and soak for 2–3 hours. Rinse and drain well through a strainer.

2 Heat the oil in a large saucepan and sauté the ham or salt pork for 2–3 minutes. Add the onion and cook gently until it softens but does not brown.

3 Stir in the celery and carrot and cook for 5 minutes more, stirring frequently. Add the lentils and stir to coat them evenly in the cooking fats.

4 Pour in the stock or water, add the herbs and bring the soup to a boil. Cook over a moderate heat for about 1 hour or until the lentils are tender. Season to taste.

5 Stir in the pasta, and cook until it is just done. Allow the soup to stand for a few minutes before serving.

Pasta and Chick-pea Soup

The addition of a fresh rosemary sprig creates a typically Mediterranean flavor in this soup.

Serves 4–6

generous 1 cup dried chick-peas
3 garlic cloves, peeled
1 bay leaf
6 tablespoons olive oil
pinch of ground black pepper
¼ cup diced salt pork, pancetta or bacon

1 fresh rosemary sprig
2½ cups water
generous 1 cup ditalini or other short hollow pasta
pinch of salt
freshly grated Parmesan cheese, to serve (optional)

1 Soak the chick-peas in water overnight. Rinse well and drain. Place in a large saucepan with water to cover. Boil for 15 minutes. Rinse and drain.

2 Return the chick-peas to the pan. Add water to cover, one garlic clove, the bay leaf, 3 tablespoons of the oil and the pinch of pepper.

3 Simmer for about 2 hours until tender, adding more water as necessary. Remove the bay leaf. Pass about half the chick-peas through a strainer or purée in a food processor with a little cooking liquid. Return the purée to the pan with the rest of the chick-peas and the remaining cooking water.

4 Sauté the diced pork, pancetta or bacon gently in the remaining oil with the rosemary and two garlic cloves until just golden. Discard the rosemary and garlic.

5 Stir the meat with its oils into the chick-pea mixture.

6 Add 2½ cups of water to the chick-peas, and bring to a boil. Add the pinch of salt if necessary. Stir in the pasta, and cook until just *al dente*. Serve with Parmesan cheese, if you wish.

Leek and Potato Soup

Scotch Broth

If you prefer a smoother textured soup, press the mixture through a strainer.

Sustaining and warming, this traditional Scottish soup makes a delicious winter soup anywhere in the world.

Serves 4
4 tablespoons butter
2 leeks, chopped
1 small onion, finely
   chopped
12 ounces potatoes,
   chopped

3¾ cups chicken or
   vegetable stock
salt and ground black
   pepper

1 Heat 2 tablespoons of the butter in a large saucepan and gently cook the leeks and onions for about 7 minutes, stirring occasionally until softened but not browned.

2 Add the chopped potatoes to the pan and cook for 2–3 minutes, stirring occasionally, then add the chicken or vegetable stock and bring to a boil. Cover the pan with a tight-fitting lid and simmer gently for 30–35 minutes, until all the vegetables are very tender.

3 Season to taste with salt and pepper. Remove the pan from the heat and stir in the remaining butter in small pieces until completely melted. Serve the soup hot with warm crusty bread and butter, if you wish.

Cook's Tip
Never use a food processor or blender to purée potatoes as the starch in the vegetable will be broken down and will create an unpleasant gluey consistency.

Serves 6–8
2 pounds lean shoulder of
   lamb, cut into large
   even-size chunks
7½ cups water
1 large onion, chopped
¼ cup pearl barley
bouquet garni
1 large carrot, chopped

1 turnip, chopped
3 leeks, chopped
½ small white cabbage,
   shredded
salt and ground black
   pepper
chopped fresh parsley, to
   garnish

1 Put the lamb and water into a large saucepan and bring to a boil. Skim off the scum, then stir in the onion, barley and bouquet garni.

2 Bring the soup back to a boil, then partly cover the saucepan and simmer gently for 1 hour. Add the remaining vegetables and season to taste with salt and pepper. Bring to a boil, partly cover again and simmer for about 35 minutes until the vegetables are tender.

3 Remove any extra fat from the top of the soup, then serve hot, sprinkled with chopped parsley.

Country Vegetable Soup

Vary the vegetables according to what you like and what is in season.

Serves 4

4 tablespoons butter
1 onion, chopped
2 leeks, sliced
2 celery stalks, sliced
2 carrots, sliced
2 small turnips, chopped
4 ripe tomatoes, skinned
  and chopped
4 cups chicken or
  vegetable stock

bouquet garni
1 cup green beans,
  chopped
salt and ground black
  pepper
chopped fresh herbs such
  as tarragon, thyme,
  chives and parsley, to
  garnish

1 Heat the butter in a large saucepan and cook the onion and leeks gently until soft but not colored.

2 Add the celery, carrots and turnips and cook them for about 3–4 minutes, stirring occasionally. Stir in the tomatoes and stock, add the bouquet garni and simmer the vegetables gently for about 20 minutes.

3 Add the beans to the soup and continue to cook until all the vegetables are tender. Season to taste with salt and pepper and serve garnished with chopped herbs.

Split Pea and Bacon Soup

This soup is also called "London Particular", because of the city's smog. The fogs in turn were named "pea-soupers".

Serves 4

1 tablespoon butter
4 ounces bacon, chopped
1 large onion, chopped
1 carrot, chopped
1 celery stalk, chopped
scant ½ cup split peas
5 cups chicken stock

2 thick slices firm bread,
  buttered and without
  crusts
2 slices lean bacon
salt and ground black
  pepper

1 Heat the butter in a saucepan and cook the chopped bacon until the fat runs. Stir in the onion, carrot and celery and cook for 2–3 minutes.

2 Add the split peas, followed by the stock. Bring to a boil, stirring occasionally, then cover with a tight-fitting lid and simmer for 45–60 minutes.

3 Meanwhile, preheat the oven to 350°F. Bake the bread for about 20 minutes, until crisp and brown, then dice.

4 Broil the lean bacon until very crisp, then chop finely.

5 When the soup is ready, season to taste and serve hot with the chopped bacon and croutons scattered on each portion.

Smoked Haddock and Potato Soup

This soup's traditional name is "cullen skink". A "cullen" is a town's port district and "skink" means stock or broth.

Serves 6

1 smoked haddock (about
   12 ounces)
1 onion, chopped
bouquet garni
3¾ cups water
1¼ pounds (about 3 large)
   potatoes, quartered

2½ cups milk
3 tablespoons butter
salt and ground black
   pepper
chopped fresh chives, to
   garnish

1 Put the haddock, onion, bouquet garni and water into a large saucepan and bring to a boil. Skim the scum from the surface, then cover the pan with a tight-fitting lid. Reduce the heat and poach for about 10–15 minutes, or until the haddock flakes easily.

2 Lift the poached fish from the pan using a fish slice and remove the skin and bones. Flake the flesh and reserve. Return the skin and bones to the pan and simmer, uncovered, for 30 minutes.

3 Strain the fish stock and return to the pan, then add the potatoes and simmer for about 25 minutes or until tender. Remove the potatoes from the pan using a slotted spoon. Add the milk to the pan and bring to a boil.

4 Meanwhile, mash the potatoes with the butter, then whisk into the milk in the pan until thick and creamy. Add the flaked fish to the pan and adjust the seasoning. Sprinkle with chives and serve at once with crusty bread, if you wish.

Mulligatawny Soup

Choose red split lentils for the best color, although green or brown lentils could also be used.

Serves 4

4 tablespoons butter or 4
   tablespoons oil
2 large chicken pieces,
   about 12 ounces each
1 onion, chopped
1 carrot, chopped
1 small turnip, chopped
about 1 tablespoon curry
   powder, to taste

4 cloves
6 black peppercorns,
   lightly crushed
¼ cup lentils
3¾ cups chicken stock
¼ cup golden raisins
salt and ground black
   pepper

1 Heat the butter or oil in a large saucepan and brown the chicken over a brisk heat. Transfer the chicken to a plate.

2 Add the onion, carrot and turnip to the pan and cook, stirring occasionally, until lightly colored. Stir in the curry powder, cloves and peppercorns and cook for 1–2 minutes, then add the lentils.

3 Pour the stock into the pan, bring to a boil, then add the raisins and chicken and any juices from the plate. Cover and simmer gently for about 1¼ hours.

4 Remove the chicken from the pan and discard the skin and bones. Chop the flesh into bite-size chunks, return to the soup and reheat. Season to taste with salt and pepper before serving the soup piping hot.

Smoked Haddock Pâté

This easily-prepared pâté is made from small haddock which have been salted and hot-smoked.

Serves 6

3 large smoked haddock, about 8 ounces each
1¼ cups medium-fat cream cheese
3 eggs, beaten
2–3 tablespoons lemon juice
pinch of freshly ground black pepper
fresh chervil sprigs, to garnish
lemon wedges and lettuce leaves, to serve

1 Preheat the oven to 325°F. Generously butter six individual ramekin dishes.

2 Lay the haddock in a baking dish and heat through in the oven for 10 minutes. Carefully remove the skin and bones from the fish, then flake the flesh into a bowl.

3 Mash the fish with a fork and work in the cheese, then the eggs. Add the lemon juice and season with pepper to taste.

4 Divide the fish mixture between the six ramekins and place in a roasting pan. Pour hot water into the roasting pan to come halfway up the dishes. Bake for 30 minutes, until just set.

5 Allow to cool for 2–3 minutes, then run a knife point around the edge of each dish and invert onto a warmed plate. Garnish with fresh chervil sprigs and serve with the lemon wedges and lettuce.

Spinach, Bacon and Shrimp Salad

Serve this hot salad with plenty of crusty bread to mop up the delicious juices.

Serves 4

7 tablespoons olive oil
2 tablespoons sherry vinegar
2 garlic cloves, finely chopped
1 teaspoon Dijon mustard
12 cooked jumbo shrimp, in the shell
4 ounces lean bacon, cut into strips
1 cup fresh young spinach leaves
½ head red lettuce, coarsely torn
salt and ground black

1 To make the dressing, whisk together 6 tablespoons of the olive oil with the vinegar, garlic, mustard and seasoning in a small saucepan. Heat gently until thickened slightly, then keep warm.

2 Carefully peel the jumbo shrimp, leaving their tails intact. Set aside until needed.

3 Heat the remaining oil in a frying pan and fry the bacon until golden and crisp, stirring occasionally. Add the shrimp and stir-fry for a few minutes until warmed through.

4 While the bacon and shrimp are cooking, arrange the spinach and torn lettuce leaves on four individual serving plates.

5 Spoon the bacon and shrimp onto the leaves, then pour over the hot dressing. Serve at once.

Cook's Tip
Sherry vinegar lends its pungent flavor to this delicious salad. It is readily available in large supermarkets or delicatessens. However, red or white wine vinegar could be substituted if you prefer.

Hot Tomato and Mozzarella Salad

A quick, easy appetizer with a Mediterranean flavor. It can be prepared in advance, then broiled just before serving.

Serves 4

1 pound plum tomatoes, sliced
8 ounces mozzarella cheese
1 red onion, chopped
4–6 pieces sun-dried tomatoes in oil, drained and chopped
4 tablespoons olive oil
1 teaspoon red wine vinegar
½ teaspoon Dijon mustard
4 tablespoons mixed chopped fresh herbs such as basil, parsley, oregano and chives
salt and ground black pepper
fresh herb sprigs, to garnish (optional)

1 Arrange the sliced tomatoes and mozzarella in circles in four shallow flameproof dishes. Scatter over the onion and sun-dried tomatoes. Whisk together the olive oil, vinegar, mustard, chopped herbs and seasoning. Pour over the salads.

2 Place the salads under a hot broiler for 4–5 minutes, until the mozzarella starts to melt. Grind over plenty of black pepper and serve garnished with fresh herb sprigs, if you wish.

Asparagus with Tarragon Butter

Eating fresh asparagus with your fingers is correct but messy, so serve this dish with finger bowls.

Serves 4

1¼ pounds fresh asparagus
½ cup butter
2 tablespoons chopped fresh tarragon
1 tablespoon chopped fresh parsley
grated rind of ½ lemon
1 tablespoon lemon juice
salt and black pepper

1 Trim the woody ends from the asparagus spears, then tie them into four equal bundles.

2 Place the bundles of asparagus in a large frying pan with about 1 inch of boiling water. Cover with a lid and cook for about 6–8 minutes, until the asparagus is tender but still firm. Drain well and discard the strings.

3 Arrange the asparagus spears on four warmed serving plates. Make the tarragon butter by creaming together the remaining ingredients; heat it gently and pour it over the asparagus. Serve immediately.

Deviled Kidneys

This tangy dish makes an impressive appetizer, although it is sometimes served as an English breakfast dish.

Serves 4

Mix 2 tablespoons Worcestershire sauce, 1 tablespoon each English mustard, lemon juice and tomato paste. Season with cayenne pepper and salt. Melt 3 tablespoons butter, add 1 chopped shallot; cook until softened. Stir in 8 prepared lambs' kidneys; cook for 3 minutes on each side. Coat with the sauce; serve sprinkled with chopped parsley.

Egg and Tomato Salad with Crab

You could also adjust the quantities in this tasty salad to make a quick, light and healthy weekday meal.

Serves 4

1 head of round lettuce
2 x 7-ounce cans
* crabmeat, drained*
4 hard-boiled eggs, sliced
16 cherry tomatoes,
* halved*
½ green bell pepper,
* seeded and thinly*
* sliced*
6 pitted black olives,
* sliced*

For the dressing
3 tablespoons chili sauce
1 cup mayonnaise
2 teaspoons fresh lemon
* juice*
½ green bell pepper,
* seeded and finely*
* chopped*
1 teaspoon prepared
* horseradish*
1 teaspoon
* Worcestershire sauce*

1 To make the dressing, place all the ingredients in a bowl and mix well. Set aside in a cool place.

2 Line four plates with the lettuce leaves. Mound the crabmeat in the center. Arrange the eggs around the outside with the tomatoes on top.

3 Spoon some of the dressing over the crabmeat. Arrange the green pepper slices on top and sprinkle with the olives. Serve immediately with the remaining dressing.

Stuffed Mushrooms

These flavorful mushrooms may also be served as an accompaniment to a main course.

Serves 4

10 ounces spinach, stalks
* removed*
14-ounces medium cap
* mushrooms*
2 tablespoons butter, plus
* extra for brushing*
1 ounce bacon, chopped
½ small onion, chopped
5 tablespoons double
* cream*

about 4 tablespoons
* grated Cheddar cheese*
2 tablespoons fresh bread
* crumbs*
salt and ground black
* pepper*
fresh parsley sprigs, to
* garnish*

1 Preheat the oven to 375 °F. Butter a baking dish. Wash but do not dry the spinach. Place it in a saucepan and cook, stirring occasionally, until wilted.

2 Place the spinach in a colander and squeeze out as much liquid as possible. Chop finely. Snap the stalks from the mushrooms and chop the stalks finely.

3 Melt the butter in a pan and cook the bacon, onion and mushroom stalks for about 5 minutes. Stir in the spinach, cook for a moment or two, then remove the pan from the heat, stir in the cream and season to taste with salt and pepper.

4 Brush the mushroom caps with melted butter, then place, gills facing upwards, in a single layer in the baking dish.

5 Divide the spinach mixture among the mushrooms. Mix together the cheese and bread crumbs, sprinkle over the mushrooms, then bake for about 20 minutes until the mushrooms are tender. Serve warm, garnished with parsley.

Cook's Tip
Squeeze out all the excess water from the cooked spinach, otherwise the stuffing will be too soggy.

Pears and Stilton

Stilton is the classic British blue cheese, but you could use blue Cheshire instead, or even Gorgonzola.

Serves 4

	For the dressing
4 ripe pears	3 tablespoons light olive
3 ounces blue Stilton	oil
cheese	1 tablespoon lemon juice
3 tablespoons curd cheese	½ tablespoon toasted
pinch of ground black	poppy seeds
pepper	salt and ground black
fresh watercress sprigs,	pepper
to garnish	

1 First make the dressing. Place the olive oil, lemon juice, poppy seeds and seasoning in a screw-top jar and shake together until thoroughly blended.

2 Cut the pears in half lengthwise, then scoop out the cores and cut away the calyx from the rounded end.

3 Beat together the Stilton, curd cheese and a little pepper. Divide this mixture among the cavities in the pears.

4 Shake the dressing to mix it again, then spoon it over the pears. Serve garnished with watercress.

Cook's Tip
The pears should be lightly chilled in the fridge before they are used in this dish.

Potted Shrimp

The brown shrimp traditionally used for potting are very messy to peel. Use peeled cooked jumbo shrimp if you prefer.

Serves 4

2 cups shelled shrimps	fresh dill sprigs, to
1 cup butter	garnish
pinch of ground mace	lemon wedges and thin
salt and cayenne pepper	slices of brown bread
	and butter, to serve

1 Chop a quarter of the shrimp. Melt ½ cup of the butter slowly, carefully skimming off any foam that rises to the surface.

2 Stir all the shrimps, the mace, salt and cayenne pepper into the saucepan and heat gently without boiling. Pour the shrimp and butter mixture into four individual pots and set it aside to cool.

3 Heat the remaining butter in a clean small pan, then carefully spoon the clear butter over the shrimp, leaving behind the residue.

4 Let stand until the butter is almost set, then place a dill sprig in the center of each pot. Let set completely, then cover and chill in the fridge.

5 Transfer the shrimp to room temperature 30 minutes before serving with lemon wedges and thin slices of brown bread and butter.

Leek Terrine with Deli Meats

This attractive appetizer is simple yet looks spectacular. It can be made a day ahead.

Serves 6

20–24 small young leeks
about 8 ounces mixed
   sliced meats, such as
   prosciutto and salami
½ cup walnuts, toasted
   and chopped

For the dressing
4 tablespoons walnut oil
4 tablespoons olive oil
2 tablespoons wine
   vinegar
1 teaspoon whole-grain
   mustard
salt and ground black
   pepper

1 Cut off the roots and most of the green part from the leeks. Wash them thoroughly under cold running water.

2 Bring a large saucepan of salted water to a boil. Add the leeks, bring the water back to a boil, then simmer for 6–8 minutes, until the leeks are just tender. Drain well.

3 Fill a 1-pound loaf pan with the leeks, placing them top to bottom one after the other and sprinkling each layer as you go with salt and pepper.

4 Put another loaf pan inside the first and gently press down on the leeks. Carefully invert both tins and let any water drain out. Place one or two weights on top of the pans and chill the terrine for at least 4 hours, or overnight.

5 To make the dressing, whisk together the walnut and olive oils, vinegar and mustard in a small bowl. Season to taste.

6 Carefully turn out the terrine onto a board and cut into slices using a large sharp knife. Lay the slices of leek terrine on serving plates and arrange the slices of meat beside them.

7 Spoon the dressing over the slices of terrine and scatter the chopped walnuts over the top. Serve immediately.

Garlic Shrimp in Phyllo Tartlets

Tartlets made with crisp layers of phyllo pastry and filled with garlic shrimp make a tempting and unusual appetizer.

Serves 4
For the tartlets
4 tablespoons butter,
   melted
2–3 large sheets phyllo
   pastry

For the filling
½ cup butter
2–3 garlic cloves,
   crushed

1 fresh red chili, seeded
   and chopped
3 cups peeled, cooked
   shrimp
2 tablespoons chopped
   fresh parsley or fresh
   chives
salt and ground black
   pepper

1 Preheat the oven to 400°F. Brush four individual 3-inch tart pans with melted butter.

2 Cut the phyllo pastry into twelve 4-inch squares and brush with the melted butter.

3 Place three squares inside each pan, overlapping them at slight angles and carefully curling the edges and points while forming a good depression in each center. Bake the pastry for 10–15 minutes, until crisp and golden. Cool slightly and remove from the pans.

4 To make the filling, melt the butter in a large frying pan, fry the garlic, chili and shrimp for 1–2 minutes to warm through. Stir in the parsley or chives and season to taste with salt and pepper.

5 Spoon the prawn filling into the tartlets and serve immediately.

Cook's Tip
Use fresh phyllo pastry rather than frozen, then simply wrap and freeze any leftover sheets.

Smoked Salmon and Dill Blinis

Blinis, small pancakes of Russian origin, are an easy to make but sophisticated dinner party appetizer.

Serves 4

1 cup buckwheat flour
1 cup all-purpose flour
pinch of salt
1 tablespoon rapid-rise dried yeast
2 eggs
1½ cups warm milk
1 tablespoon melted butter, plus extra for shallow-frying
⅔ cup crème fraîche
3 tablespoons chopped fresh dill
8 ounces smoked salmon, thinly sliced
fresh dill sprigs, to garnish

1 Mix together the buckwheat and all-purpose flour in a large bowl with the salt. Sprinkle in the yeast and mix well. Separate one of the eggs. Whisk together the whole egg and the yolk, the warm milk and the melted butter.

2 Pour the egg mixture onto the flour mixture. Beat well to form a smooth batter. Cover with plastic wrap and let rise in a warm place for 1–2 hours.

3 Whisk the remaining egg white in a large bowl until stiff peaks form, then gently fold into the batter.

4 Preheat a heavy-based frying pan or griddle and brush with melted butter. Drop tablespoons of the batter onto the pan, spacing them well apart. Cook for about 40 seconds, until bubbles appear on the surface.

5 Flip over the blinis and cook for 30 seconds on the other side. Wrap in foil and keep warm in a low oven. Repeat with the remaining mixture, buttering the pan each time.

6 Combine the crème fraîche and dill. Serve the blinis topped with the salmon and cream. Garnish with dill sprigs.

Celery Root Fritters with Mustard Dip

The combination of the hot, crispy fritters and the cold mustard dip is extremely tasty.

Serves 4

1 egg
1 cup ground almonds
3 tablespoons freshly grated Parmesan cheese
3 tablespoons chopped fresh parsley
1 celery root, about 1 pound
squeeze of lemon juice
oil, for deep-frying

For the mustard dip
⅔ cup sour cream
1–2 tablespoons wholegrain mustard
salt and ground black pepper
sea salt flakes, for sprinkling

1 Beat the egg well and pour into a shallow dish. Mix together the almonds, grated Parmesan and parsley in a separate dish. Season to taste, then set aside.

2 Peel and cut the celery root into strips about ½ inch wide and 2 inches long. Drop them immediately into a bowl of water with a little lemon juice added to prevent them from becoming discolored.

3 Heat the oil in a deep-fat fryer to 350 °F. Drain and then pat dry half the celery root strips. Dip them into the beaten egg, then into the ground almond mixture, making sure that the pieces are coated completely and evenly.

4 Deep-fry the fritters, a few at a time, for about 2–3 minutes until golden. Drain on paper towels and keep warm while you cook the remainder.

5 To make the mustard dip, mix together the sour cream, mustard and sea salt to taste. Spoon into a small serving bowl.

6 Heap the celery root fritters onto warmed individual serving plates. Sprinkle with sea salt flakes and serve immediately with the mustard dip.

Chicken Liver Pâté with Marsala

This is a really quick and simple pâté to make, yet it has a delicious – and quite sophisticated – flavor.

Serves 4

12 ounces chicken livers,
    defrosted if frozen
1 cup butter
2 garlic cloves, crushed
1 tablespoon Marsala
1 teaspoon chopped sage

salt and ground black
    pepper
8 fresh sage leaves, to
    garnish
Melba toast, to serve

1 Pick over the chicken livers, then rinse and dry with paper towels. Melt 2 tablespoons of the butter in a frying pan and fry the chicken livers with the garlic over a moderate heat for about 5 minutes, or until they are firm but still pink in their centers.

2 Transfer the livers to a food processor or blender using a slotted spoon. Add the Marsala and chopped sage.

3 Melt a generous ½ cup of the remaining butter in the frying pan, stirring to loosen any residue, then pour into the food processor or blender and process until smooth. Season well with salt and pepper.

4 Spoon the pâté into four individual pots and smooth the surface. Melt the remaining butter in a separate pan and pour over the pâtés. Garnish with sage leaves and chill in the fridge until set. Serve with triangles of Melba toast.

Cook's Tip
This delicious pâté contains Marsala, a dark, sweet, pungent dessert wine made in Sicily. If this is not available, you could substitute either brandy or a medium-dry sherry.

Salmon Rillettes

A variation on the traditional pork rillette, this appetizer is much easier to make.

Serves 6

12 ounces salmon fillets
¾ cup butter
1 celery stalk, finely
    chopped
1 leek, white part only,
    finely chopped
1 bay leaf
⅔ cup dry white wine

4 ounces smoked salmon
    trimmings
large pinch of ground
    mace
4 tablespoons ricotta
    cheese
salt and ground black
    pepper
salad greens, to serve

1 Lightly season the salmon with salt and pepper. Melt 2 tablespoons of the butter in a frying pan and cook the celery and leek for about 5 minutes. Add the salmon and bay leaf and pour over the wine. Cover with a tight-fitting lid and cook for about 15 minutes until the fish is tender.

2 Strain the cooking liquid into a saucepan and boil until reduced to 2 tablespoons. Cool. Melt 4 tablespoons of the remaining butter and gently cook the smoked salmon until it turns pale pink. Leave to cool.

3 Remove the skin and any bones from the salmon fillets. Flake the flesh into a bowl and add the cooking liquid.

4 Beat in the remaining butter, the mace and ricotta cheese. Break up the smoked salmon trimmings and fold into the mixture with the pan juices. Taste and adjust the seasoning.

5 Spoon the salmon mixture into a dish or terrine and smooth the top level. Cover and chill in the fridge.

6 To serve the salmon rillettes, shape the mixture into oval quenelles using two dessert spoons and arrange on individual plates with the salad greens. Accompany with brown bread or oatcakes, if you wish.

Mexican Dip with Chips

Omit the fresh chili and the chili powder if you prefer a dip
to have a mild flavor.

Serves 4

2 medium-ripe avocados
juice of 1 lime
½ small onion, finely
   chopped
½ red chili, seeded and
   finely chopped
3 tomatoes, skinned,
   seeded and finely
   diced
2 tablespoons chopped
   fresh cilantro
2 tablespoons sour cream
salt and ground black
   pepper

1 tablespoon sour cream
   and a pinch of cayenne
   pepper, to garnish

For the chips

5-ounce bag tortilla chips
2 tablespoons finely
   grated mature
   Cheddar cheese
¼ teaspoon chili powder
2 teaspoons chopped fresh
   parsley

1 Peel, halve and pit the avocados.

2 Place the avocado in a blender or food processor with the
remaining ingredients, reserving the sour cream and cayenne
pepper. Process until fairly smooth. Transfer to a bowl, cover
and chill in the fridge until required.

3 To make the chips, preheat the broiler, then scatter the
tortilla chips over a baking sheet. Mix the grated cheese with
the chili powder, sprinkle over the chips and broil for about
1–2 minutes, until the cheese has melted.

4 Remove the avocado dip from the fridge, top with the sour
cream and sprinkle with cayenne pepper. Serve the bowl on a
plate surrounded by the tortilla chips, garnished with the
chopped fresh parsley.

French Goat Cheese Salad

The deep, tangy flavors of this salad would also make it
satisfying enough for a light meal, if you wished.

Serves 4

7-ounce bag prepared
   mixed salad greens
4 strips bacon
16 thin slices French
   bread
4 ounces full-fat goat
   cheese

For the dressing

4 tablespoons olive oil
1 tablespoon tarragon
   vinegar
2 teaspoons walnut oil
1 teaspoon Dijon
   mustard
1 teaspoon wholegrain
   mustard

1 Preheat the broiler to a moderate heat. Rinse and dry the
salad greens, then arrange in four individual bowls. Place the
ingredients for the dressing in a screw-top jar, shake together
well and reserve.

2 Lay the bacon strips on a board, then stretch with the back
of a knife and cut each into four. Roll each piece up and broil
for about 2–3 minutes.

3 Meanwhile, slice the goat cheese into eight and halve each
slice. Top each slice of bread with a piece of goat cheese and
pop under the broiler. Turn over the bacon and continue
cooking with the goat cheese toasts until the cheese is golden
and bubbling.

4 Arrange the bacon rolls and toasts on top of the prepared
salad greens, shake the dressing well and pour a little of the
dressing over each one.

Chinese Garlic Mushrooms

High in protein and low in fat, marinated tofu makes an unusual stuffing for these mushrooms.

Serves 4

8 large open mushrooms
3 scallions, sliced
1 garlic clove, crushed
2 tablespoons oyster sauce
10-ounce packet
  marinated tofu, diced

7-ounce can corn,
  drained
2 teaspoons sesame oil
salt and ground black
  pepper

1 Preheat the oven to 400°F. Finely chop the mushroom stems and mix with the next three ingredients.

2 Stir in the diced, marinated tofu and corn, season well, then spoon the filling into the mushrooms.

3 Brush the edges of the mushrooms with the sesame oil. Arrange them in a baking dish and bake for 12–15 minutes, until the mushrooms are just tender, then serve at once.

Tomato Cheese Tarts

These crisp little tartlets are easier to make than they look and are best eaten fresh from the oven.

Serves 4

2 sheets phyllo pastry
1 egg white
½ cup skimmed-milk
  cream cheese

handful of fresh basil
  leaves
3 small tomatoes, sliced
salt and ground black
  pepper

1 Preheat the oven to 400°F. Brush the sheets of phyllo pastry lightly with egg white and cut into sixteen 4-inch squares.

2 Layer the squares in twos, in eight muffin pans. Spoon the cheese into the pastry cases. Season with salt and ground black pepper and top with basil leaves.

3 Arrange the tomato slices on the tarts, add seasoning and bake for 10–12 minutes, until golden. Serve warm.

Ricotta and Pinto Bean Pâté

A lovely light yet full-flavored pâté that can be enjoyed by vegetarians.

Serves 4

Process 14 ounces pinto beans, ¾ cup ricotta cheese, 1 garlic clove, 4 tablespoons melted butter, juice of ½ lemon and seasoning. Add 2 tablespoons fresh chopped parsley and 1 tablespoon fresh thyme or dill; blend. Spoon into one serving dish or four lightly oiled and bottom-lined ramekins. Chill. Garnish with salad greens and serve with warm crusty bread or toast. If serving the pâté individually, turn each one out of its ramekin onto a plate, then remove the paper. Top the pâté with radish slices and sprigs of dill.

Avocados with Tangy Topping

Lightly broiled with a tasty topping of red onions and cheese, this dish makes a delightful appetizer.

Serves 4

1 tablespoon sunflower
  oil
1 small red onion, sliced
1 garlic clove, crushed
dash of Worcestershire
  sauce
2 ripe avocados, pitted
  and halved
2 small tomatoes, sliced

1 tablespoon chopped
  fresh basil, marjoram
  or parsley
2 ounces mozzarella
  cheese, sliced
salt and ground black
  pepper

1 Heat the oil in a frying pan and gently fry the onion and garlic for about 5 minutes until just softened. Shake in a little Worcestershire sauce.

2 Preheat a broiler. Place the avocado halves on the broiler pan and spoon the onions into the centers.

3 Divide the tomato slices and fresh herbs between the four halves and top each one with the cheese.

4 Season well with salt and pepper and broil until the cheese melts and starts to brown.

Bruschetta with Goat Cheese

Simple to prepare in advance, this Italian dish can be served as an appetizer or at a finger buffet.

Serves 4–6
For the tapenade
14-ounce can black
  olives, pitted and
  finely chopped
2 ounces sun-dried
  tomatoes in oil,
  chopped
2 tablespoons capers,
  chopped
1 tablespoon green
  peppercorns, in juice,
  crushed
2 garlic cloves, crushed
3 tablespoons chopped
  fresh basil or 1
  teaspoon dried basil

3–4 tablespoons olive oil
salt and ground black
  pepper

For the bases
12 slices ciabatta or other
  crusty bread
olive oil, for brushing
2 garlic cloves, halved
½ cup soft goat cheese or
  other whole-milk soft
  cheese
mixed fresh herb sprigs,
  to garnish

1 To make the tapenade, mix all the tapenade ingredients together and check the seasoning. It should not need too much. Allow to marinate overnight, if possible.

2 To make the bruschetta, broil both sides of the bread lightly until golden. Brush one side with oil and then rub with a cut clove of garlic. Set aside until ready to serve.

3 Spread the bruschetta with the cheese, roughing it up with a fork, and spoon the tapenade on top. Garnish with sprigs of mixed fresh herbs.

Cook's Tip
Grill the bruschetta on a barbecue for a delicious smoky flavor if you are making this appetizer in the summer.

Grilled Garlic Mussels

Use a combination of fresh herbs, such as oregano, basil and Italian parsley.

Serves 4

3–3½ pounds live
    mussels
½ cup dry white wine
4 tablespoons butter
2 shallots, finely chopped
2 garlic cloves, crushed
½ cup dried white bread
    crumbs

4 tablespoons mixed
    chopped fresh herbs
2 tablespoons freshly
    grated Parmesan
    cheese
salt and ground black
    pepper
fresh basil leaves, to
    garnish

1 Scrub the mussels well under cold running water. Remove the beards and discard any mussels that are open. Place in a large saucepan with the wine. Cover and cook over a high heat, shaking the pan occasionally, for 5–8 minutes until the mussels have opened.

2 Strain the mussels and reserve the cooking liquid. Discard any mussels that remain closed. Allow them to cool slightly, then remove and discard the top half of each shell.

3 Melt the butter in a pan and fry the shallots until softened. Add the garlic and cook for 1–2 minutes. Stir in the dried bread crumbs and cook, stirring until lightly browned. Remove the pan from the heat and stir in the herbs. Moisten with a little of the reserved mussel liquid, then season to taste with salt and pepper.

4 Spoon the breadcrumb mixture over the mussels and arrange on baking sheets. Sprinkle with the grated Parmesan.

5 Cook the mussels under a hot broiler in batches for about 2 minutes, until the topping is crisp and golden. Keep the cooked mussels warm in a low oven while broiling the rest. Garnish with fresh basil leaves and serve hot.

Nut Patties with Mango Relish

These spicy patties can be made in advance, if you wish, and reheated just before serving.

Serves 4–6

1½ cups finely chopped
    roasted and salted
    cashew nuts
1½ cups finely chopped
    walnuts
1 small onion, finely
    chopped
1 garlic clove, crushed
1 green chili, seeded and
    chopped
1 teaspoon ground cumin
2 teaspoons ground
    coriander
2 carrots, coarsely grated
1 cup fresh white bread
    crumbs
2 tablespoons chopped
    fresh cilantro

1 tablespoon lemon juice
1–2 eggs, beaten
salt and ground black
    pepper
fresh cilantro sprigs, to
    garnish

For the relish

1 large ripe mango, diced
1 small onion, cut into
    slivers
1 teaspoon grated fresh
    ginger
pinch of salt
1 tablespoon sesame oil
1 teaspoon black mustard
    seeds

1 Preheat the oven to 350°F. In a bowl, mix together the nuts, onion, garlic, chili, spices, bread crumbs, carrots, chopped cilantro and seasoning.

2 Sprinkle the lemon juice over the mixture and add enough of the beaten egg to bind the mixture together. Shape the mixture into twelve balls, then flatten slightly into round patties. Place them on a lightly greased baking sheet and bake for about 25 minutes, until golden brown.

3 To make the relish, mix together the mango, onion, fresh ginger and salt. Heat the oil in a small frying pan and fry the mustard seeds for a few seconds until they pop, then stir into the mango mixture. Serve with the nut patties, garnished with cilantro.

Dim Sum

A popular Chinese snack, these tiny dumplings are now fashionable in many specialty restaurants.

Serves 4

For the dough
1¼ cups all-purpose flour
¼ cup boiling water
⅛ cup cold water
½ tablespoon vegetable oil

½ tablespoon light soy
   sauce
1 teaspoon dry sherry
1 teaspoon raw sugar
½ teaspoon sesame oil
1 teaspoon cornstarch
mixed fresh lettuce leaves
   such as iceberg or
   frisée

For the filling
3 ounces ground pork
3 tablespoons chopped
   canned bamboo shoots

1 To make the dough, sift the flour into a bowl. Stir in the boiling water, then the cold water together with the oil. Mix to form a ball and knead until smooth. Divide the mixture into sixteen equal pieces and shape into circles.

2 For the filling, mix together the pork, bamboo shoots, soy sauce, sherry, sugar and oil. Then stir in the corn starch

3 Place a little of the filling in the center of each dim sum circle. Carefully pinch the edges of the dough together to form little "purses".

4 Line a steamer with a damp dish towel. Place the dim sum in the steamer and steam for 5–10 minutes. Serve on a bed of lettuce with soy sauce, scallion curls, sliced red chili and prawn crackers, if you wish.

Cook's Tip
As an alternative filling, substitute the pork with cooked, peeled shrimp.

Sesame Shrimp Toasts

Serve about four of these delicious toasts per person with a soy sauce for dipping.

Serves 6
6 ounces peeled, cooked
   shrimp
2 scallions, finely
   chopped
1-inch piece fresh ginger,
   peeled and grated
2 garlic cloves, crushed
2 tablespoons cornstarch
2 teaspoons soy sauce,
   plus extra for dipping

6 slices stale bread from a
   small loaf, without
   crusts
3 tablespoons sesame
   seeds
about 2½ cups vegetable
   oil, for deep-frying

1 Place the shrimp, scallions, ginger and garlic cloves into a food processor fitted with a metal blade. Add the cornstarch and soy sauce and work the mixture into a paste.

2 Spread the bread slices evenly with the paste and cut into triangles. Sprinkle with the sesame seeds, making sure they stick to the bread. Chill in the fridge for 30 minutes.

3 Heat the oil for deep-frying in a large heavy-based saucepan until it reaches a temperature of 375°F. Using a slotted spoon, lower the toasts into the oil, sesame-seed side down, and fry for 2–3 minutes, turning over for the last minute. Drain on absorbent paper towels. Keep the toasts warm while frying the rest.

4 Serve the toasts with soy sauce for dipping.

English Ploughman's Pâté

This is a roughly modern interpretation of a traditional ploughman's lunch.

Serves 4

3 tablespoons cream
   cheese
½ cup grated hard goat
   cheese
½ cup grated Cheddar
   cheese
4 pickled onions, drained
   and finely chopped
1 tablespoon apricot
   chutney

2 tablespoons butter,
   melted
2 tablespoons chopped
   fresh chives
4 slices soft-grain bread
salt and ground black
   pepper
watercress and cherry
   tomatoes, to serve

1 Mix together the cream cheese, grated cheeses, onions, chutney and butter in a bowl and season lightly with salt and ground black pepper.

2 Spoon the mixture onto a sheet of wax paper and roll up into a cylinder, smoothing the mixture into a roll with your hands. Scrunch the ends of the paper together and twist them to seal. Place in the freezer for about 30 minutes, until the parcel is just firm.

3 Spread the chives on a plate, then unwrap the chilled cheese pâté. Roll in the chives until evenly coated. Enclose in plastic wrap and chill for 10 minutes in the fridge.

4 Preheat the broiler. To make Melba toast, lightly toast the bread on both sides. Cut off the crusts and slice each piece in half horizontally. Cut each half into two triangles. Broil, untoasted side up, until golden and curled at the edges.

5 Slice the pâté into rounds with a sharp knife and serve three or four rounds per person with the Melba toast, watercress and cherry tomatoes.

Golden Cheese Puffs

Serve these deep-fried puffs – called *aigrettes* in France – with a fruity chutney and salad.

Makes 8

½ cup all-purpose flour
2 tablespoon butter
1 egg plus 1 egg yolk
½ cup finely grated
   mature Cheddar
   cheese
2 tablespoons grated
   Parmesan cheese

½ tsp mustard powder
pinch of cayenne pepper
oil, for deep-frying
salt and ground black
   pepper
mango chutney and
   green salad, to serve

1 Sift the flour onto a square of wax paper and set aside. Place the butter and ⅔ cup water in a saucepan and heat gently until the butter has melted.

2 Bring the liquid to a boil and pour in the flour all at once. Remove from the heat and stir well with a wooden spoon until the mixture begins to leave the sides of the pan and forms a ball. Let cool slightly.

3 Beat the egg and egg yolk together in a bowl with a fork and then gradually add to the mixture in the pan, beating well after each addition.

4 Stir the cheeses, mustard powder and cayenne pepper into the mixture and season to taste with salt and pepper.

5 Heat the oil in a large pan to 375°F or until a cube of bread dropped into the pan browns in 30 seconds. Drop four spoonfuls of the cheese mixture into the oil at a time and deep-fry for 2–3 minutes until golden. Drain on paper towels and keep hot in the oven while cooking the remaining mixture. Serve two puffs per person with a spoonful of mango chutney and green salad.

Kansas City Fritters

Crispy bacon and vegetable fritters are served with a spicy tomato salsa.

Makes 8

1¾ cups canned corn, drained well

2 eggs, separated

¾ cup all-purpose flour

5 tablespoons milk

1 small zucchini, grated

2 strips bacon, diced

2 scallions, finely chopped

large pinch of cayenne pepper

3 tablespoons sunflower oil

salt and ground black pepper

fresh cilantro sprigs, to garnish

For the salsa

3 tomatoes, skinned, seeded and diced

½ small red bell pepper, seeded and diced

½ small onion, diced

1 tablespoon lemon juice

1 tablespoon chopped fresh cilantro

dash of Tabasco sauce

1 To make the salsa, mix all the ingredients together and season to taste. Cover and chill until required.

2 Empty the corn into a bowl and mix in the egg yolks. Add the flour and blend in with a wooden spoon. When the mixture thickens, gradually blend in the milk.

3 Stir in the zucchini, bacon, scallions, cayenne pepper and seasoning and set aside. Whisk the egg whites until stiff peaks form. Gently fold into the corn batter mixture.

4 Heat the oil in a large frying pan and place four large spoonfuls of the mixture into the oil. Fry over a moderate heat for 2–3 minutes on each side until golden. Drain on paper towels and keep warm in the oven while frying the remaining four fritters.

5 Serve two fritters each, garnished with cilantro sprigs and a spoonful of the chilled tomato salsa.

Spinach and Cheese Dumplings

These tasty little dumplings are known as *gnocchi* in Italy, where they are very popular.

Serves 4

6 ounces cold mashed potato

½ cup semolina

1 cup frozen leaf spinach, defrosted, squeezed and chopped

½ cup ricotta cheese

5 tablespoons freshly grated Parmesan cheese

2 tablespoons beaten egg

½ teaspoon salt

large pinch of grated nutmeg

pinch of ground black pepper

2 tablespoons freshly grated Parmesan cheese

fresh basil sprigs, to garnish

For the butter

6 tablespoons butter

1 teaspoon grated lemon rind

1 tablespoon lemon juice

1 tablespoon chopped fresh basil

1 Place all the gnocchi ingredients except the 2 tablespoons Parmesan and the basil in a bowl and mix well. Take walnut-size pieces of the mixture and roll each one back and forth along the prongs of a fork until ridged. Make twenty-eight gnocchi in this way.

2 Bring a large pan of water to a boil, reduce to a simmer and drop in the gnocchi. They will sink at first, but as they cook they will rise to the surface; this procedure will take about 2 minutes, then simmer for 1 minute. Transfer the gnocchi to a lightly-greased and warmed casserole.

3 Sprinkle the gnocchi with the Parmesan cheese and broil under a high heat for 2 minutes, or until lightly browned. Meanwhile, heat the butter in a pan and stir in the lemon rind, lemon juice and basil. Season to taste. Pour some of this butter over each portion of gnocchi and serve hot, garnished with the basil sprigs.

Tricolor Salad

This can be a simple appetizer if served on individual salad plates, or part of a light buffet meal served on a platter.

Serves 4–6

1 small red onion, thinly sliced
6 large full-flavored tomatoes
extra-virgin olive oil, to sprinkle
2 ounces arugula or watercress, chopped

6 ounces mozzarella cheese, thinly sliced
salt and ground black pepper
2 tablespoons pine nuts (optional), to garnish

1 Soak the onion slices in a bowl of cold water for about 30 minutes, then drain and pat dry. Skin the tomatoes by slashing and dipping briefly in boiling water. Remove the cores and slice the flesh.

2 Arrange half the sliced tomatoes on a large platter or divide them among small plates.

3 Sprinkle liberally with olive oil, then layer with the chopped arugula or watercress and soaked onion slices, seasoning well with salt and pepper. Add the cheese, then sprinkle over more oil and seasoning.

4 Repeat with the remaining tomato slices, salad leaves, cheese and oil.

5 Season well to finish and complete with some oil and a good scattering of pine nuts, if using. Cover the salad and chill in the fridge for at least 2 hours before serving.

Cook's Tip
When lightly salted, tomatoes make their own dressing with their natural juices. The sharpness of the arugula or watercress offsets them wonderfully.

Minted Melon Salad

Use two different varieties of melon in this salad, such as a cantaloupe and a honeydew.

Serves 4

2 ripe melons
fresh mint sprigs, to garnish

For the dressing
2 tablespoons coarsely chopped fresh mint

1 teaspoon sugar
2 tablespoons raspberry vinegar
6 tablespoons extra-virgin olive oil
salt and ground black pepper

1 Halve the melons, then scoop out the seeds using a dessertspoon. Cut the melons into thin wedges using a large sharp knife and remove the skins.

2 Arrange the two different varieties of melon wedges alternately among four individual serving plates.

3 To make the dressing, whisk together the mint, sugar, vinegar, oil and seasoning in a small bowl, or put them in a screw-top jar and shake until blended.

4 Spoon the mint dressing over the melon wedges and garnish with mint sprigs. Serve very lightly chilled.

Garlic Mushrooms

Serve these on toast for a quick, tasty appetizer or put them into ramekins and serve with slices of warm crusty bread.

Serves 4

1 pound button
   mushrooms, sliced if
   large
3 tablespoons olive oil
3 tablespoons stock or
   water
2 tablespoons dry sherry
   (optional)

3 garlic cloves, crushed
½ cup light cream cheese
2 tablespoons chopped
   fresh parsley
1 tablespoon chopped fresh
   chives
salt and ground black
   pepper

1. Put the mushrooms into a large saucepan with the olive oil, stock or water and sherry, if using. Heat until bubbling, then cover the pan with a tight-fitting lid and simmer gently for about 5 minutes.

2 Add the crushed garlic and stir well to mix. Cook for another 2 minutes. Remove the mushrooms with a slotted spoon and set them aside. Cook the liquor until it reduces down to 2 tablespoons. Remove from the heat and stir in the cream cheese, parsley and chives.

3 Stir the mixture well until the cheese has completely melted, then return the mushrooms to the pan so that they become coated with the cheese mixture. Season to taste with salt and pepper.

4 Pile the mushrooms onto thick slabs of hot toast. Alternatively, spoon them into four ramekins and serve with slices of crusty bread.

Cook's Tip
Use a mixture of different types of mushrooms for this dish, if you prefer. Shiitake mushrooms will give this appetizer a particularly rich flavor, if you can find them.

Vegetables with Tahini

This colorful appetizer is easily prepared in advance. For an *al fresco* meal, grill the vegetables on a barbecue.

Serves 4

2 red, green or yellow bell
   peppers, quartered
2 zucchini, halved
   lengthwise
2 small eggplants
   degorged and halved
   lengthways
1 fennel bulb, quartered
dash of olive oil
4 ounces Halloumi
   cheese, sliced
salt and ground black

pepper

For the tahini cream
1 cup tahini paste
1 garlic clove, crushed
2 tablespoons olive oil
2 tablespoons fresh lemon
   juice
½ cup cold water
warm pita or nan bread,
   to serve

1 Preheat the broiler or barbecue grill until hot. Brush the vegetables with the oil and cook until just browned, turning once. (If the peppers blacken, don't worry. The skins can be peeled off when cool enough to handle.) Cook the vegetables until just softened.

2 Place all the vegetables in a shallow dish and season to taste with salt and pepper. Allow to cool. Meanwhile, brush the cheese slices with olive oil and broil these on both sides until they are just charred. Remove them from the pan with a metal spatula.

3 To make the tahini cream, place all the ingredients, except the water, in a food processor or blender. Process for a few seconds to mix, then, with the motor still running, pour in the water and blend until smooth.

4 Place the vegetables and cheese slices on a platter and trickle over the tahini cream. Serve with plenty of warm pita or nan bread.

Haddock with Parsley Sauce

The parsley sauce is enriched with cream and an egg yolk in this simple supper dish.

Serves 4

4 haddock fillets (about 6
   ounces each)
4 tablespoons butter
⅔ cup milk
⅔ cup fish stock
1 bay leaf
4 teaspoons all-purpose
   flour
4 tablespoons cream

1 egg yolk
3 tablespoons chopped
   fresh parsley
grated rind and juice of
   ½ lemon
salt and ground black
   pepper

1 Place the fish in a frying pan, add half the butter, the milk, fish stock, bay leaf and seasoning, and heat over a moderately low heat to simmering point. Lower the heat, cover the pan with a tight-fitting lid and poach the fish for 10–15 minutes, depending on the thickness of the fillets, until the fish is tender and the flesh just begins to flake.

2 Transfer the fish to a warmed serving plate with a slotted spoon, cover the fish and keep warm while you make the sauce. Return the cooking liquid to the heat and bring to a boil, stirring. Simmer for about 4 minutes, then remove and discard the bay leaf.

3 Melt the remaining butter in a saucepan and add the flour, stirring continuously for 1 minute. Remove from the heat and gradually stir in the fish cooking liquid. Return to the heat and bring to a boil, stirring. Simmer for about 4 minutes, stirring frequently.

4 Remove the pan from the heat, blend the cream into the egg yolk, then stir into the sauce with the parsley. Reheat gently, stirring for a few minutes; do not allow to boil. Remove from the heat, add the lemon juice and rind, and season to taste with salt and pepper. Pour into a warmed sauceboat and serve with the fish.

Pickled Herrings

A good basic pickled herring dish which is enhanced by the grainy mustard vinaigrette.

Serves 4

4 fresh herrings
⅔ cup white wine
   vinegar
2 teaspoons salt
12 black peppercorns
2 bay leaves
4 whole cloves
2 small onions, sliced

For the dressing
1 teaspoon coarse-grain
   mustard
3 tablespoons olive oil
1 tablespoon white wine
   vinegar
salt and ground black
   pepper

1 Preheat the oven to 325°F. Clean and bone the fish. Cut each fish into two fillets.

2 Roll up the fillets tightly and place them closely packed together in a casserole so that they can't unroll.

3 Pour the vinegar over the fish and add just enough water to cover them.

4 Add the spices and onion, cover and cook for 1 hour. Leave to cool with the liquid. To make the dressing, combine all the ingredients and shake well; serve with the fish.

Herrings with Mustard Sauce

In this delicious dish, crunchy-coated herrings are served with a piquant mayonnaise sauce.

Serves 4

*1 tablespoon Dijon
    mustard
1½ teaspoons tarragon
    vinegar
¾ cup thick mayonnaise*

*4 herrings, about 8
    ounces each, cleaned
1 lemon, halved
1 cup medium oatmeal
salt and ground black
    pepper*

1 Beat the mustard and vinegar to taste into the mayonnaise. Chill lightly in the fridge.

2 Place one fish at a time on a board, cut-side down and opened out. Press firmly along the backbone with your thumbs. Turn over the fish and carefully lift away the backbone and discard.

3 Squeeze lemon juice over both sides of the fish, then season with salt and ground black pepper. Fold the fish in half, skin-side outwards.

4 Preheat a broiler until fairly hot. Place the oatmeal on a plate, then coat each herring evenly in the oatmeal, pressing it on gently with your fingers.

5 Place the herrings on a broiler rack and broil the fish for about 3 – 4 minutes on each side, until the skin is golden brown and crisp and the flesh flakes easily. Serve hot with the mustard sauce, served separately.

Fish and Chips

The traditional British combination of battered fish and thick-cut fries is served with lemon wedges.

Serves 4

*1 cup self-rising flour
⅔ cup water
1½ pound potatoes

1½ pound piece skinned
    cod fillet, cut into four*

*oil, for deep-frying
salt and ground black
    pepper
lemon wedges, to serve*

1 Stir the flour and salt together in a bowl, then form a well in the center. Gradually pour in the water, whisking in the flour to make a smooth batter. Let stand for 30 minutes.

2 Cut the potatoes into strips about ½ inch wide and 2 inches long, using a sharp knife. Place the potatoes in a colander, rinse in cold water, then drain and dry them well.

3 Heat the oil in a deep-fat fryer or large heavy-based saucepan to 300°F. Using the wire basket, lower the potatoes in batches into the oil and cook for 5–6 minutes, shaking the basket occasionally until the potatoes are soft but not browned. Remove the fries from the oil and drain them thoroughly on paper towels.

4 Heat the oil in the fryer to 375°F. Season the fish. Stir the batter, then dip the pieces of fish one by one into it, allowing the excess to drain off.

5 Working in two batches if necessary, lower the fish into the oil and fry for 6–8 minutes, until crisp and brown. Drain the fish on paper towels and keep warm.

6 Add the fries in batches to the oil and cook them for about 2 – 3 minutes, until brown and crisp. Keep hot until ready to serve, then sprinkle with salt and serve with the fish, accompanied by lemon wedges.

Trout with Hazelnuts

The hazelnuts in this recipe make an interesting change from the almonds that are more frequently used.

Serves 4

½ cup hazelnuts, chopped
5 tablespoons butter
4 trout, about 10 ounces
  each
2 tablespoons lemon juice

salt and ground black
  pepper
lemon slices and Italian
  parsley sprigs, to serve

1 Preheat the broiler. Toast the nuts in a single layer, stirring frequently, until the skins split. Then tip the nuts onto a clean dish towel and rub to remove the skins. Leave the nuts to cool, then chop them coarsely.

2 Heat 4 tablespoons of the butter in a large frying pan. Season the trout inside and out, then fry two at a time for 12–15 minutes, turning once, until the trout are brown and the flesh flakes easily when tested with the point of a sharp kitchen knife.

3 Drain the cooked trout on paper towels, then transfer to a warm serving plate and keep warm while frying the remaining trout in the same way. (If your frying pan is large enough, you could, of course, cook the trout in one batch.)

4 Add the remaining butter to the frying pan and fry the hazelnuts until evenly browned. Stir the lemon juice into the pan and mix well, then quickly pour the buttery sauce over the trout and serve at once, garnished with slices of lemon and Italian parsley sprigs.

Cook's Tip
You can use a microwave to prepare the nuts instead of the broiler. Spread them out in a shallow microwave dish and leave uncovered. Cook on full power until the skins split, then remove the skins using a dish towel as described above.

Trout Wrapped in a Blanket

The "blanket" of bacon bastes the fish during cooking, keeping it moist and adding flavor at the same time.

Serves 4

juice of ½ lemon
4 trout, about 10 ounces
  each
4 fresh thyme sprigs
8 thin strips lean bacon

salt and ground black
  pepper
chopped fresh parsley and
  thyme sprigs,
  to garnish
lemon wedges, to serve

1 Preheat the oven to 400°F. Squeeze lemon juice over the skin and in the cavity of each fish, season all over with salt and ground black pepper, then put a thyme sprig in each cavity.

2 Stretch each bacon slice using the back of a knife, then wind two slices around each fish. Place the fish in a lightly greased shallow baking dish, with the loose ends of bacon tucked underneath to prevent them unwinding.

3 Bake in the oven for 15–20 minutes, until the trout flesh flakes easily when tested with the point of a sharp knife and the bacon is crisp and beginning to brown.

4 Serve garnished with chopped parsley, sprigs of thyme and accompanied by lemon wedges.

Cook's Tip
If you prefer, use fresh chopped cilantro in place of the parsley for the garnish.

Smoked Trout Salad

Horseradish goes well with smoked trout. It combines with yogurt to make a lovely dressing.

Serves 4

1 red lettuce, such as lollo rosso	**For the dressing**
8 ounces small ripe tomatoes, cut into thin wedges	pinch of English mustard powder
½ cucumber, peeled and thinly sliced	3–4 teaspoons white wine vinegar
4 smoked trout fillets, about 7 ounces each, skinned and flaked coarsely	2 tablespoons light olive oil
	scant ½ cup natural yogurt
	2 tablespoons grated fresh or bottled horseradish
	pinch of caster sugar

1 To make the dressing, mix together the mustard powder and vinegar, then gradually whisk in the oil, yogurt, horseradish and sugar. Set aside for 30 minutes.

2 Place the lettuce leaves in a large bowl. Stir the dressing again, then pour half of it over the leaves and toss lightly using two spoons.

3 Arrange the lettuce on four individual plates with the tomatoes, cucumber and trout. Spoon over the remaining dressing and serve immediately.

Cook's Tip
The addition of salt to the horseradish salad dressing should not be necessary because of the saltiness of the smoked trout fillets.

Moroccan Fish Tagine

Tagine **is the name of the large cooking pot used for this type of cooking in Morocco.**

Serves 4

2 garlic cloves, crushed	12 ounces tomatoes, sliced
2 tablespoons ground cumin	2 green bell peppers, seeded and thinly sliced
2 tablespoons paprika	
1 small fresh red chili (optional)	salt and ground black pepper
2 tablespoons tomato paste	chopped fresh cilantro, to garnish
4 tablespoons lemon juice	
4 whiting or cod cutlets, about 6 ounces each	

1 Mix together the garlic, cumin, paprika, chili, tomato paste and lemon juice. Spread this mixture over the fish, then cover and chill in the fridge for about 30 minutes to let the flavours penetrate.

2 Preheat the oven to 400°F. Arrange half of the tomatoes and peppers in a baking dish.

3 Cover with the fish, then arrange the remaining tomatoes and peppers on top. Cover the baking dish with foil and bake for about 45 minutes, until the fish is tender. Sprinkle with chopped cilantro or parsley to serve.

Cook's Tip
Try different white fish in this dish, such as hoki or pollack. If you are preparing this dish for a dinner party, it can be assembled completely and stored in the fridge until you are ready to cook it.

Shrimp and Mint Salad

Green (uncooked) shrimp make all the difference to this salad, as the flavors penetrate well into the flesh.

Serves 4

12 large green shrimp
1 tablespoon unsalted
   butter
1 tablespoon fish sauce
juice of 1 lime
3 tablespoons thin
   coconut milk
1 inch piece of fresh
   ginger, peeled and
   grated

1 teaspoon sugar
1 garlic clove, crushed
2 fresh red chilies, seeded
   and finely chopped
2 tablespoons fresh mint
   leaves
ground black pepper
8 ounces light green
   lettuce leaves, such as
   butter lettuce, to serve

1 Peel the shrimp, leaving the tails intact.

2 Melt the butter in a large frying pan and toss in the green shrimp until they turn pink.

3 Mix the fish sauce, lime juice, coconut milk, ginger, sugar, garlic, chilies and pepper together.

4 Toss the warm shrimp into the sauce with the mint leaves. Serve the shrimp mixture on a bed of green lettuce leaves.

Cook's Tip
For a really tropical touch, garnish this flavorful salad with some shavings of fresh coconut made using a potato peeler.

Mackerel with Tomatoes and Pesto

This rich and oily fish needs the sharp tomato sauce. The aromatic pesto is excellent drizzled over the fish.

Serves 4
For the pesto sauce
½ cup pine nuts
2 tablespoons fresh basil
   leaves
2 garlic cloves, crushed
2 tablespoons freshly
   grated Parmesan
   cheese
⅔ cup extra-virgin olive
   oil

salt and ground black
   pepper

For the fish
4 mackerel, gutted
2 tablespoons olive oil
4 ounces onion, coarsely
   chopped
1 pound tomatoes,
   coarsely chopped

1 To make the pesto sauce, place the pine nuts, basil and garlic cloves in a food processor fitted with a metal blade. Process until the mixture forms a rough paste. Add the Parmesan cheese and, with the machine running, gradually add the oil. Set aside until required.

2 Heat the broiler until very hot. Season the mackerel well with salt and pepper and cook for 10 minutes on either side.

3 Meanwhile, heat the oil in a large heavy-based saucepan and sauté the onions until soft.

4 Stir in the tomatoes and cook for 5 minutes. Serve the warm fish on top of the tomato mixture and top with a dollop of pesto sauce.

Cook's Tip
The pesto sauce can be made ahead and stored in the fridge until needed. Soften it again before using. For red pesto sauce, add some puréed sun-dried tomatoes after the oil.

Mackerel with Mustard and Lemon

Mackerel must be really fresh to be enjoyed. Look for bright, firm-fleshed fish.

Serves 4

4 fresh mackerel, about
    10 ounces each
1½–2 cups spinach

For the mustard and lemon butter
½ cup butter, melted
2 tablespoons wholegrain
    mustard

grated rind of 1 lemon
2 tablespoons lemon juice
3 tablespoons chopped
    fresh parsley
salt and ground black
    pepper

1 To prepare each mackerel, use a sharp knife to cut off the head just behind the gills, then cut along the belly so that the fish can be opened out flat. Remove the innards.

2 Place the fish on a board, skin-side up, and, with the heel of your hand, press along the backbone to loosen it.

3 Turn the fish the right way up and pull the bone away from the flesh. Remove the tail and cut each fish in half lengthwise. Wash and pat dry with paper towels. Score the skin three or four times, then season the fish.

4 To make the mustard and lemon butter, mix together the melted butter, mustard, lemon rind and juice and parsley. Season with salt and pepper. Place the mackerel on a broiler rack. Brush a little of the butter over the mackerel and broil for 5 minutes each side, basting occasionally, until cooked through.

5 Arrange the spinach leaves in the center of four large plates. Place the mackerel on top. Heat the remaining butter in a small saucepan until sizzling and pour over the mackerel. Serve immediately.

Smelt with Herb Sandwiches

Smelt are the tiny fry of sprats or herring and are served whole. Cayenne pepper makes them spicy hot.

Serves 4

unsalted butter, for
    spreading
6 slices whole wheat
    bread
6 tablespoons mixed
    chopped fresh herbs,
    such as parsley,
    chervil and chives
1 pound smelt,
    defrosted if frozen

scant ¾ cup all-purpose
    flour
1 tablespoon chopped
    fresh parsley
salt and cayenne pepper
peanut oil,
    for deep-frying
lemon slices, to garnish

1 Butter the bread slices. Sprinkle the herbs over three of the slices, then top with the remaining slices of bread. Remove the crusts and cut each sandwich into eight triangles. Cover with plastic wrap and set aside.

2 Rinse the smelt thoroughly. Drain and then pat dry on paper towels.

3 Put the flour, chopped parsley, salt and cayenne pepper in a large plastic bag and shake to mix. Add the smelt and toss gently in the seasoned flour until lightly coated. Heat the oil in a deep-fat fryer to 350°F.

4 Fry the fish in batches for 2–3 minutes, until golden and crisp. Lift out of the oil and drain on paper towels. Keep warm in the oven until all the fish is cooked.

5 Sprinkle the smelt with salt and more cayenne pepper, if liked, and garnish with the lemon slices. Serve immediately with the herb sandwiches.

Sole Goujons with Lime Mayonnaise

This simple dish can be rustled up quite quickly. It makes an excellent light lunch or supper.

Serves 4

1½ pound sole fillets,
    skinned
2 eggs, beaten
2 cups fresh white
    bread crumbs
oil, for deep-frying
salt and ground black
    pepper
lime wedges, to serve

1 small garlic clove,
    crushed
2 teaspoons capers,
    rinsed and chopped
2 teaspoons chopped
    small gherkins
finely grated rind
    of ½ lime
2 teaspoons lime juice
1 tablespoon chopped
    fresh cilantro

For the mayonnaise
scant 1 cup mayonnaise

1 To make the lime mayonnaise, mix together the mayonnaise, garlic, capers, gherkins, lime rind and juice and chopped cilantro. Season to taste with salt and pepper. Transfer to a serving bowl and chill until required.

2 Cut the sole fillets into finger-length strips. Dip into the beaten egg, then into the bread crumbs.

3 Heat the oil in a deep-fat fryer to 350°F. Add the fish in batches and fry until golden brown and crisp. Drain well on paper towels.

4 Pile the goujons onto warmed serving plates and serve with the lime wedges for squeezing over. Pass the lime mayonnaise around separately.

Cook's Tip
Make sure you use good-quality mayonnaise for the sauce, or – better still – make your own. But remember that some people, including pregnant women, should not eat raw egg.

Spicy Fish Rösti

Serve these delicious fish cakes crisp and hot for lunch or supper with a green salad.

Serves 4

12 ounces large, firm
    waxy potatoes
12 ounces salmon or cod
    fillet, skinned and
    boned
3–4 scallions, finely
    chopped
2 teaspoons grated fresh
    ginger

2 tablespoons chopped
    fresh cilantro
2 teaspoons lemon juice
2–3 tablespoons
    sunflower oil
salt and cayenne pepper
lemon wedges, to serve
fresh cilantro sprigs, to
    garnish

1 Bring a saucepan of water to a boil and cook the potatoes with their skins on for about 10 minutes. Drain and leave to cool for a few minutes.

2 Meanwhile, finely chop the salmon or cod fillet and place in a bowl. Stir in the chopped scallions, grated ginger, chopped cilantro and lemon juice. Season to taste with salt and cayenne pepper.

3 When the potatoes are cool enough to handle, peel off the skins and grate the potatoes coarsely. Gently stir the grated potato into the fish mixture.

4 Form the fish mixture into twelve cakes, pressing the mixture together but leaving the edges slightly rough.

5 Heat the oil in a large frying pan, and, when hot, fry the fish cakes a few at a time for 3 minutes on each side, until golden brown and crisp. Drain on paper towels. Serve hot with lemon wedges for squeezing over. Garnish with sprigs of fresh cilantro.

Mediterranean Plaice Rolls

Sun-dried tomatoes, pine nuts and anchovies make a flavorful combination for the stuffing mixture.

Serves 4

*4 plaice fillets, about 8
    ounces each, skinned*
6 tablespoons butter
1 small onion, chopped
*1 celery stalk, finely
    chopped*
*2 cups fresh white bread
    crumbs*
*3 tablespoons chopped
    fresh parsley*

*2 tablespoons pine nuts,
    toasted*
*3 – 4 pieces sun-dried
    tomatoes in oil,
    drained and chopped*
*2-ounce can anchovy
    fillets, drained and
    chopped*
5 tablespoons fish stock
pinch of black pepper

1 Preheat the oven to 350°F/. Using a sharp knife, cut the plaice fillets in half lengthwise to make eight smaller fillets.

2 Melt the butter in a pan and add the onion and celery. Cover with a tight-fitting lid and cook over a low heat for about 15 minutes until softened. Do not allow to brown.

3 Mix together the bread crumbs, parsley, pine nuts, sun-dried tomatoes and anchovies. Stir in the softened vegetables with the buttery juices and season to taste with pepper.

4 Divide the stuffing into eight portions. Taking one portion at a time, form the stuffing into balls, then roll up each one inside a plaice fillet. Secure each roll with a toothpick.

5 Place the rolled-up fillets in a buttered casserole. Pour over the stock and cover the dish with buttered foil. Bake for about 20 minutes, or until the fish flakes easily. Remove the toothpicks, then serve with a little of the cooking juices drizzled over.

Salmon with Watercress Sauce

Adding the watercress right at the end of cooking retains much of its flavor and colour.

Serves 4

1¼ cups crème fraîche
*2 tablespoons chopped
    fresh tarragon*
2 tablespoons butter
*1 tablespoon sunflower
    oil*
*4 salmon fillets, skinned
    and boned*

1 garlic clove, crushed
½ cup dry white wine
1 bunch watercress
*salt and ground black
    pepper*

1 Gently heat the crème fraîche in a small saucepan until just beginning to boil. Remove the pan from the heat and stir in half the tarragon. Leave the herb cream to infuse while cooking the fish.

2 Heat the butter and oil in a frying pan and fry the salmon fillets for 3 – 5 minutes on each side. Remove from the pan and keep warm.

3 Add the garlic and fry for another 1 minute, then pour in the wine and let it bubble until reduced to about 1 tablespoon.

4 Meanwhile, strip the leaves off the watercress stalks and chop finely. Discard any damaged leaves. (Save the watercress stalks for soup, if you wish.)

5 Strain the herb cream into the pan and cook for a few minutes, stirring until the sauce has thickened. Stir in the remaining tarragon and watercress, then cook for a few minutes, until wilted but still bright green. Season to taste with salt and pepper and serve at once, spooned over the salmon. The dish can be accompanied by a green salad if you wish.

Warm Salmon Salad

Red Mullet with Fennel

This light salad is perfect in summer. Serve immediately, or the salad greens will lose their color.

Ask the fish seller to gut the mullet but not to discard the liver, as this is a delicacy and provides much of the flavor.

Serves 4

1 pound salmon fillet, skinned
2 tablespoons sesame oil
grated rind of ½ orange
juice of 1 orange
1 teaspoon Dijon mustard
1 tablespoon chopped fresh tarragon
3 tablespoons peanut oil
4 ounces fine green

beans, trimmed
6 ounces mixed salad greens, such as young spinach leaves, radicchio and frisée
1 tablespoon toasted sesame seeds
salt and ground black pepper

Serves 4

3 small fennel bulbs
4 tablespoons olive oil
2 small onions, sliced
2–4 fresh basil leaves
4 small or 2 large red mullet, cleaned
grated rind of ½ lemon

⅔ cup fish stock
4 tablespoons butter
juice of 1 lemon

1 Cut the salmon into bite-size pieces, then make the dressing. Mix together the sesame oil, orange rind and juice, mustard, chopped tarragon and season to taste with salt and ground black pepper. Set aside.

2 Heat the peanut oil in a frying pan and fry the salmon pieces for 3–4 minutes, or until lightly browned but still tender on the inside.

3 While the salmon is cooking, blanch the green beans in boiling salted water for about 5–6 minutes, until tender yet still slightly crisp.

4 Add the dressing to the salmon, toss together gently and cook for 30 seconds. Remove the pan from the heat.

5 Arrange the salad on serving plates. Drain the beans and toss over the salad. Spoon over the salmon and cooking juices and serve immediately, sprinkled with the toasted sesame seeds.

1 Snip off the feathery leaves from the fennel bulbs, finely chop and reserve for the garnish. Cut the fennel into wedges, being careful to leave the layers attached at the root ends so the pieces stay intact.

2 Heat the oil in a frying pan large enough to take the fish in a single layer and cook the wedges of fennel and onions for about 10–15 minutes, until softened and lightly browned.

3 Tuck a basil leaf inside each mullet, then place on top of the vegetables. Sprinkle the lemon rind on top. Pour in the stock and bring just to a boil. Cover with a tight-fitting lid and cook gently for 15–20 minutes, until the fish is tender.

4 Melt the butter in a small saucepan and, when it starts to sizzle and color slightly, add the lemon juice. Pour over the mullet, sprinkle with the reserved fennel fronds and serve.

Cook's Tip
Grey mullet can also be cooked in this way. Look for fish with bright, convex eyes, firm, gleaming flesh and red gills.

Tuna with Pan-fried Tomatoes

Meaty and filling tuna steaks are served here with juicy tomatoes and black olives.

Serves 2

2 tuna steaks, about 6
  ounces each
6 tablespoons olive oil
2 tablespoons lemon juice
2 garlic cloves, chopped
1 teaspoon chopped fresh
  thyme
4 canned anchovy fillets,
  drained and chopped

8 ounces plum tomatoes,
  halved
2 tablespoons chopped
  fresh parsley
4 – 6 black olives, pitted
  and chopped
pinch of ground black
  pepper
crusty bread, to serve

1 Place the tuna steaks in a shallow non-metallic dish. Mix 4 tablespoons of the oil with the lemon juice, garlic, thyme, anchovies and pepper. Pour this mixture over the tuna and leave to marinate for at least 1 hour.

2 Lift the tuna from the marinade and place on a broiler rack. Broil for 4 minutes on each side, or until the tuna feels firm to touch, basting with the marinade. Take care not to overcook.

3 Meanwhile, heat the remaining oil in a frying pan and fry the tomatoes for a maximum of 2 minutes on each side.

4 Divide the tomatoes equally between two serving plates and scatter the chopped parsley and olives over them. Top each with a tuna steak.

5 Add the remaining marinade to the pan juices and warm through. Pour over the tomatoes and tuna steaks and serve at once with crusty bread for mopping up the juice.

Cook's Tip
If you are unable to find fresh tuna steaks, you could replace them with salmon fillets, if you wish – just broil them for one or two minutes more on each side.

Sautéed Salmon with Cucumber

Cucumber is the classic accompaniment to salmon. Here it is served hot, but be careful not to overcook it.

Serves 4

1 pound salmon fillet,
  skinned
3 tablespoons butter
2 scallions, chopped
½ cucumber, seeded and
  cut into strips
4 tablespoons dry white
  wine

½ cup crème fraîche
2 tablespoons chopped
  fresh chives
2 tomatoes, peeled, seeded
  and diced
salt and ground black
  pepper

1 Cut the salmon into about twelve thin slices, then cut across into strips.

2 Melt the butter in a large frying pan and sauté the salmon for 1–2 minutes. Remove the salmon strips using a slotted spoon and set aside.

3 Add the scallions to the pan and cook for 2 minutes. Stir in the cucumber and sauté for 1–2 minutes, until hot. Remove the cucumber mixture and keep warm with the salmon.

4 Add the wine to the pan and let it bubble until well reduced. Stir in the cucumber mixture, crème fraîche, 1 tablespoon of the chives and season to taste with salt and pepper. Return the salmon to the pan and warm through gently. Sprinkle the tomatoes and remaining chives over the top. Serve at once.

Crunchy-topped Cod

It's easy to forget just how tasty and satisfying a simple, classic dish can be.

Serves 4
4 pieces cod fillet, about 4
  ounces each, skinned
2 tomatoes, sliced
1 cup fresh whole wheat
  bread crumbs
2 tablespoons chopped
  fresh parsley

finely grated rind and
  juice of ½ lemon
1 teaspoon sunflower oil
salt and ground black
  pepper

1 Preheat the oven to 400°F. Arrange the cod fillets in a wide casserole.

2 Arrange the tomato slices on top. Mix together the bread crumbs, fresh parsley, lemon rind and juice and the oil with seasoning to taste.

3 Spoon the crumb mixture evenly over the fish, then bake for 15–20 minutes. Serve hot.

Fish Balls in Tomato Sauce

This quick meal is a good choice for young children, as you can guarantee there are no bones.

Serves 4
1 pound hoki or other
  white fish fillets,
  skinned
4 tablespoons fresh whole
  wheat bread crumbs
2 tablespoons chopped
  chives or scallions

14-ounce can chopped
  tomatoes
2 ounces button
  mushrooms, sliced
salt and ground black
  pepper

1 Cut the fish fillets into chunks; place in a food processor. Add the bread crumbs, and chives or scallions. Season and process until the fish is chopped, but still with some texture. Divide the fish mixture into about 16 even-size pieces, then mold them into balls with your hands.

2 Place the tomatoes and mushrooms in a saucepan; cook over a medium heat until boiling. Add the fish balls, cover and simmer for about 10 minutes until cooked. Serve hot.

Tuna and Corn Fish Cakes

These economical tuna fish cakes are quick to make. Use fresh mashed potatoes or instant mash.

Serves 4
Place 1½ cups mashed potato in a bowl; stir in 7 ounces tuna fish, ¼ cup canned corn and 2 tablespoons chopped parsley. Season to taste with salt and black pepper, then shape into eight patties. Press the fish cakes into 1 cup fresh bread crumbs to coat them lightly, then place on a baking sheet. Cook under a moderate broiler until crisp and golden, turning once. Serve hot with lemon wedges and fresh vegetables.

Cod Creole

Inspired by the cuisine of the Caribbean, this fish dish is both colorful and delicious.

Serves 4

1 pound cod fillets, skinned
1 tablespoon lime or lemon juice
2 teaspoons olive oil
1 onion, finely chopped
1 green bell pepper, seeded and sliced

½ teaspoon cayenne pepper
½ teaspoon garlic salt
14-ounce can chopped tomatoes
boiled rice or potatoes, to serve

1 Cut the cod fillets into bite-size chunks and sprinkle with the lime or lemon juice.

2 Heat the oil in a large, nonstick frying pan and fry the onion and pepper gently until softened. Add the cayenne pepper and garlic salt.

3 Stir in the cod and the chopped tomatoes. Bring to a boil, then cover and simmer for about 5 minutes, or until the fish flakes easily. Serve with boiled rice or potatoes.

Cook's Tip
This flavorful dish is surprisingly light in calories, so if you are worried about your waistline, this is the meal for you.

Salmon Pasta with Parsley Sauce

The parsley sauce is added at the last moment to the salmon mixture and does not have to be cooked separately.

Serves 4

1 pound salmon fillet, skinned
2 cups pasta, such as penne
6 ounces cherry tomatoes, halved
⅔ cup low-fat crème fraîche

3 tablespoons finely chopped parsley
finely grated rind of ½ orange
salt and ground black pepper

1 Cut the salmon into bite-size pieces, arrange on a heat proof plate and cover with foil.

2 Bring a large saucepan of salted water to a boil, add the pasta and return to a boil. Place the plate of salmon on top and simmer for 10–12 minutes, until the pasta and salmon are cooked.

3 Drain the pasta and toss with the tomatoes and salmon. Mix together the crème fraîche, parsley, orange rind and pepper to taste, then toss into the salmon and pasta. Serve hot or leave to cool to room temperature.

Cook's Tip
The grated orange rind in the sauce complements the salmon beautifully in this recipe. For an alternative, try trout fillets and substitute grated lemon rind.

Monkfish with Mexican Salsa

Remove the pinkish-grey membrane from the tail before cooking, or the fish will be tough.

Serves 4

1½-pound monkfish tail
3 tablespoons olive oil
2 tablespoons lime juice
1 garlic clove, crushed
1 tablespoon chopped
 fresh cilantro
salt and ground black
 pepper
fresh cilantro sprigs and
 lime slices, to garnish

For the salsa
4 tomatoes, seeded, peeled
 and diced
1 avocado, pitted, peeled
 and diced
½ red onion, chopped
1 green chili, seeded and
 chopped
2 tablespoons chopped
 fresh cilantro
2 tablespoons olive oil
1 tablespoon lime juice

1 To make the salsa, mix the salsa ingredients and let sit at room temperature for about 40 minutes.

2 Prepare the monkfish. Using a sharp knife, remove the pinkish-grey membrane. Cut the fillets from either side of the backbone, then cut each fillet in half to give four steaks.

3 Mix together the oil, lime juice, garlic, cilantro and seasoning in a shallow non-metallic dish. Turn the monkfish several times to coat with the marinade, then cover the dish and let marinate at cool room temperature, or in the fridge, for 30 minutes.

4 Remove the monkfish from the marinade and broil for 10–12 minutes, turning once and brushing regularly with the marinade until cooked through.

5 Serve the monkfish garnished with cilantro sprigs and lime slices and accompanied by the salsa.

Seafood Pancakes

The combination of fresh and smoked haddock imparts a wonderful flavor to the pancake filling.

Serves 4–6

12 ready-made pancakes

For the filling
8 ounces smoked haddock
 fillet
8 ounces fresh haddock
 fillet
1¼ cups milk
⅔ cup light cream
3 tablespoons butter
3 tablespoons all-purpose
 flour

pinch of freshly grated
 nutmeg
2 hard-boiled eggs,
 shelled and chopped
salt and ground black
 pepper
sprinkling of Gruyère
 cheese
curly salad greens, to
 serve (optional)

1 To make the filling, put the haddock fillets in a large pan. Add the milk and poach for 6–8 minutes, until just tender. Lift out the fish using a draining spoon and, when cool enough to handle, remove skin and bones. Reserve the milk. Measure the cream into a measuring cup, then strain enough milk into the cup to measure a scant 2 cups.

2 Melt the butter in a pan, stir in the flour and cook gently for 1 minute. Gradually mix in the milk mixture, stirring constantly to make a smooth sauce. Cook for 2–3 minutes. Season to taste with salt, pepper and nutmeg. Flake the haddock and fold into the sauce with the eggs. Let cool.

3 Preheat the oven to 350°F. Divide the filling among the pancakes. Fold the sides of each pancake into the center, then roll them up to enclose the filling completely. Butter four or six individual casseroles and arrange two or three filled pancakes in each, or butter one large dish for all the pancakes. Brush with melted butter and cook for 15 minutes. Sprinkle over the Gruyère and cook for another 5 minutes, until warmed through. Serve hot with a few curly salad greens, if you wish.

Herbed Plaice Croquettes

Deep-fry with clean oil every time as the fish will flavor the oil and spoil any other foods fried in the oil.

Serves 4

1 pound plaice fillets
1¼ cups milk
1 pound cooked potatoes
1 fennel bulb, finely
    chopped
1 garlic clove, finely
    chopped
3 tablespoons chopped
    fresh parsley
2 eggs

1 tablespoon unsalted
    butter
2 cups white bread
    crumbs
2 tablespoons sesame
    seeds
oil, for deep-frying
salt and ground black
    pepper

1   Poach the fish fillets in the milk for about 15 minutes until the fish flakes. Drain the fillets and reserve the milk.

2   Peel the skin off the fish and remove any bones. Process the fish, potatoes, fennel, garlic, parsley, eggs and butter in a food processor fitted with a metal blade.

3   Add 2 tablespoons of the reserved cooking milk and season to taste with salt and pepper.

4   Chill in the fridge for about 30 minutes, then shape into 20 croquettes with your hands.

5   Mix together the bread crumbs and sesame seeds.

6   Roll the croquettes in the mixture to form a good coating. Heat the oil in a large heavy-based saucepan and deep-fry in batches for about 4 minutes until golden brown. Drain well on paper towels and serve hot.

Mixed Smoked Fish Kedgeree

An ideal breakfast dish on a cold morning. Garnish with quartered hard-boiled eggs and season well.

Serves 6

1 pound mixed smoked
    fish such as smoked
    cod, smoked haddock,
    smoked mussels or
    oysters, if available
1¼ cups milk
1 cup long grain rice
1 slice lemon
4 tablespoons butter
1 teaspoon medium-hot
    curry powder

½ tsp freshly grated
    nutmeg
1 tablespoon chopped
    fresh parsley
salt and ground black
    pepper
2 hard-boiled eggs, to
    garnish

1   Poach the uncooked smoked fish in milk for 10 minutes or until it flakes. Drain off the milk and flake the fish. Mix with the other smoked fish.

2   Cook the rice in boiling water together with a slice of lemon for 10 minutes, or according to the instructions on the package, until just cooked. Drain well.

3   Melt the butter in a large saucepan and add the rice and fish. Shake the pan to mix all the ingredients together well.

4   Stir in the curry powder, nutmeg, parsley and seasoning. Serve immediately, garnished with quartered eggs.

Cook's Tip
When flaking the fish, keep the pieces fairly large to give this dish a chunky consistency.

Spanish-style Hake

Cod and haddock cutlets will work just as well as hake in this tasty fish dish.

Serves 4

2 tablespoons olive oil
2 tablespoons butter
1 onion, chopped
3 garlic cloves, crushed
1 tablespoon all-purpose flour
½ teaspoon paprika
4 hake cutlets, about 6 ounces each
8 ounces fine green beans, cut into 1-inch lengths

1½ cups fish stock
generous ½ cup dry white wine
2 tablespoons dry sherry
15–20 live mussels in the shell, cleaned
3 tablespoons chopped fresh parsley
salt and ground black pepper
crusty bread, to serve

1 Heat the oil and butter in a sauté or frying pan and cook the onion for 5 minutes, until softened but not browned. Add the crushed garlic and cook for 1 minute more.

2 Mix together the all-purpose flour and paprika, then lightly dust over the hake cutlets. Push the sautéed onion and garlic to one side of the pan.

3 Add the hake cutlets to the pan and fry until golden on both sides. Stir in the beans, stock, wine and sherry and season to taste with salt and pepper. Bring to a boil and cook for about 2 minutes.

4 Add the mussels and parsley, cover the pan with a tight-fitting lid and cook for 5–8 minutes, until the mussels have opened. Discard any that do not open.

5 Serve the hake in warmed, shallow soup bowls with crusty bread to mop up the juice.

Fish Goujons

Any white fish fillets can be used for the goujons – you could try a mixture of haddock and cod for a change.

Serves 4

4 tablespoons mayonnaise
2 tablespoons plain yogurt
grated rind of ½ lemon
squeeze of lemon juice
1 tablespoon chopped fresh parsley
1 tablespoon capers, chopped
2 x 6-ounce sole fillets, skinned

2 x 6-ounces plaice fillets, skinned
1 egg, lightly beaten
2 cups fresh white bread crumbs
1 tablespoon sesame seeds
pinch of paprika
oil, for frying
salt and ground black pepper
4 lemon wedges, to serve

1 To make the lemon mayonnaise, mix the mayonnaise, yogurt, lemon rind and juice, parsley and capers in a bowl. Cover and chill.

2 Cut the fish fillets into thin strips. Place the beaten egg in one shallow bowl. Mix together the bread crumbs, sesame seeds, paprika and seasoning in another bowl. Dip the fish strips, one at a time, into the beaten egg, then into the bread crumb mixture and toss until coated evenly. Lay on a clean plate.

3 Heat about 1 inch of oil in a frying pan until a cube of bread browns in 30 seconds. Deep-fry the strips in batches for 2-3 minutes, until lightly golden.

4 Remove with a slotted spoon, drain on paper towels and keep warm in the oven while frying the rest. Garnish with watercress and serve hot with lemon wedges and the chilled lemon mayonnaise.

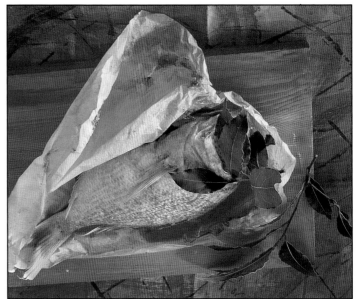

Pan-fried Garlic Sardines

Lightly fry a sliced garlic clove to garnish the fish. This dish could also be made with sprats or fresh anchovies.

Serves 4

2½ pounds fresh sardines
2 tablespoons olive oil
4 garlic cloves
finely grated rind of
2 lemons
2 tablespoons chopped
fresh parsley

salt and ground black
pepper

For the tomato bread
8 slices crusty bread,
toasted
2 large ripe beefsteak
tomatoes

1 Gut and clean the sardines thoroughly.

2 Heat the oil in a frying pan and cook the garlic cloves until they are softened.

3 Add the sardines and fry for 4–5 minutes. Sprinkle the lemon rind, parsley and seasoning over the top.

4 Cut the tomatoes in half and rub them onto the toast. Discard the skins. Serve the sardines with the tomato toast.

Cook's Tip
Make sure you use very ripe beefsteak tomatoes for this dish so they will rub onto the toast easily.

Sea Bass en Papillote

Bring the unopened packages to the table and let your guests unfold their own fish to release the delicious aroma.

Serves 4

4 small sea bass, gutted
generous ½ cup butter
1 pound spinach
3 shallots, finely chopped
4 tablespoons white wine

4 bay leaves
salt and ground black
pepper
new potatoes and glazed
carrots, to serve

1 Preheat the oven to 350°F. Season both the inside and outside of the fish with salt and pepper. Melt 4 tablespoons of the butter in a large heavy-based saucepan and add the spinach. Cook gently until the spinach has broken down into a smooth purée. Set aside to cool.

2 Melt another 4 tablespoons of the butter in a clean pan and add the shallots. Gently sauté for 5 minutes until soft. Add to the spinach and let cool.

3 Stuff the insides of the fish with the spinach filling.

4 For each fish, fold a large sheet of wax paper in half and cut around the fish laid on one half, to make a heart shape when unfolded. It should be at least 2 inches larger than the fish. Melt the remaining butter and brush a little onto the paper. Set the fish on one side of the paper.

5 Add a little wine and a bay leaf to each package.

6 Fold the other side of the paper over the fish and make small pleats to seal the two edges, starting at the curve of the heart. Brush the outsides with butter. Transfer the packages to a baking sheet and bake for 20–25 minutes until the packages are brown. Serve with new potatoes and glazed carrots.

Chili Shrimp

This delightful, spicy combination makes a lovely light main course for a casual supper.

Serves 3–4

3 tablespoons olive oil
2 shallots, chopped
2 garlic cloves, chopped
1 fresh red chili, chopped
1 pound ripe tomatoes, peeled, seeded and chopped
1 tablespoon tomato paste
1 bay leaf
1 fresh thyme sprig
6 tablespoons dry white wine
4 cups peeled, cooked large shrimp
salt and ground black pepper
coarsely torn fresh basil leaves, to garnish

1 Heat the oil in a saucepan and fry the shallots, garlic and chili until the garlic starts to brown.

2 Add the tomatoes, tomato paste, bay leaf, thyme, wine and seasoning. Bring to a boil, then reduce the heat and cook gently for about 10 minutes, stirring occasionally until the sauce has thickened. Remove the herbs.

3 Stir the shrimp into the sauce and heat through for a few minutes. Taste and adjust the seasoning. Scatter the basil leaves over the top and serve immediately.

Scallops with Ginger

Scallops are at their best in winter. Rich and creamy, this dish is very simple to make and quite delicious.

Serves 4

8–12 shelled scallops
3 tablespoons butter
1-inch piece fresh ginger, finely chopped
1 bunch scallions, diagonally sliced
4 tablespoons white vermouth
1 cup crème fraîche
salt and ground black pepper
chopped fresh parsley, to garnish

1 Remove the tough muscle opposite the coral on each scallop. Separate the coral and cut the white part of the scallop in half horizontally.

2 Melt the butter in a frying pan. Add the scallops, including the corals, and sauté for about 2 minutes until lightly browned. Take care not to overcook the scallops as this will toughen them.

3 Lift out the scallops with a draining spoon and transfer to a warmed serving dish. Keep warm.

4 Add the ginger and scallions to the pan and stir-fry for 2 minutes. Pour in the vermouth and allow to bubble until it has almost evaporated. Stir in the crème fraîche and cook for a few minutes until the sauce has thickened. Season to taste with salt and pepper.

5 Pour the sauce over the scallops, sprinkle with parsley and serve immediately.

Smoked Trout Pilaf

Smoked trout might seem an unusual partner for rice, but this is a winning combination.

Serves 4

1¼ cups white basmati rice	4 smoked trout fillets, skinned
3 tablespoons butter	½ cup slivered almonds, toasted
2 onions, sliced into rings	generous ½ cup seedless raisins
1 garlic clove, crushed	
2 bay leaves	2 tablespoons chopped fresh parsley
2 whole cloves	mango chutney and poppadoms, to serve
2 green cardamom pods	
2 cinnamon sticks	
1 teaspoon cumin seeds	

1 Wash the rice thoroughly in water and drain well. Set aside. Melt the butter in a large frying pan and fry the onions until well browned, stirring frequently.

2 Add the garlic, bay leaves, cloves, cardamom pods, cinnamon and cumin seeds, and stir-fry for 1 minute.

3 Stir in the rice, then add 2 ½ cups boiling water. Bring to a boil. Cover the pan with a tight-fitting lid, reduce the heat and cook very gently for 20–25 minutes, until the water has been absorbed and the rice is tender.

4 Flake the smoked trout and add to the pan with the almonds and raisins. Fork through gently. Re-cover the pan and allow the smoked trout to warm in the rice for a few minutes. Scatter the parsley over the top and serve with mango chutney and poppadoms.

Cod with Spiced Red Lentils

This is a very tasty and filling dish, yet it is a healthy option at the same time.

Serves 4

¾ cup red lentils	1 tablespoon lemon juice
¼ teaspoon ground turmeric	2 tablespoons chopped fresh cilantro
2½ cups fish stock	1 pound cod fillets, skinned and cut into large chunks
pinch of salt, to taste	
2 tablespoons oil	
1½ teaspoons cumin seeds	fresh cilantro leaves and lemon wedges, to garnish
1 tablespoon grated fresh ginger	
½ teaspoon cayenne pepper	

1 Put the lentils in a saucepan with the turmeric and stock. Bring to a boil, cover with a tight-fitting lid and simmer for 20–25 minutes, until the lentils are just tender. Remove from the heat and add salt, if needed.

2 Heat the oil in a small frying pan. Add the cumin seeds and, when they begin to pop, add the ginger and cayenne pepper. Stir-fry the spices for a few seconds, then pour onto the lentils. Add the lemon juice and cilantro and stir them gently into the mixture.

3 Lay the pieces of cod on top of the lentils, cover the pan and then cook gently over a low heat for 10–15 minutes, or until the fish is tender.

4 Transfer the lentils and cod to warmed serving plates with a spatula. Sprinkle over the cilantro leaves and garnish each serving with one or two lemon wedges. Serve hot.

Mediterranean Fish Stew

Use any combination of fish you wish in this stew, which is served with an authentic rouille sauce.

Serves 4

2 cups cooked shrimp in the shell
1 pound mixed white fish, skinned and chopped (reserve skin for the stock)
3 tablespoons olive oil
1 onion, chopped
1 leek, sliced
1 carrot, diced
1 garlic clove, chopped
½ teaspoon ground turmeric
⅔ cup dry white wine or cider
14-ounce can chopped tomatoes
sprig of fresh parsley, thyme and fennel
1 bay leaf

small piece of orange peel
1 prepared squid, body cut into rings and tentacles chopped
12 mussels in the shell
salt and ground black pepper
2–3 tablespoons fresh Parmesan cheese shavings and fresh parsley, to garnish

For the rouille sauce
2 slices white bread, without crusts
2 garlic cloves, crushed
½ fresh red chili
1 tablespoon tomato paste
3–4 tablespoons olive oil

1 Peel the shrimp, leaving the tails on. Make stock with the prawn and fish skins and 1¾ cups water. Fry the onion, leek, carrot and garlic in the oil for about 6–7 minutes; stir in the turmeric. Add the wine, tomatoes, the fish stock, herbs and orange peel. Bring to a boil, cover and simmer for 20 minutes.

2 To make the rouille sauce, purée all the sauce ingredients in a food processor or blender.

3 Add the fish and seafood to the pan and simmer for about 5–6 minutes, until the mussels open. Remove the bay leaf and peel; season to taste. Serve with a spoonful of the rouille, garnished with Parmesan cheese and parsley.

Salmon with Herb Butter

Other fresh herbs could be used to flavor the butter – try mint, fennel, parsley or oregano.

Serves 4

4 tablespoons butter, softened
finely grated rind of ½ small lemon
1 tablespoon lemon juice
1 tablespoon chopped fresh dill

4 salmon steaks
2 lemon slices, halved
4 fresh dill sprigs
salt and ground black pepper

1 Place the butter, lemon rind, lemon juice, chopped dill and seasoning in a small bowl and mix together with a fork until thoroughly blended.

2 Spoon the butter onto a piece of wax paper and roll up, smoothing with your hands into a sausage shape. Twist the ends tightly, enclose in plastic wrap and place in the freezer for 20 minutes until firm.

3 Meanwhile, preheat the oven to 375°F. Cut out four squares of foil big enough to enclose the salmon steaks and grease lightly. Place a salmon steak in the center of each square.

4 Remove the butter from the freezer and slice into eight rounds. Place two rounds on top of each salmon steak with a halved lemon slice in the center and a sprig of dill on top. Lift up the edges of the foil and crinkle them together until they are well sealed.

5 Lift the parcels onto a baking sheet and bake for about 20 minutes. Remove from the oven and place the unopened parcels on warmed plates. Open the parcels and slide the contents onto the plates with the juice.

Spanish Seafood Paella

Use monkfish instead of the cod, if you wish, and add a red mullet cut into chunks.

Serves 4

4 tablespoons olive oil	⅔ cup white wine
8 ounces cod, skinned and cut into chunks	¼ cup frozen peas
3 prepared baby squid, body cut into rings and tentacles chopped	4–5 saffron strands, soaked in 2 tablespoons hot water
1 onion, chopped	1 cup peeled, cooked shrimp
3 garlic cloves, finely chopped	8 fresh mussels in the shell, scrubbed
1 red bell pepper, seeded and sliced	salt and ground black pepper
4 tomatoes, skinned and chopped	1 tablespoon chopped fresh parsley, to garnish
1¼ cups arborio rice	lemon wedges, to serve
scant 2 cups fish stock	

1 Heat 2 tablespoons of the oil in a frying pan and stir-fry the cod and the squid for 2 minutes. Transfer to a bowl.

2 Heat the remaining oil in the pan and fry the onion, garlic and pepper for 6–7 minutes, stirring, until softened.

3 Stir in the tomatoes and fry for another 2 minutes, then add the rice, stirring to coat the grains with oil, and cook for 2–3 minutes more. Pour on the stock and wine and add the peas, saffron and water. Season to taste.

4 Gently stir in the reserved cooked fish with all the juice, followed by the shrimp, and then push the mussels into the rice. Cover with a tight-fitting lid and cook over a gentle heat for about 30 minutes, or until the stock has been absorbed. Remove from the heat, keep covered and let stand for 5 minutes. Sprinkle with parsley; serve with lemon wedges.

Spaghetti with Seafood Sauce

The Italian name for this tomato-based sauce is *marinara*. It is very popular in coastal regions.

Serves 4

3 tablespoons olive oil	6 ounces cooked clam meat (rinsed well if canned or bottled)
1 onion, chopped	
8 ounces spaghetti	
2½ cups tomato sauce	1 tablespoon lemon juice
1 tablespoon tomato paste	3 tablespoons chopped fresh parsley
1 teaspoon dried oregano	2 tablespoons butter
1 bay leaf	salt and ground black pepper
1 teaspoon sugar	
2 cups peeled, cooked shrimp	4 whole cooked shrimp, to garnish

1 Heat the oil in a saucepan and fry the onion and garlic for 6–7 minutes until softened. Meanwhile, cook the spaghetti in a large pan of boiling salted water for 10–12 minutes or according to the instructions on the package, until *al dente*.

2 Stir the tomato sauce, tomato paste, oregano, bay leaf and sugar into the onions and season to taste with salt and pepper. Bring to a boil, then simmer for 2–3 minutes.

3 Add the shellfish, lemon juice and 2 tablespoons of the parsley. Stir well, then cover and cook for 6–7 minutes more.

4 Drain the spaghetti and add the butter to the pan. Return the drained spaghetti to the pan and toss in the butter. Season well.

5 Divide the spaghetti among four warmed plates and top with the seafood sauce. Sprinkle with the remaining parsley, garnish with whole shrimp and serve immediately.

Garlic Chili Shrimp

Deep-fried Spicy Smelt

In Spain *gambas al ajillo* are traditionally cooked in small earthenware dishes, but a frying pan is just as suitable.

This is a delicious British dish – serve these tiny fish very hot and crisp.

Serves 4

4 tablespoons olive oil	1 tablespoon chopped
2 – 3 garlic cloves, finely	fresh parsley
chopped	salt and ground black
½–1 fresh red chili,	pepper
seeded and chopped	lemon wedges and
16 cooked whole shrimp	French bread, to serve

Serves 4

1 pound smelt	oil, for
3 tablespoons all-purpose	deep-frying
flour	salt and ground black
1 teaspoon paprika	pepper
pinch of cayenne pepper	4 lemon wedges, to
12 fresh parsley sprigs	garnish

1 Heat the oil in a large frying pan and stir-fry the garlic and chili for 1 minute, until the garlic begins to turn brown.

2 Add the shrimp and stir-fry for about 3–4 minutes, coating them well with the flavored oil.

3 Add the parsley, remove from the heat and serve four shrimp per person in heated bowls, with the flavored oil spooned over them. Serve with lemon wedges for squeezing and French bread to mop up the juice.

1 If using frozen smelt, defrost in the bag, then drain off any water. Spread the fish on paper towels and pat dry.

2 Place the flour, paprika, cayenne and seasoning in a large plastic bag. Add the smelt and shake gently until all the fish is lightly coated with the flour. Transfer to a plate.

3 Heat about 2 inches of oil in a saucepan or deep-fat fryer to 375°F, or until a cube of bread dropped into the oil browns in about 30 seconds.

4 Add the smelt in batches and deep-fry in the hot oil for 2–3 minutes, until the coating is lightly golden and crispy. Remove, drain on paper towels and keep warm in the oven while frying the rest.

5 When all the smelt is cooked, drop the sprigs of parsley into the hot oil (don't worry if the oil spits a bit) and fry for a few seconds until crisp. Drain on paper towels. Serve the smelt garnished with the deep-fried parsley sprigs and lemon wedges.

Baked Fish Creole-style

Fish fillets cooked in a colorful pepper and tomato sauce are topped with a cheesy crust.

Serves 4

1 tablespoon oil	3 – 4 drops Tabasco sauce
2 tablespoons butter	4 tail end pieces cod or
1 onion, thinly sliced	haddock fillets, about
1 garlic clove, chopped	6 ounces each, skinned
1 red bell pepper, halved,	6 basil leaves, shredded
seeded and sliced	3 tablespoons fresh bread
1 green bell pepper,	crumbs
halved, seeded and	¼ cup grated Cheddar
sliced	cheese
14-ounce can chopped	2 teaspoons chopped fresh
tomatoes with basil	parsley
1 tablespoon tomato	salt and ground black
paste	pepper
2 tablespoons chopped	fresh basil sprigs,
capers	to garnish

1 Preheat the oven to 450°F. Heat the oil and half of the butter in a saucepan, and fry the sliced onion for about 6–7 minutes until softened. Add the garlic, peppers, chopped tomatoes, tomato paste, capers and Tabasco and season to taste. Cover and cook for 15 minutes, then uncover and simmer gently for 5 minutes to reduce slightly.

2 Place the fish fillets in a buttered casserole, dot with the remaining butter and season lightly. Spoon the tomato and pepper sauce over the top and sprinkle with the shredded basil. Bake in the oven for about 10 minutes.

3 Meanwhile, mix together the bread crumbs, cheese and parsley in a bowl. Remove the fish from the oven and scatter the cheese mixture over the top. Return to the oven and bake for about another 10 minutes. Let the fish stand for about a minute, then, using a spatula, carefully transfer each topped fillet to a warmed plate. Garnish with sprigs of fresh basil and serve while still hot.

Tuna Fishcake Bites

An updated version of a traditional British tea-time dish, these little cakes would also make an elegant appetizer.

Serves 4

1½ pounds potatoes	salt and ground black
knob of butter	pepper
2 hard-boiled eggs,	green salad, to serve
chopped	
3 scallions, chopped	**For the tartar sauce**
grated rind of ½ lemon	4 tablespoons
1 teaspoon lemon juice	mayonnaise
2 tablespoons chopped	1 tablespoon plain yogurt
fresh parsley	1 tablespoon finely
7-ounce can tuna in oil,	chopped small
drained	gherkins
2 teaspoons capers,	1 tablespoon capers,
chopped	chopped
2 eggs, lightly beaten	1 tablespoon chopped
2 cups fresh white bread	fresh parsley
crumbs	
sunflower oil, for	
shallow-frying	

1 Boil the potatoes. Drain and mash with the butter.

2 Mix the hard-boiled eggs, scallions, lemon rind and juice, parsley, tuna, capers and 1 tablespoon of the beaten egg into the cooled potato. Season to taste, cover and chill.

3 Mix all the sauce ingredients together. Chill in the fridge.

4 Roll the fishcake mixture into about 24 balls. Dip these into the egg and then roll gently in the bread crumbs until evenly coated. Transfer to a plate.

5 Heat 6 tablespoons of the oil in a frying pan and fry the balls over a moderate heat, in batches, for about 4 minutes, turning two or three times until browned all over. Drain on paper towels and keep warm in the oven while frying the rest. Serve with the tartare sauce and a salad.

Kashmir Coconut Fish Curry

Mussels with Wine and Garlic

The combination of spices in this dish gives an interesting depth of flavor to the creamy curry sauce.

This famous French dish is traditionally known as *moules marinière*, and can be served as an appetizer or a main course.

Serves 4

2 tablespoons vegetable
   oil
2 onions, sliced
1 green bell pepper,
   seeded and sliced
1 garlic clove, crushed
1 dried chili, seeded and
   chopped
1 teaspoon ground
   coriander
1 teaspoon ground cumin
½ teaspoon ground
   turmeric
½ teaspoon hot chili
   powder
½ teaspoon garam masala

1 tablespoon all-purpose
   flour
4 ounces creamed
   coconut, chopped
1½ pounds haddock fillet,
   skinned and chopped
4 tomatoes, skinned,
   seeded and chopped
1 tablespoon lemon juice
2 tablespoons ground
   almonds
2 tablespoons heavy
   cream
fresh cilantro sprigs, to
   garnish
naan bread and boiled
   rice, to serve

1 Heat the oil in a large saucepan and add the onions, pepper and garlic. Cook for 6–7 minutes, until the onions and pepper have softened. Stir in the chopped dried chili, all the ground spices, the chili powder, garam masala and flour, and cook for 1 minute.

2 Dissolve the coconut in 2½ cups boiling water and stir into the spicy vegetable mixture. Bring to the boil, cover and then simmer gently for 6 minutes.

3 Add the fish and tomatoes and cook for 5–6 minutes, or until the fish has turned opaque. Uncover and gently stir in the lemon juice, ground almonds and cream. Season well, garnish with cilantro and serve with nan bread and rice.

Serves 4

4 pounds live mussels
1 tablespoon oil
2 tablespoons butter
1 small onion or 2
   shallots, finely
   chopped
2 garlic cloves, finely
   chopped

⅔ cup dry white wine or
   hard cider
fresh parsley sprigs
ground black pepper
2 tablespoons chopped
   fresh parsley, to
   garnish
French bread, to serve

1 Check that the mussels are closed. (Throw away any that are cracked or won't close when tapped.) Scrape the shells under cold running water and pull off the hairy beard attached to the hinge of the shell. Rinse well in two or three changes of water.

2 Heat the oil and butter in a large pan and fry the onions and garlic for 3–4 minutes.

3 Pour on the wine or cider and add the parsley sprigs, stir well, bring to a boil, then add the mussels. Cover with a tight-fitting lid and cook for about 5–7 minutes, shaking the pan once or twice until the shells open (throw away any that have not opened).

4 Serve the mussels and their juice sprinkled with the chopped parsley and some ground black pepper. Serve with hot French bread.

Thai Shrimp Salad

This salad has the distinctive flavor of lemon grass, the bulbous grass used widely in South-East Asian cooking.

Serves 2

2¼ cups peeled, cooked, jumbo shrimp
1 tablespoon oriental fish sauce
2 tablespoons lime juice
½ tablespoon soft light brown sugar
1 small fresh red chili, finely chopped
1 scallion, finely chopped
1 small garlic clove, crushed
1-inch piece fresh lemon grass, finely chopped
2 tablespoons chopped fresh cilantro
3 tablespoons dry white wine
8–12 Bibb lettuce leaves, to serve
fresh cilantro sprigs, to garnish

1 Place the jumbo shrimp in a bowl and add all the remaining ingredients. Stir well, cover and leave to marinate in the fridge for 2–3 hours, mixing and turning the shrimp occasionally.

2 Arrange two or three of the lettuce leaves on each of four individual serving plates.

3 Spoon the shrimp salad into the lettuce leaves. Garnish with fresh cilantro and serve immediately.

Cajun Spiced Fish

Fillets of fish are coated with an aromatic blend of herbs and spices and pan-fried in butter.

Serves 4

1 teaspoon dried thyme
1 teaspoon dried oregano
1 teaspoon ground black pepper
¼ teaspoon cayenne pepper
2 teaspoons paprika
½ teaspoon garlic salt
4 tail end pieces of cod fillet, about 6 ounces each
6 tablespoons butter
½ fresh red bell pepper, sliced
½ green bell pepper, sliced
fresh thyme sprigs, to garnish
grilled tomatoes and sweet potato purée, to serve

1 Place all the herbs and spices in a bowl and mix well. Dip the fish fillets in the spice mixture until lightly coated.

2 Heat 2 tablespoons of the butter in a large frying pan, add the peppers and fry for 4–5 minutes, until softened. Remove the peppers and keep warm.

3 Add the remaining butter to the pan and heat until sizzling. Add the cod fillets and fry over a moderate heat for about 3–4 minutes on each side, until browned and cooked.

4 Transfer the fish to a warmed serving dish, surround with the peppers and garnish with thyme. Serve the spiced fish with some grilled tomatoes and sweet potato purée.

Golden Fish Pie

This lovely light pie with a crumpled phyllo pastry topping makes a delicious lunch or supper dish.

Serves 4–6

1½ pounds white fish fillets
1¼ cups milk
flavoring ingredients such as onion slices, bay leaf and black peppercorns
1 cup peeled, cooked shrimp, defrosted if frozen
½ cup butter

½ cup all-purpose flour
1¼ cups light cream
¾ cup grated Gruyère cheese
1 bunch watercress, leaves only, chopped
1 teaspoon mustard
5 sheets phyllo pastry
salt and ground black pepper

1 Place the fish in a saucepan, pour over the milk and add the flavoring ingredients. Bring to a boil, cover with a lid and simmer for 10–12 minutes, until the fish is almost tender. Skin and bone the fish, then coarsely flake into a shallow ovenproof dish. Scatter the shrimp over the fish. Strain the milk and reserve.

2 Melt 4 tablespoons of the butter in a pan. Stir in the flour; cook for 1 minute. Stir in the milk and cream. Bring to the boil, stirring, then simmer for 2–3 minutes, until thickened. Remove from the heat, stir in the Gruyère, watercress and then mustard, season. Pour the mixture over the fish and leave to cool.

3 Preheat the oven to 375°F, then melt the remaining butter. Brush one sheet of phyllo pastry with a little butter, then crumple up loosely and place on top of the filling. Repeat with the remaining phyllo sheets and butter until they are all used up and the pie is completely covered.

4 Bake in the oven for 25–30 minutes, until the pastry is golden and crisp. Serve immediately.

Special Fish Pie

This fish pie is colorful, healthy and best of all, it is very simple to make.

Serves 4

12 ounces haddock fillet, skinned
2 tablespoons cornstarch
1 cup peeled, cooked shrimp
7-ounce can corn, drained
scant 1 cup frozen peas
¾ cup milk

¾ cup yogurt
1½ cups fresh whole wheat bread crumbs
generous ¼ cup grated Cheddar cheese
salt and ground black pepper

1 Preheat the oven to 375°F. Cut the haddock into bite-size pieces and toss in cornstarch to coat evenly.

2 Place the fish, shrimp, corn and peas in a baking dish. Beat together the milk, yogurt and seasoning, then pour into the dish.

3 Mix together the bread crumbs and grated cheese, then spoon evenly over the top. Bake for 25–30 minutes, or until golden brown. Serve hot with fresh vegetables.

Cook's Tip
For a more economical version of this dish, omit the shrimp and replace with more fish fillet.

Smoked Trout with Cucumber

Smoked trout provides an easy and delicious first course or light meal. Serve at room temperature for the best flavor.

Serves 4

1 large cucumber
4 tablespoons crème fraîche or strained plain yogurt
1 tablespoon chopped fresh dill
4 smoked trout fillets
salt and ground black pepper
dill sprigs, to garnish
crusty whole wheat bread, to serve

1 Peel the cucumber, cut in half lengthwise and scoop out the seeds using a teaspoon. Dice the flesh.

2 Put the cucumber in a colander, place over a plate and sprinkle with salt. Alow to drain for at least 1 hour to draw out the excess moisture.

3 Rinse the cucumber well, then pat dry on paper towels. Transfer the cucumber to a bowl and stir in the crème fraîche or yogurt, chopped dill and some freshly ground pepper. Chill the cucumber salad for about 30 minutes.

4 Arrange the trout fillets on individual plates. Spoon the cucumber and dill salad on one side and grind over a little black pepper. Garnish the dish with dill sprigs and serve with crusty bread.

Fish Cakes

Homemade fish cakes are an underrated food which bear little resemblance to the store-bought type.

Serves 4

1 pound cooked, mashed potatoes
1 pound cooked, mixed white and smoked fish such as haddock or cod, flaked
2 tablespoons butter, cubed
3 tablespoons chopped fresh parsley
1 egg, separated
1 egg, beaten
fine bread crumbs made with stale bread (about 1 cup)
pinch of pepper
oil, for shallow frying
crisp salad, to serve

1 Place the potatoes in a bowl and beat in the fish, butter, parsley and egg yolk. Season to taste with pepper.

2 Divide the fish mixture into eight equal portions, then, with floured hands, form each into a flat cake.

3 Beat the remaining egg white with the whole egg. Dip each fish cake in the beaten egg, then in bread crumbs.

4 Heat the oil in a frying pan and fry the fish cakes for about 3–5 minutes on each side, until crisp and golden. Drain on paper towels and serve hot with a crisp salad.

Cook's Tip
Make smaller fish cakes to serve as an appetizer with a salad garnish. For an extra-special version, make them with cooked fresh salmon or drained, canned red or pink salmon.

Stuffed Plaice Rolls

Plaice fillets are a good choice for families because they are economical, easy to cook and free of bones.

Serves 4

1 zucchini, grated
2 carrots, grated
4 tablespoons fresh whole wheat bread crumbs
1 tablespoon lime or lemon juice
4 plaice fillets
salt and ground black pepper
new potatoes, to serve

1 Preheat the oven to 400°F. Mix together the carrots and zucchini. Stir in the bread crumbs, lime or lemon juice and season with salt and pepper.

2 Lay the fish fillets skin-side up and divide the stuffing between them, spreading it evenly.

3 Roll up to enclose the stuffing and place in a baking dish. Cover and bake for about 30 minutes, or until the fish flakes easily. Serve hot with new potatoes.

Mackerel Kebabs with Parsley

Oily fish such as mackerel is ideal for broiling as it cooks quickly and needs no extra oil.

Serves 4

1 pound mackerel fillets
finely grated rind and juice of 1 lemon
3 tablespoons chopped fresh parsley
12 cherry tomatoes
8 pitted black olives
salt and ground black pepper
boiled rice or noodles and green salad, to serve

1 Cut the fish into 1½-inch chunks and place in a bowl with half the lemon rind and juice, half of the parsley and some seasoning. Cover the bowl and allow to marinate for about 30 minutes.

2 Thread the chunks of fish on to eight long wooden or metal skewers, alternating them with the cherry tomatoes and olives. Cook the kebabs under a hot broiler for 3–4 minutes, turning the kebabs occasionally, until the fish is cooked.

3 Mix the remaining lemon rind and juice with the remaining parsley in a small bowl, then season to taste with salt and pepper. Spoon the dressing over the kebabs. Serve hot with plain boiled rice or noodles and a leafy green salad.

Grilled Salmon Steaks with Fennel

Fennel grows wild all over the south of Italy. Its mild aniseed flavor goes well with fish.

Serves 4

juice of 1 lemon
3 tablespoons chopped
 fresh fennel, or the
 green feathery leaves
 from the top of a
 fennel bulb
1 teaspoon fennel seeds

3 tablespoons olive oil
4 salmon steaks of the
 same thickness, about
 1½ pounds
salt and ground black
 pepper
lemon wedges, to garnish

1 Combine the lemon juice, chopped fennel and fennel seeds with the olive oil in a bowl. Add the salmon steaks, turning them to coat them with the marinade. Sprinkle with salt and ground black pepper. Cover and place in the fridge. Allow to stand for about 2 hours.

2 Preheat the broiler. Arrange the fish in one layer on a broiler pan or shallow baking pan. Broil about 4 inches from the broiler element for 3–4 minutes.

3 Turn the steaks over and spoon on the remaining marinade. Broil for 3–4 minutes, or until the edges begin to brown. Serve hot, garnished with lemon wedges.

Cook's Tip
If you wish, remove the skin from the salmon steaks before serving. Simply insert the prongs of a fork between the flesh and the skin at one end and roll the skin around the prongs in a smooth motion.

Seafood Pilaf

This one-pan dish makes a satisfying meal. For a special occasion, use dry white wine instead of orange juice.

Serves 4

2 teaspoons olive oil
1½ cups long-grain rice
1 teaspoon ground
 turmeric
1 red bell pepper, seeded
 and diced
1 small onion, finely
 chopped
2 zucchini, sliced
5 ounces button
 mushrooms, wiped
 and halved

1½ cups fish or chicken
 stock
⅔ cup orange juice
12 ounces white fish
 fillets
12 live mussels (or
 cooked shelled
 mussels)
salt and ground black
 pepper
grated rind of 1 orange,
 to garnish

1 Heat the oil in a large nonstick frying pan and fry the rice and turmeric over a gentle heat for about 1 minute.

2 Add the pepper, onion, zucchini and mushrooms. Stir in the stock and orange juice. Bring to a boil.

3 Reduce the heat and add the fish. Cover with a tight-fitting lid and simmer gently for about 15 minutes, until the rice is tender and the liquid absorbed. Stir in the mussels and heat thoroughly. Adjust the seasoning, sprinkle with orange rind and serve hot.

Cook's Tip
If you wish, bring the pan to the table, rather than transferring the pilaf to a serving dish, and let everyone help themselves.

Grilled Fresh Sardines

Fresh sardines are flavorful, firm-fleshed and rather different in taste and consistency from those canned in oil.

Serves 4–6

2 pounds very heavy fresh sardines, gutted and with heads removed	salt and ground black pepper
olive oil, for brushing	3 tablespoons chopped fresh parsley, to serve
	lemon wedges, to garnish

1 Preheat the broiler. Rinse the sardines in water. Pat dry with kitchen paper.

2 Brush the sardines lightly with olive oil and sprinkle generously with salt and pepper. Place the sardines in one layer in a broiler pan. Broil for about 3–4 minutes.

3 Turn, and cook for 3–4 minutes more, or until the skin begins to brown. Serve immediately, sprinkled with parsley and garnished with lemon wedges.

Cook's Tip
For a fuller flavor, you might like to leave the sardines whole, as they do in some Mediterranean countries.

Red Mullet with Tomatoes

Red mullet is a popular fish in Italy, and in this recipe both its flavor and color are accentuated.

Serves 4

4 red mullet, about 6–7 ounces each	2 cloves garlic, finely chopped
1 pound tomatoes, peeled, or 14-ounce can plum tomatoes	½ cup dry white wine
4 tablespoons olive oil	4 thin lemon slices, cut in half
4 tablespoons finely chopped fresh parsley	salt and ground black pepper

1 Scale and clean the fish without removing the liver. Wash and pat dry with paper towels.

2 Finely chop the tomatoes. Heat the oil in a saucepan or flameproof casserole large enough to hold the fish in one layer. Add the parsley and garlic, and sauté for 1 minute. Stir in the tomatoes and cook over a moderate heat for 15–20 minutes. Season to taste with salt and pepper.

3 Add the red mullet to the tomato sauce and cook over a moderate to high heat for 5 minutes. Add the wine and the lemon slices. Bring the sauce back to a boil, and cook for about 5 minutes more. Turn the fish over and continue to cook for 4–5 minutes more. Remove the fish to a warmed serving platter and keep warm until needed.

4 Boil the sauce for 3–4 minutes to reduce it slightly, then spoon it over the fish and serve immediately.

Cook's Tip
To peel fresh tomatoes, use a sharp knife to make a slit in their bases, plunge into boiling water for 30 seconds, or until the skins split, and then plunge into cold water. The skins should then slip off easily.

Middle Eastern Sea Bream

Buy the smallest sea bream you can find to cook whole, allowing one for two people.

Serves 4

4-pound sea bream or
   2 smaller sea bream
2 tablespoons olive oil
¾ cup pine nuts
1 large onion, finely
   chopped
1 pound ripe tomatoes,
   coarsely chopped
½ cup raisins

ground cinnamon
mixed spice
3 tablespoons chopped
   fresh mint
1¼ cups long-grain rice
3 lemon slices
1¼ cups fish stock
salt

1 Trim, gut and scale the sea bream. Meanwhile, preheat the oven to 350°F.

2 Heat the oil in a large heavy-based saucepan and stir-fry the pine nuts for 1 minute. Add the onions and continue to stir-fry until softened but not colored.

3 Add the tomatoes and simmer for 10 minutes, then stir in the raisins, ¼ teaspoon each cinnamon and mixed spice and the mint.

4 Add the rice and lemon slices. Transfer to a large roasting pan and pour the fish stock over the top.

5 Place the fish on top and cut several slashes in the skin. Sprinkle on a little salt, mixed spice and cinnamon and bake in the preheated oven for 30–35 minutes for large fish or 20–25 minutes for smaller fish.

Cook's Tip
If you prefer, use almonds instead of pine nuts. Use the same quantity of blanched almonds and split them in half before stir-frying.

Salmon with Spicy Pesto

This pesto uses sunflower seeds and chili as its flavoring rather than the classic basil and pine nuts.

Serves 4

4 x 8-ounce salmon
   steaks
2 tablespoons sunflower
   oil
finely grated rind and
   juice of 1 lime
pinch of salt

For the pesto
6 mild fresh red chilies
2 garlic cloves
2 tablespoons pumpkin
   or sunflower seeds
freshly grated rind and
   juice of 1 lime
5 tablespoons olive oil
salt and ground black
   pepper

1 Insert a very sharp knife close to the top of the salmon's backbone. Working closely to the bone, cut halfway through the steak all round. repeat with the other side and pull out the bone. Remove any extra visible bones with a pair of tweezers.

2 Sprinkle a little salt on the surface and take hold of the end of the salmon, skin-side down. Insert a small sharp knife under the skin and, working away from you, cut off the skin keeping as close to the skin as possible. Repeat with the three remaining pieces of fish.

3 Rub the sunflower oil into the boneless fish rounds. Add the lime juice and rind and marinate in the fridge for 2 hours.

4 To make the pesto, seed the chilies and place them together with the garlic cloves, pumpkin or sunflower seeds, lime juice, rind and seasoning in a food processor or blender. Process until well mixed. Pour the olive oil gradually over the moving blades until the sauce has thickened and emulsified. Drain the salmon from its marinade. Broil the fish steaks for about 5 minutes on either side and serve with the spicy pesto.

Roast Chicken with Celery Root

Celery root and whole wheat bread crumbs give the stuffing an unusual and delicious twist.

Serves 4

3½-pound chicken
1 tablespoon butter

For the stuffing

1 pound celery root, chopped
3 tablespoons butter
3 slices bacon, chopped
1 onion, finely chopped
leaves from 1 fresh thyme sprig, chopped
leaves from 1 fresh small tarragon sprig, chopped
2 tablespoons chopped fresh parsley
1½-cups fresh whole wheat bread crumbs
dash of Worcestershire sauce
1 egg
salt and ground black pepper

1 To make the stuffing, cook the celery root in boiling water until tender. Drain well and chop finely. Heat 2 tablespoons of the butter in a saucepan and gently cook the bacon and onion until the onion is soft. Stir in the celery root and herbs and cook, stirring occasionally, for 2–3 minutes. Meanwhile, preheat the oven to 400°F.

2 Remove the pan from the heat and stir in the fresh bread crumbs, Worcestershire sauce, enough egg to bind the mixture, and season it with salt and pepper. Use this mixture to stuff the neck cavity of the chicken. Season the bird's skin, then rub it with the remaining butter.

3 Roast the chicken, basting occasionally with the pan drippings, for 1¼–1½ hours, until the juices run clear when the thickest part of the leg is pierced. Turn off the oven, open the door slightly and allow the chicken to rest for about 10 minutes before carving.

Chicken with Lemon and Herbs

The herbs can be changed according to what is available; for example, parsley or thyme could be used.

Serves 2

4 tablespoons butter
2 scallions, white part only, finely chopped
1 tablespoon chopped fresh tarragon
1 tablespoon chopped fresh fennel
juice of 1 lemon
4 chicken thighs
salt and ground black pepper
lemon slices and herb sprigs, to garnish

1 Preheat the broiler to moderate. In a small saucepan, melt the butter, then add the scallions, herbs and lemon juice; season with salt and pepper.

2 Brush the chicken thighs generously with the herb mixture, then broil for 10–12 minutes, basting frequently with the herb mixture.

3 Turn the chicken over and baste again, then cook for another 10–12 minutes or until the chicken juices run clear.

4 Serve the chicken garnished with lemon slices and herb sprigs, and accompanied by any remaining herb mixture.

Chicken with Peppers

This colorful dish comes from the south of Italy, where sweet peppers are plentiful.

Serves 4

3-pound chicken, cut into serving pieces
6 tablespoons olive oil
2 red onions, finely sliced
2 garlic cloves, finely chopped
small piece of dried chili, crumbled (optional)
½ cup dry white wine

3 large bell peppers (red, yellow or green), seeded and sliced into strips
2 tomatoes, fresh or canned, peeled and chopped
3 tablespoons chopped fresh parsley
salt and ground black

1 Trim any fat off the chicken and remove all excess skin.

2 Heat half the oil in a large heavy saucepan or flameproof casserole and cook the onion over a gentle heat until soft. Reserve. Add the remaining oil to the pan, raise the heat to moderate, add the chicken pieces and brown them on all sides, 6–8 minutes. Return the onions to the pan, and add the garlic and dried chili, if using.

3 Pour in the wine and cook until it has reduced by half. Add the peppers and stir well to coat. Season to taste. After 3–4 minutes, stir in the tomatoes. Lower the heat, cover the pan with a tight-fitting lid, and cook for about 25–30 minutes, until the peppers are soft and the chicken is cooked. Stir occasionally. Stir in the parsley and serve.

Cook's Tip

For a more elegant version of this dish to serve at a dinner party, use skinless, boneless chicken breasts. Substitute the fresh parsley with different chopped fresh herbs, such as cilantro, tarragon, rosemary, chervil or marjoram.

Golden Parmesan Chicken

Served cold with the garlic mayonnaise, these morsels of chicken make good picnic food.

Serves 4

4 chicken breast fillets, skinned
1½ cups fresh white bread crumbs
½ cup finely grated Parmesan cheese
2 tablespoons chopped fresh parsley
2 eggs, beaten
4 tablespoons butter, melted

salt and ground black pepper
crisp green salad, to serve

For the garlic mayonnaise
½ cup good-quality mayonnaise
½ cup plain yogurt
1–2 garlic cloves, crushed

1 Cut each chicken fillet into four or five large chunks. Mix together the bread crumbs, Parmesan cheese, parsley and salt and pepper in a shallow dish.

2 Dip the chicken pieces in the beaten egg, then into the bread crumb mixture. Place in a single layer on a baking sheet and chill in the fridge for at least 30 minutes.

3 Meanwhile, to make the garlic mayonnaise, mix the mayonnaise, yogurt, garlic and pepper to taste. Spoon the mayonnaise into a small serving bowl. Chill in the fridge until ready to serve.

4 Preheat the oven to 350°F. Drizzle the melted butter over the chicken pieces and cook for about 20 minutes, until crisp and golden. Serve the chicken immediately with a crisp green salad and the garlic mayonnaise for dipping.

Chicken in Green Sauce

Slow, gentle cooking makes the chicken in this dish very succulent and tender.

Serves 4

2 tablespoons butter
1 tablespoon olive oil
4 chicken portions – legs,
   breasts or quarters
1 small onion, finely
   chopped
⅔ cup medium-bodied
   dry·white wine
⅔ cup chicken stock

2 fresh thyme sprigs
2 fresh tarragon sprigs
6 ounces watercress
   leaves
⅔ cup heavy cream
salt and ground black
   pepper
watercress leaves, to
   garnish

1 Heat the butter and oil in a frying pan and brown the chicken evenly. Transfer the chicken to a plate using a slotted spoon and keep warm in the oven.

2 Add the onion to the pan juices and cook until softened but not colored. Stir in the wine, then boil for 2–3 minutes. Add the stock and bring to the boil. Return the chicken to the pan, cover with a tight-fitting lid and cook very gently for about 30 minutes, until the chicken juices run clear when pierced with the point of a knife. Then transfer the chicken to a warm dish, cover and keep warm.

3 Boil the pan juices hard until they are reduced to about 4 tablespoons. Remove the leaves from the herbs and add to the pan with the watercress leaves and cream. Simmer over a moderate heat until slightly thickened.

4 Return the chicken to the casserole, season to taste with salt and pepper and heat through for a few minutes. Garnish with watercress leaves to serve.

Spatchcocked Deviled Cornish Hens

"Spatchcock" refers to birds that have been split and skewered flat. This shortens the cooking time considerably.

Serves 4

1 tablespoon English
   mustard powder
1 tablespoon paprika
1 tablespoon ground
   cumin
4 teaspoons tomato
   ketchup

1 tablespoon lemon juice
5 tablespoons butter,
   melted
4 Cornish hens, about 1
   pound each
pinch of salt

1 Mix together the mustard, paprika, cumin, ketchup, lemon juice and salt until smooth, then gradually stir in the butter.

2 Using game shears or strong kitchen scissors, split each Cornish hen along one side of the backbone, then cut down the other side of the backbone to remove it.

3 Open out a Cornish hen, skin-side up, then press down firmly with the heel of your hand. Pass a long skewer through one leg and out through the other to secure the bird open and flat. Repeat with the remaining birds.

4 Spread the mustard mixture evenly over the skin of the birds. Cover loosely and leave in a cool place for at least 2 hours to marinate. Preheat the broiler.

5 Place the birds, skin-side up, under the broiler and cook for about 12 minutes. Turn the birds over, baste with any pan juices, and cook for another 7 minutes, until the juices run clear when pierced with the point of a knife.

Cook's Tip
For an al fresco *meal in the summer, these spatchcocked Cornish hens may be cooked on a barbecue.*

Stoved Chicken

"Stoved" is derived from the French *étouffer*, meaning to cook in a covered pot.

Serves 4

2 pounds potatoes, cut
  into ¼-inch slices
2 large onions, thinly
  sliced
1 tablespoon chopped
  fresh thyme
2 tablespoons butter
1 tablespoon
  sunflower oil

2 large slices bacon,
  chopped
4 large chicken pieces,
  cut in half
1 bay leaf
2½ cups chicken stock
salt and ground black
  pepper

1 Preheat the oven to 300°F. Make a thick layer of half the potato slices in a large heavy-based casserole, then cover with half the onion. Sprinkle with half of the thyme and season.

2 Heat the butter and oil in a large frying pan and brown the bacon and chicken. Using a slotted spoon, transfer the chicken and bacon to the casserole. Reserve the fat in the pan. Sprinkle the rest of the thyme and some seasoning over the chicken and add the bayleaf. Cover with the rest of the onion, followed by a neat layer of overlapping potato slices. Sprinkle with seasoning.

3 Pour the stock into the casserole, brush the potatoes with the reserved fat, then cover with a tight-fitting lid and cook in the oven for about 2 hours, until the chicken is tender.

4 Preheat the broiler. Uncover the casserole and place under the broiler. Cook until the slices of potatoes are beginning to brown and crisp. Serve hot.

Cook's Tip
Instead of using large chicken pieces, use thighs or drumsticks, or a mixture of the two.

Chicken with Red Cabbage

Crushed juniper berries provide a distinctive flavor in this unusual casserole.

Serves 4

4 tablespoons butter
4 large chicken pieces,
  cut in half
1 onion, chopped
8¼ cups finely shredded
  red cabbage

4 juniper berries, crushed
12 cooked chestnuts
½ cup full-bodied red
  wine
salt and ground black
  pepper

1 Heat the butter in a heavy-based flameproof casserole and lightly brown the chicken pieces. Transfer to a plate.

2 Add the onion to the casserole and fry gently until soft and light golden brown. Stir the cabbage and juniper berries into the casserole, season and cook over a moderate heat for about 6–7 minutes, stirring once or twice.

3 Stir the chestnuts into the casserole, then tuck the chicken pieces under the cabbage so they are on the bottom of the casserole. Pour in the red wine.

4 Cover and cook gently for about 40 minutes until the chicken juices run clear and the cabbage is very tender. Adjust the seasoning to taste and serve immediately.

Italian Chicken

Use chicken legs, breasts or quarters in this colorful dish, and a different type of pasta if you prefer.

Serves 4

2 tablespoons all-purpose
  flour
4 chicken pieces
2 tablespoons olive oil
1 onion, chopped
2 garlic cloves, chopped
1 red bell pepper, seeded
  and chopped
14-ounce can chopped
  tomatoes
2 tablespoons red pesto
  sauce

4 sun-dried tomatoes in
  oil, chopped
⅔ cup chicken stock
1 teaspoon dried oregano
8 black olives, pitted
salt and ground black
  pepper
chopped fresh basil and
  whole basil leaves, to
  garnish
tagliatelle, to serve

1 Place the flour and seasoning in a plastic bag. Add the chicken pieces and shake well until coated. Heat the oil in a flameproof casserole and brown the chicken quickly. Remove with a slotted spoon and set aside.

2 Lower the heat and add the onion, garlic and pepper and cook for 5 minutes. Stir in the remaining ingredients, except the olives, and bring to a boil.

3 Return the sautéed chicken pieces to the casserole, season lightly, cover with a tight-fitting lid and simmer for 30–35 minutes, or until the chicken is cooked.

4 Add the black olives and simmer for another 5 minutes. Transfer to a warmed serving dish, sprinkle with the chopped basil and garnish with basil leaves. Serve with hot tagliatelle.

Cook's Tip
If you do not have red pesto sauce, use green pesto instead. Finely chop, then purée two sun-dried tomato pieces in a blender or food processor and add with the other ingredients.

Honey and Orange Glazed Chicken

This dish is popular in the United States and Australia and is ideal for an easy meal served with baked potatoes.

Serves 4

4–6 ounce boneless
  chicken breasts
1 tablespoon sunflower
  oil
4 scallions, chopped
1 garlic clove, crushed
3 tablespoons honey
4 tablespoons fresh
  orange juice

1 orange, peeled and
  segmented
2 tablespoons soy sauce
fresh lemon balm or
  Italian parsley, to
  garnish
baked potatoes and mixed
  salad, to serve

1 Preheat the oven to 375°F. Place the chicken breasts, with skins on, in a single layer in a shallow roasting pan and set aside.

2 Heat the sunflower oil in a small saucepan, and gently fry the scallions and garlic for about 2 minutes until softened but not browned. Add the honey, orange juice, orange segments and soy sauce to the pan, stirring well, and cook until the honey has completely dissolved.

3 Pour the sauce over the chicken and bake, uncovered, for about 45 minutes, basting once or twice until the chicken is cooked. Check by piercing with the point of a knife; the juices should run clear. Garnish with lemon balm or flat leaf parsley and serve with baked potatoes and a salad.

Cook's Tip
For a slightly spicier version, look out for mustard that has been flavored with honey to add to this dish instead of the honey. Use the same amount.

Cajun Chicken Jambalaya

Wonderfully spicy Cajun cooking was developed by the French-speaking immigrants in Louisiana, USA.

Serves 4

2½ pound fresh chicken
1½ onions
1 bay leaf
4 black peppercorns
2 tablespoons oil
2 garlic cloves, chopped
1 green bell pepper,
    seeded and chopped
1 celery stalk, chopped
1¼ cups long-grain rice
4 ounces chorizo sausage,
    sliced
1 cup chopped, cooked
    ham

14-ounce can chopped
    tomatoes
½ teaspoon hot chili
    powder
½ teaspoon cumin seeds
½ teaspoon ground
    cumin
1 teaspoon dried thyme
1 cup peeled, cooked
    shrimp
dash of Tabasco sauce
salt and ground black
    pepper
chopped fresh parsley, to
    garnish

1 Place the chicken in a flameproof casserole and pour over 2½ cups water. Add half an onion, the bay leaf and peppercorns and bring to a boil. Cover and simmer for 1½ hours. Then lift the chicken out of the pan. Skin, bone and chop the meat. Strain the stock and reserve.

2 Chop the remaining whole onion. Heat the oil in a large frying pan and fry the onion, garlic, green pepper and celery for 5 minutes. Stir in the rice. Add the sausage, ham and chicken and fry for 2–3 minutes, stirring frequently.

3 Pour in the tomatoes and 1¼ cups of the reserved stock, then and add the chili, cumin and thyme. Bring to a boil, cover and simmer gently for 20 minutes, or until the rice is tender and the liquid absorbed.

4 Stir in the shrimp and Tabasco. Cook for 5 minutes more, then season to taste with salt and ground black pepper. Serve hot, garnished with chopped fresh parsley.

Moroccan Chicken Couscous

The combination of sweet and spicy flavors in the sauce and couscous makes this dish irresistible.

Serves 4

1 tablespoon butter
1 tablespoon sunflower oil
4 chicken pieces
2 onions, finely chopped
2 garlic cloves, crushed
½ teaspoon ground
    cinnamon
¼ teaspoon ground
    ginger
¼ teaspoon ground
    turmeric
2 tablespoons orange
    juice
2 teaspoons honey
pinch of salt
fresh mint sprigs,
    to garnish

For the couscous
2¼ cups couscous
1 teaspoon salt
2 teaspoons caster sugar
1 tablespoon sunflower
    oil
½ teaspoon ground
    cinnamon
pinch of grated nutmeg
1 tablespoon orange
    blossom water
2 tablespoons golden
    raisins
½ cup chopped toasted
    almonds
3 tablespoons chopped
    pistachios

1 Fry the chicken pieces skin-side down in the butter and oil until golden. Turn them over. Add the onions, garlic, spices, a pinch of salt, the orange juice and 1¼ cups water. Cover and bring to a boil, then simmer for about 30 minutes.

2 Mix the couscous with the salt and 1½ cups water. Leave for 5 minutes. Add the rest of the ingredients for the couscous.

3 Line a steamer with parchment paper and spoon in the couscous. Set over the chicken and steam for 10 minutes.

4 Remove the steamer and keep covered. Stir the honey into the chicken liquid and boil rapidly for 3–4 minutes. Serve the chicken on a bed of couscous with some sauce spooned over. Garnish with fresh mint and serve with the remaining sauce.

Rabbit with Mustard

Rabbit is increasingly available in butchers and larger supermarkets, ready prepared and in serving pieces.

Serves 4

1 tablespoon all-purpose
   flour
1 tablespoon English
   mustard powder
4 large rabbit pieces
2 tablespoons butter
2 tablespoons oil
1 onion, finely chopped
⅔ cup beer
1¼ cups chicken or veal
   stock
1 tablespoon tarragon
   vinegar
2 tablespoons dark brown
   sugar

2 – 3 teaspoons prepared
   English mustard
salt and ground black
   pepper

To finish
4 tablespoons butter
2 tablespoons oil
1 cup fresh bread crumbs
1 tablespoon chopped
   fresh chives
1 tablespoon chopped
   fresh tarragon

1 Preheat the oven to 325°F. Mix the flour and mustard powder together, then put on a plate. Dip the rabbit pieces in the flour mixture; reserve any excess flour. Heat the butter and oil in a heavy flameproof casserole and brown the rabbit. Transfer to a plate. Stir in the onion and cook until soft.

2 Stir any reserved flour mixture into the casserole, cook for 1 minute, then stir in the beer, stock and vinegar. Bring to a boil and add the sugar and pepper. Simmer for 2 minutes. Return the rabbit and any juices that have collected on the plate to the casserole, cover with a tight-fitting lid and cook in the oven for 1 hour. Stir the mustard and salt to taste into the casserole, cover again and cook for another 15 minutes.

3 To finish, heat together the butter and oil in a frying pan and fry the bread crumbs, stirring frequently, until golden, then stir in the herbs. Transfer the rabbit to a warmed serving dish and sprinkle the bread crumb mixture over the top.

Turkey Hot-pot

Turkey and sausages combine well with kidney beans and other vegetables in this hearty stew.

Serves 4

scant ½ cup kidney
   beans, soaked
   overnight, drained
   and rinsed
3 tablespoons butter
2 herbed pork sausages
1 pound turkey casserole
   meat
3 leeks, sliced

2 carrots, finely chopped
4 tomatoes, chopped
2 – 3 teaspoons tomato
   paste
bouquet garni
1½ cups chicken stock
salt and ground black
   pepper

1 Cook the kidney beans in unsalted boiling water for 10 minutes, drain, cover with cold water, bring to the boil, and cook for about 30 minutes.

2 Meanwhile, heat the butter in a flameproof casserole, then cook the sausages until browned and the fat runs. Drain on paper towels, stir the turkey into the casserole and cook until lightly browned all over, then transfer to a bowl using a slotted spoon. Stir the leeks and carrot into the casserole and brown them lightly, stirring occasionally.

3 Add the chopped tomatoes and tomato paste and simmer gently for about 5 minutes.

4 Chop the sausages and return to the casserole with the beans, turkey, bouquet garni, stock and seasoning. Cover with a tight-fitting lid and cook gently for about 1¼ hours, until the meat is tender and there is very little liquid.

Duck with Cumberland Sauce

A sophisticated dish: the sauce contains both port and brandy, making it very rich.

Serves 4

4 duck portions	4 tablespoons port
grated rind and juice of 1 lemon	pinch of ground mace or ginger
grated rind and juice of 1 large orange	1 tablespoon brandy
4 tablespoons redcurrant jelly	salt and ground black pepper
	orange slices, to garnish

1 Preheat the oven to 375°F. Place a rack in a roasting pan. Prick the duck portions all over, sprinkle with salt and pepper. Place on the rack and cook in the oven for 45–50 minutes, until the duck skin is crisp and the juices run clear when pricked with the point of a knife.

2 Meanwhile, simmer the lemon and orange rinds and juices together in a saucepan for 5 minutes.

3 Add the redcurrant jelly and stir until melted, then stir in the port. Bring to a boil and add mace or ginger and salt and pepper, to taste.

4 Transfer the duck to a serving plate; keep warm. Pour the fat from the roasting pan, leaving the pan juices. With the pan over a gentle heat, stir in the brandy, dislodge the residue and bring to a boil. Stir in the port sauce and serve with the duck, garnished with orange slices.

Coronation Chicken

A cold chicken dish with a mild, curry-flavored sauce, ideal for summer lunch parties.

Serves 8

½ lemon	1 tablespoon curry paste
5-pound chicken	1 tablespoon tomato paste
1 onion, quartered	½ cup red wine
1 carrot, quartered	1 bay leaf
large bouquet garni	juice of ½ lemon, or more to taste
8 black peppercorns, crushed	2–3 teaspoons apricot jelly
pinch of salt	1¼ cups mayonnaise
fresh watercress sprigs, to garnish	½ cup whipping cream, whipped

For the sauce

1 small onion, chopped	salt and ground black pepper
1 tablespoon butter	

1 Put the lemon half in the chicken cavity, then place the chicken in a saucepan that it just fits. Add the vegetables, bouquet garni, peppercorns and salt.

2 Add enough water to come two-thirds of the way up the chicken, bring to a boil, then cover and cook gently for about 1½ hours, until the chicken juices run clear.

3 Transfer the chicken to a large bowl, pour the cooking liquid over and allow to cool. When cool, skin and bone the chicken, then chop. (Use the liquid for making soup.)

4 To make the sauce, cook the onion in the butter until soft. Add the curry paste, tomato paste, wine, bay leaf and lemon juice, then cook for 10 minutes. Add the jelly; strain and cool.

5 Beat the sauce mixture into the mayonnaise. Fold in the cream, season to taste with salt and pepper and add the lemon juice, then stir in with the chicken.

Tandoori Chicken Kebabs

This popular dish originates from the Punjab, where it is traditionally cooked in clay ovens known as *tandoors*.

Serves 4

4 boneless chicken breasts,
  about 6 ounces each,
  skinned
1 tablespoon lemon juice
3 tablespoons tandoori
  paste
3 tablespoons plain
  yogurt
1 garlic clove, crushed
2 tablespoons chopped
  fresh cilantro

1 small onion, cut into
  wedges and separated
  into layers
a little oil, for brushing
salt and ground black
  pepper
fresh cilantro sprigs, to
  garnish
pilau rice and nan bread,
  to serve

1 Dice the chicken breasts into 1-inch pieces, place in a bowl and add the lemon juice, tandoori paste, yogurt, garlic, cilantro and seasoning. Cover and allow to marinate in the fridge for 2–3 hours.

2 Preheat the broiler. Thread alternate pieces of marinated chicken and onion onto four skewers.

3 Brush the onions with a little oil, lay the skewers on a broiler rack and cook under a high heat for 10–12 minutes, turning once. Garnish the kebabs with fresh cilantro and serve at once with pilau rice and nan bread.

Cook's Tip
If you are using wooden skewers, soak them first in cold water to prevent them catching fire under the broiler. For an economical alternative, use chicken thighs instead of breasts.

Chinese Chicken with Cashew Nuts

The cashew nuts give this oriental dish a delightful crunchy texture that contrasts well with the noodles.

Serves 4

4 boneless chicken breasts,
  about 6 ounces each,
  skinned
3 garlic cloves, crushed
4 tablespoons soy sauce
2 tablespoons cornstarch
4 cups dried egg noodles
3 tablespoons peanut or
  sunflower oil

1 tablespoon sesame oil
1 cup roasted cashew
  nuts
6 scallions, cut into
  2-inch pieces and
  halved lengthwise
scallion curls and a little
  chopped fresh red chili,
  to garnish

1 Slice the chicken into strips, then combine with the garlic, soy sauce and cornflour. Cover and chill in the fridge for about 30 minutes.

2 Meanwhile, bring a saucepan of water to the boil and add the egg noodles. Turn off the heat and let stand for 5 minutes. Drain well and reserve.

3 Heat the oils in a large frying pan or wok and stir-fry the chilled chicken and marinade juices over a high heat for about 3–4 minutes, or until golden brown.

4 Add the cashew nuts and scallions to the pan or wok and stir-fry for another 2–3 minutes.

5 Add the drained noodles and stir-fry for 2 minutes more. Toss the noodles well and serve immediately, garnished with the scallion curls and chopped chili.

Cook's Tip
For a milder garnish, seed the red chili before chopping or finely dice some red bell pepper instead and use with the scallion curls.

Chinese-style Chicken Salad

For a variation and to add more color, add some cooked, peeled shrimp to this lovely salad.

Serves 4

4 boneless chicken breasts, about 6 ounces each
4 tablespoons dark soy sauce
pinch of Chinese five-spice powder
squeeze of lemon juice
½ cucumber, peeled and cut into matchsticks
1 teaspoon salt
3 tablespoons sunflower oil
2 tablespoons sesame oil
1 tablespoon sesame seeds

2 tablespoons dry sherry
2 carrots, cut into matchsticks
8 scallions, shredded
1 cup bean sprouts

For the sauce
4 tablespoons crunchy peanut butter
2 teaspoons lemon juice
2 teaspoons sesame oil
¼ teaspoon hot chili powder
1 scallion, finely chopped

1 Put the chicken into a saucepan and cover with water. Add 1 tablespoon of the soy sauce, the Chinese five-spice powder and lemon juice. Cover, bring to a boil, then simmer for 20 minutes. Then skin and slice into thin strips.

2 Sprinkle the cucumber matchsticks with salt, leave for 30 minutes, then rinse and pat dry.

3 Fry the sesame seeds in the oils for 30 seconds, then stir in the remaining soy sauce and the sherry. Add the carrots and stir-fry for 2 minutes, then remove from the heat.

4 Mix together the cucumber, scallions, bean sprouts, carrots, pan juices and chicken. Transfer to a shallow dish. Cover and chill for 1 hour.

5 For the sauce, cream the first four ingredients together, then stir in the scallion. Serve the chicken with the sauce.

Duck, Avocado and Berry Salad

Duck breasts are roasted until crisp with a honey and soy glaze to serve warm with fresh raspberries and avocado.

Serves 4

4 small or 2 large duck breasts, halved if large
1 tablespoon honey
1 tablespoon dark soy sauce
mixed chopped fresh salad greens such as lamb's lettuce, red chicory or frisée
2 avocados, pitted, peeled and cut into chunks
1 cup raspberries

salt and ground black pepper

For the dressing
4 tablespoons olive oil
1 tablespoon raspberry vinegar
1 tablespoon redcurrant jelly
salt and ground black pepper

1 Preheat the oven to 425°F. Prick the skin of each duck breast with a fork. Blend the honey and soy sauce together in a small bowl, then brush all over the skin.

2 Place the duck breasts on a rack set over a roasting pan and season with salt and pepper. Roast in the oven for about 15–20 minutes, until the skins are crisp and the meat cooked.

3 Meanwhile, to make the dressing, put the oil, vinegar, redcurrant jelly and seasoning in a small bowl and whisk well until evenly blended.

4 Slice the duck breasts diagonally and arrange on four individual plates with the salad greens, avocados and raspberries. Spoon the dressing over the top and serve.

Cook's Tip
Small avocados contain the most flavor and have a good texture. They should be ripe but not too soft, so avoid any with skins that are turning black.

Crumbed Turkey Steaks

The authentic Austrian dish, *Wiener schnitzel*, uses veal scallops, but turkey breasts make a tasty alternative.

Serves 4

4 turkey breast steaks, about 5 ounces each
3 tablespoons all-purpose flour, seasoned
1 egg, lightly beaten
1½ cups fresh bread crumbs

5 tablespoons finely grated Parmesan cheese
2 tablespoons butter
3 tablespoons sunflower oil
fresh parsley sprigs, to garnish
4 lemon wedges, to serve

1 Lay the turkey steaks between two sheets of pastic wrap. Hit each one with a rolling pin until flattened. Snip the edges of the steaks with scissors a few times to prevent them from curling during cooking.

2 Place the seasoned flour on one plate, the egg in a shallow bowl and the bread crumbs and Parmesan mixed together on another plate.

3 Dip each side of the steaks into the flour and shake off any extra. Next, dip them into the egg and then gently press each side into the bread crumbs and cheese until evenly coated.

4 Heat the butter and oil in a large frying pan and fry the turkey steaks over a moderate heat for 2–3 minutes on each side, until golden. Garnish with the fresh parsley sprigs and serve with lemon wedges.

Country Cider Hot-pot

Rabbit meat is regaining popularity and is a healthy, low-fat option, as is all game.

Serves 4

2 tablespoons all-purpose flour
4 boneless rabbit pieces
2 tablespoons butter
1 tablespoon oil
15 baby onions
4 slices bacon, chopped
2 teaspoons mustard
1¾ cups hard cider
3 carrots, chopped

2 parsnips, chopped
12 ready-to-eat dried prunes, pitted
1 fresh rosemary sprig
1 bay leaf
salt and ground black pepper

1 Preheat the oven to 325°F. Place the flour and seasoning in a plastic bag, add the rabbit portions and shake until coated. Set aside.

2 Heat the butter and oil in a flameproof casserole and add the onions and bacon. Fry for 4 minutes, until the onions have softened. Remove with a slotted spoon and reserve.

3 Fry the seasoned rabbit pieces in the oil left in the flameproof casserole until they are browned all over, then spread a little of the mustard over the top of each piece.

4 Return the onions and bacon to the pan. Pour on the cider and add the carrots, parsnips, prunes, rosemary and bay leaf. Season well. Bring to a boil, then cover with a tight-fitting lid and transfer to the oven. Cook for about 1½ hours until the meat and vegetables are tender.

5 Remove the rosemary sprig and bay leaf and serve the rabbit hot with creamy mashed potatoes, if you wish.

Turkey Pastitsio

A traditional Greek pastitsio is a rich, high-fat dish made with ground beef, but this lighter version is just as tasty.

Serves 4–6

1 pound lean ground turkey
1 large onion, finely chopped
4 tablespoons tomato paste
1 cup red wine or stock
1 teaspoon ground cinnamon
2½ cups macaroni
1¼ cups skimmed milk
2 tablespoons sunflower margarine

2 tablespoons all-purpose flour
1 teaspoon grated nutmeg
2 tomatoes, sliced
4 tablespoon whole wheat bread crumbs
salt and ground black pepper
green salad, to serve

1 Preheat the oven to 425°F. Fry the turkey and onion in a nonstick frying pan without fat, stirring until lightly browned.

2 Stir in the tomato paste, red wine or stock and cinnamon. Season with salt and pepper, then cover with a tight-fitting lid and simmer for 5 minutes.

3 Cook the macaroni in boiling salted water until just tender, then drain. Layer with the meat mixture in a wide casserole.

4 Place the milk, margarine and flour in a saucepan and whisk over a moderate heat until thickened and smooth. Add the nutmeg, and salt and pepper to taste.

5 Pour the sauce evenly over the pasta and meat. Arrange the tomato slices on top and sprinkle lines of bread crumbs over the surface. Bake for 30–35 minutes, or until golden brown and bubbling. Serve hot with a green salad.

Tuscan Chicken

A simple peasant casserole with all the flavors of Tuscan ingredients. The wine can be replaced by chicken stock.

Serves 4

1 teaspoon olive oil
8 chicken thighs, skinned
1 onion, thinly sliced
2 red bell peppers, seeded and sliced
1 garlic clove, crushed
1¼ cups tomato sauce
½ cup dry white wine

large fresh oregano sprig, or 1 teaspoon dried oregano
14-ounce can navy or white beans, drained
3 tablespoons fresh bread crumbs
salt and ground black pepper

1 Heat the oil in a nonstick or heavy saucepan and fry the chicken until golden brown. Remove and keep hot. Add the onion and peppers to the pan and gently sauté until softened, but not brown. Stir in the garlic.

2 Add the chicken, tomato sauce, wine and oregano. Season well with salt and pepper, bring to a boil, then cover the pan with a tight lid.

3 Lower the heat and simmer gently, stirring occasionally, for 30–35 minutes or until the chicken is tender and the juices run clear, not pink, when pierced with the point of a knife.

4 Stir in the beans and simmer for another 5 minutes until heated through. Sprinkle with the bread crumbs and cook under a hot broiler until golden brown.

Cornish Hens with Grapes in Vermouth

This sauce could also be served with roast chicken, but poussin have the stronger flavor.

Serves 4

4 oven-ready Cornish
   hens, about 1 pound
   each
4 tablespoons butter,
   softened
2 shallots, chopped
4 tablespoons chopped
   fresh parsley
2 cups white grapes,
   preferably Muscatel,
   halved and seeded

⅔ cup white vermouth
1 teaspoon cornstarch
4 tablespoons heavy
   cream
2 tablespoons pine nuts,
   toasted
salt and ground black
   pepper
watercress sprigs, to
   garnish

1 Preheat the oven to 400°F. Wash and dry the Cornish hens. Spread the softened butter all over the Cornish hens and put a hazelnut-sized piece in the cavity of each bird.

2 Mix together the shallots and parsley and place a quarter of the mixture inside each Cornish hen. Put the Cornish hens side by side in a large roasting pan and roast for 40–50 minutes, or until the juices run clear when the thickest part of the flesh is pierced with a skewer. Transfer the Cornish hens to a warmed serving plate. Cover and keep warm.

3 Skim off most of the fat from the roasting pan, then add the grapes and vermouth. Place the tin directly over a low heat for a few minutes to warm and slightly soften the grapes.

4 Lift the grapes out of the tin using a slotted spoon and scatter them around the Cornish hens. Keep covered. Stir the cornstarch into the cream, then add to the pan juices. Cook gently for a few minutes, stirring, until the sauce has thickened. Season to taste with salt and pepper. Pour the sauce around the Cornish hens. Sprinkle with the toasted pine nuts and garnish with watercress sprigs.

Chicken Parcels with Herb Butter

These delightful, individual phyllo pastry parcels contain a wonderfully moist and herby filling.

Serves 4

4 chicken breast fillets,
   skinned
generous ½ cup butter,
   softened
6 tablespoons mixed
   chopped fresh herbs
   such as thyme, parsley,
   oregano and rosemary
1 teaspoon lemon juice

5 large sheets phyllo
   pastry, defrosted if
   frozen
1 egg, beaten
2 tablespoons freshly
   grated Parmesan
   cheese
salt and ground black
   pepper

1 Season the chicken fillets. Melt 2 tablespoons of the butter in a frying pan and fry the chicken fillets to seal and brown lightly. Allow to cool.

2 Preheat the oven to 375°F. Put the remaining butter, the herbs, lemon juice and seasoning in a food processor or blender and process until smooth. Melt half of this herb butter.

3 Take one sheet of phyllo pastry and brush with melted herb butter. Keep the other sheets covered with a damp dish towel. Fold the phyllo pastry sheet in half and brush again with butter. Place a chicken fillet about 1 inch from the top end.

4 Dot the chicken with a quarter of the remaining unmelted herb butter. Fold in the sides of the pastry, then roll up to enclose it completely. Place seam-side down on a lightly greased baking sheet. Repeat with the other chicken fillets.

5 Brush the phyllo parcels with beaten egg. Cut the last sheet of filo into strips, then scrunch and arrange on top. Brush the parcels once again with the egg glaze, then sprinkle with Parmesan cheese. Bake for about 35–50 minutes, until golden brown. Serve hot.

Pot-roast of Venison

The venison is marinated for 24 hours before preparation to give this rich dish an even fuller flavor.

Serves 4–5

4 – 4½ pound boned leg
  of venison
5 tablespoons oil
4 cloves
8 black peppercorns,
  lightly crushed
12 juniper berries, lightly
  crushed
1 cup full-bodied red
  wine
4 ounces lean bacon,
  chopped

2 onions, finely chopped
2 carrots, chopped
5 ounces large
  mushrooms, sliced
1 tablespoon all-purpose
  flour
1 cup veal stock
2 tablespoons redcurrant
  jelly
salt and ground black
  pepper

1   Put the venison in a bowl, add half the oil, the spices and wine, cover and leave in a cool place for 24 hours, turning the meat occasionally.

2   Preheat the oven to 325°F. Remove the venison from the bowl and pat dry. Reserve the marinade. Heat the remaining oil in a shallow saucepan, then brown the venison evenly. Transfer to a plate.

3   Stir the bacon, onions, carrots and mushrooms into the pan and cook for about 5 minutes. Stir in the flour and cook for 2 minutes, then remove from the heat and stir in the marinade, stock, redcurrant jelly and seasoning. Return to the heat, bring to a boil, stirring, then simmer for 2–3 minutes.

4   Transfer the venison and sauce to a casserole and cover with a tight-fitting lid. Cook in the oven for about 3 hours, turning the meat from time to time, until tender.

Pheasant with Mushrooms

The wine and mushroom sauce in this recipe is given a lift by including anchovy fillets.

Serves 4

1 pheasant, cut in pieces
1 cup red wine
3 tablespoons oil
4 tablespoons Spanish
  sherry vinegar
1 large onion, chopped
2 strips bacon
12 ounces chestnut
  mushrooms, sliced

3 anchovy fillets,
  soaked for 10 minutes
  and drained
1½ cups game, veal or
  chicken stock
bouquet garni
salt and ground black
  pepper

1   Place the pheasant in a dish, add the wine, half the oil and half the vinegar, and scatter over half the onion. Season with salt and pepper, then cover the dish and leave in a cool place for about 8–12 hours, turning the pheasant occasionally.

2   Preheat the oven to 325°F. Lift the pheasant from the dish and pat dry with paper towels. Reserve the marinade for later.

3   Heat the remaining oil in a flameproof casserole, then brown the pheasant pieces. Transfer to a plate.

4   Add the bacon with the remaining onion to the casserole and cook until the onion is soft. Stir in the mushrooms and cook for about 3 minutes.

5   Stir in the anchovies and remaining vinegar and boil until reduced. Add the marinade, cook for 2 minutes, then add the stock and bouquet garni. Return the pheasant to the casserole, cover and bake for about 1½ hours. Transfer the pheasant to a serving dish. Boil the cooking juices to reduce. Discard the bouquet garni. Pour over the pheasant and serve at once.

Minty Yogurt Chicken

Marinated, broiled chicken thighs make a tasty light lunch or supper. Use drumsticks if you prefer.

Serves 4

8 chicken thigh portions
1 tablespoon honey
2 tablespoons lime juice
2 tablespoons plain
  yogurt

4 tablespoons chopped
  fresh mint
salt and ground black
  pepper

1 Skin the chicken thighs and slash the flesh at intervals with a sharp knife. Place in a bowl. Mix together the honey, lime juice, yogurt, seasoning and half the mint.

2 Spoon the marinade over the chicken and allow to marinate for 30 minutes. Line a broiler pan with foil and cook the chicken under a moderately hot broiler until thoroughly cooked and golden brown, turning occasionally.

3 Sprinkle with the remaining mint and serve with potatoes and tomato salad, if you wish.

Mandarin Sesame Duck

The rind, juice and flesh of sweet mandarin oranges are used in this delightful roast dish.

Serves 4

4 duck leg or boned breast
  portions
2 tablespoons light soy
  sauce
3 tablespoons clear honey

1 tablespoon sesame seeds
4 mandarin oranges
1 teaspoon cornstarch
salt and ground black
  pepper

1 Preheat the oven to 350°F. Prick the duck skin all over. Slash the breast skin diagonally at intervals. Roast the duck for 1 hour. Mix 1 tablespoon soy sauce with 2 tablespoons honey and brush over the duck. Sprinkle with sesame seeds. Roast for 15 minutes more.

2 Grate the rind from one mandarin and squeeze the juice from two. Mix in the cornstarch, remaining soy sauce and honey. Heat, stirring, until thickened and clear. Season. Peel and slice the remaining mandarins. Serve the duck with the mandarin slices and the sauce.

Sticky Ginger Chicken

For a fuller flavor, marinate the chicken drumsticks in the glaze for 30 minutes before cooking.

Serves 4

Mix 2 tablespoons lemon juice, 1 ounce light brown sugar, 1 teaspoon grated fresh ginger, 2 teaspoons, soy sauce and ground pepper to taste. Using a sharp knife, slash 8 chicken drumsticks about three times through the thickest part of the flesh, then toss the chicken in the glaze. Cook it under a hot broiler or on a barbecue, turning occasionally and brushing with the glaze, until it is golden and the juices run clear when pierced. Serve on a bed of lettuce, with crusty bread, if you wish.

Oat-crusted Chicken with Sage

Oats make a good, crunchy coating for savory foods, and offer a good way to add extra fiber.

Serves 4

3 tablespoons milk
2 teaspoons English
  mustard
½ cup rolled oats
3 tablespoons chopped
  fresh sage leaves
8 chicken thighs or
  drumsticks, skinned

½ cup plain yogurt
1 teaspoon whole-grain
  mustard
salt and ground black
  pepper
fresh sage leaves, to
  garnish

1 Preheat the oven to 400°F. Mix together the milk and English mustard.

2 Mix the oats with 2 tablespoons of the chopped sage and the seasoning on a plate. Brush the chicken with the milk and press into the oats to coat evenly.

3 Place the chicken on a baking sheet and bake for about 40 minutes, or until the juices run clear, not pink, when pierced through the thickest part.

4 Meanwhile, mix together the yogurt, whole-grain mustard, remaining sage and seasoning, transfer to a serving dish and serve with the chicken. Garnish the chicken with fresh sage leaves.

Cook's Tip
If fresh sage is not available, choose another fresh herb such as thyme or parsley rather than using a dried alternative. These chicken thighs or drumsticks may be served hot or cold.

Chicken in Creamy Orange Sauce

The brandy adds a rich flavor to the sauce, but omit it if you prefer and use orange juice alone.

Serves 4

8 chicken thighs or
  drumsticks, skinned
3 tablespoons brandy
1¼ cups orange juice
3 scallions, chopped

2 teaspoons cornstarch
6 tablespoons plain
  yogurt
salt and ground black
  pepper

1 Fry the chicken pieces without fat in a nonstick or heavy frying pan, turning until evenly browned.

2 Stir in the brandy, orange juice and scallions. Bring to the boil, then cover and simmer for 15 minutes, or until the chicken is tender and the juices run clear, not pink, when pierced with the point of a sharp knife.

3 Blend the cornstarch with a little water, then mix into the yogurt. Stir this into a small saucepan and cook over a moderate heat until boiling.

4 Adjust the seasoning to taste and serve with boiled rice or pasta and green salad, if you wish.

Normandy Roast Chicken

The chicken is turned over halfway through roasting so that it cooks evenly and stays wonderfully moist.

Serves 4

4 tablespoons butter,
    softened
2 tablespoons chopped
    fresh tarragon
1 small garlic clove,
    crushed
3-pound fresh chicken

1 teaspoon all-purpose
    flour
⅔ cup light cream
squeeze of lemon juice
salt and ground black
    pepper
fresh tarragon and lemon
    slices, to garnish

1 Preheat the oven to 400°F. Mix together the butter, a tablespoon of the chopped tarragon, the garlic and seasoning in a bowl. Spoon half the butter mixture into the cavity of the chicken.

2 Carefully lift the skin at the neck cavity of the bird from the breast flesh on each side, then gently push a little of the butter mixture into each pocket and smooth it down over the breasts with your fingers.

3 Season the bird and lay it, breast-side down, in a roasting pan. Roast in the oven for 45 minutes, then turn the chicken over and baste with the juices. Cook for another 45 minutes.

4 When the chicken is cooked, lift it to drain out any juices from the cavity into the pan, then transfer the bird to a warmed platter and keep warm.

5 Place the roasting pan on the stove top and heat until sizzling. Stir in the flour and cook for 1 minute, then stir in the cream, the remaining tarragon, ⅔ cup water, the lemon juice and seasoning. Boil and stir for 2–3 minutes, until thickened. Garnish the chicken with tarragon and lemon slices and serve with the sauce.

Duck Breasts with Orange Sauce

A simple variation on the classic French whole roast duck, which makes for a more elegant presentation.

Serves 4

4 duck breasts
1 tablespoon sunflower
    oil
2 oranges
⅔ cup fresh orange juice
1 tablespoon port

2 tablespoons orange
    marmalade
1 tablespoon butter
1 teaspoon cornstarch
salt and ground black
    pepper

1 Season the duck breast skin. Heat the oil in a frying pan over a moderate heat and add the duck breasts, skin-side down. Cover and cook for 3–4 minutes, until just lightly browned. Turn the breasts over, lower the heat slightly and cook uncovered for 5–6 minutes.

2 Peel the skin and pith from the oranges. Working over a bowl to catch any juice, slice either side of the membranes to release the orange segments, then set aside with the juice.

3 Remove the duck breasts from the pan with a slotted spoon, drain on paper towels and keep warm in the oven while making the sauce.

4 Drain off the fat from the frying pan. Add the segmented oranges, all but 2 tablespoons of the orange juice, the port and the orange marmalade. Bring to a boil and then reduce the heat slightly. Whisk small pats of the butter into the sauce and season with salt and pepper.

5 Blend the cornstarch with the reserved orange juice, pour into the pan and stir until slightly thickened. Add the duck breasts and cook gently for about 3 minutes. To serve, arrange the sliced breasts on plates with the sauce.

Pot-roast Cornish Hens

This dish is inspired by the French method of cooking these birds. Pot-roasting keeps them moist and succulent.

Serves 4

1 tablespoon olive oil
1 onion, sliced
1 large garlic clove, sliced
½ cup diced bacon
2 fresh Cornish hens, about 1 pound each
2 tablespoons melted butter
2 baby celery hearts, each cut into 4 pieces
8 baby carrots
2 small zucchini, cut into chunks
8 small new potatoes
2½ cups chicken stock
⅔ cup dry white wine
1 bay leaf
2 fresh thyme sprigs
2 fresh rosemary sprigs
1 tablespoon butter, softened
1 tablespoon all-purpose flour
salt and ground black pepper
fresh herbs, to garnish

1 Preheat the oven to 375°F. Heat the olive oil in a large flameproof casserole and sauté the onions, garlic and bacon for 5–6 minutes until the onions have softened. Brush the Cornish hens with half the melted butter and season. Add to the casserole with the vegetables. Pour in the stock and wine and add the herbs. Cover and bake for 20 minutes.

2 Remove the lid and brush the birds with the remaining butter. Bake for 25–30 minutes more until golden. Transfer the Cornish hens to a warmed serving platter and cut each in half with poultry shears or scissors. Remove the vegetables with a slotted spoon and arrange them around the birds. Cover with foil and keep warm.

3 Discard the herbs from the casserole. Mix the butter and flour to a paste. Bring the cooking liquid to a boil then whisk in spoonfuls of paste until thickened. Season and serve with the Cornish hens and vegetables, garnished with herbs.

Coq au Vin

Chicken is flamed in brandy, then braised in red wine with bacon, mushrooms and onions in this classic dish.

Serves 4

½ cup all-purpose flour
3-pound chicken, cut into 8 pieces
1 tablespoon olive oil
5 tablespoons butter
20 baby onions
3 ounces bacon, diced
about 20 button mushrooms
2 tablespoons brandy
1 bottle red Burgundy
bouquet garni
3 garlic cloves
1 teaspoon soft light brown sugar
salt and ground black pepper
1 tablespoon chopped fresh parsley and croûtons, to garnish

1 Place 3 tablespoons of the flour and seasoning in a large plastic bag and coat the chicken pieces. Heat the oil and 4 tablespoons of the butter in a large flameproof casserole and sauté the onions and bacon until the onions have browned lightly. Add the mushrooms and fry for 2 minutes more. Remove with a slotted spoon and reserve.

2 Add the chicken pieces to the hot oil and cook for about 5–6 minutes until browned. Add the brandy and, standing back, light it with a match, then shake the casserole gently until the flames die.

3 Add the wine, bouquet garni, garlic and sugar, and season. Bring to a boil, cover and simmer for 1 hour, stirring from time to time. Add the onions, bacon and mushrooms, cover and cook for 30 minutes. Transfer the chicken, vegetables and bacon to a warmed dish.

4 Remove the bouquet garni; boil the liquid for 2 minutes. Cream the remaining butter and flour. Whisk in spoonfuls of the mixture to thicken the liquid. Pour the sauce over the chicken and serve garnished with parsley and croûtons.

Moroccan Spiced Roast Cornish Hens

The Cornish hens are stuffed with an aromatic rice mixture and glazed with spiced yogurt in this flavorful dish.

Serves 4

1 cup cooked long-grain
   rice
1 small onion, chopped
finely grated rind and
   juice of 1 lemon
2 tablespoons chopped
   fresh mint
3 tablespoons chopped
   dried apricots
2 tablespoons plain
   yogurt

2 teaspoons ground
   turmeric
2 teaspoons ground
   cumin
2 x 1-pound Cornish
   hens
salt and ground black
   pepper
lemon slices and fresh
   mint sprigs, to
   garnish

1 Preheat the oven to 400°F. Mix together the rice, onion, lemon rind, mint and apricots. Stir in half each of the lemon juice, yogurt, turmeric, cumin, and salt and pepper.

2 Stuff the Cornish hens with the rice mixture at the neck cavity only. The spare stuffing can be served separately. Place the Cornish hens on a rack in a roasting pan.

3 Mix together the remaining lemon juice, yogurt, turmeric and cumin, then brush this over the Cornish hens. Cover loosely with foil and cook in the oven for 30 minutes.

4 Remove the foil and roast for another 15 minutes more, or until golden brown and the juices run clear, not pink, when the thickest part of the flesh is pierced with a skewer.

5 Cut both the Cornish hens in half with a sharp knife or poultry shears, and serve with warmed reserved rice. Garnish with slices of lemon and fresh mint sprigs.

Chili Chicken Couscous

Couscous is a very easy alternative to rice and makes a good base for all kinds of ingredients.

Serves 4

2 cups couscous
4 cups boiling water
1 teaspoon olive oil
14 ounces boneless,
   skinless chicken, diced
1 yellow bell pepper,
   seeded and sliced
2 large zucchini, sliced
   thickly

1 small green chili, thinly
   sliced, or 1 teaspoon
   chili sauce
1 large tomato, diced
15-ounce can
   chick-peas, drained
salt and ground black
   pepper
fresh cilantro or parsley
   sprigs, to garnish

1 Place the couscous in a large bowl and pour the boiling water over. Cover and let stand for 30 minutes.

2 Heat the oil in a large nonstick frying pan and stir-fry the chicken quickly to seal, then reduce the heat.

3 Stir in the pepper, zucchini and chili or chili sauce and cook for 10 minutes, until the vegetables are softened.

4 Stir in the tomato and chick-peas, then add the couscous. Adjust the seasoning and stir over a moderate heat until hot. Serve garnished with sprigs of fresh cilantro or parsley.

Cook's Tip
If you prefer, use 7 ounces of dried chick-peas in this recipe. Soak them overnight, then drain, place in a saucepan and add water to cover. Bring to a boil, then cook until tender, 45–60 minutes.

Mediterranean Turkey Skewers

These skewers are easy to assemble, and can be cooked under a broiler or on a charcoal barbecue.

Serves 4

6 tablespoons olive oil
3 tablespoons lemon juice
1 garlic clove, finely chopped
2 tablespoons chopped fresh basil
2 zucchini
1 long thin eggplant
11 ounces boned turkey, cut into 2-inch cubes
12–16 pickled onions
1 red or yellow bell pepper, cut into 2-inch squares
salt and ground black pepper

1 Mix the oil with the lemon juice, garlic and basil in a small bowl. Season with salt and pepper.

2 Slice the zucchini and eggplant lengthwise into strips ¼ inch thick. Cut them crosswise about two-thirds of the way along their length. Discard the shorter length. Wrap half the turkey pieces with the zucchini slices, and the other half with the eggplant slices.

3 Prepare the skewers by alternating the turkey, onions, and pepper pieces. If you are using wooden skewers, soak them in water for several minutes. This will prevent them from charring during broiling. Lay the prepared skewers on a platter and sprinkle with the flavored oil. Then let them marinate for at least 30 minutes. Preheat the broiler or light the coals to prepare a barbecue.

4 Broil or barbecue for 10 minutes, until the vegetables are tender, turning occasionally. Serve hot.

Duck with Chestnut Sauce

This autumnal dish makes use of the sweet chestnuts that are gathered in Italian woods.

Serves 4–5

1 fresh rosemary sprig
1 garlic clove, sliced
2 tablespoons olive oil
4 boned duck breasts, fat removed

For the sauce
4 cups chestnuts
1 teaspoon oil
1½ cups milk
1 small onion, finely chopped
1 carrot, finely chopped
1 small bay leaf
salt and ground black pepper
2-4 tablespoons light cream, warmed

1 Pull the leaves from the sprig of rosemary. Combine them with the garlic and oil in a shallow bowl. Pat the duck breasts dry with paper towels. Brush them with the marinade and allow to stand for at least 2 hours before cooking.

2 Preheat the oven to 350°F. Cut a cross in the flat side of each chestnut with a sharp knife. Place the chestnuts on a baking sheet with the oil and shake the sheet until they are coated with oil. Bake for 20 minutes, then peel.

3 Place the peeled chestnuts in a heavy saucepan with the milk, onion, carrot and bay leaf. Cook slowly for about 10–15 minutes until the chestnuts are tender, then season. Discard the bay leaf. Press the mixture through a strainer.

4 Return the sauce to the pan. Heat gently while the duck breasts are cooking. Just before serving, stir in the cream. If the sauce is too thick, add a little more cream. Preheat the broiler, or prepare a barbecue.

5 Broil the duck breasts until medium-rare, for about 6–8 minutes. They should be pink inside. Slice into rounds and arrange on warmed plates. Serve with the heated sauce.

Turkey Spirals

These little spirals may look difficult, but they're so easy to make, and a very good way to pep up all-purpose turkey.

Serves 4

4 thinly sliced turkey
  breast steaks, about
  3½ ounces each
4 teaspoons tomato paste
½ ounce large fresh basil
  leaves
1 garlic clove, crushed
1 tablespoon skim milk

2 tablespoons whole
  wheat flour
salt and ground black
  pepper
fresh tomato sauce and
  pasta with fresh basil,
  to serve

1 Place the turkey steaks on a board. If too thick, flatten them slightly by beating with a rolling pin.

2 Spread each turkey breast steak with tomato paste, then top with a few leaves of basil, a little crushed garlic, and salt and pepper.

3 Roll up firmly around the filling and secure with a toothpick. Brush with milk and sprinkle with flour to coat lightly.

4 Place the spirals on a foil-lined broiler pan. Cook under a moderately hot broiler for 15–20 minutes, turning them occasionally, until thoroughly cooked. Serve hot, sliced with a spoonful or two of fresh tomato sauce and pasta, sprinkled with fresh basil.

Caribbean Chicken Kebabs

These kebabs have a rich, sunshine Caribbean flavor and the marinade keeps them moist without the need for oil.

Serves 4

1¼ pounds boned chicken
  breasts, skinned
finely grated rind of
  1 lime
2 tablespoons lime juice
1 tablespoon rum or
  sherry

1 tablespoon light brown
  sugar
1 teaspoon ground
  cinnamon
2 mangoes, peeled and
  diced
rice and salad, to serve

1 Cut the chicken into bite-size chunks and place in a bowl with the lime rind and juice, rum, sugar and cinnamon. Toss well, cover and let stand for 1 hour.

2 Save the juice and thread the chicken onto four wooden skewers, alternating with the mango cubes.

3 Cook the skewers under a hot broiler or on a barbecue for about 8-10 minutes, turning occasionally and basting with the juice until the chicken is tender and golden brown. Serve at once with rice and salad.

Cook's Tip
These kebabs may be served with a colorful salad and rice. The rum or sherry adds a lovely rich flavor but it is optional, so leave it out if you prefer.

Autumn Pheasant

Pheasant is well worth buying as it is low in fat, full of flavor and never dry when cooked in this way.

Serves 4

1 oven-ready pheasant	2 tablespoons
2 small onions, quartered	Worcestershire sauce
3 celery stalks, thickly	pinch of freshly grated
sliced	nutmeg
2 red eating apples,	2 tablespoons toasted
thickly sliced	hazelnuts
½ cup stock	salt and ground black
1 tablespoon honey	pepper

1 Preheat the oven to 350°F. Fry the pheasant without fat in a nonstick frying pan, turning occasionally until golden. Remove and keep hot.

2 Fry the onions and celery in the pan to brown lightly. Spoon into a casserole and place the pheasant on top. Tuck the apple slices around it.

3 Spoon over the stock, honey and Worcestershire sauce. Sprinkle with nutmeg, salt and pepper, cover with a tight-fitting lid and bake for 1¼–1½ hours or until tender. Sprinkle with nuts and serve hot.

Cook's Tip
Pheasant should be hung by the neck to develop its distinctive flavor for 7–14 days, according to the degree of gaminess preferred. If you are buying the bird ready-prepared, make sure all the tendons have been removed from the legs. This recipe provides an excellent method of cooking older, cock birds which tend to be rather tough and dry if just roasted.

Chicken Stroganoff

This dish is based on the classic Russian dish, which is made with fillet of beef, and it is just as good.

Serves 4

4 boneless, skinless	1¼ cups sour cream
chicken breasts,	salt and ground black
3 tablespoons olive oil	pepper
1 large onion, thinly	1 tablespoon chopped
sliced	fresh parsley, to
8 ounces mushrooms,	garnish
sliced	

1 Divide the chicken breasts into two natural fillets, place between two sheets of plastic wrap and flatten each to a thickness of ¼inch with a rolling pin.

2 Cut into 1-inch strips diagonally across the fillets.

3 Heat 2 tablespoons of the oil in a large frying pan and cook the sliced onion slowly until soft but not colored.

4 Add the mushrooms and cook until golden brown. Remove and keep warm.

5 Increase the heat, add the remaining oil and fry the chicken very quickly, in small batches, for 3–4 minutes until lightly colored. Remove and keep warm while frying the rest of the chicken.

6 Return all the chicken, onions and mushrooms to the pan and season with salt and pepper. Stir in the sour cream and bring to a boil. Sprinkle with fresh parsley and serve immediately.

Chicken Tikka

The red food coloring give this dish its traditional bright color. Serve with lemon wedges and a crisp mixed salad.

Serves 4
3½ pound chicken
mixed fresh salad greens
  such as frisée or
  radichio, to serve

For the marinade
⅔ cup plain yogurt
1 teaspoon ground
  paprika

2 teaspoons grated fresh
  root ginger
1 garlic clove, crushed
2 teaspoons garam masala
½ teaspoon salt
2-3 drops red food
  coloring
juice of 1 lemon
salad greens, to serve

1 Cut the chicken into eight even-size pieces, using a sharp knife.

2 Mix all the marinade ingredients in a large dish, add the chicken pieces to coat and chill for 4 hours or overnight to allow the flavors to penetrate the flesh.

3 Preheat the oven to 400°F. Remove the chicken pieces from the marinade and arrange them in a single layer in a large casserole. Bake for 30–40 minutes or until tender.

4 Baste with a little of the marinade while cooking. Arrange on a bed of salad greens and serve hot or cold.

Cook's Tip
This dish would also make an excellent appetizer. Cut the chicken into smaller pieces and reduce the cooking time slightly, then serve with lemon wedges and just a simple salad garnish.

Simple Chicken Curry

Curry powder can be bought in three different strengths – mild, medium and hot. Use the type you prefer.

Serves 4
8 chicken legs, each piece
  including thigh and
  drumstick
2 tablespoons olive oil
1 onion, thinly sliced
1 garlic clove, crushed
1 tablespoon medium
  curry powder
1 tablespoon all-purpose
  flour

1¾ cups chicken stock
1 beefsteak tomato
1 tablespoon mango
  chutney
1 tablespoon lemon juice
salt and ground black
  pepper
2½ cups boiled rice, to
  serve

1 Cut the chicken legs in half. Heat the olive oil in a large flameproof casserole and brown the chicken pieces on both sides. Remove and keep warm.

2 Add the onion and garlic clove to the casserole and cook them until tender. Add the curry powder and cook gently for another 2 minutes.

3 Add the flour and gradually blend in the chicken stock and seasoning.

4 Bring to a boil, replace the chicken pieces, cover and simmer for 20–30 minutes or until tender.

5 Skin the beefsteak tomato by blanching in boiling water for about 15 seconds, then running it under cold water to loosen the skin. Peel and dice.

6 Add to the chicken with the mango chutney and lemon juice. Heat through gently and adjust the seasoning to taste. Serve with boiled rice and Indian accompaniments.

Chicken Biryani

A *biryani* – from the Urdu – is a dish mixed with rice which resembles a risotto. It provides a one-pan meal.

Serves 4

1½ cups basmati rice, rinsed
½ teaspoon salt
5 whole cardamom pods
2–3 whole cloves
1 cinnamon stick
3 tablespoons oil
3 onions, sliced
1½ pounds boneless, skinless, diced chicken
¼ teaspoon ground cloves
5 cardamom pods, seeds removed and ground
¼ teaspoon hot chili powder
1 teaspoon ground cumin
1 teaspoon ground coriander

½ teaspoon freshly ground black pepper
3 garlic cloves, finely chopped
1 teaspoon finely chopped fresh ginger
juice of 1 lemon
4 tomatoes, sliced
2 tablespoons chopped fresh cilantro
⅔ cup plain yogurt
½ teaspoon saffron strands soaked in 2 teaspoons hot milk
3 tablespoons toasted flaked almonds and fresh cilantro sprigs, to garnish
plain yogurt, to serve

1 Preheat the oven to 375°F. Boil the rice mixture, salt, cardamom pods, cloves and cinnamon stick for 2 minutes. Then drain, leaving the whole spices in the rice.

2 Brown the onions in the oil. Add the chicken, ground spices, garlic, ginger and lemon juice. Stir-fry for 5 minutes.

3 Transfer to a casserole; top with the tomatoes. In layers, add the cilantro, yogurt and rice. Drizzle over the saffron and milk, then ⅔ cup water.

4 Cover and bake for 1 hour. Transfer to a warmed serving platter and remove the whole spices. Garnish with toasted almonds and cilantro and serve with yogurt.

Spatchcock of Cornish Hen

Allow one poussin per person and sharp knives to tackle them. Serve with new potatoes and salad, if wished.

Serves 4

4 Cornish hens
1 tablespoon mixed chopped fresh herbs such as rosemary and parsley, plus extra to garnish

1 tablespoon lemon juice
4 tablespoons butter, melted
salt and ground black pepper
lemon slices, to garnish

1 Remove any trussing strings from the birds, and, using a pair of kitchen scissors, cut down on either side of the backbone. Lay them flat and flatten with the help of a rolling pin or mallet, or use the heel of your hand.

2 Thread the legs and wings onto skewers to keep the poussins flat while they are cooking.

3 Brush both sides with melted butter and season with salt and pepper. Sprinkle with lemon juice and herbs.

4 Preheat the broiler to moderate heat and cook skin-side first for 6 minutes until golden brown. Turn over, brush with butter and broil for another 6–8 minutes or until cooked. Garnish with chopped herbs and lemon slices.

Chicken, Leek and Parsley Pie

A filling pie with a two-cheese sauce, this dish is ideal for serving on a cold winter's day.

Serves 4–6

3 boneless chicken breasts
flavorings: carrot, onion,
   peppercorns, bouquet
   garni
piecrust, made with
   2½ cups all-purpose
   flour
4 tablespoons butter
2 leeks, thinly sliced
½ cup grated Cheddar
   cheese
¼ cup grated Parmesan
   cheese

3 tablespoons chopped
   fresh parsley
2 tablespoons whole-
   grain mustard
1 teaspoon cornstarch
1¼ cups heavy cream
salt and ground black
   pepper
beaten egg, to glaze
mixed fresh green salad,
   to serve

1 Poach the chicken breasts with the flavorings in water to cover, until tender. Cool in the liquid, then cut into strips.

2 Preheat the oven to 400°F. Divide the pastry into two pieces, one slightly larger than the other. Use the larger piece to line a 7 x 11 inch baking pan. Prick the bottom, bake for 15 minutes, then let cool.

3 Fry the leeks in the butter until soft. Stir in the cheeses and parsley. Spread half the leek mixture over the pastry bottom, cover with the chicken strips, then top with the remaining leek mixture. Mix the mustard, cornstarch and cream. Season and pour into the pie.

4 Moisten the pastry bottom edges. Use the remaining pastry to cover the pie. Brush with beaten egg and bake for 30–40 minutes until golden and crisp. Serve with salad.

Hampshire Farmhouse Quiche

A traditional dish from the south of England, this quiche will satisfy the hungriest person.

Serves 4

2 cups whole wheat flour
2 ounces butter, cubed
4 tablespoons vegetable
   shortening
1 teaspoon caraway seeds
1 tablespoon oil
1 onion, chopped
1 garlic clove, crushed
2 cups cooked chicken,
   chopped
3 ounces watercress
   leaves, chopped

grated rind of ½ lemon
2 eggs, lightly beaten
¼ cup heavy cream
3 tablespoons plain
   yogurt
large pinch of grated
   nutmeg
3 tablespoons grated
   Cheddar cheese
beaten egg, to glaze
salt and ground black
   pepper

1 Rub the fats into the flour with a pinch of salt until the mixture resembles bread crumbs.

2 Stir in the caraway seeds and 3 tablespoons iced water and mix to a firm dough. Knead until smooth, then use to line a 7 x 11 inch loose-bottom tart pan. Reserve the dough scraps. Prick the bottom and chill for 20 minutes. Heat a baking sheet in the oven at 400°F.

3 Sauté the onion and garlic in the oil until softened. Remove from the heat and cool. Meanwhile, line the pastry case with wax paper and baking beans. Bake for 10 minutes, remove the paper and beans and cook for 5 minutes.

4 Mix the onion, chicken, watercress and lemon rind; spoon into the pastry shell. Beat the eggs, cream, yogurt, nutmeg, cheese and seasoning; pour over the chicken mixture. Cut the pastry scraps into ½ inch strips. Brush with egg, then twist and lay in a lattice over the quiche. Press on the ends. Bake for 35 minutes, until golden.

Chicken Charter Pie

A light pie with a fresh taste; it is versatile enough to use for light meals or informal dinners.

Serves 4

4 tablespoons butter	8 ounces ready-made puff
4 chicken legs	pastry
1 onion, finely chopped	½ cup heavy cream
⅔ cup milk	2 eggs, beaten, plus extra
⅔ cup sour cream	for glazing
4 scallions, quartered	salt and ground black
¾ ounce fresh parsley	pepper
leaves, finely chopped	

1 Melt the butter in a frying pan and brown the chicken legs. Transfer to a plate. Add the chopped onion to the pan and cook until softened but not browned. Stir the milk, sour cream, scallions, parsley and seasoning into the pan, bring to a boil, then simmer for 2 minutes.

2 Return the chicken to the pan with any juice, cover and cook gently for 30 minutes. Transfer the chicken mixture to a 5-cup pie pan. Leave to cool.

3 Preheat the oven to 425°F. Place a narrow strip of pastry on the edge of the pie pan. Moisten the strip, then cover the pan with the pastry. Press the edges together. Make a hole in the center of the pastry and insert a small funnel of foil. Brush the pastry with beaten egg, then bake for 15–20 minutes.

4 Reduce the oven temperature to 350°F. Mix the cream and eggs, then pour into the pie through the funnel. Shake the pie to distribute the cream, then return to the oven for 5–10 minutes. Leave the pie in a warm place for about 5–10 minutes before serving, or cool completely.

Chicken and Ham Pie

This is a rich pie flavored with fresh herbs and lightly spiced with mace – ideal for taking on a picnic.

Serves 8

14 ounces ready-made	2 teaspoons chopped fresh
piecrust	thyme
1¾ pounds chicken breast	grated rind and juice of
12 ounces uncooked	½ large lemon
smoked ham	1 teaspoon freshly
4 tablespoons heavy	ground mace
cream	salt and ground black
6 scallions, finely chopped	pepper
1 tablespoon chopped	beaten egg or milk, to
fresh tarragon	glaze

1 Preheat the oven to 375°F. Roll out one-third of the pastry and use it to line an 8-inch pie pan, 2 inches deep. Place on a baking sheet.

2 Grind 4 ounces of the chicken with the ham, then mix with the cream, scallions, herbs, lemon rind and 1 tablespoon of the lemon juice; season lightly. Cut the remaining chicken into ½-inch pieces and mix with the remaining lemon juice, the mace and seasoning.

3 Make a layer of one-third of the ham mixture in the pastry shell, cover with half the chopped chicken, then add another layer of one-third of the ham. Add all the remaining chicken followed by the remaining ham.

4 Moisten the edges of the pastry shell and roll out the remaining pastry to make a lid for the pie. Use the scraps to make a lattice decoration. Make a small hole in the center of the pie, brush the top with beaten egg or milk, then bake for 20 minutes. Reduce the temperature to 325°F and bake for another 1–1¼ hours. Transfer the pie to a wire rack and allow to cool.

Venison with Cranberry Sauce

Venison steaks are now readily available. Lean and low in fat, they make a healthy choice for a special occasion.

Serves 4

1 orange
1 lemon
¾ cup fresh or frozen (unthawed) cranberries
1 teaspoon grated fresh ginger
1 fresh thyme sprig
1 teaspoon Dijon mustard
4 tablespoons redcurrant jelly

⅔ cup ruby port
2 tablespoons sunflower oil
4 venison steaks
2 shallots, finely chopped
salt and ground black pepper
fresh thyme sprigs, to garnish
mashed potatoes and broccoli, to serve

1 Pare the rind from half the orange and half the lemon using a vegetable peeler, then cut into very fine strips. Blanch the strips in a small saucepan of boiling water for 5 minutes until tender. Drain the strips and refresh under cold water.

2 Squeeze the juice from the citrus fruit and pour into a small pan. Add the cranberries, ginger, thyme, mustard, redcurrant jelly and port. Cook gently until the jelly melts. Bring to a boil, stirring, cover and reduce the heat. Cook for 15 minutes, until the cranberries are just tender.

3 Fry the venison steaks in the oil over a high heat for 2–3 minutes. Turn them over and add the shallots. Cook on the other side for 2–3 minutes, to taste. Just before the end of cooking, pour in the sauce and add the strips of orange and lemon rind. Allow the sauce to bubble for a few seconds to thicken slightly, then remove the thyme sprig and adjust the seasoning to taste.

4 Transfer the venison steaks to warmed plates and spoon over the sauce. Garnish with thyme sprigs and serve accompanied by creamy mashed potatoes and broccoli.

Turkey and Snow Peas Stir-fry

Have all the ingredients prepared before you start cooking this dish, as it will be ready in minutes.

Serves 4

2 tablespoons sesame oil
6 tablespoons lemon juice
1 garlic clove, crushed
½-inch piece fresh ginger, peeled and grated
1 teaspoon honey
1 pound turkey fillets, cut into strips
1 cup snow peas, trimmed

2 tablespoons peanut oil
½ cup cashew nuts
6 scallions, cut into strips
8-ounce can water chestnuts, drained and thinly sliced
pinch of salt
saffron rice, to serve

1 Mix together the sesame oil, lemon juice, garlic, ginger and honey in a shallow non-metallic dish. Add the turkey and mix well. Cover and let marinate for 3–4 hours.

2 Blanch the snow peas in boiling salted water for about 1 minute. Drain and refresh under cold running water.

3 Drain the marinade from the turkey strips and reserve the marinade. Heat the peanut oil in a wok or large frying pan, add the cashew nuts and stir-fry for about 1–2 minutes until golden brown. Remove the cashew nuts from the wok or frying pan using a slotted spoon and set aside.

4 Add the turkey and stir-fry for 3–4 minutes, until golden brown. Add the scallions, snow peas, water chestnuts and the reserved marinade. Cook for a few minutes, until the turkey is tender and the sauce is bubbling and hot. Stir in the cashew nuts and serve with saffron rice.

Cook's Tip
This dish could be served on a bed of medium-width egg noodles for a quick meal.

Farmhouse Venison Pie

A simple and satisfying pie; the venison is cooked in a rich gravy, topped with potato and parsnip mash.

Serves 4

3 tablespoons sunflower
  oil
1 onion, chopped
1 garlic clove, crushed
3 slices bacon, chopped
1½ lb minced venison
4 ounces button
  mushrooms, chopped
2 tablespoons all-purpose
  flour
1¾ cups beef stock
⅔ cup ruby port
2 bay leaves
1 teaspoon chopped fresh
  thyme

1 teaspoon Dijon mustard
1 tablespoon redcurrant
  jelly
1½ pounds potatoes
1 pound parsnips
1 egg yolk
4 tablespoons butter
pinch of freshly grated
  nutmeg
3 tablespoons chopped
  fresh parsley
salt and ground black
  pepper

1 Heat the oil in a large frying pan and fry the onion, garlic and bacon for 5 minutes. Add the venison and mushrooms and cook for a few minutes, stirring, until browned.

2 Stir in the flour and cook for 1–2 minutes, then add the stock, port, herbs, mustard, redcurrant jelly and seasoning. Bring to a boil, cover with a tight-fitting lid and simmer for 30–40 minutes, until tender. Spoon into a large pie pan or four individual baking dishes.

3 While the venison and mushroom mixture is cooking, preheat the oven to 400°F. Cut the potatoes and parsnips into large chunks. Cook together in boiling salted water for 20 minutes or until tender. Drain and mash, then beat in the egg yolk, butter, nutmeg, parsley and seasoning.

4 Spread the potato and parsnip mixture over the meat and bake for 30–40 minutes, until piping hot and golden brown. Serve immediately with a green vegetable, if you wish.

Normandy Pheasant

Calvados, cider, apples and cream – the produce of Normandy – make this a rich and flavorful dish.

Serves 4

2 oven-ready pheasants
1 tablespoon olive oil
2 tablespoons butter
4 tablespoons Calvados
1¾ cups hard cider
bouquet garni

3 tart apples
⅔ cup heavy cream
salt and ground black
  pepper
fresh thyme sprigs, to
  garnish

1 Preheat the oven to 325°F. Cut both the pheasants into four pieces using a large sharp knife. Discard the backbones and knuckles.

2 Heat the oil and butter in a large flameproof casserole. Working in two batches, add the pheasant pieces to the casserole and brown them over a high heat. Return all the pheasant pieces to the casserole.

3 Standing far back, pour over the Calvados and set it alight with a match. Shake the casserole and when the flames have died, pour in the cider, then add the bouquet garni and season to taste with salt and pepper. Bring to a boil, cover with a tight-fitting lid and cook for about 50 minutes.

4 Peel, core and thickly slice the apples. Tuck the apple slices around the pheasant. Cover and cook for 5–10 minutes, or until the pheasant is tender. Transfer the pheasant and apples to a warmed serving plate. Keep warm.

5 Remove the bouquet garni, then boil the sauce rapidly to reduce by half to a syrupy consistency. Stir in the heavy cream and simmer for another 2–3 minutes until thickened. Taste the sauce and adjust the seasoning if necessary. Spoon the sauce over the pheasant pieces and serve immediately, garnished with fresh thyme sprigs.

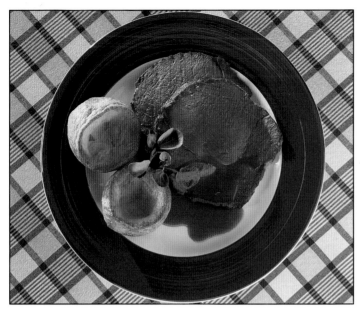

Roast Beef with Yorkshire Pudding

This classic British dish is often served at Sunday lunch, accompanied by potatoes, mustard and horseradish sauce.

Serves 6

4-pound piece of beef
2–4 tablespoons
 dripping or oil
1¼ cups beef stock, wine
 or water
salt and ground black
 pepper

For the puddings

½ cup all-purpose flour
1 egg, beaten
⅔ cup water mixed with
 milk
dripping or oil, for
 cooking

1 Weigh the beef and calculate the cooking time. Allow 15 minutes per pound plus 15 minutes for rare meat, 20 minutes plus 20 minutes for medium, and 25–30 minutes plus 25 minutes for well-done.

2 Preheat the oven to 425°F. Heat the dripping or oil in a roasting pan in the oven. Place the meat on a rack, fat-side up, then place the rack in the roasting pan. Baste the beef with the dripping or oil, and cook for the required time, basting occasionally.

3 To make the Yorkshire puddings, stir the flour, salt and pepper together in a bowl and form a well in the centre. Pour the egg into the well, then slowly pour in the milk, stirring in the flour to give a smooth batter. Stand for 30 minutes.

4 A few minutes before the meat is ready, spoon a little dripping or oil in each of twelve patty pans and place in the oven until very hot. Remove the meat, season, then cover loosely with foil and keep warm. Quickly divide the batter among the patty tins, then bake for 15–20 minutes, until well risen and brown.

5 Spoon off the fat from the roasting pan. Add the stock, wine or water, stirring, and boil for a few minutes. Season to taste, then serve with the beef and Yorkshire puddings.

Beef Olives

So-called because of their shape, these beef rolls contain a delicious filling made with bacon and mushrooms.

Serves 4

2 tablespoons butter
2 slices bacon, finely
 chopped
4 ounces mushrooms,
 chopped
1 tablespoon chopped
 fresh parsley
grated rind and juice of
 1 lemon
2 cups fresh bread
 crumbs

1½ pounds topside of
 beef, cut into 8 thin slices
3 tablespoons all-purpose
 flour
3 tablespoons oil
2 onions, sliced
1¾ cups beef stock
salt and ground black
 pepper

1 Preheat the oven to 325°F. Melt the butter in a saucepan and fry the bacon and mushrooms for 3 minutes. Mix them with the chopped parsley, lemon rind and juice, bread crumbs and seasoning.

2 Spread an equal amount of the bread crumb mixture evenly over the beef slices, leaving a narrow border clear around the edge. Roll up the slices and tie securely with fine string, then dip the beef rolls in the flour to coat lightly, shaking off any excess flour.

3 Heat the oil in a frying pan, then fry the beef rolls until lightly browned. Remove and keep warm. Add the onions and fry until browned. Stir in the remaining flour and cook until lightly browned. Pour in the stock, stirring constantly, bring to a boil, stirring, and simmer for 2–3 minutes.

4 Transfer the rolls to a casserole, pour the sauce over the top, then cover with a tight-fitting lid and cook in the oven for 2 hours. Lift out the "olives" using a slotted spoon and remove the string. Return them to the sauce and serve hot.

Lamb and Spring Vegetable Stew

Known as a *blanquette* in France, this stew may have blanched asparagus spears or French beans added.

Serves 4

5 tablespoons butter
2 pound lean boned shoulder of lamb, diced into 1¼-inch pieces
2½ cups lamb stock or water
⅔ cup dry white wine
1 onion, quartered
2 fresh thyme sprigs
1 bay leaf
8 ounces baby onions, halved
8 ounces young carrots

2 small turnips, quartered
¾ cup shelled lima beans
1 tablespoon all-purpose flour
1 egg yolk
2 tablespoons heavy cream
2 teaspoons lemon juice
salt and ground black pepper
2 tablespoons chopped fresh parsley, to garnish

1 Sauté the lamb in 2 tablespoons of the butter to seal. Add the stock or water and wine, bring to the boil and skim. Add the quartered onion, thyme and bay leaf. Cover and simmer for 1 hour.

2 Brown the baby onions in 1 tablespoon of the butter. Add to the lamb with the carrots and turnips. Cook for 20 minutes. Add the beans and cook for 10 minutes.

3 Arrange the lamb and vegetables on a serving dish. Cover and keep warm. Discard the onion quarters and herbs. Strain the stock; skim off the fat. Bring to the boil and reduce the stock to 1¾ cups. Mix the remaining butter and flour to a paste. Whisk into the stock, then simmer briefly.

4 Combine the egg yolk and cream. Add a little hot sauce then stir into the pan. Do not boil. Add the lemon juice, and season. Pour the sauce over the lamb; garnish with parsley.

Beef Paprika with Roasted Peppers

This dish is perfect for family suppers – and roasting the peppers gives an added dimension.

Serves 4

2 tablespoons olive oil
1½ pounds chuck steak, cut into 1½-inch pieces
2 onions, chopped
1 garlic clove, crushed
1 tablespoon all-purpose flour
1 tablespoon paprika, plus extra to garnish

14-ounce can chopped tomatoes
2 red bell peppers, halved and seeded
⅔ cup crème fraîche
salt and ground black pepper
buttered noodles, to serve

1 Preheat the oven to 275°F. Heat the oil in a large flameproof casserole and brown the diced chuck steak in batches. Remove the meat from the casserole using a slotted spoon and set aside.

2 Add the onions and garlic and fry gently until softened but not browned. Stir in the flour and paprika and continue cooking for 1–2 minutes more, stirring continuously to prevent sticking.

3 Return the meat and any juice that has collected on the plate to the casserole, then add the chopped tomatoes and salt and ground black pepper. Bring to a boil while stirring continuously, then cover with a tight-fitting lid and cook in the oven for 2½ hours.

4 Meanwhile, place the peppers skin-side up on a broiler rack and broil until the skins have blistered and charred. Cool, then peel off the skins. Cut the flesh into strips, then add to the casserole and cook for another 15–30 minutes, or until the meat is tender.

5 Stir in the crème fraîche and sprinkle with a little paprika. Serve hot with buttered noodles.

Beef in Guinness

Guinness gives this stew a deep, rich flavor. Use another stout if you prefer.

Serves 6

2 pounds chuck steak, cut into 1½ inch pieces
all-purpose flour, for coating
3 tablespoons oil
1 large onion, sliced
1 carrot, thinly sliced
2 celery stalks, thinly sliced
2 teaspoons granulated sugar
1 teaspoon English mustard powder
1 teaspoon tomato paste
1 x 3inch strip orange rind
2½ cups Guinness
bouquet garni
salt and ground black pepper

1 Toss the beef in flour to coat. Heat 2 tablespoons of the oil in a large shallow saucepan, then cook the beef in batches until lightly browned. Transfer to a bowl.

2 Add the remaining oil to the pan, then cook the onion until well browned, adding the thinly sliced carrot and celery towards the end.

3 Stir in the sugar, mustard, tomato paste, orange rind, Guinness and seasoning, then add the bouquet garni and bring to a boil. Return the meat, and any juice in the bowl, to the pan; add water, if necessary, so that the meat is covered. Cover the pan with a tight-fitting lid and cook gently for 2–2½ hours, until the meat is very tender.

Cottage Pie

This traditional dish is always a favorite with adults and children alike.

Serves 4

2 tablespoons oil
1 onion, finely chopped
1 carrot, finely chopped
4 ounces mushrooms, chopped
1¼ pounds ground lean chuck steak
1¼ cups ground beef stock or water
1 tablespon all-purpose flour
1 bay leaf
2–3 teaspoons Worcestershire sauce
1 tablespoon tomato paste
1½ pounds potatoes, boiled
2 tablespoons butter
3 tablespoons hot milk
1 tablespoon chopped fresh tarragon
salt and ground black pepper

1 Heat the oil in a saucepan and cook the onion, carrot and mushrooms, stirring occasionally, until browned. Stir the beef into the pan and cook, stirring to break up the lumps, until lightly browned.

2 Blend a few spoonfuls of the stock or water with the flour, then stir into the pan. Stir in the remaining stock or water and bring to a simmer, stirring. Add the bay leaf, Worcestershire sauce and tomato paste, then cover with a tight-fitting lid and cook very gently for 1 hour, stirring occasionally. Uncover towards the end of cooking to allow any excess liquid to evaporate, if necessary.

3 Preheat the oven to 375°F. Gently heat the potatoes for a couple of minutes, then mash with the butter, milk and seasoning.

4 Add the tarragon to the beef and season to taste with salt and pepper, then pour into a pie pan. Cover the beef with an even layer of potato and mark the top with the prongs of a fork. Bake for about 25 minutes, until golden brown.

Irish Stew

This wholesome and filling stew is given a slight piquancy by including a little anchovy sauce.

Serves 4

4 slices bacon
2 celery stalks, chopped
2 large onions, sliced
8 middle neck lamb
    chops, about 2¼
    pound s total weight
2¼ pounds potatoes, sliced

1¼ cups lamb stock
1½ teaspoons
    Worcestershire sauce
1 teaspoon anchovy sauce
salt and ground black
    pepper
fresh parsley, to garnish

1 Preheat the oven to 325°F. Chop and then fry the bacon for 3–5 minutes until the fat runs, then add the celery and one-third of the onions and continue to cook, stirring occasionally, until browned.

2 Layer the lamb chops, potatoes, vegetables and bacon and remaining onions in a heavy flameproof casserole, seasoning each layer with salt and pepper as you go. Finish with a layer of potatoes.

3 Pour the veal stock, Worcestershire sauce and anchovy sauce into the bacon and vegetable cooking juices in the pan, stir, and bring to a boil. Pour the mixture into the casserole, adding water if necessary so that the liquid comes halfway up the sides of the casserole.

4 Cover the casserole with a tight-fitting lid, then cook in the oven for 3 hours, until the meat and vegetables are tender. Return to the oven for longer if necessary. Serve hot, sprinkled with chopped fresh parsley.

Cook's Tip
This is a good way of cooking cheaper cuts of lamb but for a more elegant dish, use diced lamb or lamb steaks instead of the chops and cook in the oven for 2 hours.

Oatmeal and Herb Rack of Lamb

Ask the butcher to remove the chine bone that runs along the eye of the meat – this will make carving easier.

Serves 6

2 best end necks of lamb,
    about 2 pound each
finely grated rind of
    1 lemon
4 tablespoons medium
    oatmeal
1 cup fresh white bread
    crumbs
4 tablespoons chopped
    fresh parsley

2 tablespoons butter,
    melted
2 tablespoons honey
salt and ground black
    pepper
roasted baby vegetables
    and gravy, to serve
fresh herb sprigs, to
    garnish

1 Preheat the oven to 400°F. Using a small sharp knife, cut through the skin and meat of both pieces of lamb about 1 inch from the tips of the bones. Pull off the fatty meat to expose the bones, then scrape around each bone tip until completely clean.

2 Trim all the skin and most of the fat from the meat, then lightly score the remaining fat with a sharp knife. Repeat with the second rack.

3 Mix together the lemon rind, oatmeal, bread crumbs, the parsley and seasoning, then stir in the melted butter.

4 Brush the fatty side of each rack of lamb with honey, then press the oatmeal mixture evenly over the surface with your fingers until well coated.

5 Place the racks in a roasting pan with the oatmeal sides up. Roast for 40–50 minutes, depending on whether you like rare or medium lamb. Cover loosely with foil if browning too much. To serve, slice each rack into three and accompany with roasted baby vegetables and gravy made with the pan juices. Garnish with herb sprigs.

Beef Wellington

This dish is so-named because of a supposed resemblance of shape and color to the Duke of Wellington's boot.

Serves 8

3 pounds fillet of beef
1 tablespoon butter
2 tablespoons oil
½ small onion, finely
   chopped
6 ounces mushrooms,
   chopped
6 ounces liver pâté

freshly squeezed lemon
   juice
a few drops of
   Worcestershire sauce
14 ounces ready-made
   puff pastry
salt and ground black
   pepper
beaten egg, to glaze

1 Preheat the oven to 425°F. Season the beef with pepper, then tie it at intervals with string.

2 Heat the butter and oil in a roasting pan. Brown the beef over a high heat, then cook in the oven for 20 minutes. Cool and remove the string.

3 Scrape the pan juices into another pan, add the onion and mushrooms and cook until tender. Cool, then mix with the pâté. Add lemon juice and Worcestershire sauce.

4 Roll out the pastry to a large ¼-inch-thick rectangle. Spread the pâté mixture on the beef, then place it in the centre of the pastry. Moisten the edges of the pastry, then fold it over the beef to make a neat package, tucking in the ends neatly; press to seal.

5 Place the package on a baking sheet with the seam on the underneath and brush with beaten egg. Bake in the oven for 25–45 minutes, depending how well done you like the beef. Serve in generous slices.

Butterflied Cumin and Garlic Lamb

Ground cumin and garlic give the lamb a wonderful Middle-Eastern flavor in this recipe.

Serves 6

4-pound leg of lamb
4 tablespoons extra-
   virgin olive oil
2 tablespoons ground
   cumin
4–6 garlic cloves,
   crushed

salt and ground black
   pepper
toasted almond and
   raisin rice, to serve
fresh cilantro sprigs and
   lemon wedges,
   to garnish

1 To butterfly the lamb, cut away the meat from the bone using a small sharp knife. Remove any excess fat and the thin, parchment-like membrane. Bat out the meat with a rolling pin to an even thickness, then prick the fleshy side of the lamb well with the tip of the knife.

2 In a bowl, mix together the olive oil, cumin and garlic and season with pepper. Spoon the mixture all over the lamb, then rub it well into the crevices. Cover the bowl and allow the lamb to marinate overnight.

3 Preheat the oven to 400°F. Spread the lamb, skin-side down, on a rack in a roasting tin. Season with salt and roast for 45–60 minutes, until crusty brown on the outside but still pink in the center.

4 Remove the lamb from the oven and let it rest for about 10 minutes. Cut into diagonal slices and serve with the toasted almond and raisin rice. Garnish with the fresh cilantro sprigs and lemon wedges.

Cook's Tip
The lamb may be barbecued rather than roasted. Thread it on to two long skewers and barbecue for about 20-25 minutes on each side, until it is cooked to your liking.

Lamb with Mint Sauce

In this flavorful dish, the classic combination of lamb and mint is given an original twist.

Serves 4

8 lamb noisettes, ³⁄₄ – 1
   inch thick
2 tablespoons oil
3 tablespoons medium-
   bodied dry white wine,
   or light stock
salt and ground black
   pepper
fresh mint sprigs, to
   garnish

For the sauce
2 tablespoons boiling
   water
1 – 2 teapoons sugar
leaves from a small
   bunch of fresh mint,
   finely chopped
2-3 tablespoons white
   wine vinegar

1 To make the sauce, stir the water and sugar together, then add the mint, vinegar to taste and season with salt and black pepper. Leave for 30 minutes.

2 Season the lamb with pepper. Heat the oil in a large frying pan and fry the lamb, in batches if necessary so that the pan is not crowded, for about 3 minutes on each side for meat that is pink in the middle.

3 Transfer the lamb to a warmed plate and season with salt, then cover and keep warm.

4 Stir the wine or stock into the pan juices, dislodging the residue, and bring to a boil. Bubble for a couple of minutes, then pour over the lamb. Garnish the lamb noisettes with small sprigs of mint and serve hot with the mint sauce.

Somerset Pork with Apples

A creamy cider sauce accompanies tender pieces of pork and sliced apples to make a rich supper dish.

Serves 4

2 tablespoons butter
1¼-pounds pork loin, cut
   into bite-size pieces
12 baby onions, peeled
2 teaspoons grated lemon
   rind
1¼ cups hard cider
²⁄₃ cup ham or veal stock

2 crisp eating apples such
   as Granny Smith,
   cored and sliced
3 tablespoons chopped
   fresh parsley
scant ½ cup whipping
   cream
salt and ground black
   pepper

1 Heat the butter in a large sauté or frying pan and brown the pork in batches. Transfer the pork to a bowl.

2 Add the onions to the pan, brown lightly, then stir in the lemon rind, cider and stock and boil for about 3 minutes. Return all the pork to the pan and cook gently for about 25 minutes, until tender.

3 Add the apples to the pan and continue to cook for another 5 minutes. Using a slotted spoon, transfer the pork, onions and apples to a warmed serving dish, cover and keep warm. Stir the parsley and cream into the pan and allow to bubble to thicken the sauce slightly. Season, then pour over the pork and serve hot.

Pork with Plums

Plums poached in apple juice are used here to make a delightfully fruity sauce for pork chops.

Serves 4

3 tablespoons butter	1 onion, finely chopped
1 tablespoon oil	pinch of freshly ground
4 pork chops, about	mace
7 ounces each	salt and ground black
1 pound ripe plums,	pepper
halved and stoned	fresh sage leaves, to
1¼ cups apple juice	garnish

1 Heat the butter and oil in a large frying pan and fry the chops until brown on both sides, then transfer them to a plate.

2 Meanwhile, simmer the plums in the apple juice until tender. Strain off and reserve the juice, then purée half the plums with a little of the juice.

3 Add the onion to the pan and cook gently until soft, but not colored. Return the chops to the pan. Pour over the plum purée and all the juice.

4 Simmer, uncovered, for 10–15 minutes, until the chops are cooked through. Add the remaining plums to the pan, then add the mace and seasoning. Warm the sauce through over a moderate heat and serve garnished with fresh sage leaves.

Lancashire Hot-pot

Browning the lamb and kidneys, plus the extra vegetables and herbs, adds flavor to the traditional basic ingredients.

Serves 4

3 tablespoons dripping,	3 celery stalks, sliced
or 3 tablespoons oil	1 tablespoon chopped
8 medium lamb chops,	fresh thyme
about 2 pounds total	2 tablespoons chopped
weight	fresh parsley
6 ounces lambs' kidneys,	small fresh rosemary
cut into large pieces	sprig
2 pounds potatoes, thinly	2½ cups lamb stock
sliced	salt and ground black
3 carrots, thickly sliced	pepper
1 pound leeks, sliced	

1 Preheat the oven to 325°F. Heat the dripping or oil in a frying pan and brown the chops and kidneys in batches, then reserve the fat.

2 In a large casserole, make alternate layers of lamb chops, kidneys, three-quarters of the potatoes and the carrots, leeks and celery, sprinkling the herbs and seasoning over each layer as you go. Tuck the rosemary sprig down the side.

3 Arrange the remaining potatoes on top. Pour over the stock, brush with the reserved fat, then cover the casserole with a tight-fitting lid and bake for 2½ hours. Increase the oven temperature to 425°F. Uncover and cook for another 30 minutes.

Pork Loin with Celery

Have a change from a plain Sunday roast and try this whole loin of pork in a celery and cream sauce instead.

Serves 4

1 tablespoon oil
4 tablespoons butter
2¼-pound boned, rolled
   loin of pork, rind
   removed and trimmed
1 onion, chopped
bouquet garni
3 fresh dill sprigs
⅔ cup dry white wine
⅔ cup water

stalks from 1 celery head,
   cut into 1-inch lengths
2 tablespoons all-purpose
   flour
⅔ cup heavy cream
squeeze of lemon juice
salt and ground black
   pepper
chopped fresh dill, to
   garnish

1 Heat the oil and half the butter in a heavy flameproof casserole just large enough to hold the pork and celery, then brown the pork evenly. Transfer the pork to a plate.

2 Add the onion to the casserole and cook until softened but not browned. Place the bouquet garni and the dill sprigs on the onion, then place the pork on top and add any juice from the plate. Pour the wine and water over the pork, season to taste, cover and simmer gently for 30 minutes.

3 Turn the pork, arrange the celery around it, cover again and cook for 40 minutes, until the pork and celery are tender. Transfer the pork and celery to a serving plate, cover and keep warm. Discard the bouquet garni and dill.

4 Cream the remaining butter and flour, then whisk into the cooking liquid while it is barely simmering. Cook for about 2–3 minutes, stirring occasionally. Stir the cream into the casserole, bring to a boil and add a squeeze of lemon juice.

5 Slice the pork, pour some sauce over the slices and garnish with dill. Serve the remaining sauce separately.

Spiced Lamb with Apricots

Inspired by Middle Eastern cooking, this fruity, spicy casserole is simple to make yet looks impressive.

Serves 4

4 ounces ready-to-eat
   dried apricots
scant ½ cup seedless
   raisins
½ teaspoon saffron
   strands
⅔ cup orange juice
1 tablespoon red wine
   vinegar
2–3 tablespoons olive oil
3-pound leg of lamb,
   boned and diced
1 onion, chopped
2 garlic cloves, crushed
2 teaspoons ground
   cumin

¼ teaspoon ground cloves
1 tablespoon ground
   coriander
2 tablespoons all-purpose
   flour
2½ cups lamb stock
3 tablespoons chopped
   fresh cilantro
salt and ground black
   pepper
saffron rice mixed with
   toasted almonds and
   chopped fresh cilantro,
   to serve

1 Mix together the dried apricots, raisins, saffron, orange juice and vinegar. Cover and let soak for 2–3 hours.

2 Preheat the oven to 325°F. Heat 2 tablespoons oil in a large flameproof casserole and brown the lamb in batches. Remove and set aside. Add the onion and garlic with a little more of the remaining oil and cook until softened.

3 Stir in the spices and flour and cook for 1–2 minutes more. Return the meat to the casserole. Stir in the stock, fresh cilantro and the soaked fruit with its liquid. Season to taste with salt and pepper, then bring to a boil. Cover the casserole with a tight-fitting lid and cook for 1½ hours (adding extra stock if necessary), or until the lamb is tender. Serve with saffron rice mixed with toasted almonds and fresh cilantro.

Beef and Mushroom Burgers

It's worth making your own burgers to cut down on fat – in these the meat is extended with mushrooms for extra fiber.

Serves 4

1 small onion, chopped
2 cups small cup
    mushrooms
1 pound lean ground beef
1 cup fresh bread crumbs
1 teaspoon dried mixed
    herbs

1 tablespoon tomato
    paste
flour, for shaping
salt and black pepper

1 Process the onion and mushrooms until finely chopped. Add the beef, bread crumbs, herbs, tomato paste and seasoning. Process until the mixture binds but still has some texture. Divide into 8–10 pieces and press into burger shapes.

2 Cook the burgers in a nonstick frying pan, or under a hot broiler for 12–15 minutes, turning once, until evenly cooked. Serve with relish and salad, in burger buns or pita bread.

Ruby Chops

This dish can be prepared with the minimum of effort, yet would still impress at an informal dinner party.

Serves 4

1 ruby grapefruit
4 lean pork loin chops

3 tablespoons redcurrant
    jelly
ground black pepper

1 Using a sharp knife, cut away all the peel and pith from the grapefruit. Carefully remove the segments, catching the juice in a bowl.

2 Fry the pork loin chops in a nonstick frying pan without fat, turning them once, until golden. Add the reserved grapefruit juice and redcurrant jelly to the pan and stir until melted. Add the grapefruit segments, then season with pepper and serve hot with fresh vegetables.

Beef Strips with Orange and Ginger

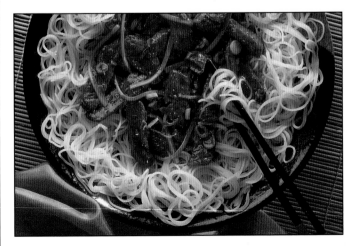

Stir-frying is a good way of cooking with the minimum of fat. It's also one of the quickest ways to cook.

Serves 4

Place 1 pound beef strips in a bowl; sprinkle over the rind and juice of 1 orange. Allow to marinate for at least 30 minutes. Drain the liquid and set aside, then mix the meat with 1 tablespoon soy sauce, 1 tablespoon cornstarch and 1 inch ginger. Heat 2 teaspoons sesame oil in a wok or large frying pan and add the beef. Stir-fry for 1 minute, add 1 carrot, cut into small strips and stir-fry for another 2–3 minutes. Stir in 2 sliced scallions and the reserved liquid, then boil, stirring, until thickened.

Steak, Kidney and Mushroom Pie

If you prefer, omit the kidneys from this pie and substitute more chuck steak in their place.

Serves 4

2 tablespoons sunflower oil
1 onion, chopped
4 ounces bacon, finely chopped
1¼ pounds chuck steak, diced
2 tablespoons all-purpose flour

4 ounces lambs' kidneys
1¾ cups beef stock
large bouquet garni
4 ounces button mushrooms
8 ounces ready-made puff pastry
beaten egg, to glaze
salt and ground black pepper

1 Preheat the oven to 325°F. Heat the oil in a heavy-based saucepan and cook the bacon and onion until lightly browned.

2 Toss the steak in the flour. Stir the meat into the pan in batches and cook, stirring, until browned. Toss the kidneys in flour; add to the pan with the bouquet garni. Transfer to a casserole then pour in the stock, cover with a tight-fitting lid and cook in the oven for 2 hours. Stir in the mushrooms and seasoning and leave to cool.

3 Preheat the oven to 425°F. Roll out the pastry to ¾ inch larger than the top of a 5-cup pie dish. Cut off a pastry strip and then fit it around the moistened rim of the dish. Brush the pastry strip with water.

4 Turn the meat mixture into the dish. Lay the pastry over the dish, crimp the edges together to seal, cut a small vent in the pastry, brush with beaten egg and bake for 20 minutes. Lower the oven temperature to 350°F and bake for another 20 minutes, until the pastry has risen, and is golden and crisp.

Lamb Pie with Mustard Thatch

This makes a pleasant change from a classic shepherd's pie – and it is a healthier option, as well.

Serves 4

1½ pounds old potatoes, diced
2 tablespoons skim milk
1 tablespoon wholegrain or French mustard
1 pound lean minced lamb
1 onion, chopped
2 celery stalks, sliced
2 carrots, diced
⅔ cup beef stock

4 tablespoons rolled oats
1 tablespoon Worcestershire sauce
2 tablespoons fresh rosemary, chopped, or 2 teaspoons dried rosemary
salt and ground black pepper
fresh vegetables, to serve

1 Cook the potatoes in lightly salted boiling water until tender. Drain and mash until smooth, then stir in the milk and mustard. Meanwhile, preheat the oven to 400°F.

2 Break up the lamb with a fork and fry without any fat in a nonstick pan until lightly browned. Add the onion, celery and carrots to the saucepan and cook for 2–3 minutes, stirring constantly.

3 Stir in the stock and rolled oats. Bring to a boil, then add the Worcestershire sauce and rosemary and season to taste with salt and pepper.

4 Turn the meat mixture into a 7½-cup casserole and spread the potato topping evenly over the top, swirling with the edge of a knife. Bake for 30–35 minutes, or until golden. Serve hot with fresh vegetables.

Sausage and Bean Ragoût

An economical and nutritious main course that children will love. Serve with garlic and herb bread, if you wish.

Serves 4

*2 cups dried flageolet
  beans, soaked
  overnight
3 tablespoons olive oil
1 onion, finely chopped
2 garlic cloves, crushed
1 pound good-quality
  chunky sausages,
  skinned and thickly
  sliced
1 tablespoon tomato
  paste*

*2 tablespoons chopped
  fresh parsley
1 tablespoon chopped
  fresh thyme
14-ounce can chopped
  tomatoes
salt and ground black
  pepper
chopped fresh thyme and
  parsley, to garnish*

1 Drain and rinse the soaked beans and place them in a saucepan with enough water to cover. Bring to a boil, cover the pan with a tight-fitting lid and simmer for about 1 hour, or until tender. Drain the beans and set aside.

2 Heat the oil in a frying pan and fry the onion, garlic and sausages until golden.

3 Stir in the tomato paste, tomatoes, chopped parsley and thyme. Season with salt and pepper, then bring to a boil.

4 Add the beans, then cover with a lid and cook gently for about 15 minutes, stirring occasionally, until the sausage slices are cooked through. Garnish with chopped fresh thyme and parsley and serve immediately.

Cook's Tip
For a spicier version, add some skinned, thinly sliced chorizo sausage along with the flageolet beans for the last 15 minutes of cooking.

Pepper Steaks with Madeira

A really easy dish for special occasions. Mixed peppercorns have an excellent flavor, though black pepper will do.

Serves 4

*1 tablespoon mixed dried
  peppercorns (green,
  pink and black)
4 fillet or sirloin steaks,
  about 6 ounces each
1 tablespoon olive oil,
  plus extra oil for
  shallow frying*

*1 garlic clove, crushed
4 tablespoons Madeira
  wine
6 tablespoons beef stock
⅔ cup heavy cream
pinch of salt*

1 Finely crush the peppercorns using a coffee grinder or mortar and pestle, then press them evenly onto both sides of the steaks.

2 Place the steaks in a shallow non-metallic dish, then add the olive oil, garlic and Madeira wine. Cover the dish and allow to marinate in a cool place for at least 4–6 hours, or preferably overnight for a more intense flavour.

3 Remove the steaks from the dish, reserving the marinade. Brush a little oil over a large heavy-based frying pan and heat until it is hot.

4 Add the steaks and cook over a high heat, according to taste. Allow about 3 minutes' cooking time per side for a medium steak or 2 minutes per side for rare. Remove the steaks from the frying pan and keep them warm.

5 Add the reserved marinade and the beef stock to the pan and bring to a boil, then let the sauce bubble until it is well reduced.

6 Add the heavy cream to the pan, with salt to taste, and stir until it has slightly thickened. Serve the pepper steaks on warmed plates with the sauce.

Pork with Mozzarella and Sage

Here is a variation of the famous dish *saltimbocca alla romana* – the mozzarella adds a delicious creamy flavor.

Serves 2–3

8 ounces pork tenderloin
1 garlic clove, crushed
3 ounces mozzarella, cut
   into 6 slices
6 slices Parma ham
6 large sage leaves

2 tablespoons butter
salt and ground black
   pepper
potato wedges roasted in
   olive oil and green
   beans, to serve

1 Trim any excess fat from the pork, then cut the pork crosswise into six pieces about 1 inch thick.

2 Stand each piece of tenderloin on its end and bat down with a rolling pin to flatten. Rub with garlic and set aside for 30 minutes in a cool place.

3 Place a slice of mozzarella on top of each pork steak and season with salt and pepper. Lay a slice of Parma ham on top of each, crinkling it a little to fit.

4 Press a sage leaf onto each and secure with a toothpick. Melt the butter in a large heavy-based frying pan and cook the pork for about 2 minutes on each side until you see the mozzarella melting. Remove the toothpicks and serve immediately with roasted potatoes and green beans.

Five-spice Lamb

This aromatic lamb casserole is a perfect dish to serve at an informal supper party.

Serves 4

2–3 tablespoons oil
3–3½ pound leg of lamb,
   boned and cubed
1 onion, chopped
2 teaspoons grated fresh
   ginger
1 garlic clove, crushed
1 teaspoon five-spice
   powder
2 tablespoons hoisin
   sauce
1 tablespoon soy sauce

1¼ cups tomato paste
1 cup lamb stock
1 red bell pepper, seeded
   and diced
1 yellow bell pepper,
   seeded and diced
2 tablespoons chopped
   fresh cilantro
1 tablespoon sesame
   seeds, toasted
salt and ground black
   pepper

1 Preheat the oven to 325°F. In a large, flameproof casserole, heat 2 tablespoons of the oil and then brown the diced lamb in batches over a high heat. Remove to a plate and set aside.

2 Add the onion, ginger and garlic to the casserole with a little more of the oil, if necessary, and cook for 5 minutes, or until softened.

3 Return the lamb to the casserole. Stir in the five-spice powder, hoisin sauce, soy sauce, tomato purée and stock, and season to taste with salt and pepper. Bring to a boil, then cover with a tight-fitting lid and cook in the oven for about 1¼ hours.

4 Remove the casserole from the oven, stir in the peppers, then cover and return to the oven for another 15 minutes, or until the lamb is very tender.

5 Sprinkle with the chopped fresh cilantro and toasted sesame seeds. Serve hot accompanied by rice, if you wish.

Rich Beef Casserole

Use a full-bodied red wine such as a Burgundy to create the flavorful sauce in this casserole.

Serves 4–6

2 pounds chuck steak, cubed
2 onions, coarsely chopped
1 bouquet garni
6 black peppercorns
1 tablespoon red wine vinegar
1 bottle red wine
3–4 tablespoons olive oil
3 celery stalks, thickly sliced
½ cup all-purpose flour
1¼ cups beef stock
2 tablespoons tomato paste
2 garlic cloves, crushed
6 ounces chestnut mushrooms, halved
14-ounce can artichoke hearts, drained and halved
chopped fresh parsley and thyme, to garnish

1 Combine the meat, onions, bouquet garni, peppercorns, vinegar and wine. Cover and let marinate overnight.

2 The next day, preheat the oven to 325°F. Strain the meat, reserving the marinade, and pat dry. Heat the oil in a large flameproof casserole and fry the meat and onions in batches, adding a little more oil if necessary. Remove and set aside. Add the celery and fry until browned, then remove this also and set it aside with the meat.

3 Sprinkle the flour into the casserole and cook for 1 minute. Gradually add the reserved marinade and the stock, and bring to a boil, stirring continuously. Return the meat, onions and celery to the casserole, then stir in the tomato paste and crushed garlic.

4 Cover the casserole with a tight-fitting lid and cook in the oven for about 2¼ hours. Stir in the mushrooms and artichokes, cover again and cook for 15 minutes more, until the meat is tender. Garnish with parsley and thyme, and serve hot with creamy mashed potatoes, if you wish.

Pork Steaks with Gremolata

Gremolata is a popular Italian dressing of garlic, lemon and parsley – it adds a hint of sharpness to the pork.

Serves 4

2 tablespoons olive oil
4 pork shoulder steaks
1 onion, chopped
2 garlic cloves, crushed
14-ounce can tomatoes
2 tablespoons tomato paste
⅔ cup dry white wine
bouquet garni
3 anchovy fillets, drained and chopped
salt and ground black pepper
salad greens, to serve

For the gremolata
3 tablespoons chopped fresh parsley
grated rind of ½ lemon
grated rind of 1 lime
1 garlic clove, chopped

1 Heat the oil in a large flameproof casserole and brown the pork steaks on both sides. Remove and set aside.

2 Add the onions to the casserole and cook until soft. Add the garlic and cook for 1–2 minutes. Chop the tomatoes and add with the tomato paste and wine. Add the bouquet garni, then boil rapidly for 3–4 minutes to reduce and thicken the sauce slightly. Return the pork to the casserole, then cover with a tight-fitting lid and cook for about 30 minutes. Stir in the chopped anchovies. Cover the casserole and cook for another 15 minutes, or until the pork is tender.

3 Meanwhile, to make the gremolata, mix together the parsley, lemon and lime rinds and garlic.

4 Remove the pork steaks and discard the bouquet garni. Reduce the sauce over a high heat, if it is not already thick. Taste and adjust the seasoning if necessary.

5 Return the pork to the casserole, then sprinkle with the gremolata. Cover and cook for another 5 minutes more, then serve hot with salad greens.

Beef Casserole and Dumplings

A traditional English recipe, this delicious casserole is topped with light herb dumplings for a filling meal.

Serves 4

1 tablespoon oil
1 pound ground beef
16 button onions
2 carrots, thickly
    sliced
2 celery stalks, thickly
    sliced
2 tablespoons all-purpose
    flour
2½ cups beef stock

salt and ground black
    pepper

For the dumplings
4 tablespoons shredded
    beef suet
1 cup self-rising flour
1 tablespoon chopped
    fresh parsley

1 Preheat the oven to 350°F. Heat the oil in a flameproof casserole and fry the ground beef for 5 minutes until brown and sealed.

2 Add the onions; fry over a moderate heat for 5 minutes, stirring all the time.

3 Stir in the sliced carrots, the celery and the flour, then cook for another 1 minute more.

4 Add the beef stock and season to taste with salt and ground black pepper. Bring to a boil. Cover and cook in the oven for 1¼ hours.

5 For the dumplings, mix together the suet, flour and fresh parsley. Add enough cold water to form a smooth dough.

6 Roll the dumpling mixture into eight equal-size balls and place them around the top of the casserole. Return the casserole, uncovered, to the oven for another 20 minutes. Serve with broccoli florets, if liked.

Stilton Burgers

This tasty recipe contains a delicious surprise. The lightly melted Stilton cheese is enclosed in the crunchy burger.

Serves 4

1 pound ground beef
1 onion, finely chopped
1 celery stalk, chopped
1 teaspoon mixed
    dried herbs
1 teaspoon mustard

½ cup crumbled Stilton
    cheese
4 burger buns
salt and ground black
    pepper
green salad and mustard
    pickle, to serve

1 Place the ground beef in a bowl with the chopped onion and celery. Mix together, then season with salt and pepper.

2 Stir in the herbs and mustard, and bring together to form a firm mixture.

3 Divide the mixture into eight equal portions. Place four on a cutting board and flatten each one slightly.

4 Place the crumbled cheese in the center of each.

5 Flatten the remaining mixture and place on top. Mold the mixture together, enclosing the crumbled cheese, and shape into four burgers.

6 Broil under a moderate heat for turning once 10 minutes, or until cooked through. Split the burger buns and place a burger inside each. Serve with a freshly made salad and some mustard pickle.

Cook's Tip
These burgers could be made with ground lamb or pork for a variation, but make sure they are thoroughly cooked and not pink inside.

Indian Curried Lamb Samosas

Authentic samosa pastry is rather difficult to make but these samosas work equally well using puff pastry.

Serves 4

1 tablespoon oil
1 garlic clove, crushed
6 ounces ground lamb
4 scallions, finely chopped
2 teaspoons medium-hot
   curry paste
4 ready-to-eat dried
   apricots, chopped
1 small potato, diced
2 teaspoons apricot
   chutney
2 tablespoons frozen peas
squeeze of lemon juice

1 tablespoon chopped fresh
   cilantro
8 ounces ready-made
   puff pastry
beaten egg, to glaze
1 teaspoon cumin seeds
salt and ground black
   pepper
3 tablespoons plain
   yogurt with chopped
   fresh mint, to serve
fresh mint sprigs, to
   garnish

1 Preheat the oven to 425°F and moisten a large nonstick baking sheet. Fry the garlic in the oil for 30 seconds, then add the lamb. Fry for about 5 minutes, stirring, until the meat is well browned.

2 Stir in the scallions, curry paste, apricots and potato, and cook for 2–3 minutes. Then add the chutney, peas and 4 tablespoons water. Cover and simmer for 10 minutes, stirring occasionally. Stir in the lemon juice and cilantro, season to taste, remove and let cool.

3 Roll out the pastry and cut into four 6-inch squares. Place a quarter of the curry mixture in the center of each square and brush the edges with beaten egg. Fold over to make a triangle and seal the edges. Make a small vent in the top of each.

4 Brush each samosa with beaten egg and sprinkle with cumin seeds. Place on the damp baking sheet and bake for about 20 minutes. Serve garnished with mint sprigs and with the minty yogurt passed around separately.

Breton Pork and Bean Casserole

This is a traditional French dish, called *cassoulet*. There are many variations in the different regions of France.

Serves 4

2 tablespoons olive oil
1 onion, chopped
2 garlic cloves, chopped
1 pound lean shoulder of
   pork, diced
12 ounces lean lamb
   (preferably leg), diced
8 ounces coarse pork and
   garlic sausage, cut
   into chunks
14-ounce can chopped
   tomatoes

2 tablespoons red wine
1 tablespoon tomato paste
bouquet garni
14-ounce can navy or
   white beans, drained
   and rinsed
1 cup whole wheat bread
   crumbs
salt and ground black
   pepper
green salad and French
   bread, to serve

1 Preheat the oven to 325°F. Heat the oil in a large flameproof casserole and fry the onions and garlic until softened. Remove with a slotted spoon and reserve.

2 Add the pork, lamb and sausage chunks to the casserole and fry over a high heat until browned on all sides. Add the onions and garlic to the meat.

3 Stir in the chopped tomatoes, wine and tomato paste and add 1¼ cups water. Season to taste with salt and pepper and add the bouquet garni. Cover and bring to a boil, then transfer the casserole to the preheated oven and cook for 1½ hours.

4 Remove the bouquet garni, stir in the beans and sprinkle the bread crumbs over the top. Return to the oven, uncovered, for another 30 minutes, until the top is golden brown. Serve hot with a green salad and French bread to mop up the juice.

Cook's Tip
Replace the lamb with duck breast, but be sure to drain off any fat before adding the bread crumbs.

Pan-fried Mediterranean Lamb

The warm, summery flavors of the Mediterranean are combined for a simple weekday meal.

Serves 4

8 lean lamb cutlets
1 onion, thinly sliced
2 red bell peppers, seeded and sliced
14-ounce can plum tomatoes
1 garlic clove, crushed
3 tablespoons chopped fresh basil leaves
2 tablespoons chopped black olives
salt and ground black pepper

1 Trim any excess fat from the lamb, then fry without fat in a nonstick frying pan until golden brown.

2 Add the onion and red peppers to the pan. Cook, stirring, for a few minutes to soften, then add the plum tomatoes, garlic and fresh basil leaves.

3 Cover and simmer for 20 minutes or until the lamb is tender. Stir in the olives, season to taste with salt and pepper and serve hot, with pasta if you wish.

Cook's Tip
The red peppers give this dish a slightly sweet taste. If you prefer, use green peppers for a more savory dish.

Greek Lamb Pie

Ready-made phyllo pastry is so easy to use and gives a most professional look to this lamb and spinach pie.

Serves 4

1 pound ground lamb
1 onion, sliced
1 garlic clove, crushed
14-ounce can plum tomatoes
2 tablespoons chopped fresh mint
1 teaspoon grated nutmeg
12 ounces young spinach leaves
10-ounce package ready-made phyllo pastry
sunflower oil, for brushing
1 teaspoon sesame seeds
salt and ground black pepper

1 Preheat the oven to 400°F. Lightly oil an 8½-inch round springform pan.

2 Fry the lamb and onion without fat in a nonstick pan until golden. Add the garlic, tomatoes, mint and nutmeg and season with salt and pepper. Bring to a boil, stirring from time to time. Simmer, stirring occasionally, until most of the liquid has evaporated.

3 Wash the spinach and remove any tough stalks, then cook in only the water clinging to the leaves for about 2 minutes, until just wilted.

4 Lightly brush each sheet of phyllo pastry with oil and lay in overlapping layers in the pan, leaving enough hanging over to wrap over the top.

5 Spoon in the meat and spinach, then wrap the pastry over to enclose, scrunching it slightly. Sprinkle with sesame seeds and bake for about 25–30 minutes, or until golden and crisp. Serve hot, with salad or vegetables, as you wish.

Pasta Bolognese with Cheese

If you like lasagne, you will love this dish. It is especially popular with children too.

Serves 4

2 tablespoons olive oil
1 onion, chopped
1 garlic clove, crushed
1 carrot, diced
2 celery stalks, chopped
2 slices bacon, finely
 chopped
5 button mushrooms,
 chopped
1 pound lean ground beef
½ cup red wine
1 tablespoon tomato paste
7-ounce can chopped
 tomatoes

sprig of fresh thyme
2 cups dried penne pasta
1¼ cups milk
2 tablespoons butter
2 tablespoons all-purpose
 flour
1 cup diced mozzarella
 cheese
4 tablespoons grated
 Parmesan cheese
salt and ground black
 pepper
fresh basil sprigs, to
 garnish

1 Fry the onion, garlic, carrot and celery in the olive oil until softened. Add the bacon and fry for 3–4 minutes. Add the mushrooms, fry for 2 minutes, then fry the beef until brown.

2 Add the wine, tomato paste, 3 tablespoons water, tomatoes and the sprig of fresh thyme. Bring to a boil, cover, and simmer for 30 minutes.

3 Preheat the oven to 400°F. Cook the pasta. Meanwhile, place the milk, butter and flour in a saucepan; heat gently, whisking until thickened. Stir in the mozzarella and Parmesan cheeses, and season.

4 Drain the pasta and stir into the cheese sauce. Uncover the Bolognese sauce and boil rapidly for 2 minutes. Spoon the sauce into a casserole, top with the pasta mixture and sprinkle with the remaining Parmesan. Bake for 25 minutes, or until golden. Garnish with basil and serve hot.

Corned Beef and Egg Hash

This classic American hash is a popular brunch dish and should be served with chili sauce for an authentic touch.

Serves 4

2 tablespoons oil
2 tablespoons butter
1 onion, finely chopped
1 small green bell pepper,
 seeded and diced
2 large boiled potatoes,
 diced
12-ounce can corned beef,
 diced

¼ teaspoon grated
 nutmeg
¼ teaspoon paprika
4 eggs
salt and ground black
 pepper
chopped fresh parsley, to
 garnish
chili sauce, to serve

1 Heat the oil and butter together in a large frying pan and fry the onion for 5–6 minutes until softened. In a bowl, mix together the pepper, potatoes, corned beef, nutmeg and paprika; season to taste with salt and pepper. Add to the pan and toss gently to distribute the cooked onion. Press down lightly; fry over a moderate heat for 3–4 minutes, until a golden brown crust has formed on the bottom.

2 Stir the mixture through to distribute the crust, then repeat the frying twice, until the mixture has browned.

3 Make four wells in the hash and crack an egg into each one. Cover and cook gently for about 4–5 minutes, until the egg whites are just set.

4 Sprinkle with chopped parsley and cut the hash into quarters. Serve hot with chili sauce.

Cook's Tip
Put the can of corned beef in the fridge for about 30 minutes before using. It will firm up and you will be able to cut it into cubes more easily than if it is used at room temperature.

Best-ever American Burgers

These meaty quarter-pounders are far superior in taste and texture to anything you can buy ready-made.

Makes 4 burgers

1 tablespoon oil
1 small onion, chopped
1 pound lean ground beef
1 large garlic clove, crushed
1 teaspoon ground cumin
2 teaspoons ground coriander
2 tablespoons tomato paste or ketchup
1 teaspoon wholegrain mustard
dash of Worcestershire sauce

2 tablespoons mixed chopped fresh herbs such as parsley, thyme and oregano or marjoram
1 tablespoon lightly beaten egg
salt and ground black pepper
flour, for shaping
oil, for frying (optional)
mixed salad, chips and relish, to serve

1 Heat the oil in a frying pan, add the onion and cook for 5 minutes, until softened. Remove from the pan, drain on paper towels and allow to cool.

2 Mix together the beef, garlic, spices, tomato paste or ketchup, mustard, Worcestershire sauce, herbs, beaten egg and seasoning in a bowl. Stir in the cooled onions.

3 Sprinkle a board with flour and shape the mixture into four burgers with floured hands and a palette knife. Cover and chill in the fridge for 15 minutes.

4 Heat a little oil in a pan and fry the burgers over a moderate heat for about 5 minutes each side, depending on how rare you like them. Alternatively, cook under a moderate broiler for the same time. Serve with salad, fries and relish.

Cook's Tip
If you prefer, make eight smaller burgers to serve in buns, with melted cheese and tomato slices.

Bacon and Sausage Sauerkraut

Juniper berries and crushed cilantro seeds flavour this traditional dish from Alsace.

Serves 4

2 tablespoons oil
1 large onion, thinly sliced
1 garlic clove, crushed
1 pound bottled sauerkraut, rinsed and drained
1 eating apple, cored and chopped
5 juniper berries
5 coriander seeds, crushed

1-pound piece of lightly smoked bacon loin roast
8 ounces whole smoked pork sausage, pricked
¾ cup unsweetened apple juice
⅔ cup chicken stock
1 bay leaf
8 small salad potatoes

1 Preheat the oven to 350°F. Heat the oil in a flameproof casserole and fry the onion and garlic for about 3–4 minutes, until softened. Stir in the sauerkraut, apple, juniper berries and coriander seeds.

2 Lay the piece of bacon loin and the sausage on top of the sauerkraut, pour on the apple juice and stock, and add the bay leaf. Cover and bake in the oven for about 1 hour.

3 Remove from the oven and pop the potatoes into the casserole. Add a little more stock if necessary, cover and bake for another 30 minutes, or until the potatoes are tender.

4 Just before serving, lift out the bacon and sausages onto a board and slice. Spoon the sauerkraut onto a warmed platter, top with the meat and surround with the potatoes.

Ginger Pork with Black Bean Sauce

Preserved black beans provide a unique flavor in this dish. Look for them in specialty Chinese food stores.

Serves 4

12-ounce pork fillet
1 garlic clove, crushed
1 tablespoon grated fresh ginger
6 tablespoons chicken stock
2 tablespoons dry sherry
1 tablespoon light soy sauce
1 teaspoon sugar
2 teaspoons cornstarch
3 tablespoons peanut oil

2 yellow bell peppers, seeded and cut into strips
2 red bell peppers, seeded and cut into strips
1 bunch scallions, sliced diagonally
3 tablespoons preserved black beans, coarsely chopped
fresh cilantro sprigs, to garnish

1 Cut the pork into thin slices across the grain of the meat. Put the slices into a dish and mix them with the garlic and ginger. Let marinate at room temperature for 15 minutes.

2 Blend together the stock, sherry, soy sauce, sugar and cornstarch in a small bowl, then set the sauce mixture aside.

3 Heat the oil in a wok or large frying pan and stir-fry the marinated pork for 2–3 minutes. Add the peppers and scallions and continue to stir-fry for another 2 minutes.

4 Add the beans and sauce mixture and cook, stirring, until thick. Serve hot, garnished with the fresh cilantro sprigs.

Cook's Tip
If you cannot find preserved black beans, use the same amount of black bean sauce instead.

Golden Pork and Apricot Casserole

The rich golden color and warm spicy flavor of this simple casserole make it ideal for a chilly winter's day.

Serves 4

4 lean pork loin chops
1 onion, thinly sliced
2 yellow bell peppers, seeded and sliced
2 teaspoons medium curry powder
1 tablespoon all-purpose flour

1 cup chicken stock
4 ounces ready-to-eat dried apricots
2 tablespoons wholegrain mustard
salt and ground black pepper

1 Trim the excess fat from the pork and fry without fat in a large heavy or nonstick saucepan until lightly browned.

2 Add the onion and yellow peppers to the pan and stir over a moderate heat for 5 minutes. Then stir in the curry powder and the flour.

3 Add the stock, stirring, then add the apricots and mustard. Cover with a tight-fitting lid and simmer for 25–30 minutes, until tender. Adjust the seasoning to taste and serve hot, with rice or new potatoes, if you wish.

Sukiyaki-style Beef

This dish incorporates all the traditional Japanese elements – meat, vegetables, noodles and bean curd.

Serves 4

1 pound thick round
  steak
3½ cups Japanese rice
  noodles
1 tablespoon shredded
  suet
7 ounces hard bean curd,
  cut into dice
8 shiitake mushrooms,
  trimmed
2 leeks, sliced into 1-inch
  lengths

scant 1 cup baby spinach,
  to serve

For the stock

1 tablespoon caster sugar
6 tablespoons rice wine
3 tablespoons dark soy
  sauce
½ cup water

1 Cut the beef into thin even-size slices.

2 Blanch the rice noodles in boiling water for 2 minutes, then strain well.

3 Mix together all the stock ingredients in a bowl.

4 Heat a wok, then add the suet. When the suet is melted, stir-fry the beef for 2–3 minutes until it is cooked, but still pink in color.

5 Pour the stock over the beef.

6 Add the remaining ingredients and cook for 4 minutes, until the leeks are tender. Serve a selection of the different ingredients, with a few baby spinach leaves, to each person.

Cook's Tip
Add a touch of authenticity and serve this complete meal with chopsticks and a porcelain spoon to collect the stock juices.

Stir-fried Pork with Mustard

Fry the apples for this dish very carefully, because they will disintegrate if they are overcooked.

Serves 4

1¼ pound pork fillet
1 tart apple, such as
  Granny Smith
3 tablespoons unsalted
  butter
1 tablespoon sugar
1 small onion, finely
  chopped
2 tablespoons Calvados
  or brandy

1 tablespoon Meaux or
  coarse grain mustard
⅔ cup heavy cream
2 tablespoons chopped
  fresh parsley
salt and ground black
  pepper
fresh Italian parsley
  sprigs, to garnish

1 Cut the pork fillet into thin even-size slices.

2 Peel and core the apple. Cut into thick slices.

3 Heat a wok, then add half the butter. When the butter is hot, add the apple slices, sprinkle on the sugar, and stir-fry for 2–3 minutes. Remove the apple and set aside. Wipe out the wok with paper towels.

4 Reheat the wok, then add the remaining butter and stir-fry the pork fillet and onion together for 2–3 minutes, until the pork is golden and the onion has begun to soften.

5 Stir in the Calvados or brandy and boil until it is reduced by half. Stir in the mustard.

6 Add the cream and simmer for about 1 minute, then stir in the parsley. Serve garnished with sprigs of Italian parsley.

Cook's Tip
If you don't have a wok, use a large frying pan, preferably with deep, sloping sides.

Hungarian Beef Goulash

Spicy beef stew served with caraway-flavored dumplings will satisfy even the largest appetites.

Serves 4

2 tablespoons oil
2 pounds beef round, cubed
2 onions, chopped
1 garlic clove, crushed
1 tablespoon all-purpose flour
2 teaspoons paprika
1 teaspoon caraway seeds
14-ounce can chopped tomatoes
1¼ cups beef stock
1 large carrot, chopped
1 red bell pepper, seeded and chopped

sour cream, to serve
paprika, to garnish

For the dumplings
1 cup self-rising flour
½ cup shredded suet
1 tablespoon chopped fresh parsley
½ teaspoon caraway seeds
salt and ground black pepper

1 Heat the oil in a flameproof casserole and fry the meat for 5 minutes over a high heat, stirring, until browned. Remove with a slotted spoon. Add the onions and garlic and fry gently for 5 minutes, until softened. Add the flour, paprika and caraway seeds, stir and cook for 2 minutes.

2 Return the meat to the casserole; stir in the tomatoes and stock. Bring to a boil, cover, simmer for 2 hours.

3 To make the dumplings, sift the flour and seasoning into a bowl, add the suet, parsley, caraway seeds and about 3–4 tablespoons water and mix to a soft dough. Divide into eight pieces and roll into balls. Cover and reserve.

4 After 2 hours, stir the carrot and red pepper into the goulash, and season. Drop the dumplings into the goulash, cover and simmer for 25 minutes. Serve in bowls topped with a spoonful of sour cream sprinkled with paprika.

Pork Satay with Peanut Sauce

These delightful little satay sticks from Thailand make a good light meal or a party snack.

Makes 8

½ small onion, chopped
2 garlic cloves, crushed
2 tablespoons lemon juice
1 tablespoon soy sauce
1 teaspoon ground coriander
½ teaspoon ground cumin
1 teaspoon ground turmeric
2 tablespoons oil
1 pound pork tenderloin
fresh cilantro sprigs, to garnish
boiled rice, to serve

For the sauce
2 ounces creamed coconut, chopped
4 tablespoons crunchy peanut butter

1 tablespoon lemon juice
½ teaspoon ground cumin
½ teaspoon ground coriander
1 teaspoon brown sugar
1 tablespoon soy sauce
1–2 dried red chilies, seeded and chopped
1 tablespoon chopped fresh cilantro

For the salad
½ small cucumber, peeled and diced
1 tablespoon white wine vinegar
1 tablespoon chopped fresh cilantro
salt and ground black pepper

1 Process the first eight ingredients until smooth. Cut the pork into strips, mix with the marinade, and chill. Preheat the broiler to hot. Thread two or three pork pieces onto each of eight soaked woodenskewers and broil for 2–3 minutes each side, basting with the marinade.

2 To make the sauce, dissolve the creamed coconut in ⅔ cup boiling water. Put the remaining ingredients into a saucepan, stir in the coconut, bring to a boil, stirring, and simmer for 5 minutes.

3 Mix together all the salad ingredients. Arrange the satay sticks on a platter, garnish with cilantro sprigs and season.

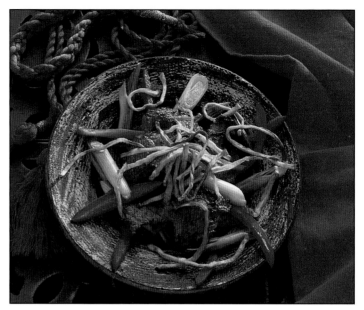

Stir-fried Pork with Lychees

No extra oil or fat is needed to cook this dish, as the pork produces enough on its own.

Serves 4

1 pound fatty pork, with
  the skin on or off
2 tablespoons hoisin
  sauce
4 scallions, sliced
  diagonally

6 ounces lychees, peeled,
  pitted and cut into
  slivers
salt and ground black
  pepper
fresh lychees and parsley
  sprigs, to garnish

1 Cut the pork into bite-size pieces.

2 Pour the hoisin sauce over the pork and leave to marinate for at least 30 minutes.

3 Heat a wok, then add the pork and stir-fry for 5 minutes until crisp and golden. Add the scallions and stir-fry for another 2 minutes.

4 Scatter the lychee slivers over the pork, and season well with salt and pepper. Garnish with fresh lychees and fresh parsley sprigs, to serve.

Cook's Tip
Lychees have a very pretty pink skin which, when peeled, reveals a soft fleshy berry with a hard shiny pit. If you cannot buy fresh lychees, this dish can be made with drained canned lychees.

Sizzling Beef with Celery Root Straw

The crisp celery root matchsticks look like fine pieces of straw when cooked and have a mild celery-like flavor.

Serves 4

1 pound celery root
⅔ cup oil
1 red bell pepper
6 scallions
1 pound rump steak
4 tablespoons beef stock
2 tablespoons sherry
  vinegar

2 teaspoons
  Worcestershire sauce
2 teaspoons tomato paste
salt and ground black
  pepper

1 Peel the celery root and then cut it into fine matchsticks, using a cleaver if you have one, or a large sharp knife.

2 Heat the wok, then add two-thirds of the oil. When the oil is hot, fry the celery root matchsticks in batches until golden brown and crispy. Drain well on paper towels.

3 Chop the red pepper and the scallions into 1-inch lengths, using diagonal cuts.

4 Chop the beef into strips, across the grain of the meat.

5 Heat the wok, then add the remaining oil. When the oil is hot, stir-fry the chopped scallions and red pepper for about 2–3 minutes.

6 Add the beef strips and stir-fry for another 3–4 minutes until well browned. Add the stock, vinegar, Worcestershire sauce and tomato paste. Season well with salt and pepper and serve with the celery root "straw".

Cook's Tip
The Chinese use a large cleaver for preparing most vegetables. With a little practice, you will discover that it is the ideal kitchen utensil for cutting fine vegetable matchsticks and chopping thin strips of meat.

Turkish Lamb and Apricot Stew

Almond and parsley–flavored couscous accompanies this rich stew of lamb, apricots and chick-peas.

Serves 4

1 large eggplant, diced	1 cup canned chick-peas,
2 tablespoons sunflower	drained
oil	1 teaspoon honey
1 onion, chopped	salt and ground black
1 garlic clove, crushed	pepper
1 teaspoon ground	couscous, to serve
cinnamon	2 tablespoons olive oil
3 whole cloves	2 tablespoons chopped
1 pound boned leg of	almonds, fried in a
lamb, cubed	little oil
14-ounce can chopped	chopped fresh parsley, to
tomatoes	garnish
4 ounces ready-to-eat	
dried apricots	

1 Place the diced eggplant in a colander, sprinkle with salt and set aside for about 30 minutes. Heat the oil in a large flameproof casserole and fry the onion and garlic for about 5 minutes, until softened but not browned.

2 Stir in the ground cinnamon and whole cloves and fry for another 1 minute. Add the lamb and cook for 5–6 minutes more, stirring occasionally to brown the pieces evenly.

3 Rinse, drain and pat dry the eggplant with paper towels, add to the casserole and cook for 3 minutes, stirring well. Add the chopped tomatoes, 1¼ cups water and the apricots, and season to taste with salt and pepper. Bring to a boil, then cover and simmer gently for about 45 minutes.

4 Stir the chick-peas and honey into the stew, then cook for a final 15–20 minutes, or until the lamb is tender. Serve the dish accompanied by couscous with the olive oil, fried almonds and chopped parsley stirred into it.

Curried Lamb and Lentils

This colorful curry is packed with protein and low in fat, and makes a flavorful yet healthy meal.

Serves 4

8 lean boned lamb leg	2 tablespoons tomato
steaks, about 1¼	paste
pounds total weight	2 cups stock
1 onion, chopped	1 cup green lentils
2 carrots, diced	salt and ground black
1 celery stalk, chopped	pepper
1 tablespoon hot curry	fresh cilantro leaves, to
paste	garnish
	boiled rice, to serve

1 In a large nonstick saucepan, fry the lamb steaks without fat until browned, turning once.

2 Add the vegetables and cook for 2 minutes, then stir in the curry paste, tomato paste, stock and lentils.

3 Bring to a boil, cover with a tight-fitting lid and simmer gently for 30 minutes until tender. Add some extra stock, if necessary. Season to taste and serve garnished with cilantro and accompanied by rice.

Cook's Tip
Pick over the lentils carefully before adding them to the saucepan. They sometimes contain small stones which are unpleasant to find while eating a meal.

Middle-Eastern Lamb Kebabs

Skewered, broiled meats are a staple of Middle Eastern cooking. Here, marinated lamb is broiled with vegetables.

Makes 4

1 pound boned leg of
   lamb, cubed
5 tablespoons olive oil
5 tablespoon chopped
   fresh oregano or
   thyme, or 2 teaspoons
   dried oregano
1 tablespoon chopped
   fresh parsley
juice of ½ lemon

½ small eggplant, thickly
   sliced and quartered
4 baby onions, halved
2 tomatoes, quartered
4 fresh bay leaves
salt and ground black
   pepper
pita bread and plain
   yogurt, to serve

1 Place the lamb in a bowl. Mix together the olive oil, oregano or thyme, parsley, lemon juice, salt and pepper. Pour over the lamb; mix well. Cover and marinate for about 1 hour.

2 Preheat the broiler. Thread the marinated lamb, eggplant, onions, tomatoes and bay leaves alternately onto four large skewers. (If using wooden skewers, soak them first.)

3 Place the kebabs on a broiler rack and brush the vegetables liberally with the leftover marinade. Cook the kebabs under a medium heat for about 8–10 minutes on each side, basting once or twice with the juices that have collected in the bottom of the broiler pan. Serve the kebabs hot, accompanied by hot pita bread and plain yogurt.

Cook's Tip
For a more piquant marinade, add one or two cloves of garlic, peeled and crushed.

Mexican Spiced Roast Leg of Lamb

Make sure you push the garlic slices deeply into the meat or they will burn and develop a bitter flavor.

Serves 4

1 small leg or half leg of
   lamb, about 2½
   pounds
1 tablespoon dried
   oregano
1 teaspoon ground cumin
1 teaspoon hot chili
   powder

2 garlic cloves
3 tablespoons olive oil
2 tablespoons red wine
   vinegar
salt and ground black
   pepper
fresh oregano sprigs, to
   garnish

1 Preheat the oven to 425°F. Place the leg of lamb on a large cutting board.

2 Place the oregano, cumin, chili powder and one of the garlic cloves, crushed, into a bowl. Pour on half of the olive oil and mix well to form a paste. Set the paste aside.

3 Using a sharp knife, make a criss-cross pattern of fairly deep slits going through the skin and just into the meat of the leg of lamb. Press the spice paste into the meat slits with the back of a round-bladed knife. Peel and slice the remaining garlic clove thinly and cut each slice in half again. Push the pieces of garlic deeply into the slits made in the meat.

4 Mix the vinegar and remaining oil, pour over the leg and season with salt and pepper.

5 Bake for about 15 minutes at the higher temperature, then reduce the heat to 350°F and cook for another 1¼ hours (or a little longer if you like your meat well done). Serve the lamb with a delicious gravy made with the spicy pan juices and garnish with fresh oregano sprigs.

Burgundy Beef

This French classic is named after the region it comes from, Burgundy, where the local red wine is used to flavor it.

Serves 4

2 tablespoons olive oil
8 ounces piece streaky
   bacon, diced
12 whole baby onions
2 pounds stewing beef,
   cut into 2-inch
   squares
1 large onion, thickly
   sliced
1 tablespoon all-purpose
   flour

about 1¾ cups red
   Burgundy wine
bouquet garni
1 garlic clove
8 ounces button
   mushrooms, halved
salt and ground black
   pepper
chopped fresh parsley, to
   garnish

1 Heat the oil in a flameproof casserole and fry the bacon and baby onions for 7–8 minutes, until the onions have browned and the bacon fat is transparent. Remove with a slotted spoon and reserve.

2 Add the beef to the casserole and fry quickly on all sides until evenly browned. Add the sliced onion and continue cooking for 4–5 minutes.

3 Sprinkle on the flour and stir well. Pour on the wine and add the bouquet garni and garlic. Cover with a tightly fitting lid and simmer gently for about 2 hours. Stir in the reserved sautéed onions and bacon and add a little extra wine, if necessary.

4 Add the mushrooms. Cover again and cook for another 30 minutes more. Remove the bouquet garni and garlic and garnish with chopped fresh parsley.

Spiced Lamb Bake

A quite delicious South African shepherd's pie. The recipe was originally poached from the Afrikaners' Malay slaves.

Serves 4

1 tablespoon oil
1 onion, chopped
1½ pounds ground lamb
2 tablespoons medium
   curry paste
2 tablespoons mango
   chutney
2 tablespoons freshly
   squeezed lemon juice
4 tablespoons chopped,
   blanched almonds

2 tablespoons golden
   raisins
3 ounces creamed
   coconut, crumbled
2 eggs
2 bay leaves
salt and ground black
   pepper

1 Preheat the oven to 350°F. Heat the oil in a frying pan and cook the chopped onion for 5–6 minutes, until softened but not browned.

2 Add the lamb and cook over a moderate heat, turning frequently, until browned all over. Stir in the curry paste, chutney, lemon juice, almonds and raisins, season well with salt and pepper and cook for about 5 minutes.

3 Transfer the mixture to a casserole and cook in the oven, uncovered, for 10 minutes.

4 Meanwhile, dissolve the crumbled creamed coconut in a scant 1 cup of boiling water and cool slightly. Beat in the eggs and a little seasoning.

5 Remove the dish from the oven and pour the coconut custard over the meat mixture. Lay the bay leaves on the top and return the dish to the oven for 30–35 minutes, or until the top is set and golden. Serve hot.

Greek Pasta Bake

Another excellent main meal (called *pastitsio* in Greece), this recipe is both economical and filling.

Serves 4

1 tablespoon oil	2 large tomatoes
1 pound groundlamb	4-ounce cup pasta shapes
1 onion, chopped	1-pound tub strained
2 garlic cloves, crushed	plain yogurt
2 tablespoons tomato	2 eggs
paste	salt and ground black
2 tablespoons all-purpose	pepper
flour	green salad, to serve
1¼ cups lamb stock	

1 Preheat the oven to 375°F. Heat the oil in a large saucepan and fry the lamb for 5 minutes. Add the onion and garlic and continue to fry for another 5 minutes.

2 Stir in the tomato paste and flour. Cook for 1 minute.

3 Stir in the lamb stock and season to taste with salt and pepper. Bring to a boil and cook for 20 minutes.

4 Slice the tomatoes, place the meat in a baking dish and arrange the tomatoes on top.

5 Bring a pan of salted water to a boil and cook the pasta shapes for 8–10 minutes until *al dente*. Drain well.

6 Mix together the pasta, yogurt and eggs. Spoon on top of the tomatoes and cook in the preheated oven for 1 hour. Serve hot with a crisp green salad.

Cook's Tip
Choose pasta shapes for this dish rather than tubes so the sauce coats the pasta all over. Try shells, spirals or twists.

Bacon Koftas

These easy koftas are good for barbecues and summer parties, served with lots of salad.

Serves 4

8 ounces lean bacon,	ground black pepper
coarsely chopped	pinch of paprika
1½ cups fresh whole	lemon rind and fresh
wheat bread crumbs	parsley leaves, to
2 scallions, chopped	garnish
1 tablespoon chopped	lemon rice and salad, to
fresh parsley	serve
finely grated rind of	
1 lemon	
1 egg white	

1 Place the bacon in a food processor with the bread crumbs, scallions, parsley, lemon rind, egg white and pepper. Process the mixture until it is finely chopped and begins to bind together. Alternatively, use a chopper.

2 Divide the bacon mixture into eight even-size pieces and shape into long ovals around eight previously soaked wooden or bamboo skewers.

3 Sprinkle the koftas with paprika and cook under a hot broiler or on a barbecue for about 8–10 minutes, turning them occasionally, until browned and cooked through. Garnish with lemon rind and parsley leaves, then serve hot with lemon rice and salad.

Cook's Tip
This is a good way to spread a little meat a long way as each portion only requires 2 ounces of bacon. Use good quality bacon for this recipe.

Peking Beef and Pepper Stir-fry

Once the steak has marinated, this colorful dish can be prepared in just a few minutes.

Serves 4

12 ounces round or sirloin steak, sliced into strips	1 tablespoon grated fresh ginger
2 tablespoons soy sauce	1 red bell pepper, seeded and sliced
2 tablespoons medium sherry	1 yellow bell pepper, seeded and sliced
1 tablespoon cornstarch	1 cup snow peas
1 teaspoon brown sugar	4 scallions, cut into 2-inch pieces
1 tablespoon sunflower oil	2 tablespoons Chinese oyster sauce
1 tablespoon sesame oil	hot noodles, to serve
1 garlic clove, finely chopped	

1 In a bowl, mix together the steak strips, soy sauce, sherry, cornstarch and brown sugar. Cover and allow to marinate for 30 minutes.

2 Heat the oils in a wok or large frying pan and stir-fry the garlic and ginger for about 30 seconds. Add the peppers, peas and scallions and stir-fry over a high heat for 3 minutes.

3 Add the beef with the marinade juices to the wok or frying pan and stir-fry for another 3–4 minutes.

4 Finally, pour in the oyster sauce and 4 tablespoons water and stir until the sauce has thickened slightly. Serve immediately with hot noodles.

Texan Barbecued Ribs

This barbecue or oven-roast dish of pork spareribs cooked in a sweet and sour sauce is a favorite in the United States.

Serves 4

3 pounds (about 16) lean pork spareribs	2 teaspoons honey
1 onion, finely chopped	2 tablespoons light brown sugar
1 large garlic clove, crushed	dash of Worcestershire sauce
½ cup tomato paste	2 tablespoons vegetable oil
2 tablespoons orange juice	salt and ground black pepper
2 tablespoons red wine vinegar	chopped fresh parsley, to garnish
1 teaspoon mustard	

1 Preheat the oven to 400°F. Place the pork spareribs in a large shallow roasting pan; bake for 20 minutes.

2 Meanwhile, in a saucepan mix together the onion, garlic, tomato paste, orange juice, wine vinegar, mustard, honey, brown sugar, Worcestershire sauce, oil and seasoning. Bring to a boil and simmer for about 5 minutes.

3 Remove the ribs from the oven and then reduce the oven temperature to 350°F. Spoon on half the sauce, covering the ribs well, and bake for 20 minutes. Turn them over, baste with the remaining sauce and cook for about another 25 minutes.

4 Sprinkle the spareribs with parsley before serving and allow three or four ribs per person. Provide finger bowls for washing sticky fingers.

Skewers of Lamb with Mint

For a more substantial meal, serve these skewers on a bed of flavored rice or couscous.

Serves 4

1¼ cups plain strained yogurt
½ garlic clove, crushed
generous pinch of saffron powder
2 tablespoons chopped fresh mint
2 tablespoons honey
3 tablespoons olive oil
3 lamb neck fillets (about 1½ pounds total)

1 eggplant, in 1-inch pieces
2 small red onions, quartered
salt and ground black pepper
small fresh mint leaves, to garnish
mixed salad and hot pita bread, to serve

1 Mix the yogurt, garlic, saffron, mint, honey, oil and pepper together in a shallow dish.

2 Trim the lamb and cut into 1-inch cubes. Add to the marinade and stir until well coated. Cover and let marinate for at least 4 hours, or preferably overnight.

3 Blanch the diced eggplant in a saucepan of boiling salted water for about 1–2 minutes. Drain well and then pat dry on paper towels.

4 Remove the diced lamb from the marinade. Thread the lamb, eggplant and onion pieces alternately onto skewers. (If you are using wooden skewers, soak them in water first. This will prevent them from charring during broiling.) Broil for 10–12 minutes, turning and basting occasionally with the marinade, until the lamb is tender.

5 Serve the skewers garnished with mint leaves and accompanied by a mixed salad and hot pita bread.

Beef Stew with Red Wine

A slow-cooked casserole of tender beef in a red wine and tomato sauce, with black olives and red pepper.

Serves 6

5 tablespoons olive oil
2½ pounds boned beef chuck, in 1½-inch pieces
1 onion, very finely sliced
2 carrots, chopped
3 tablespoons finely chopped fresh parsley
1 garlic clove, chopped
1 bay leaf
a few fresh thyme sprigs
pinch of freshly ground nutmeg

1 cup red wine
14-ounce can plum tomatoes, chopped, with their juice
½ cup beef or chicken stock
about 15 black olives, pitted and halved
salt and ground black pepper
1 large red bell pepper, cut into strips

1 Preheat the oven to 350°F. Brown the meat, in batches, in 3 tablespoons of the oil in a large heavy-based flameproof casserole. Remove to a side plate as the meat is browned, and set aside until needed.

2 Add the remaining oil, the onion and carrots to the casserole. Cook over a low heat until the onion softens. Add the parsley and garlic, and cook for another 3–4 minutes.

3 Return the meat to the casserole, raise the heat, and stir well to mix the vegetables with the meat. Stir in the bay leaf, thyme and nutmeg. Add the wine, bring to a boil and cook, stirring, for 4–5 minutes. Stir in the tomatoes, stock and olives, and mix well. Season to taste with salt and pepper. Cover the casserole with a tight-fitting lid and place in the center of the preheated oven. Bake for 1½ hours.

4 Remove the casserole from the oven. Stir in the strips of pepper. Return the casserole to the oven and cook, uncovered, for 30 minutes more, or until the beef is tender.

Mixed Peppers and Salsa

Soft smoky broiled peppers make a lovely combination with the slightly tart salsa.

Serves 4

4 medium bell peppers in different colors

3 tablespoons chopped fresh Italian parsley

3 tablespoons chopped fresh dill

3 tablespoons chopped fresh mint

1 small red onion, finely chopped

1 tablespoon capers, coarsely chopped

¼ cup Greek olives, pitted and sliced

1 fresh green chili, seeded and finely chopped

4 tablespoons pistachios, chopped

5 tablespoons extra-virgin olive oil

3 tablespoons fresh lime juice

½ cup medium-fat feta cheese, crumbled

2 tablespoons finely chopped small gherkins

1 Preheat the broiler. Place the whole peppers on a tray and broil until charred and blistered.

2 Place the peppers in a plastic bag and let cool.

3 Peel, seed and cut the peppers into even strips.

4 To make the salsa, mix all the remaining ingredients together, and stir in the pepper strips.

Vegetable and Bean Curd Kebabs

A colorful mixture of vegetables and bean curd, skewered, glazed and broiled until tender.

Serves 4

1 yellow bell pepper

2 small zucchini

8 ounce piece of firm bean curd

8 cherry tomatoes

6 button mushrooms

1 tablespoon wholegrain mustard

1 tablespoon honey

2 tablespoons olive oil

salt and ground black pepper

cooked mixed rice and wild rice, to serve

lime wedges and Italian parsley, to garnish

1 Cut the pepper in half and remove the seeds. Cut each half into quarters and cut each quarter in half.

2 Cut the ends off the zucchini. Cut each zucchini into seven or eight chunks.

3 Cut the beans curd into 1½-inch pieces.

4 Thread the pepper pieces, zucchini chunks, tofu, cherry tomatoes and mushrooms alternately on to four metal or bamboo skewers. (If you are using bamboo skewers, soak them in a bowl of cold water first. This will prevent them from charring during broiling.)

5 Whisk the mustard, honey and olive oil in a small bowl. Season to taste with salt and pepper.

6 Put the kebabs onto a baking sheet. Brush them with the mustard and honey glaze. Cook under the broiler for 8 minutes, turning once or twice during cooking. Serve with a mixture of long-grain and wild rice, and garnish with lime wedges and Italian parsley.

Soufflé Omelet

This delectable soufflé omelet is light and delicate enough to melt in the mouth.

Serves 1

2 eggs, separated
2 tablespoons cold water
1 tablespoon chopped
   fresh cilantro
½ tablespoon olive oil

2 tablespoons mango
   chutney
¼ cup grated Jarlsberg
   cheese
salt and ground black
   pepper

1 Beat the egg yolks together with the cold water, cilantroand salt and pepper.

2 Whisk the egg whites until stiff peaks form and gently fold into the egg yolk mixture.

3 Heat the oil in a frying pan, pour in the egg mixture and reduce the heat. Do not stir. Cook until the omelet becomes puffy and golden brown underneath (carefully lift one edge with a spatula to check).

4 Spoon on the chutney and sprinkle on the Jarlsberg. Fold over and slide onto a warm plate. Eat immediately. (If preferred, before adding the chutney and cheese, place the pan under a hot broiler to set the top.)

Cook's Tip
A light hand is essential to the success of this dish. Do not overmix the egg whites into the egg yolks or the mixture will be heavy.

Bubble-and-Squeak

This London breakfast dish was originally made on Mondays with leftover vegetables from the Sunday lunch.

Serves 4

3 cups mashed potato
4 cups shredded cooked
   cabbage or kale
1 egg, beaten
1 cup grated Cheddar
   cheese
pinch of freshly grated
   nutmeg

salt and ground black
   pepper
all-purpose flour, for
   coating
oil, for frying

1 Mix the potatoes with the cabbage or kale, egg, cheese, nutmeg and seasoning. Divide and shape into eight patties.

2 Chill in the fridge for an hour or so, if possible, as this allows the mixture to become firm and makes it easier to fry. Toss the patties in the flour. Heat about ½ inch oil in a frying pan until it is quite hot.

3 Carefully slide the patties into the oil and fry on each side for about 3 minutes until golden and crisp. Drain on paper towels and serve hot and crisp.

Eggplant and Red Pepper Pâté

This simple pâté of baked eggplant, pink peppercorns and red bell peppers, has more than a hint of garlic.

Serves 4

3 eggplant
2 fresh large red bell
   peppers
5 garlic cloves,
   unpeeled

1½ teaspoons pink
   peppercorns in brine,
   drained and crushed
2 tablespoons chopped
   fresh cilantro

1 Preheat the oven to 400°F. Arrange the whole eggplant, peppers and garlic cloves on a baking sheet and place in the oven. After 10 minutes remove the garlic cloves and turn over the eggplant and peppers.

2 Peel the garlic cloves and place in the bowl of a blender or food processor.

3 After another 20 minutes remove the blistered and charred peppers from the oven and place in a plastic bag. Leave to cool.

4 After another 10 minutes take out the eggplant. Split in half and scoop the flesh into a strainer placed over a bowl. Press the flesh with a spoon to remove the bitter juices.

5 Add the mixture to the garlic and process until smooth. Place in a large mixing bowl.

6 Peel and chop the red peppers and stir into the eggplant mixture. Mix in the pink peppercorns and chopped fresh cilantro and serve at once.

Cook's Tip
Serve the pâté with Melba toast, if you like. Simply grill some slices of crustless white bread on both sides, being careful to remove any loose crumbs, then slice the crispy golden toasts horizontally.

Red Pepper Watercress Parcels

The peppery watercress flavor combines well with sweet red pepper in these crisp little phyllo pastry parcels.

Makes 8

3 red peppers
6 ounces watercress
1 cup ricotta cheese
¼ cup toasted, chopped
   almonds

8 sheets phyllo pastry,
   thawed if frozen
2 tablespoons olive oil
salt and ground black
   pepper

1 Preheat the oven to 375°F. Place the peppers under a hot broiler until blistered and charred. Place in a plastic bag. When cool enough to handle, peel, seed and pat dry on paper towels.

2 Place the peppers and watercress in a food processor and pulse until coarsely chopped. Spoon into a bowl.

3 Mix in the ricotta and almonds, and season to taste with salt and pepper.

4 Working with one sheet of phyllo pastry at a time, cut out two 7-inch and two 2-inch squares from each sheet. Brush one large square with a little olive oil and place a second large square at an angle of 45 degrees to form a star shape.

5 Place one of the small squares in the center of the star shape, brush lightly with olive oil and top with a second small square.

6 Top with one-eighth of the red pepper mixture. Bring the edges together to form a purse shape and twist to seal. Place on a lightly greased baking sheet and cook for 25–30 minutes until golden. Serve immediately.

Nutty Cheese Balls

An extremely quick and simple recipe. Try making a small version to serve as canapés at a cocktail party.

Serves 4

1 cup low-fat soft cheese such as Quark	1 teaspoon brandy or port (optional)
½ cup dolcelatte cheese	pinch of paprika
1 tablespoon finely chopped onion	½ cup walnuts, coarsely chopped
1 tablespoon finely chopped celery	6 tablespoons chopped fresh chives
1 tablespoon finely chopped fresh parsley	salt and ground black pepper
1 tablespoon finely chopped gherkin	

1 Beat the soft cheese and dolcelatte together using a spoon, until quite smooth.

2 Mix in all the remaining ingredients, except the chopped chives, stirring well to combine.

3 Divide the mixture into 12 pieces and roll into balls.

4 Roll each ball gently in the chopped chives. Leave to chill in the fridge for about an hour before serving.

Cook's Tip
For an alternative look, mix the chives with the rest of the ingredients but omit the walnuts. Instead, chop the walnuts finely and use to roll on to the cheese balls.

Fried Tomatoes with Polenta Crust

This recipe works well with green tomatoes freshy picked from the garden or greenhouse.

Serves 4

4 large firm under-ripe tomatoes	all-purpose flour, for dredging
1 cup polenta or coarse cornmeal	1 egg, beaten with seasoning
1 teaspoon dried oregano or marjoram	oil, for deep-frying
½ teaspoon garlic powder	green salad, to serve

1 Cut the tomatoes into thick slices. Mix the polenta or cornmeal with the oregano or marjoram and garlic powder.

2 Put the flour, egg and polenta into different bowls. Dip the tomato slices into the flour, then into the egg and finally into the polenta or cornmeal.

3 Fill a shallow frying pan one-third full of oil and heat steadily until quite hot.

4 Slip the tomato slices into the oil carefully, a few at a time, and fry on each side until crisp. Remove and drain. Repeat with the remaining tomatoes, reheating the oil in between each batch. Serve with salad.

Bean Purée with Grilled Vegetables

The slightly bitter radicchio and chicory make a wonderful marriage with the creamy citrus bean purée.

Serves 4

14-ounce can navy beans
3 tablespoons plain
    yogurt
finely grated rind and
    juice of 1 large orange
1 tablespoon finely
    chopped fresh
    rosemary

4 heads of chicory
2 radicchio
1 tablespoon walnut oil

1 Drain the beans, rinse, and drain again. Purée the beans in a food processor or blender with the yogurt, half the orange rind, orange juice and rosemary. Set aside.

2 Cut the heads of chicory in half lengthwise.

3 Cut each radicchio into eight wedges.

4 Lay out the chicory and radicchio on a baking sheet and brush with walnut oil. Broil for 2–3 minutes. Serve with the purée and scatter over the remaining orange rind.

Cook's Tip
Substitute different beans for the navy beans, if you like. Try white, mung or lima beans instead.

Broccoli and Chestnut Terrine

Served hot or cold, this versatile terrine is just as suitable for a dinner party as for a picnic.

Serves 4–6

4 cups broccoli florets
2 cups cooked chestnuts,
    coarsely chopped
1 cup fresh whole wheat
    bread crumbs
4 tablespoons low-fat
    plain yogurt

2 tablespoons finely
    grated Parmesan
    cheese
2 eggs, beaten
salt, freshly grated
    nutmeg and ground
    black pepper

1 Preheat the oven to 350°F. Bottom-line a 2-pound loaf pan with nonstick baking parchment.

2 Blanch or steam the broccoli for 3–4 minutes until just tender. Drain well. Reserve a quarter of the smallest florets and chop the rest finely.

3 Mix together the chestnuts, bread crumbs, yogurt and Parmesan, and season to taste with salt and pepper.

4 Fold in the chopped broccoli, reserved florets and the beaten eggs.

5 Spoon the broccoli mixture into the prepared pan.

6 Place in a roasting pan and pour in boiling water to come halfway up the sides of the loaf pan. Bake for 20–25 minutes. Remove from the oven and turn out onto a plate or tray. Serve cut into even slices.

Cook's Tip
If you do not have a nonstick loaf pan, grease it lightly with olive or sunflower oil after bottom-lining.

Baked Squash with Parmesan

Spaghetti squash is an unusual vegetable – when baked, the flesh separates into long strands.

Serves 2

1 spaghetti squash
½ cup butter
3 tablespoons mixed
   chopped fresh herbs
   such as parsley, chives
   and oregano
1 garlic clove, crushed

1 shallot, chopped
1 teaspoons lemon juice
scant ¾ cup freshly
   grated Parmesan
   cheese
salt and ground black
   pepper

1   Preheat the oven to 350°F. Cut the squash in half lengthwise. Place the halves, cut-side down, in a roasting pan. Pour a little water around them, then bake for about 40 minutes, until tender.

2   Meanwhile, put the butter, herbs, garlic, shallot and lemon juice in a food processor or blender and process until thoroughly blended and creamy in consistency. Season to taste with salt and pepper.

3   When the squash is tender, scrape out any seeds and cut a thin slice from the bottom of each half, so that they will sit level. Place the squash halves on warmed serving plates.

4   Using a fork, pull out a few of the spaghetti-like strands in the center of each. Add a dollop of herb butter, then sprinkle with a little of the grated Parmesan. Serve the remaining herb butter and Parmesan separately, adding them as you pull out more strands.

Asparagus Rolls with Herb Sauce

Tender asparagus spears wrapped in crisp phyllo pastry, served with a buttery herb sauce, tastes sensational.

Serves 2

4 tablespoons butter
5 sheets phyllo pastry
10 asparagus spears

For the sauce
2 shallots, finely chopped
1 bay leaf
⅔ cup dry white wine

¾ cup butter, softened
1 tablespoon chopped
   fresh herbs
salt and ground black
   pepper
chopped fresh chives, to
   garnish

1   Preheat the oven to 400°F. Melt the butter. Cut the phyllo pastry sheets in half. Brush a half sheet with melted butter. Fold one corner of the sheet down to the bottom edge to give a wedge shape.

2   Trim the asparagus, then lay a spear on top at the longest pastry edge and roll up towards the shortest edge. Make nine more rolls in the same way.

3   Lay the rolls on a greased baking sheet. Brush with the remaining melted butter. Bake in the preheated oven for about 8 minutes until golden.

4   Meanwhile, put the shallots, bay leaf and wine into a saucepan. Cover with a tight-fitting lid and cook over a high heat until the wine is reduced to 3–4 tablespoons.

5   Strain the wine mixture into a bowl. Whisk in the butter, a little at a time, until the sauce is smooth and glossy.

6   Stir in the herbs and season to taste with salt and pepper. Return to the pan and keep the sauce warm. Serve the rolls on individual plates with a salad garnish, if liked. Serve the butter sauce separately, sprinkled with a few chopped chives.

Multi-mushroom Stroganoff

A pan-fry of sliced mushrooms swirled with sour cream makes a delicious accompaniment to pasta or rice.

Serves 3–4

3 tablespoons olive oil
1 pound fresh mixed wild
  and cultivated
  mushrooms such as
  ceps, shiitakes or
  oysters, sliced
3 scallions, sliced
2 garlic cloves, crushed
2 tablespoons dry sherry
  or vermouth

1¼ cups sour cream or
  crème fraîche
1 tablespoon chopped
  fresh marjoram or
  thyme leaves
chopped fresh parsley, to
  garnish
rice, pasta or boiled new
  potatoes, to serve

1 Heat the oil in a large frying pan and fry the mushrooms gently, stirring them from time to time until they are softened and just cooked.

2 Add the scallions, garlic and sherry or vermouth and cook for 1 minute more. Season well with salt and pepper.

3 Stir in the sour cream or crème fraîche and heat to just below boiling. Stir in the marjoram or thyme, then scatter over the parsley. Serve with rice, pasta or boiled new potatoes.

Cook's Tip
To create the most interesting flavor in this dish, use at least three different varieties of mushrooms, preferably incorporating some woodland or wild mushrooms.

Ratatouille with Cheese Croûtons

Crunchy croûtons and creamy Camembert provide a tasty topping on hot, bought or home-made ratatouille.

Serves 2

3 thick slices white bread
8 ounces firm
  Camembert cheese
4 tablespoons olive oil

1 garlic clove, chopped
14-ounce can ratatouille
fresh parsley sprigs, to
  garnish

1 Trim the crusts from the bread slices and discard. Cut the bread into 1-inch squares. Cut the Camembert cheese into 1-inch cubes.

2 Heat 3 tablespoons of the oil in a frying pan and cook the bread over a high heat for 5 minutes, stirring constantly, until golden all over. Reduce the heat, add the garlic and cook for 1 minute more. Remove the croûtons with a slotted spoon.

3 Pour the ratatouille into a saucepan and place over a moderate heat, stirring occasionally, until hot.

4 Heat the remaining oil in the frying pan. Add the cheese cubes and sear over a high heat for 1 minute. Divide the hot ratatouille between two serving bowls, spoon the croûtons and cheese on top, garnish with parsley and serve at once.

Bean Curd and Crunchy Vegetables

High protein bean curd is nicest if marinated lightly before it is cooked. If you use the smoked bean curd, it's even tastier.

Serves 4

*2 – 8 ounces packages
    smoked bean curd,
    diced*
3 tablespoons soy sauce
*2 tablespoons dry sherry
    or vermouth*
1 tablespoon sesame oil
*3 tablespoons peanut or
    sunflower oil*
2 leeks, thinly sliced
2 carrots, cut into sticks

*1 large zucchini, thinly
    sliced*
*4 ounces baby corn,
    halved*
*4 ounces button or
    shiitake mushrooms,
    sliced*
*1 tablespoon sesame
    seeds*
*1 packet egg noodles,
    cooked*

1 Marinate the bean curd in the soy sauce, sherry or vermouth and sesame oil for at least 30 minutes. Drain and reserve the marinade for later.

2 Heat the peanut or sunflower oil in a wok and stir-fry the bean curd cubes until browned all over. Remove and reserve.

3 Stir-fry the leeks, carrots, zucchini and baby corn, stirring and tossing for about 2 minutes. Add the mushrooms and cook for another 1 minute.

4 Return the bean curd to the wok and pour in the marinade. Heat until bubbling, then scatter over the sesame seeds.

5 Serve as soon as possible with the hot cooked noodles, dressed in a little sesame oil, if you wish.

Cook's Tip
*The actual cooking of this dish takes just a few minutes,
so have all the ingredients prepared before you start.*

Sprouting Beans and Pak Choi

Supermarkets are becoming more cosmopolitan and many stock fresh ethnic vegetables.

Serves 4

3 tablespoons peranut oil
3 scallions, sliced
*2 garlic cloves, cut into
    slivers*
*1-inch piece fresh ginger,
    cut into slivers*
*1 carrot, cut into thick
    sticks*
*scant 1 cup sprouting
    beans (lentils, mung
    beans, chick-peas)*
*7 ounces pak choi
    cabbage, shredded*
*½ cup unsalted cashew
    nuts or halved
    almonds*

For the sauce
*3 tablespoons light soy
    sauce*
2 tablespoons dry sherry
1 tablespoon sesame oil
⅔ cup cold water
1 teaspoon cornflour
1 teaspoon honey
*salt and ground black
    pepper*

1 Heat the peanut oil in a large wok and stir-fry the onions, garlic, ginger and carrot for 2 minutes. Add the sprouting beans and fry for another 2 minutes, stirring and tossing all the ingredients together.

2 Add the pak choi and cashew nuts or almonds and stir-fry until the cabbage leaves are just wilting. Quickly mix all the sauce ingredients together in a bowl and pour them, stirring all the time, into the wok.

3 The vegetables will be coated in a thin glossy sauce. Season with salt and pepper and serve as soon as possible.

Cook's Tip
*If you cannot find pak choi, use Chinese cabbage
instead and prepare and cook in the same way.*

Tomato Omelet Envelopes

These delicious chive omelets are folded and filled with tomato and melting Camembert cheese.

Serves 2

1 small onion
4 tomatoes
2 tablespoons oil
4 eggs
2 tablespoons chopped
    fresh chives

4 ounces Camembert
    cheese, rind removed
    and diced
salt and ground black
    pepper

1 Cut the onion in half. Cut each half into thin wedges. Cut the tomatoes into wedges of similar size.

2 Heat 1 tablespoon of the oil in a frying pan and cook the onion for 2 minutes over a moderate heat, then raise the heat and add the tomatoes. Cook for another 2 minutes, then remove the pan from the heat.

3 Beat the eggs with the chives in a bowl. Season to taste with salt and pepper. Heat the remaining oil in an omelet pan. Add half the egg mixture and tilt the pan to spread thinly. Cook for 1 minute.

4 Flip the omelet over and cook for 1 minute more. Remove from the pan and keep hot. Make a second omelette with the remaining egg mixture.

5 Return the tomato mixture to a high heat. Add the cheese and toss the mixture over the heat for 1 minute.

6 Divide the mixture between the omelets and fold them over. Serve immediately. Add crisp lettuce leaves and chunks of whole wheat bread, if you wish.

Cook's Tip
Add a few sliced mushrooms to the filling, if you wish, or use them in place of the tomatoes for a change.

Curried Eggs

Hard-boiled eggs are served on a mild creamy sauce base with just a hint of curry.

Serves 2

4 eggs
1 tablespoon sunflower
    oil
1 small onion, chopped
1-inch piece of fresh root
    ginger, peeled and
    grated
½ teaspoon ground
    cumin
½ teaspoon garam masala
1½ tablespoons tomato
    paste

2 teaspoons tandoori
    paste
2 teaspoons freshly
    squeezed lemon juice
¼ cup light cream
1 tablespoon finely
    chopped fresh cilantro
salt and ground black
    pepper
fresh cilantro sprigs, to
    garnish

1 Put the eggs in a saucepan of water. Bring to a boil, lower the heat and simmer for 10 minutes.

2 Meanwhile, heat the oil in a frying pan and cook the onion for 2–3 minutes. Add the fresh ginger and cook for another 1 minute.

3 Stir in the ground cumin, garam masala, tomato paste, tandoori paste, lemon juice and cream. Cook for 1–2 minutes more, then stir in the cilantro. Season with salt and pepper.

4 Drain the eggs, remove the shells and cut each egg in half. Spoon the sauce into a serving bowl, top with the eggs and garnish with fresh cilantro. Serve immediately.

Cook's Tip
If you store your eggs in the fridge, make sure you allow them to come to room temperature before you boil them. This way, they are less likely to crack.

Potatoes with Blue Cheese

We are so used to eating potatoes as a side dish, we tend to forget they can make a good main meal too, as here.

Serves 4

1 pound small new
  potatoes
small head of celery,
  sliced
small red onion, thinly
  sliced
4 ounces blue cheese,
  mashed

⅔ cup light cream
salt and ground black
  pepper
scant 1 cup walnut
  pieces
2 tablespoons chopped
  fresh parsley

1 Cover the potatoes with water and then boil for about 15 minutes, adding the sliced celery and onion to the pan for the last 5 minutes or so.

2 Drain the vegetables and put them into a shallow serving dish, making sure they are evenly distributed.

3 In a small saucepan slowly melt the cheese in the cream, stirring occasionally. Do not allow the mixture to boil.

4 Season the sauce to taste. Pour it over the vegetables and scatter the walnuts and parsley over the top. Serve hot.

Cook's Tip
Choose any blue cheese you like, such as Stilton, Danish blue, blue vinney or blue brie.

Greek Spinach and Cheese Pies

These individual spinach, feta and Parmesan cheese pies are easy to make using ready-made phyllo pastry.

Makes 4

1 tablespoon olive oil
1 small onion, finely
  chopped
2½ cups fresh spinach,
  stalks removed
4 tablespoons butter,
  melted
4 sheets phyllo pastry
1 egg

large pinch of freshly
  grated nutmeg
¾ cup crumbled feta
  cheese
1 tablespoon grated
  Parmesan cheese
salt and ground black
  pepper

1 Preheat the oven to 375°F. Fry the onion in the oil for 5–6 minutes, until softened. Add the spinach leaves and cook, stirring, until the spinach has wilted and some of the liquid evaporated. Allow to cool.

2 Brush four 4-inch diameter loose-bottom tartlet pans with melted butter. Cut two sheets of phyllo into eight 4½-inch squares each. Cover the remaining sheets with a dish towel.

3 Brush four squares at a time with melted butter. Line the first tartlet pan with one square, gently easing it into the bottom and up the sides. Leave the edges overhanging. Lay the remaining squares on top of the first, turning them so the corners form a star shape. Repeat for the remaining pans.

4 Beat the egg with the nutmeg and seasoning, then stir in the cheeses and spinach. Divide the mixture between the pans and smooth level. Fold the overhanging edges over the filling.

5 Cut the third pastry sheet into eight 4-inch rounds. Brush with butter and place two on top of each tartlet. Press around the edges to seal. Brush the last pastry sheet with butter and cut into strips. Gently twist each strip and lay them on top of the tartlets. Bake for about 30–35 minutes, until golden. Serve hot or cold.

Chili Beans with Basmati Rice

**Red kidney beans, chopped tomatoes and hot chili make a
great combination in this colorful, flavorful dish.**

Serves 4

2 cups basmati rice
2 tablespoons olive oil
1 large onion, chopped
1 garlic clove, crushed
1 tablespoon hot chili
  powder
1 tablespoon all-purpose
  flour
1 tablespoon tomato
  paste

14-ounce can chopped
  tomatoes
14-ounce can red kidney
  beans, drained
⅔ cup hot vegetable stock
chopped fresh parsley, to
  garnish
salt and ground black
  pepper

1 Wash the rice under cold running water. Drain well. Bring
a large saucepan of water to a boil. Add the rice and cook for
10–12 minutes, until tender. Meanwhile, heat the oil in a
frying pan and cook the chopped onion and garlic for about 2
minutes.

2 Stir the chili powder and flour into the onion and garlic
mixture. Cook for 2 minutes more, stirring frequently.

3 Stir in the tomato paste and chopped tomatoes. Rinse and
drain the kidney beans well and add to the pan with the hot
vegetable stock. Cover and cook for a final 12 minutes,
stirring from time to time.

4 Season the chili sauce to taste with salt and pepper. Drain
the rice and serve immediately with the chili beans, garnished
with a little chopped fresh parsley.

Cook's Tip
*Serve the chili beans with a pasta of your choice or hot
pitta bread, if you prefer.*

Lentil Stir-fry

**Mushrooms, artichoke hearts, sugar snap peas and green
lentils make a satisfying stir-fry supper.**

Serves 2–3

1 cup snow peas
2 tablespoons butter
1 small onion, chopped
4 ounces cup chestnut
  mushrooms, sliced
14-ounce can artichoke
  hearts, drained and
  halved

14-ounce can green
  lentils, drained
4 tablespoons light cream
¼ cup flaked almonds,
  toasted
salt and ground black
  pepper
French bread, to serve

1 Bring a saucepan of salted water to the boil, add the snow
peas and cook for about 4 minutes until just tender. Drain,
refresh under cold running water, then drain again. Pat the
peas dry with paper towels and set aside.

2 Melt the butter in a frying pan and cook the chopped
onion for 2–3 minutes, stirring occasionally.

3 Add the sliced mushrooms to the onions. Stir until well
combined, then cook for 2–3 minutes until just tender. Add
the artichoke hearts, snow peas and lentils to the pan. Stir-fry
for 2 minutes.

4 Stir in the cream and almonds and cook for 1 minute.
Season to taste with salt and pepper. Serve at once, with
chunks of French bread.

Cook's Tip
*Use dried green lentils if you prefer. Cook them
according to the manufacturer's instructions first and
then add them to the stir-fry with the artichokes and
snow peas.*

Arabian Spinach

Stir-fry spinach with onions and spices, then mix in a can of chick-peas and you have a quick, delicious main meal.

Serves 4

2 tablespoons olive or
   sunflower oil
1 onion, sliced
2 garlic cloves, crushed
3½ cups spinach, washed
   and shredded

1 teaspoon cumin seeds
15-ounce can chick-peas,
   drained
pat of butter
salt and ground black
   pepper

1 Heat the oil in a large frying pan or wok and fry the onion for about 5 minutes until softened. Add the garlic and cumin seeds, then fry for another minute.

2 Add the spinach, in stages, stirring until the leaves begin to wilt. Fresh spinach leaves condense dramatically when they are cooked and they will all fit into the pan.

3 Stir in the chick-peas and butter and season with salt and pepper. Reheat until just bubbling, then serve hot. Drain off any pan juices, if you wish, but this dish is rather good served with a little sauce.

Zucchini en Papillote

An impressive dinner party accompaniment, these puffed paper parcels should be broken open at the table.

Serves 4

2 zucchini
1 leek
8 ounces young
   asparagus, trimmed
4 tarragon sprigs

4 garlic cloves, unpeeled
1 egg, beaten
salt and ground black
   pepper

1 Preheat the oven to 400°F. Using a potato peeler, slice the zucchini lengthwise into thin strips.

2 Cut the leek into very fine julienne strips and cut the asparagus evenly into 2-inch lengths.

3 Cut out four sheets of baking parchment measuring about 12 x 15 inches and fold in half. Draw a large curve to make a heart shape when unfolded. Cut along the inside of the line and open out.

4 Divide the zucchini, asparagus and leek evenly between each paper heart, positioning the filling on one side of the fold line, and topping each with a sprig of fresh tarragon and an unpeeled garlic clove. Season to taste with salt and pepper.

5 Brush the edges lightly with the beaten egg and fold over.

6 Pleat the edges together so that each parcel is completely sealed. Lay the parcels on a baking sheet and cook for about 10 minutes. Serve immediately.

Cook's Tip
Experiment with other vegetables and herbs such as sugar snow and mint, or baby carrots and rosemary. The possibilities are endless.

Green Lentil and Cabbage Salad

This warm crunchy salad makes a satisfying meal if served with crusty French bread or whole wheat rolls.

Serves 4–6

1 cup Puy lentils
6 cups cold water
1 garlic clove
1 bay leaf
1 small onion, peeled and
    studded with 2 cloves
1 tablespoon olive oil
1 red onion, finely sliced
2 garlic cloves, crushed

1 tablespoon thyme
    leaves
6 cups finely shredded
    cabbage
finely grated rind and
    juice of 1 lemon
1 tablespoon raspberry
    vinegar
salt and ground black
    pepper

1 Rinse the lentils in cold water and place in a large saucepan with the water, garlic clove, bay leaf and clove-studded onion. Bring to a boil and cook for about 10 minutes. Reduce the heat, cover the pan with a tight-fitting lid and simmer gently for 15–20 minutes. Drain and remove the onion, garlic and bay leaf.

2 Heat the oil in a large pan and cook the red onion, crushed garlic and thyme for 5 minutes until softened.

3 Add the shredded cabbage and cook for 3–5 minutes until just cooked but still crunchy.

4 Stir in the cooked lentils, grated lemon rind and juice and the raspberry vinegar. Season with salt and pepper and serve.

Cook's Tip
Vary the type of cabbage you use in this recipe, if you like. Choose a white cabbage or a Savoy, or try fresh spring greens instead.

Tomato and Basil Tart

You could make individual tartlets instead of one large tart if you prefer, but reduce the baking time slightly.

Serves 6–8

1½ cups flour
½ teaspoon salt
½ cup butter or
    margarine, chilled
3–5 tablespoons water

For the filling
6 ounces mozzarella
    cheese, thinly sliced
12 fresh basil leaves,
    6 coarsely torn

4–5 tomatoes, cut into
    ¼-inch slices
salt and ground black
    pepper
4 tablespoons freshly
    grated Parmesan
    cheese
2 tablespoons extra-
    virgin olive oil

1 Place the flour and salt in a bowl, then rub in the butter until the mixture resembles bread crumbs. Add 3 tablespoons water and combine with a fork until the dough holds together. Mix in more water if needed. Gather the dough into a ball, wrap in wax paper and chill for 40 minutes. Preheat the oven to 375°F.

2 Roll out the pastry to a thickness of ¼ inch and use to line an 11-inch fluted loose-bottom quiche pan. Prick the base and chill for 20 minutes in the fridge.

3 Line the pastry with a sheet of baking parchment. Fill with dried beans. Place the quiche pan on a baking sheet; bake blind for 15 minutes. Remove from the oven. Leave the oven on.

4 Remove the beans and paper. Brush the pastry with oil. Line with the mozzarella. Sprinkle the torn basil over the top.

5 Arrange the tomato slices over the cheese. Dot with the whole basil leaves. Season with salt and pepper, Parmesan and oil. Bake for 35 minutes. If the cheese oozes a lot of liquid during baking, tilt the pan and spoon it off to keep the pastry crisp. Serve hot or at room temperature.

Spinach and Potato Galette

Creamy layers of potato, spinach and fresh herbs make a warming and filling supper dish.

Serves 6

2 pounds large potatoes
4 cups fresh spinach
1¾ cups low-fat cream
   cheese
1 tablespoon grainy
   mustard
2 eggs

2 ounces mixed chopped
   fresh herbs such as
   chives, parsley, chervil
   or sorrel
salt and ground black
   pepper

1 Preheat the oven to 350°F. Base-line a deep 9-inch round cake pan with nonstick baking parchment. Place the potatoes in a large saucepan and cover with cold water. Bring to a boil and cook for 10 minutes. Drain well and allow to cool slightly before slicing thinly.

2 Wash the spinach and place in a large pan with only the water that is clinging to the leaves. Cover and cook, stirring once, until the spinach has just wilted. Drain well in a strainer and squeeze out the excess moisture with the back of a spoon. Chop the spinach finely.

3 Beat together the cream cheese, mustard and eggs, then stir in the chopped spinach and fresh herbs.

4 Place a layer of the sliced potatoes in the lined tin, arranging them in concentric circles. Top with a spoonful of the cream cheese mixture and spread out. Continue layering, seasoning with salt and pepper as you go, until all the potatoes and the cream cheese mixture are used up.

5 Cover the pan with a piece of foil, scrunched around the edge, and place in a roasting pan.

6 Half-fill the roasting pan with boiling water and cook the galette in the oven for 45–50 minutes. Turn out onto a plate and serve hot or cold.

Cowboy Hot-pot

A great dish to serve as a children's main meal, which adults will enjoy too – if they are allowed to join the posse.

Serves 4–6

3 tablespoons sunflower
   oil
1 onion, sliced
1 red bell pepper, sliced
1 sweet potato or
   2 carrots, chopped
scant ½ cup chopped
   green beans
14-ounce can baked
   beans
7-ounce can corn
1 tablespoon tomato
   paste

1 teaspoon barbecue spice
   seasoning
4 ounces cheese
   (preferably smoked),
   diced
1 pound potatoes, thinly
   sliced
2 tablespoons butter,
   melted
salt and ground black
   pepper

1 Preheat the oven to 375°F. Heat the oil in a frying pan and gently fry the onion, pepper and sweet potato or carrots until softened but not browned. Transfer to a flameproof casserole.

2 Add the green beans, baked beans, corn (and liquid), tomato paste and barbecue spice seasoning. Bring to a boil, then simmer for 5 minutes.

3 Cover the vegetable and cheese mixture with the sliced potato, brush with butter, season with salt and pepper and bake for 30–40 minutes until golden brown on top and the potato is cooked.

Cook's Tip
Use any vegetable mixture you like in this versatile hot-pot, according to what you have available.

Bean Curd with Ginger Chili

Bean curd easily absorbs different flavors and retains a good firm texture, making it ideal for stir-frying.

Serves 4

8-ounce packet bean curd, diced
3 tablespoons dark soy sauce
2 tablespoons dry sherry or vermouth
2 teaspoons honey
⅔ cup vegetable stock
2 teaspoons cornstarch
3 tablespoons sunflower or peanut oil
3 leeks, thinly sliced
1 red chili, seeded and sliced
1 inch piece fresh ginger, peeled and shredded
salt and ground black pepper

1 Toss the bean curd in the soy sauce and sherry or vermouth until well coated and allow to marinate for about 30 minutes.

2 Strain the bean curd from the marinade and reserve the juices in a bowl. Mix the marinade with the honey, vegetable stock and cornstarch to make a paste.

3 Heat the oil in a wok or large frying pan and when hot, stir-fry the bean curd until it is crisp on the outside. Remove the bean curd and set aside.

4 Reheat the oil and stir-fry the leeks, chili and ginger for about 2 minutes until they are just soft. Season to taste with salt and pepper.

5 Return the bean curd to the pan, together with the marinade, and stir well until the liquid is thick and glossy. Serve hot with rice or egg noodles.

Cook's Tip
Bean curd tastes bland, allowing it to absorb the flavor of marinades and ingredients with which it is cooked.

Chinese Potatoes with Chili Beans

This oriental-inspired dish gains particular appeal by way of its tasty sauce.

Serves 4

4 potatoes, cut into thick chunks
3 scallions, sliced
1 large fresh chili, seeded and sliced
2 tablespoons sunflower or groundnut oil
2 garlic cloves, crushed
14-ounce can red kidney beans
2 tablespoons dark soy sauce
1 tablespoon sesame oil
salt and ground black pepper
1 tablespoon sesame seeds, to sprinkle
chopped fresh cilantro or parsley, to garnish

1 Boil the potatoes until they are just tender. Take care not to overcook them. Drain and reserve.

2 In a large frying pan or wok, stir-fry the scallions and chili in the oil for about 1 minute, then add the garlic and fry for a few seconds longer.

3 Rinse and drain the kidney beans then add them to the pan with the potatoes, stirring well. Finally add the soy sauce and sesame oil.

4 Season to taste with salt and pepper and cook the vegetables until they are well heated through. Sprinkle with the sesame seeds and the chopped fresh cilantro or parsley.

Corn and Bean Tamale Pie

This is a hearty dish with a polenta and cheese topping which covers corn and kidney beans in a rich hot sauce.

Serves 4

2 corn on the cob
2 tablespoons oil
1 onion, chopped
2 garlic cloves, crushed
1 red bell pepper, seeded and chopped
2 green chilies, seeded and chopped
2 tablespoons ground cumin
1 pound ripe tomatoes, peeled, seeded and chopped
1 tablespoon tomato paste
15-ounce can red kidney beans, drained and rinsed

1 tablespoon chopped fresh oregano
oregano leaves, to garnish

For the topping
1 cup polenta
1 tablespoon all-purpose flour
½ teaspoon salt
2 teaspoons baking powder
1 egg, lightly beaten
½ cup milk
1 tablespoon butter, melted
½ cup grated smoked Cheddar cheese

1 Preheat the oven to 425°F. Husk the corn on the cob, then parboil for 8 minutes. Drain, let cool slightly, then remove the kernels with a sharp knife.

2 Fry the onion, garlic and pepper in the oil for 5 minutes, until softened. Add the chilies and cumin; fry for 1 minute. Stir in the tomatoes, tomato paste, beans, corn kernels and oregano. Season to taste. Simmer, uncovered, for 10 minutes.

3 To make the topping, mix the polenta, flour, salt, baking powder, egg, milk and butter to form a thick batter.

4 Transfer the bean mixture to an baking dish, spoon the polenta mixture over and spread evenly. Bake for 30 minutes. Remove from the oven, sprinkle the cheese over the top, then bake for another 5–10 minutes, until golden.

Pepper and Potato Tortilla

Traditionally a Spanish dish, tortilla is best eaten cold in chunky wedges and makes an ideal picnic food.

Serves 4

2 potatoes
3 tablespoons olive oil
1 large onion, thinly sliced
2 garlic cloves, crushed
1 green bell pepper, thinly sliced
1 red bell pepper, thinly sliced

6 eggs, beaten
1 cup grated mature Cheddar cheese
salt and ground black pepper

1 Do not peel the potatoes, but wash them well. Parboil them for about 10 minutes, then drain and, when they are cool enough to handle, slice them thickly. Switch on the broiler so that it warms up while you prepare the rest of the dish.

2 In a large nonstick or well seasoned frying pan, heat the oil and fry the onion, garlic and pepper over a moderate heat for 5 minutes until softened.

3 Add the potatoes and continue frying, stirring from time to time until the potatoes are completely cooked and the vegetables are soft. Add a little extra oil if the pan seems rather too dry.

4 Pour in half the beaten eggs, then sprinkle over half the grated Cheddar cheese, then the rest of the egg. Season with salt and pepper and finish with a layer of cheese.

5 Continue to cook over a low heat, without stirring, half covering the pan with a lid to help set the eggs.

6 When the mixture is firm, flash the pan under the hot broiler to seal the top just lightly. Leave the tortilla in the pan to cool. This helps it firm up further and makes it easier to turn out. Cut into generous wedges to serve.

Chick-pea Stew

This hearty chick-pea and vegetable stew is delicious served with garlic-flavored mashed potato.

Serves 4

2 tablespoons olive oil	8 ounces zucchini, sliced
1 small onion, finely chopped	7-ounce can corn, drained
8 ounces carrots, halved lengthwise and thinly sliced	14-ounce can chick-peas, drained
½ teaspoon ground cumin	2 tablespoons tomato paste
1 teaspoon ground coriander	scant 1 cup hot vegetable stock
2 tablespoons all-purpose flour	salt and ground black pepper
	mashed potato, to serve

1 Heat the oil in a frying pan. Add the onion and carrots. Toss the vegetables to coat them in the oil, then cook over a moderate heat for 4 minutes.

2 Add the ground cumin, coriander and flour. Stir and cook for 1 minute more.

3 Cut the zucchini slices in half. Add them to the pan with the corn, chick-peas, tomato paste and vegetable stock. Stir well. Cook for 10 minutes, stirring frequently.

4 Taste the stew and season to taste with salt and pepper. Serve immediately with mashed potato.

Cook's Tip
To make garlic-flavored mashed potato, peel and crush a garlic clove, fry it lightly in butter, then stir into the mashed potato until well combined.

Potato and Broccoli Stir-fry

This wonderful stir-fry combines potato, broccoli and red pepper with just a hint of fresh ginger.

Serves 2

1 pound potatoes	8 ounces broccoli, broken into florets
3 tablespoons peanut oil	1-inch piece fresh ginger, peeled and grated
4 tablespoons butter	salt and ground black pepper
1 small onion, chopped	
1 red pepper, seeded and chopped	

1 Peel the potatoes and dice them into ½-inch pieces.

2 Heat the oil in a large frying pan and cook the potatoes for 8 minutes over a high heat, stirring and tossing occasionally, until browned and just tender.

3 Drain off the oil. Add the butter to the potatoes in the pan. As soon as it melts, add the chopped onion and red pepper. Stir-fry for 2 minutes.

4 Add the broccoli florets and ginger to the pan. Stir-fry for 2–3 minutes more, taking care not to break up the potatoes. Season to taste with salt and pepper and serve at once.

Vegetables with Lentil Bolognese

Instead of a cheese sauce, it makes a pleasant change to top lightly steamed vegetables with a delicious lentil sauce.

Serves 6

1 small cauliflower
    broken into florets
2 cups broccoli florets
2 leeks, thickly sliced
8 ounces Brussels
    sprouts, halved if large

**For the lentil
Bolognese sauce**
1 onion, chopped
2 garlic cloves, crushed
2 carrots, coarsely grated
2 celery stalks, chopped

3 tablespoons olive oil
½ cup red lentils
14-ounce can chopped
    tomatoes
2 tablespoons tomato
    paste
2 cups vegetable stock
1 tablespoon fresh
    marjoram, chopped,
    or 1 teaspoon dried
    marjoram
salt and ground black
    pepper

1 First make the sauce in a large saucepan, gently fry the onion, garlic, carrots and celery in the oil for about 5 minutes, until they are soft. Add the lentils, tomatoes, tomato paste, stock, marjoram and seasoning. Bring the mixture to a boil, then partially cover with a lid and simmer for 20 minutes until thick and soft.

2 Place all the vegetables in a steamer over a pan of boiling water and cook for 8–10 minutes until just tender.

3 Drain and place in a shallow serving dish. Spoon the sauce on top, stirring slightly to mix. Serve hot.

Black Bean and Vegetable Stir-fry

This colorful and very flavorful vegetable mixture is coated in a classic Chinese sauce.

Serves 4

8 scallions
8 ounces button
    mushrooms
1 red bell pepper
1 green bell pepper
2 large carrots
4 tablespoons sesame oil
2 garlic cloves, crushed

4 tablespoons black bean
    sauce
6 tablespoons warm
    water
scant 3 cups bean sprouts
salt and ground black
    pepper

1 Thinly slice the scallions and button mushrooms. Set aside in separate bowls.

2 Cut both the peppers in half, remove the seeds and slice the flesh into thin strips.

3 Cut the carrots in half. Cut each half into thin strips lengthwise. Stack the slices and cut through them to make very fine strips.

4 Heat the oil in a large wok or frying pan until very hot and stir-fry the scallions and garlic for 30 seconds.

5 Add the mushrooms, peppers and carrots. Stir-fry for another 5–6 minutes over a high heat until the vegetables are just beginning to soften.

6 Mix the black bean sauce with the water. Add to the wok or pan and cook for another 3–4 minutes. Stir in the bean sprouts and stir-fry for a final 1 minute until all the vegetables are coated in the sauce. Season to taste with salt and pepper. Serve immediately.

Tomato and Okra Stew

Okra is an unusual and delicious vegetable. It releases a sticky sap when cooked, which helps to thicken the stew.

Serves 4

1 tablespoon olive oil
1 onion, chopped
14-ounce can pimientos, drained
2 x 14-ounce cans chopped tomatoes
10 ounces okra
2 tablespoons chopped fresh parsley
salt and ground black pepper

1 Heat the oil in a saucepan and cook the chopped onion for about 2–3 minutes.

2 Coarsely chop the pimientos and add to the onion. Add the chopped tomatoes and mix well.

3 Cut the tops off the okra and cut into halves or quarters if large. Add to the tomato sauce in the pan. Season to taste with plenty of salt and pepper.

4 Bring the vegetable stew to a boil, then lower the heat, cover the pan with a tight-fitting lid and simmer for 12 minutes until the vegetables are tender and the sauce has thickened. Stir in the chopped parsley and serve immediately.

Cook's Tip
Okra is now available all year round. Do not buy them any longer than 3–4 inches and look for clean, dark green pods – a brown tinge indicates staleness. When preparing, if the ridges look tough or damaged, scrape them with a sharp knife.

Chunky Vegetable Paella

This Spanish rice dish is now enjoyed the world over. This version includes eggplant and chick-peas.

Serves 6

large pinch of saffron strands
1 eggplant, cut into thick chunks
6 tablespoons olive oil
1 large onion, thickly sliced
3 garlic cloves, crushed
1 yellow bell pepper, sliced
1 red bell pepper, sliced
2 teaspoons paprika
1¼ cups risotto rice
2½ cups stock
1 pound fresh tomatoes, skinned and chopped
4 ounces sliced mushrooms
scant ½ cup cut green beans
14-ounce can chick-peas

1 Steep the saffron in 3 tablespoons hot water. Sprinkle the eggplant with salt, let drain in a colander for 30 minutes, then rinse and dry.

2 In a large paella or frying pan, heat the oil and fry the onion, garlic, peppers and eggplant for about 5 minutes, stirring occasionally. Sprinkle in the paprika and stir again.

3 Mix in the rice, then pour in the stock, tomatoes, saffron and seasoning. Bring to a boil, then simmer the mixture for about 15 minutes, uncovered, shaking the pan frequently and stirring from time to time.

4 Stir in the mushrooms, green beans and chick-peas (with their liquid). Continue cooking for another 10 minutes, then serve hot, direct from the pan.

Onion and Gruyère Tart

The secret of this tart is to cook the onions very slowly until they almost caramelize.

Serves 4
1½ cups all-purpose flour
pinch of salt
6 tablespoons butter,
    diced
1 egg yolk

1–2 tablespoons
    wholegrain mustard
2 eggs, plus 1 egg yolk
1 cup heavy cream
generous ½ cup grated
    Gruyère cheese
pinch of freshly grated
    nutmeg
salt and ground black
    pepper

For the filling
4 tablespoons butter
1 pound onions, thinly
    sliced

1 To make the pastry, sift the flour and salt into a bowl. Add the butter and rub into the flour with your fingertips until the mixture resembles fine bread crumbs. Add the egg yolk and 1 tablespoon cold water and mix to a firm dough. Chill in the fridge for 30 minutes.

2 Preheat the oven to 400°F. Knead the pastry, then roll it out on a lightly floured work surface and use to line a 9-inch loose-bottomed tart pan. Prick the base all over with a fork, line the pastry case with greaseproof paper and fill with baking beans.

3 Bake the pastry case blind for 15 minutes. Remove the paper and beans and bake for another 10–15 minutes, until the pastry case is crisp. Meanwhile, melt the butter in a saucepan, add the onions, cover with a tight-fitting lid and cook for 20 minutes, stirring occasionally, until golden.

4 Reduce the oven temperature to 350°F. Spread the pastry case with mustard and top with the onions. Mix together the eggs, egg yolk, cream, cheese, nutmeg and seasoning. Pour over the onions. Bake for 30–35 minutes, until golden. Serve warm.

Potato and Spinach Gratin

Pine nuts add a satisfying crunch to this gratin of wafer-thin potato slices and spinach in a creamy cheese sauce.

Serves 2
1 pound potatoes
1 garlic clove, crushed
3 scallions, thinly sliced
⅔ cup light cream
1 cup milk
8 ounces frozen chopped
    spinach, thawed

1 cup grated mature
    Cheddar cheese
¼ cup pine nuts
salt and ground black
    pepper
lettuce and tomato salad,
    to serve

1 Peel the potatoes and cut them carefully into wafer-thin slices. Spread them out in a large, heavy-based, nonstick frying pan.

2 Scatter the crushed garlic and sliced scallions evenly over the potatoes.

3 Pour the cream and milk over the potatoes. Place the pan over a gentle heat, cover and cook for 8 minutes or until the potatoes are tender.

4 Using both hands, squeeze the spinach dry. Add the spinach to the potatoes, mixing lightly. Cover the pan with a tight-fitting lid and cook for 2 minutes more.

5 Season to taste with salt and pepper, then spoon the mixture into a gratin dish. Preheat the broiler.

6 Sprinkle the grated cheese and pine nuts over the spinach mixture. Lightly toast under the broiler for 2–3 minutes until the topping is golden. A simple lettuce and tomato salad makes an excellent accompaniment to this dish.

Stuffed Peppers

Sweet peppers can be stuffed and baked with a variety of fillings, from cooked vegetables to rice or pasta.

Serves 6

6 peppers, any color
generous 1 cup rice
4 tablespoons olive oil
1 large onion, chopped
3 anchovy fillets, chopped
2 garlic cloves, finely
   chopped
3 tomatoes, peeled and
   diced

4 tablespoons white wine
3 tablespoons finely
   chopped fresh parsley
scant ½ cup mozzarella
6 tablespoons freshly
   grated Parmesan
   cheese
salt and ground black
   pepper

1   Cut the tops off the peppers. Scoop out the seeds and the fibrous insides. Blanch the peppers and their tops in a large saucepan of boiling water for 3–4 minutes. Remove, and stand upside down on wire racks to drain.

2   Boil the rice according to the package instructions, but drain and rinse it in cold water 3 minutes before the recommended cooking time has elapsed. Drain again.

3   Sauté the onion in the oil until soft. Mash in the anchovies and garlic. Add the tomatoes and wine; cook for 5 minutes.

4   Preheat the oven to 375°F. Remove the tomato mixture from the heat. Stir in the rice, parsley, the mozzarella and 4 tablespoons of the Parmesan cheese. Season to taste with salt and pepper.

5   Pat the insides of the peppers dry with paper towels. Sprinkle with salt and pepper. Stuff the peppers. Sprinkle the tops with the remaining Parmesan and a little oil. Arrange the peppers in a shallow baking dish. Pour in enough water to come ½ inch up the sides of the peppers. Bake for 25 minutes. Serve immediately.

Broccoli and Ricotta Cannelloni

When piping the filling into the cannelloni tubes, hold them upright on the work surface.

Serves 4

12 dried cannelloni tubes,
   3 inches long
4 cups broccoli florets
1½ cups fresh bread
   crumbs
⅔ cup milk
4 tablespoons olive oil,
   plus extra for brushing
1 cup ricotta cheese
pinch of grated nutmeg
6 tablespoons freshly
   grated Parmesan or
   Pecorino cheese
salt and ground black
   pepper

2 tablespoons pine nuts,
   for sprinkling

For the tomato sauce
2 tablespoons olive oil
1 onion, finely chopped
1 garlic clove, crushed
2 x 14-ounce cans
   chopped tomatoes
1 tablespoon tomato paste
4 black olives, pitted and
   chopped
1 teaspoon dried thyme

1   Preheat the oven to 375°F and grease a casserole . Bring a saucepan of water to a boil, add a little olive oil and simmer the pasta, uncovered, until nearly cooked. Boil the broccoli until tender. Drain the pasta and rinse under cold water. Drain the broccoli, then process in a food processor or blender until smooth.

2   Mix together the bread crumbs, milk and oil. Add the ricotta, broccoli purée, nutmeg, 4 tablespoons Parmesan cheese and seasoning.

3   For the sauce, fry the onions and garlic in the oil for 5 minutes. Stir in the tomatoes, tomato paste, olives and thyme, and season. Boil for 2 minutes; pour in the dish.

4   Open the pasta tubes. Pipe in the filling using a ½-inch nozzle. Arrange in the dish. Brush with olive oil, then sprinkle over the remaining cheese and pine nuts. Bake for 30 minutes, or until golden on top.

Pasta with Spring Vegetables

If you are not fond of fennel, use a small onion instead. Prepare in the same way.

Serves 4
1 cup broccoli florets
4 ounces baby leeks
8 ounces asparagus
1 small fennel bulb
1 cup fresh or frozen peas
3 tablespoons butter
1 shallot, chopped
1¼ cups heavy cream

3 tablespoons mixed
   chopped fresh herbs,
   such as parsley, thyme
   and sage
12 ounces penne
salt and ground black
   pepper
freshly grated Parmesan
   cheese, to serve

1 Divide the broccoli florets into tiny sprigs. Cut the leeks and asparagus diagonally into 2-inch lengths. Trim the fennel bulb and remove any tough outer leaves. Cut into wedges, leaving the layers attached at the root ends so the pieces stay intact.

2 Cook each vegetable separately in boiling salted water until just tender – use the same water for each vegetable. Drain well and keep warm.

3 Melt the butter in a separate saucepan, and cook the chopped shallot, stirring occasionally, until softened but not browned. Stir in the herbs and cream and cook for a few minutes, until slightly thickened.

4 Meanwhile, cook the pasta in boiling salted water for 10 minutes or according to the instructions on the package. Drain well and add to the sauce with all the vegetables. Toss gently to combine and season to taste with plenty of pepper.

5 Serve the pasta hot, with plenty of freshly grated Parmesan cheese.

Pasta Carbonara

A classic Roman dish traditionally made with spaghetti, which is equally delicious with fresh egg tagliatelle.

Serves 4
12 ounces–1 pound fresh
   tagliatelle
1 tablespoon olive oil
8-ounce piece of ham,
   bacon or pancetta, cut
   into 1-inch sticks
4 ounces button
   mushrooms, sliced
4 eggs, lightly beaten

5 tablespoons light cream
salt and ground black
   pepper
2 tablespoons finely
   grated Parmesan
   cheese
fresh basil sprigs, to
   garnish

1 Cook the pasta in a pan of boiling salted water, with a little oil added, for 6–8 minutes or until *al dente*.

2 Meanwhile, heat the oil in a frying pan and fry the ham for 3–4 minutes, then add the mushrooms and fry for another 3–4 minutes. Turn off the heat and reserve. Lightly beat the eggs and cream together in a bowl and season well with salt and pepper.

3 When the pasta is cooked, drain it well and return to the pan. Add the ham, mushrooms and any pan juices and stir into the pasta.

4 Pour in the eggs, cream and half the Parmesan cheese. Stir well and as you do this the eggs will cook in the heat of the pasta. Pile on to warmed serving plates, sprinkle with the remaining Parmesan and garnish with basil.

Spinach and Hazelnut Lasagne

Use frozen spinach in this hearty and satisfying dish if you are short of time.

Serves 4

8 cups fresh spinach
1¼ cups vegetable stock
1 onion, finely chopped
1 garlic clove, crushed
¾ cup hazelnuts
2 tablespoons chopped fresh basil
6 sheets lasagne

14-ounce can chopped tomatoes
1 cup ricotta cheese
salt and ground black pepper
flaked hazelnuts and chopped fresh parsley

1 Preheat the oven to 400°F. Wash the spinach; cook with no extra water over a low or medium heat for 2 minutes until wilted. Drain well. Simmer the onion and garlic in 2 tablespoons of the stock until soft. Stir in the spinach, hazelnuts and basil.

2 In a large baking dish, layer the spinach, lasagne and tomatoes; season as you go. Pour in the remaining stock. Spread the ricotta over the top. Bake for 45 minutes. Serve hot, sprinkled with hazelnuts and chopped parsley.

Tagliatelle with Hazelnut Pesto

Hazelnuts are used instead of pine nuts in the pesto sauce, providing a healthier, lower-fat option.

Serves 4

2 garlic cloves, crushed
1 ounce fresh basil leaves
¼ cup chopped hazelnuts

scant 1 cup cream cheese
8 ounces tagliatelle
ground black pepper

1 Place the garlic, basil, hazelnuts and cheese in a food processor or blender and process to a thick paste.

2 Cook the tagliatelle in lightly salted boiling water until just tender, then drain well.

3 Spoon the sauce into the hot pasta, tossing until melted. Sprinkle with pepper and serve hot.

Spaghetti with Tuna Sauce

Use 1 pound fresh spaghetti in place of the dried pasta in this piquant dish, if you prefer.

Serves 4

Cook 8 ounces spaghetti, drain and keep hot. Boil 1 garlic clove and 14-ounce can chopped tomatoes and simmer for 2–3 minutes. Add 15 ounces canned tuna or 1 pound fresh tuna, cut into small chunks, and ½ teaspoon chili sauce (optional), 4 black olives and the spaghetti. Simmer until the tuna is cooked, and season to taste.

Penne with Broccoli and Chili

For a milder sauce you could omit the chili, but it does give this dish a great kick.

Serves 4

4 cups small broccoli
    florets
2 tablespoons stock
1 garlic clove, crushed
1 small red chili, finely
    sliced, or ½ teaspoon
    chili sauce

4 tablespoons plain
    low-fat yogurt
2 tablespoons toasted
    pine nuts or cashew
    nuts
12 ounces penne
salt and ground black
    pepper

1 Add the pasta to a large pan of lightly salted boiling water and return to a boil. Place the broccoli in a steamer basket over the top. Cover and cook for 8–10 minutes until both are just tender. Drain.

2 Heat the stock and add the crushed garlic and chili or chili sauce. Stir over a low heat for 2–3 minutes.

3 Stir in the broccoli, pasta and yogurt. Adjust the seasoning, sprinkle with nuts and serve hot.

Linguine with Pesto Sauce

Pesto originates in Liguria, where the sea breezes are said to give the local basil a particularly fine flavor.

Serves 5–6

2½ ounces fresh basil
    leaves
3–4 garlic cloves, peeled
3 tablespoons pine nuts
½ teaspoon salt
5 tablespoons extra-
    virgin olive oil

scant ¾ cup freshly
    grated Parmesan
    cheese
4 tablespoons freshly
    grated Pecorino cheese
salt and ground black
    pepper
1¼ pounds linguine

1 Place the basil, garlic, pine nuts, salt and olive oil in a food processor or blender and process until smooth. Place in a bowl. (If desired, the sauce may be frozen at this point, before the cheeses are added.)

2 Add the cheeses and stir to combine thoroughly. Season to taste with salt and pepper.

3 Cook the pasta in a large saucepan of rapidly boiling salted water until it is *al dente.* Just before draining it, take about 4 tablespoons of the cooking water and stir it into the pesto sauce.

4 Drain the pasta and toss with the sauce. Serve immediately, with extra cheese if desired.

Cook's Tip
Pecorino cheese is not as widely available as Parmesan. If you cannot find it, use all Parmesan instead.

Spaghetti with Herb Sauce

Fresh herbs make a wonderful aromatic sauce – the heat from the pasta releases their flavor to delicious effect.

Serves 4

2 ounces chopped mixed
   fresh herbs such as
   parsley, basil and
   thyme
2 garlic cloves, crushed
4 tablespoons pine nuts,
   toasted
⅔ cup olive oil

12 ounces dried spaghetti
4 tablespoons freshly
   grated Parmesan
   cheese
salt and ground black
   pepper
fresh basil leaves, to
   garnish

1 Put the herbs, garlic and half the pine nuts into a food processor or blender. With the machine running slowly, add the oil and process to form a thick purée.

2 Cook the spaghetti in plenty of boiling salted water for about 8 minutes, until *al dente*. Drain thoroughly.

3 Transfer the herb purée to a large warm bowl, then add the spaghetti and Parmesan. Toss well to coat the pasta with the sauce. Season with salt and peppper, sprinkle the remaining pine nuts and the basil leaves on top and serve hot.

Tagliatelle with Saffron Mussels

Tagliatelle is served with mussels in a saffron and cream sauce in this recipe, but use other pasta if you prefer.

Serves 4

4–4½ pounds live
   mussels in the shell
⅔ cup dry white wine
2 shallots, finely
   chopped
12 ounces dried
   tagliatelle
2 tablespoons butter
2 garlic cloves, crushed

1 cup heavy cream
large pinch of saffron
   strands
1 egg yolk
salt and ground black
   pepper
2 tablespoons chopped
   fresh parsley, to
   garnish

1 Scrub the mussels well under cold running water. Remove the beards and discard any mussels that are open. Place the mussels in a large saucepan with the wine and shallots. Cover with a tight-fitting lid and cook over a high heat, shaking the pan occasionally, for 5–8 minutes until the mussels have opened. Drain the mussels, reserving the liquid. Discard any that remain closed. Shell all but a few of the mussels and keep warm. Bring the reserved cooking liquid to a boil, then reduce by half. Strain into a jug.

2 Cook the pasta in a large pan of boiling salted water for 10 minutes or according to the instructions on the package.

3 Meanwhile, melt the butter in a frying pan and fry the garlic for 1 minute. Pour in the mussel liquid, cream and saffron strands. Heat gently until the sauce thickens slightly. Remove the pan from the heat and stir in the egg yolk and shelled mussels, and season to taste with salt and pepper.

4 Drain the tagliatelle and transfer to warmed serving bowls. Spoon the sauce over and sprinkle with chopped parsley. Garnish with the mussels in shells and serve immediately.

Pasta Rapido with Parsley Pesto

Here's a fresh, lively sauce that will stir the appetite and pep up any pasta supper.

Serves 4

1 pound pasta shapes
¾ cup whole almonds
½ cup flaked almonds toasted
generous ¼ cup freshly grated Parmesan cheese
pinch of salt

For the sauce
1½ ounces fresh Italian parsley
2 garlic cloves, crushed
3 tablespoons olive oil
3 tablespoons lemon juice
1 teaspoon sugar
1 cup boiling water

1 Bring a large saucepan of salted water to a boil and cook the pasta according to the instructions on the package. Toast the whole and flaked almonds separately under a moderate broiler until golden brown. Set the flaked almonds aside.

2 To make the sauce, chop the parsley finely in a food processor. Add the whole almonds and reduce to a fine consistency. Add the garlic, olive oil, lemon juice, sugar and water. Combine to make a sauce.

3 Drain the pasta and combine with half of the sauce. (The remainder of the sauce will keep in a screw-top jar in the fridge for up to ten days.) Top with freshly grated Parmesan cheese and the flaked almonds.

Macaroni and Cheese with Mushrooms

This macaroni and cheese is served in a light creamy sauce with mushrooms and topped with pine nuts.

Serves 4

1 pound quick-cooking elbow macaroni
3 tablespoons olive oil
8 ounces button mushrooms, sliced
2 fresh thyme sprigs
4 tablespoons all-purpose flour
1 vegetable stock cube
2½ cups milk

½ teaspoon celery salt
1 teaspoon Dijon mustard
1½ cups grated Cheddar
generous ¼ cup freshly grated Parmesan cheese
¼ cup pine nuts
salt and ground black pepper

1 Bring a saucepan of salted water to a boil and cook the macaroni according to the instructions on the package.

2 Heat the oil in a heavy saucepan and cover, add mushrooms and thyme, cook over a gentle heat for 2–3 minutes. Stir in the flour and remove from the heat, add the stock cube and stir constantly until evenly blended. Return to the heat and add the milk a little at a time, stirring after each addition. Add the celery salt, mustard and Cheddar cheese and season to taste with salt and pepper. Stir and simmer for about 1–2 minutes, until the sauce has thickened.

3 Preheat a moderate broiler. Drain the macaroni well, toss into the sauce and put into four individual dishes or one large flameproof gratin dish. Scatter with grated Parmesan cheese and pine nuts, then broil until brown and bubbly.

Pasta with Roasted Pepper Sauce

Add other vegetables such as green beans or zucchini or even chick-peas to make this sauce more substantial.

Serves 4

2 red bell peppers
2 yellow bell peppers
3 tablespoons olive oil
1 onion, sliced
2 garlic cloves, crushed
14-ounce can chopped
   plum tomatoes
½ teaspoon mild chili
   powder
1 pound pasta shells or
   spirals
salt and ground black
   pepper
freshly grated Parmesan
   cheese, to serve

1 Preheat the oven to 400°F. Place the peppers on a baking sheet and bake for about 20 minutes or until they are beginning to char. Alternatively, broil the peppers, turning them from time to time.

2 Rub the skins off the peppers under cold water. Halve, remove the seeds and coarsely chop the flesh.

3 Heat the oil in a saucepan and cook the onion and garlic gently for 5 minutes until soft and golden.

4 Stir in the chili powder, cook for 2 minutes, then add the tomatoes and peppers. Bring to a boil and simmer for about 10–15 minutes until slightly thickened and reduced. Season with salt and pepper to taste.

5 Bring a pan of salted water to a boil and cook the pasta according to the instructions on the package. Drain well and toss with the sauce. Serve piping hot with lots of freshly grated Parmesan cheese.

Stir-fried Vegetables with Pasta

This is a colorful oriental-style dish, easily prepared using pasta instead of Chinese noodles.

Serves 4

1 carrot
6 ounces small zucchini
6 ounces green beans
6 ounces baby corn cobs
1 pound ribbon pasta
   such as tagliatelle
pinch of salt
2 tablespoons corn oil,
   plus extra for tossing
   the pasta
½-inch piece fresh ginger,
   peeled and finely
   chopped
2 garlic cloves, finely
   chopped
6 tablespoons yellow
   bean sauce
6 scallions, sliced into 1-
   inch pieces
2 tablespoons dry sherry
1 teaspoon sesame seeds

1 Slice the carrot and zucchini diagonally into chunks. Slice the beans diagonally, then cut the baby corn cobs diagonally in half.

2 Cook the pasta in plenty of boiling salted water according to the instructions on the package. Drain, then rinse under hot water. Toss in a little oil.

3 Heat 2 tablepoons oil until smoking in a wok or frying pan and add the ginger and garlic. Stir-fry for 30 seconds, then add the carrots, beans and zucchini.

4 Stir-fry for 3–4 minutes then stir in the yellow bean sauce. Stir-fry for 2 minutes, add the scallions, sherry and pasta and stir-fry for another minute until piping hot. Sprinkle with sesame seeds and serve immediately.

Tagliatelle with Gorgonzola Sauce

Gorgonzola is a creamy Italian blue cheese. You could use Danish Blue or Pipo Crème instead.

Serves 4

2 tablespoons butter, plus
    extra for tossing the
    pasta
8 ounces Gorgonzola
    cheese
⅔ cup heavy or whipping
    cream
2 tablepoons dry
    vermouth

1 teaspoon cornstarch
1 tablespoon chopped
    fresh sage
1 pound tagliatelle
salt and ground black
    pepper

1 Melt 2 tablepoons butter in a heavy saucepan (it needs to be thick-based to prevent the cheese from burning). Stir in 1½ cups crumbled Gorgonzola cheese and stir over very gentle heat for 2–3 minutes until the cheese is melted.

2 Pour in the cream, vermouth and cornstarch, whisking well to amalgamate. Stir in the chopped sage, then season to taste with salt and pepper. Cook, whisking all the time, until the sauce boils and thickens. Set aside.

3 Boil the pasta in plenty of salted water according to the instructions on the package. Drain well and toss with a little butter to coat evenly.

4 Reheat the sauce gently, whisking well. Divide the pasta among four serving bowls, top with the sauce and sprinkle on the remaining cheese. Serve immediately.

Cook's Tip
If you do not have vermouth, use a good-quality dry sherry in its place.

Rigatoni with Garlic Crumbs

A hot and spicy dish – halve the quantity of chili if you would prefer a milder flavor.

Serves 4–6

3 tablespoons olive oil
2 shallots, chopped
8 slices bacon, chopped
2 teaspoons crushed
    dried chilies
14-ounce can chopped
    tomatoes with herbs

6 slices white bread,
    crusts removed
½ cup butter
2 garlic cloves, chopped
1 pound rigatoni
salt and ground black
    pepper

1 Heat the oil in a saucepan and fry the shallots and bacon gently for 6–8 minutes until golden. Add the dried chilies and chopped tomatoes, half-cover with a lid and simmer for about 20 minutes.

2 Meanwhile, place the bread in a blender or food processor and process to fine crumbs.

3 Heat the butter in a frying pan and stir-fry the garlic and bread crumbs until golden and crisp. (Be careful not to let the crumbs catch and burn.)

4 Bring a pan of lightly salted water to a boil and cook the pasta according to the instructions on the package. Drain well.

5 Toss the pasta with the tomato sauce and divide among four serving bowls.

6 Sprinkle with the crumbs and serve immediately.

Cook's Tip
If you are preparing this dish for vegetarians leave out the bacon, or replace it with sliced mushrooms.

Pasta with Tomatoes and Arugula

This pretty-colored pasta dish relies for its success on the slightly peppery taste of the arugula.

Serves 4

1 pound pasta shells	3 ounces fresh arugula
1 pound ripe cherry	salt and ground black
tomatoes	pepper
3 tablespoons olive oil	Parmesan cheese

1 Bring a saucepan of water to a boil and cook the pasta according to the instructions on the package. Drain well.

2 Halve the tomatoes. Trim, wash and dry the arugula.

3 Heat the oil in a large saucepan and gently cook the tomatoes for barely 1 minute. The tomatoes should only just be heated through and not be allowed to disintegrate.

4 Add the pasta to the pan, then the arugula. (Coarsely tear any arugula leaves that are too large.) Carefully stir to mix and heat through. Season to taste with salt and pepper. Serve hot, with plenty of shaved Parmesan cheese.

Cook's Tip
Arugula is increasingly available in supermarkets. However, if you cannot find it, it is easy to grow in the garden.

Pasta Spirals with Pepperoni

A warming supper dish, this pepperoni and tomato sauce could be served on any type of pasta.

Serves 4

1 onion	2 teaspoons paprika
1 red bell pepper	6 ounces pepperoni or
1 green bell pepper	chorizo
2 tablepoons olive oil,	3 tablepoons chopped
plus extra for tossing	fresh parsley
the pasta	1 pound dried green
2 x 14-ounce cans	pasta spirals
chopped tomatoes	salt and ground black
2 tablespoons tomato	pepper
paste	

1 Chop the onion. Halve and seed the peppers, removing the cores, then dice.

2 Heat the oil in a saucepan and cook the onion for about 2 minutes, until beginning to color. Stir in the peppers, tomatoes, tomato paste and paprika, bring to a boil and simmer uncovered for 15–20 minutes until the sauce is reduced and thickened.

3 Slice the sausage and stir into the sauce with about half the chopped parsley. Season to taste with salt and pepper.

4 While the sauce is simmering, cook the pasta in plenty of boiling salted water according to the instructions on the package. Drain well. Toss the pasta with the remaining parsley in a little extra olive oil. Divide among warmed bowls and top with the sauce.

Cook's Tip
All types of sausages are suitable to include in this dish. If using raw sausages, add them with the onion and cook thoroughly.

Pasta with Tuna and Capers

Pasta shapes are tossed in a flavorful sauce made with tuna, capers, anchovies and fresh basil.

Serves 4

14-ounce can tuna fish in oil
2 tablespoons olive oil
2 garlic cloves, crushed
2 x 14-ounce chopped tomatoes
6 canned anchovy fillets, drained

2 tablespoons capers in vinegar, drained
2 tablespoons chopped fresh basil
salt and ground black pepper
4 cups garganelle, penne or rigatoni
fresh basil sprigs, to garnish

1 Drain the oil from the tuna into a saucepan, add the olive oil and heat gently until it stops spitting.

2 Add the garlic and fry until golden. Stir in the tomatoes and simmer for 25 minutes until thickened.

3 Flake the tuna and cut the anchovies in half. Stir into the sauce with the capers and chopped basil. Season to taste with salt and pepper.

4 Cook the pasta in plenty of boiling salted water according to the instructions on the package. Drain well and toss with the sauce. Garnish with fresh basil sprigs.

Cook's Tip
This piquant sauce could be made without the addition of tomatoes – just heat the oil, add the other ingredients and heat through gently before tossing with the pasta.

Pasta Bows with Smoked Salmon

In Italy, pasta cooked with smoked salmon is becoming very fashionable. This is a quick and luxurious sauce.

Serves 4

6 scallions, sliced
4 tablepoons butter
6 tablespoons dry white wine or vermouth
1¾ cups heavy cream
pinch of freshly grated nutmeg
8 ounces smoked salmon

2 tablespoons chopped fresh dill or 1 tablespoon dried dill
freshly squeezed lemon juice
1 pound pasta bows
salt and ground black pepper

1 Slice the scallions finely. Melt the butter in a saucepan and fry the scallions for about 1 minute until they begin to soften.

2 Add the wine or vermouth and boil hard to reduce to about 2 tablespoons. Stir in the cream and add salt, pepper and nutmeg to taste. Bring to a boil and simmer for about 2–3 minutes until slightly thickened.

3 Cut the smoked salmon into 1-inch squares and stir into the sauce with the dill. Taste and add a little lemon juice. Keep the sauce warm.

4 Cook the pasta in plenty of boiling salted water according to the instructions on the package. Drain well. Toss the pasta with the sauce and serve immediately.

Cook's Tip
This dish could also be prepared with canned salmon, broken into bite-size pieces, if you prefer.

Pasta with Shrimp and Feta Cheese

This dish contains a delicious combination of fresh shrimp and sharp-tasting feta cheese.

Serves 4

4 cups medium raw shrimp	small bunch fresh chives
6 scallions	1 pound garganelle or rigatoni
4 tablespoons butter	salt and ground black pepper
8 ounces feta cheese	

1 Remove the heads from the shrimp by twisting and pulling off. Peel the shrimp and discard the shells. Chop the scallions.

2 Melt the butter in a frying pan and cook the shrimp. When they turn pink, add the scallions and cook gently for 1 minute more.

3 Dice the feta cheese into ½-inch pieces. Stir into the shrimp mixture and season to taste with pepper.

4 Cut the chives into 1-inch pieces and stir half into the shrimp mixture.

5 Bring a saucepan of salted water to a boil and cook the pasta according to the instructions on the package. Drain well, pile into a warmed serving dish and top with the sauce. Scatter with the remaining chives and serve.

Cook's Tip
Substitute goat cheese for the feta cheese if you like; prepare the dish in the same way.

Tagliatelle with Prosciutto

This is a simple dish, prepared in minutes from the best ingredients, with a thick covering of Parmesan cheese.

Serves 4

4 ounces prosciutto	salt and ground black pepper
1 pound tagliatelle	a few fresh sage leaves, to garnish
6 tablepoons butter	
½ cup grated Parmesan cheese	

1 Cut the prosciutto into strips of the same width as the tagliatelle. Cook the pasta in plenty of boiling salted water according to the instructions on the package.

2 Meanwhile, melt the butter gently in a saucepan and heat the prosciutto strips through, but do not fry.

3 Drain the tagliatelle well and pile into a warm serving dish. Sprinkle all the Parmesan cheese over the top.

4 Pour the buttery prosciutto over the top of the tagliatelle and Parmesan. Season well with pepper and garnish with the sage leaves.

Cook's Tip
Buy Parmesan cheese in a block and grate it yourself. The flavor is far superior to that of already-grated Parmesan cheese.

Cannelloni al Forno

This recipe provides a lighter, healthier alternative to the usual beef-filled, béchamel-coated version.

Serves 4–6

1 pound boned chicken breast, skinned and cooked	squeeze of lemon juice
8 ounces mushrooms	12–18 cannelloni tubes
2 garlic cloves, crushed	1 jar of tomato sauce
2 tablespoons chopped fresh parsley	scant ¾ cup freshly grated Parmesan cheese
1 tablespoon chopped fresh tarragon	salt and ground black pepper
1 egg, beaten	fresh parsley sprig, to garnish

1 Preheat the oven to 400°F. Place the chicken in a food processor and blend until finely minced. Transfer to a bowl and set aside.

2 Place the mushrooms, garlic, parsley and tarragon in the food processor and blend until finely ground. Beat the mushroom mixture into the chicken with the egg, salt and pepper and lemon juice to taste.

3 Bring a saucepan of salted water to a boil and cook the cannelloni according to the instructions on the package. Drain well on a clean dish towel.

4 Place the filling in an icing bag fitted with a large plain nozzle. Use this to fill each tube of cannelloni.

5 Lay the filled cannelloni tightly together in a single layer in a buttered shallow dish. Spoon on the tomato sauce and sprinkle with Parmesan cheese. Bake in the oven for 30 minutes or until brown and bubbling. Serve garnished with a sprig of parsley.

Alfredo's Noodles

A classic from Rome, this dish is simply pasta tossed with heavy cream, butter and freshly grated Parmesan cheese.

Serves 4

2 tablespoons butter	salt and ground black pepper
⅔ cup heavy cream, plus 4 tablespoons extra	scant ¾ cup freshly grated Parmesan cheese, plus extra to serve
1 pound fettuccine	
pinch of freshly grated nutmeg	

1 Place the butter and ⅔ cup cream in a heavy saucepan, bring to a boil and simmer for 1 minute until slightly thickened.

2 Bring a saucepan of salted water to a boil and cook the fettuccine according to the instructions on the package, but for about 2 minutes' less time. The pasta should still be a little firm or *al dente*.

3 Drain the pasta very thoroughly and turn into the pan with the cream sauce.

4 Place the pan on the heat and turn the pasta in the sauce to coat it evenly.

5 Add the remaining cream, the cheese, salt and pepper to taste and a little grated nutmeg. Toss until well coated and heated through. Serve immediately with some extra grated Parmesan cheese.

Cook's Tip
Popular additions to this recipe are fresh or frozen peas, and thin strips of ham if you are not catering for vegetarians.

Onion and Gorgonzola Pizzettes

Serves 4

1 quantity Basic Pizza
   Dough (see below)
2 tablespoons garlic oil
2 small red onions
5 ounces Gorgonzola

2 garlic cloves
2 teaspoons chopped fresh
   sage
pinch of black pepper

Preheat the oven to 425°F. Divide the dough into eight pieces and roll out each one on a lightly floured surface to a small oval about ¼-inch thick. Space well apart on two greased baking sheets and prick with a fork. Brush the bases well with 1 tablespoon of the garlic oil. Halve, then slice the onions into thin wedges. Scatter over the pizza bases. Remove the rind from the Gorgonzola. Cut the cheese into small cubes, then scatter it on the onions. Cut the garlic lengthwise into thin strips and sprinkle on, along with the sage. Drizzle the remaining oil on top and grind on plenty of pepper. Bake for 10–15 minutes until crisp and golden. Serve immediately.

Basic Pizza Dough

Makes one 10–12 inch round pizza base

1½ cups flour
¼ teaspoon salt
1 teaspoon rapid-rise
   dried yeast

½–¾ cup lukewarm
   water
1 tablespoon olive oil

Sift the flour and salt into a large mixing bowl and stir in the yeast. Make a well in the center; pour in the water and oil. Mix to a soft dough. Knead the dough on a lightly floured board for 10 minutes until smooth and elastic. Place in a greased bowl, cover with plastic wrap and leave until doubled in size – about 1 hour. Turn out on to a lightly floured surface, knead gently for 2–3 minutes and use as required.

Feta and Roasted Garlic Pizza

This is a pizza for garlic lovers. Mash down the cloves as you eat – they should be soft and sweet-tasting.

Serves 4

1 garlic bulb, unpeeled
3 tablespoons olive oil
1 red bell pepper, seeded
   and quartered
1 yellow bell pepper,
   seeded and quartered
2 plum tomatoes

1 batch Basic Pizza
   Dough (see below left)
1½ cups feta, crumbled
pinch of black pepper
1–2 tablespoons chopped
   fresh oregano, to
   garnish

1 Preheat the oven to 425°F. Break the garlic into cloves, discarding the outer papery layers. Toss in 1 tablespoon of the olive oil.

2 Place the peppers skin-side up on a baking sheet and broil, turning them until the skins are evenly charred. Place in a covered bowl for 10 minutes, then peel off the skins. Cut the flesh into strips.

3 Make a slash in the skin of each tomato, then put them in a bowl and pour over boiling water. Leave for 30 seconds, then plunge into cold water. Peel, seed and coarsely chop the flesh. Divide the pizza dough into four pieces and roll out each one on a lightly floured surface to an equal-sized circle of about 5 inches diameter.

4 Space the dough circles well apart on two greased baking sheets, then push up the dough edges to form a thin rim. Brush the dough circles with half the remaining oil and scatter with the chopped tomatoes. Top with the peppers, crumbled feta cheese and garlic cloves. Drizzle on the remaining oil and season to taste with pepper. Bake in the oven for 15–20 minutes until crisp and golden. Garnish with chopped oregano; serve immediately.

Mussel and Leek Pizzettes

Serve these subtly flavored seafood pizzettes with a crisp green salad for a light lunch.

Serves 4

1 pound live mussels
½ cup dry white wine
1 batch Basic Pizza
  Dough (see page 158)
1 tablespoon olive oil

2 ounces Gruyère cheese
2 ounces mozzarella
2 small leeks
salt and ground black
  pepper

1 Preheat the oven to 425°F. Place the mussels in a bowl of cold water to soak, and scrub well. Remove the beards and discard any mussels that are open.

2 Place the mussels in a saucepan. Pour over the dry white wine, cover with a tight-fitting lid and cook over high heat, shaking the pan occasionally, for 5–10 minutes until the mussels have opened.

3 Drain off the cooking liquid. Remove the mussels from their shells, discarding any that remain closed. Let cool.

4 Divide the dough into four pieces and roll out each one on a lightly floured surface to a 5-inch circle. Space well apart on two greased baking sheets, then push up the dough edges to form a thin rim. Brush the pizza bases with the oil. Grate the cheeses and sprinkle half evenly over the bases.

5 Thinly slice the leeks, then scatter on the cheese. Bake for 10 minutes, then remove from the oven.

6 Arrange the mussels on top. Season with salt and pepper and sprinkle with the remaining cheese. Bake for another 5–10 minutes until crisp and golden. Serve immediately.

Cook's Tip
Frozen or canned mussels can also be used but will give a different flavor and texture to these pizzettes.

Wild Mushroom Pizzettes

Fresh wild mushrooms add a distinctive flavor to these pizzettes, which make an ideal starter.

Serves 4

3 tablespoons olive oil
12 ounces fresh mixed
  wild mushrooms,
  washed and sliced
2 shallots, chopped
2 garlic cloves, finely
  chopped
2 tablespoons chopped
  fresh mixed thyme and
  Italian parsley

1 batch Basic Pizza
  Dough (see page 158)
generous ¼ cup grated
  Gruyère cheese
2 tablespoons freshly
  grated Parmesan
salt and ground black
  pepper

1 Preheat the oven to 425°F. Heat 2 tablespoons of the oil in a frying pan and fry the mushrooms, shallots and garlic over medium heat, stirring occasionally, until all the juice has evaporated.

2 Stir in half the herbs and seasoning, then set aside to cool.

3 Divide the dough into four pieces and roll out each one on a lightly floured surface to a 5-inch circle. Place well apart on two greased baking sheets, then push up the dough edges to form a thin rim. Brush the pizza bases with the remaining oil and top with the wild mushroom mixture.

4 Mix together the Gruyère and Parmesan, then sprinkle on. Bake for 15–20 minutes until crisp and golden. Remove from the oven and scatter with the remaining herbs to serve.

Cook's Tip
If you cannot find wild mushrooms, a mixture of cultivated mushrooms, such as shiitake, oyster and chestnut, would do just as well.

Ham, Pepper and Mozzarella Pizzas

Succulent roasted peppers, salty prosciutto and creamy mozzarella make a delicious topping for these pizzas.

Serves 2

4 thick slices ciabatta
    bread
1 red bell pepper, roasted
    and peeled
1 yellow bell pepper,
    roasted and peeled

4 slices prosciutto, cut
    into thick strips
3 ounces mozzarella
pinch of black pepper
tiny fresh basil leaves, to
    garnish

1 Lightly toast the slices of ciabatta bread on both sides until they are golden.

2 Cut the roast peppers into thick strips and arrange on the toasted bread with the prosciutto ham.

3 Thinly slice the mozzarella and arrange on top. Grind on plenty of pepper. Place under a hot broiler for 2–3 minutes until the cheese is bubbling.

4 Arrange the basil leaves on top and serve immediately.

Fruity French Bread Pizza

This recipe uses French bread as a base instead of the more usual pizza dough, for a change.

Serves 4

2 small baguettes
1 jar ready-made tomato
    sauce or pizza topping
3 ounces sliced cooked
    ham
4 rings canned pineapple,
    drained and chopped

½ small green bell pepper,
    seeded and cut into
    thin strips
3 ounces mature Cheddar
    cheese
salt and ground black
    pepper

1 Preheat the oven to 400°F. Cut the baguettes in half lengthwise and toast the outsides under a broiler until crisp and golden.

2 Spread the tomato sauce or pizza topping on the toasted baguette halves.

3 Cut the ham into strips and arrange on the baguettes with the pineapple and pepper. Season with salt and pepper.

4 Grate the Cheddar and sprinkle on top. Bake for 15–20 minutes until crisp and golden. Serve immediately.

Cook's Tip
These pizzas may be broiled instead of baked in the oven. Cook them for the same length of time under a moderate heat but check that they do not burn.

Marinara Pizza

The combination of garlic, good-quality olive oil and oregano gives this pizza an unmistakably Italian flavor.

Serves 2–3

4 tablespoons olive oil
1½ pounds plum
    tomatoes, peeled,
    seeded and chopped
1 pizza base, 10–12
    inches diameter
    (see page 158)

4 garlic cloves, cut into
    slivers
1 tablespoon chopped
    fresh oregano
salt and ground black
    pepper

1 Preheat the oven to 425°F. In a saucepan, heat 2 tablespoons of the oil. Add the tomatoes and cook, stirring frequently, for about 5 minutes until soft.

2 Place the tomatoes in a metal strainer and allow them to drain for about 5 minutes.

3 Transfer the tomatoes to a food processor or blender and purée until smooth.

4 Brush the pizza base with half the remaining oil. Spoon on the tomatoes and sprinkle with garlic and oregano. Drizzle on the remaining oil and season to taste. Bake for 15–20 minutes until crisp and golden. Serve immediately.

Cook's Tip
Ready-made pizza bases are available from most supermarkets and come in a range of sizes. It is useful to keep a few in the freezer.

Four-Cheese Pizza

Rich and cheesy, these individual pizzas are quick to make, and the aroma of melting cheese is irresistible.

Serves 4

1 batch Basic Pizza
    Dough (see page 158)
1 tablespoon garlic oil
½ small red onion, very
    thinly sliced
2 ounces dolcelatte
2 ounces mozzarella

½ cup grated Gruyère
2 tablespoons freshly
    grated Parmesan
1 tablespoon chopped
    fresh thyme
pinch of black pepper

1 Preheat the oven to 425°F. Divide the dough into four pieces and roll out each one on a lightly floured surface into a 5-inch circle. Space well apart on two greased baking sheets, then push up the dough edges to make a thin rim. Brush with garlic oil and top with the red onion.

2 Dice the dolcelatte and mozzarella and scatter over the bases. Mix together the Gruyère, Parmesan and thyme and sprinkle them on.

3 Grind on plenty of pepper. Bake for 15–20 minutes until crisp and golden and the cheeses are bubbling. Serve hot.

Pizza with Fresh Vegetables

This pizza can be made with any vegetable combination. Blanch or sauté the vegetables before baking them.

Serves 4

14 ounces peeled plum
    tomatoes, weighed
    whole (or canned
    without their juice)
2 broccoli spears
8 ounces fresh asparagus
2 small zucchini
5 tablespoons olive oil
½ cup shelled peas, fresh
    or frozen
4 scallions, sliced

1 batch Basic Pizza
    Dough (see page 158)
generous ½ cup diced
    mozzarella cheese
10 fresh basil leaves, torn
    into pieces
2 garlic cloves, finely
    chopped
salt and ground black
    pepper

1 Preheat the oven to 475°F for at least 20 minutes before baking the pizza. Strain the tomatoes through the medium holes of a food mill placed over a bowl, scraping in all the pulp.

2 Peel the broccoli stems and asparagus, and blanch with the zucchini in a large saucepan of boiling unsalted water for 4–5 minutes. Drain and cut into bite-size pieces.

3 Heat 2 tablespoons of the olive oil in a small saucepan. Stir in the peas and scallions, and cook for 5–6 minutes, stirring frequently. Remove from the heat.

4 Roll out the pizza dough to a 10-inch circle and place on a greased baking sheet. Spread the puréed tomatoes onto the dough, leaving the rim uncovered. Add all the other vegetables, spreading them evenly over the tomatoes.

5 Sprinkle with the mozzarella, basil, garlic, salt and pepper and remaining olive oil. Immediately place the pizza in the oven. Bake for about 20 minutes, or until the crust is golden brown and the cheese has melted.

Four Seasons Pizza

The topping on this pizza is divided into four quarters, one for each "season", creating a colorful effect.

Serves 4

1 pound peeled plum
    tomatoes, weighed
    whole (or canned
    without their juice)
5 tablespoons olive oil
4 ounces mushrooms,
    thinly sliced
1 garlic clove, finely
    chopped
1 batch Basic Pizza
    Dough (see page 158)
scant 2½ cups diced
    mozzarella

4 thin slices of ham, cut
    into 2-inch squares
32 black olives, pitted
    and halved
8 artichoke hearts,
    preserved in oil,
    drained and cut in
    half
1 teaspoon oregano
    leaves, fresh or dried
salt and ground black
    pepper

1 Preheat the oven to 475°F for at least 20 minutes before baking the pizza. Strain the tomatoes through the medium holes of a food mill placed over a bowl, scraping in all the pulp.

2 Heat 2 tablespoons of the oil in a saucepan and lightly sauté the mushrooms. Stir in the garlic and set aside.

3 Roll out the pizza dough to a 10-inch circle and place on a greased baking sheet. Spread the puréed tomatoes on the prepared pizza dough, leaving the rim uncovered. Sprinkle evenly with the mozzarella. Spread the mushrooms on one quarter of the pizza.

4 Arrange the ham on another quarter, and the olives and artichoke hearts on the two remaining quarters. Sprinkle with oregano, salt and pepper, and the remaining olive oil. Immediately place the pizza in the oven. Bake for about 15–20 minutes, or until the crust is golden brown and the topping is bubbling.

Florentine Pizza

Spinach is the star ingredient of this pizza. A grating of nutmeg heightens its flavor.

Serves 2–3

1½ cups fresh spinach	pinch of freshly grated
3 tablespoons olive oil	nutmeg
1 small red onion, thinly	5 ounces mozzarella
sliced	1 egg
1 pizza base, 10–12	¼ cup grated Gruyère
inches in diameter	cheese
(see page 158)	
1 jar ready-made tomato	
sauce or pizza topping	

1 Preheat the oven to 425°F. Remove the stalks from the spinach and wash the leaves in plenty of cold water. Drain well and pat dry with paper towels.

2 Heat 1 tablespoon of the oil in a large frying pan and fry the onion until softened. Add the spinach and continue to fry until just wilted. Drain off any excess liquid.

3 Brush the pizza base with half the remaining oil. Spread on the tomato sauce or pizza topping, then top with the spinach mixture. Grate on some nutmeg.

4 Thinly slice the mozzarella and arrange over the spinach. Drizzle on the remaining oil. Bake for 10 minutes, then remove from the oven.

5 Make a small well in the center of the pizza and drop the egg into the hole.

6 Sprinkle on the Gruyère and return to the oven for another 5–10 minutes until crisp and golden.

Chili Beef Pizza

Minced beef and red kidney beans combined with oregano, cumin and chilies give this pizza a Mexican character.

Serves 4

2 tablespoons olive oil	1 jar ready-made tomato
1 red onion, finely	sauce or pizza topping
chopped	1 tablespoon chopped
1 garlic clove, crushed	fresh oregano
½ red pepper, seeded and	½ cup grated mozzarella
finely chopped	¾ cup grated oak-smoked
6 ounces lean ground	Cheddar
beef	1 pizza base, 10-12
½ teaspoon ground	inches in diameter
cumin	(see page 158)
2 fresh red chilies, seeded	salt and ground black
and chopped	pepper
scant ½ cup (drained	
weight) canned red	
kidney beans, rinsed	

1 Preheat the oven to 425°F. Heat 1 tablespoon of the oil in a frying pan and gently fry the onion, garlic and pepper until soft. Increase the heat, add the beef, and brown well, stirring constantly.

2 Add the cumin and chilies and continue to cook, stirring, for about 5 minutes. Add the beans and seasoning.

3 Spread the tomato sauce on the pizza base.

4 Spoon on the beef mixture, then scatter on the oregano. Then bake.

Tuna, Anchovy and Caper Pizza

This pizza makes a substantial supper dish for two to three people when accompanied by a simple salad.

Serves 2–3
For the pizza dough
1 cup self-rising flour
1 cup self-rising whole
    wheat flour
pinch of salt
4 tablespoons butter,
    diced
⅔ cup milk

For the topping
2 tablespoons olive oil
1 jar ready-made tomato
    sauce or pizza topping

1 small red onion
7-ounce can tuna,
    drained
1 tablespoon capers
12 black olives, pitted
3 tablespoons freshly
    grated Parmesan
    cheese
2-ounce can anchovy
    fillets, drained and
    halved lengthwise
ground black pepper

1 Place the flour and salt in a bowl and rub in the butter until the mixture resembles fine bread crumbs. Add the milk and mix to a soft dough with a wooden spoon. Knead on a lightly floured surface until smooth.

2 Preheat the oven to 425°F. Roll out the dough on a lightly floured surface to a 10-inch circle. Place on a greased baking sheet and brush with 4 tablespoons of the oil. Spread the tomato sauce or pizza topping evenly over the dough, leaving the edge uncovered.

3 Cut the onion into thin wedges and arrange on top. Roughly flake the tuna with a fork and scatter on the onion. Sprinkle with the capers, black olives and Parmesan cheese. Place the anchovy fillets on the top of the pizza in a criss-cross pattern. Drizzle on the remaining oil, then grind on plenty of pepper. Bake for 15–20 minutes until crisp and golden. Serve immediately.

Salmon and Avocado Pizza

Smoked and fresh salmon make a delicious pizza topping when mixed with avocado.

Serves 3–4
5 ounces salmon fillet
½ cup dry white wine
1 pizza base, 10–12
    inches in diameter (see
    page 158)
1 tablespoon olive oil
14-ounce can chopped
    tomatoes, drained well
scant 1 cup grated
    mozzarella
1 small avocado

2 teaspoons lemon juice
2 tablespoons crème
    fraîche
3 ounces smoked salmon,
    cut into strips
1 tablespoon capers
2 tablespoons chopped
    fresh chives, to
    garnish
ground black pepper

1 Preheat the oven to 425°F. Place the salmon fillet in a frying pan, pour on the wine and season with pepper. Bring slowly to a boil over a gentle heat, remove from the heat, cover with a tight-fitting lid and cool. (The fish will cook in the cooling liquid.) Skin and flake the salmon into small pieces, removing any bones.

2 Brush the pizza base with the oil and spread the drained tomatoes on the top. Sprinkle on a scant ½ cup of mozzarella. Bake for 10 minutes, then remove from the oven.

3 Meanwhile, halve, pit and peel the avocado. Dice the flesh and toss carefully in the lemon juice.

4 Dot teaspoonfuls of the crème fraîche over the pizza base.

5 Arrange the fresh and smoked salmon, avocado, capers and remaining mozzarella on top. Season to taste with pepper. Bake for 5–10 minutes until crisp and golden.

6 Sprinkle on the chives and serve immediately.

Mushroom and Pancetta Pizzas

Use any type and combination of mushrooms you like for these simple yet tasty individual pizzas.

Serves 4

1 batch Basic Pizza Dough (see page 158)	3 ounces pancetta, coarsely chopped
4 tablespoons olive oil	1 tablespoon chopped fresh oregano
2 garlic cloves, crushed	3 tablespoons freshly grated Parmesan cheese
8 ounces fresh mixed ceps and chestnut mushrooms, coarsely chopped	salt and ground black pepper

1 Preheat the oven to 425°F. Divide the dough into four pieces and roll out each one on a lightly floured surface to a 5-inch circle. Place far apart on two greased baking sheets.

2 Heat 2 tablespoons of the olive oil in a frying pan and fry the garlic and mushrooms gently until the mushrooms are tender and the juices have evaporated. Season to taste with salt and pepper, then cool.

3 Brush the pizza bases with 1 tablespoon oil, then spoon on the mushrooms. Scatter with the pancetta and oregano. Sprinkle with Parmesan and drizzle on the remaining oil. Bake for 10–15 minutes, until crisp. Serve immediately.

Cook's Tip
Pancetta is available in larger supermarkets and Italian delicatessens. If you cannot find it, use thickly sliced fried bacon instead.

Pepperoni Pizza

Mixed peppers, mozzarella cheese and pepperoni make a delicious topping for this luxurious pizza.

Serves 4
For the sauce

2 tablespoons olive oil	
1 onion, finely chopped	
1 garlic clove, crushed	
14-ounce can chopped tomatoes with herbs	
1 tablespoon tomato paste	

For the topping

½ each red, yellow and green bell pepper, sliced into rings
5 ounces mozzarella cheese, sliced
3 ounces pepperoni sausage, thinly sliced
8 black olives, pitted
3 sun-dried tomatoes, chopped
½ teaspoon dried oregano
olive oil, for drizzling

For the pizza base
2½ cups all-purpose flour
½ teaspoon salt
1 teaspoon rapid-rise dried yeast
2 tablespoons olive oil

1 For the sauce, fry the onions and garlic in the oil until softened. Add the tomatoes and tomato paste. Boil rapidly for 5 minutes until reduced slightly. Let cool.

2 To make the pizza base, sift the flour and salt into a bowl. Sprinkle on the yeast and make a well in the center. Pour in ¾ cup warm water and the olive oil. Mix to a soft dough. Knead the dough on a lightly floured surface for about 5–10 minutes, until smooth. Roll out to a 10-inch round, press up the edges slightly and place on a greased baking sheet.

3 Spread on the tomato sauce and top with the peppers, mozzarella, pepperoni, olives and tomatoes. Sprinkle with the oregano and drizzle with olive oil. Cover loosely and leave in a warm place for 30 minutes. Meanwhile, preheat the oven to 425°F. Bake for 25–30 minutes then serve.

Farmhouse Pizza

This is the ultimate party pizza. Served cut into fingers, it is ideal for a large and hungry gathering.

Serves 8

6 tablespoons olive oil
8 ounces button
  mushrooms, sliced
2 batches Basic Pizza
  Dough (see page 158)
1 jar ready-made tomato
  sauce or pizza topping
10 ounces mozzarella
  cheese, thinly sliced
4 ounces wafer-thin
  smoked ham slices

6 bottled artichoke hearts
  in oil, drained and
  sliced
2-ounce can anchovy
  fillets, drained and
  halved lengthwise
10 black olives, pitted
  and halved
2 tablespoons chopped
  fresh oregano
3 tablespoons grated
  Parmesan cheese
ground black pepper

1 Preheat the oven to 425°F. In a large frying pan, heat 2 tablespoons of the oil. Gently fry the mushrooms for 5 minutes until all the juices have evaporated. Remove from the heat and allow to cool.

2 Roll out the dough on a lightly floured surface to make a 12 x 10-inch rectangle. Transfer to a greased baking sheet, then push up the dough edges to form a thin rim. Brush with 2 tablespoons of the oil.

3 Spread the tomato sauce or pizza topping on the dough, then arrange the sliced mozzarella over the sauce.

4 Scrunch up the ham and arrange on top with the artichoke hearts, mushrooms and anchovies.

5 Dot with the olives, then sprinkle with the oregano and Parmesan. Drizzle with the remaining oil and season to taste with pepper. Bake for about 25 minutes until crisp and golden. Serve immediately.

Crab and Parmesan Calzonelli

These miniature calzone owe their popularity to their impressive presentation.

Makes 10 – 12

1 batch Basic Pizza
  Dough (see page 158)
4 ounces mixed prepared
  crabmeat, defrosted if
  frozen
1 tablespoon heavy cream
2 tablespoons freshly
  grated Parmesan

2 tablespoons chopped
  fresh parsley
1 garlic clove, crushed
salt and ground black
  pepper
fresh parsley sprigs, to
  garnish

1 Preheat the oven to 400°F. Roll out the pizza dough on a lightly floured surface to ⅛-inch thick. Using a 3-inch plain round pastry cutter, stamp out ten to twelve circles of dough.

2 In a bowl, mix together the crabmeat, cream, Parmesan, parsley and garlic, and season to taste with salt and pepper.

3 Spoon a little of the filling onto one half of each circle. Moisten the edges of the dough with water and fold over to enclose the filling.

4 Seal the edges by pressing with a fork. Space well apart on two greased baking sheets. Bake for 10 – 15 minutes until golden. Garnish with parsley sprigs.

Cook's Tip
If you prefer, use shrimp instead of crabmeat. If frozen, make sure they are fully thawed first.

Ham and Mozzarella Calzone

A calzone is a kind of "inside-out" pizza – the dough is on the outside and the filling on the inside.

Serves 2

1 batch Basic Pizza
    Dough (see page 158)
½ cup ricotta cheese
2 tablespoons freshly
    grated Parmesan
1 egg yolk
2 tablespoons chopped
    fresh basil

3 ounces cooked ham,
    finely chopped
3 ounces mozzarella,
    diced
olive oil, for brushing
salt and ground black
    pepper

1 Preheat the oven to 425°F. Divide the dough in half and roll out each piece on a lightly floured surface to a 7-inch circle.

2 In a bowl, mix together the ricotta and Parmesan cheeses, egg yolk, basil and seasoning.

3 Spread the mixture on half of each circle, leaving a 1-inch border, then scatter the ham and mozzarella on top. Moisten the edges with water, then fold over the other half of the dough to enclose the filling.

4 Press the edges firmly together to seal. Place on two greased baking sheets. Brush with oil and make a small hole in the top of each to allow the steam to escape. Bake for 15–20 minutes until golden. Serve immediately.

Cook's Tip
For a vegetarian version, replace the ham with fried mushrooms or chopped cooked spinach.

Eggplant and Shallot Calzone

Eggplant, shallots and sun-dried tomatoes make an unusual filling for calzone.

Serves 2

3 tablespoons olive oil
3 shallots, chopped
4 baby eggplant
1 garlic clove, chopped
2 ounces (drained
    weight) sun-dried
    tomatoes in oil,
    chopped
¼ teaspoon dried red chili
    flakes

2 teaspoons chopped fresh
    thyme
1 batch Basic Pizza
    Dough (see page 158)
generous ½ cup diced
    mozzarella
salt and ground black
    pepper
1–2 tablespoons freshly
    grated Parmesan
    cheese, to serve

1 Preheat the oven to 425°F. Trim the baby eggplant, then dice.

2 Fry the shallots in some oil until soft. Add the eggplant, garlic, sun-dried tomatoes, red chili flakes, thyme and season to taste. Cook for 4–5 minutes, stirring frequently, until the eggplant is beginning to soften.

3 Divide the dough in half and roll out each piece on a lightly floured surface to a 7-inch circle. Spread the eggplant mixture over half of each circle, leaving a 1-inch border, then scatter on the mozzarella.

4 Moisten the edges with water, then fold the other half of the dough over to enclose the filling. Press the edges firmly together to seal. Place on two greased baking sheets.

5 Brush with half the remaining oil and make a small hole in the top of each to allow the steam to escape. Bake for about 15–20 minutes until golden. Remove from the oven and brush with the remaining oil. Sprinkle on the Parmesan and serve the calzone immediately.

Root Vegetable Couscous

Harissa is a very fiery Tunisian chili sauce which can be bought ready-made from Middle-Eastern shops.

Serves 4

2¼ cups couscous
3 tablespoons olive oil
4 baby onions, halved
1½ pounds fresh mixed
    root vegetables such as
    carrots, rutabaga,
    turnip, celery root and
    sweet potatoes, cubed
2 garlic cloves, crushed
pinch of saffron strands
½ teaspoon each ground
    cinnamon and ginger
½ teaspoon ground
    turmeric
1 teaspoon each ground
    cumin and coriander
1 tablespoon tomato paste
1¾ cups hot vegetable
    stock

1 small fennel bulb,
    quartered
1 cup cooked or canned
    chick-peas
½ cup seedless raisins
2 tablespoons chopped
    fresh cilantro
2 tablespoons chopped
    fresh Italian parsley
salt and ground black
    pepper

For the spiced sauce

1 tablespoon olive oil
1 tablespoon lemon juice
1 tablespoon chopped
    fresh cilantro
½–1 teaspoon harissa

1 Put the couscous in a bowl, cover with hot water; drain. Gently fry the onions for 3 minutes, then add the root vegetables and fry for 5 minutes. Add the garlic and spices and cook for 1 minute, stirring. Transfer the vegetable mixture to a large deep saucepan. Stir in the tomato paste, stock, fennel, chick-peas, raisins, chopped cilantro and Italian parsley. Bring to a boil. Put the couscous into a cheesecloth-lined steamer and place this over the vegetable mixture. Cover and simmer for 20 minutes, or until the vegetables are tender.

2 To make the sauce, mix all the ingredients into 1 cup of the vegetable liquid. Spoon the couscous onto a plate and pile the vegetables on top. Serve immediately, handing around the sauce separately.

Risotto with Mushrooms

The addition of wild mushrooms gives a lovely woodland flavor to this risotto.

Serves 3–4

1 ounce dried wild
    mushrooms, preferably
    porcini
6 ounces fresh cultivated
    mushrooms
juice of ½ lemon
6 tablespoons butter
2 tablespoons finely
    chopped fresh parsley
3¾ cups meat or chicken
    stock, preferably
    homemade

2 tablespoons olive oil
1 small onion, finely
    chopped
1½ cups medium-grain
    risotto rice, such as
    arborio
½ cup dry white wine
salt and ground black
    pepper
3 tablespoons freshly
    grated Parmesan
    cheese

1 Place the dried mushrooms in a small bowl with about 1½ cups warm water. Let soak for at least 40 minutes. Rinse the mushrooms. Filter the soaking water through a strainer lined with paper towels, and reserve. Place in a pan with the stock; simmer until needed.

2 Slice the mushrooms. Toss with the lemon juice. Melt a third of the butter in a large frying pan. Stir in the mushrooms and cook until they begin to brown. Stir in the parsley, cook for 30 seconds more, and remove to another dish.

3 Heat another third of the butter with the olive oil in the mushroom pan. Cook the onion until golden. Add the rice and stir for 1–2 minutes. Add all the mushrooms. Pour in the wine, cook until it evaporates. Add the stock until it evaporates; cook the rice until *al dente*, about 20–35 minutes.

4 Remove the risotto pan from the heat. Stir in the remaining butter and the Parmesan. Grind in a little pepper, and taste again for salt; adjust if necessary. Allow the risotto to rest for 3–4 minutes before serving.

Tomato Risotto

Use plum tomatoes in this dish, if possible, for their fresh vibrant flavor and meaty texture.

Serves 4

1½ pounds firm ripe
    tomatoes
4 tablespoons butter
1 onion, finely chopped
5 cups vegetable stock
1¾ cups arborio rice
14-ounce can navy or
    white beans

½ cup finely grated
    Parmesan cheese
salt and ground black
    pepper
10–12 fresh basil leaves,
    shredded, and freshly
    grated Parmesan
    cheese, to serve

1 Halve the tomatoes and scoop out the seeds into a sieve placed over a bowl. Press the seeds with a spoon to extract all the juice. Set aside.

2 Broil the tomatoes skin-side up until the skins are evenly blackened and blistered. Rub off the skins and dice the flesh.

3 Melt the butter in a large frying pan and cook the onion for 5 minutes until beginning to soften. Add the tomatoes, the reserved juice and seasoning, then cook, stirring occasionally, for about 10 minutes. Meanwhile, bring the vegetable stock to a boil in another pan.

4 Add the rice to the tomatoes and stir to coat, then add a ladleful of the stock and stir gently until absorbed. Repeat, adding a ladleful of stock at a time, until all the stock is absorbed and the rice is tender and creamy.

5 Stir in the beans and grated Parmesan and heat through for a few minutes. Just before serving the risotto, sprinkle each portion with shredded basil leaves and shavings of Parmesan.

Grilled Polenta with Peppers

Grilled slices of herb-flavored polenta are topped with yellow and red pepper strips for a delicious, colorful dish.

Serves 4

scant 1 cup polenta
2 tablespoons butter
1–2 tablespoons mixed
    chopped herbs such as
    parsley, thyme and
    sage
melted butter, for
    brushing
4 tablespoons olive oil
1–2 garlic cloves, cut
    into slivers

2 roasted red bell
    peppers, peeled and
    cut into strips
2 roasted yellow bell
    peppers, peeled and
    cut into strips
1 tablespoon balsamic
    vinegar
salt and ground black
    pepper
fresh herb sprigs, to
    garnish

1 Bring 2½ cups salted water to a boil in a heavy saucepan. Trickle in the polenta, beating constantly, then cook gently for 15–20 minutes, stirring occasionally, until the mixture is no longer grainy and comes away from the sides of the pan.

2 Remove the pan from the heat and beat in the butter, herbs and plenty of pepper.

3 Pour the polenta into a small ovenproof bowl, smooth the surface and let stand until cold and firm.

4 Turn out the polenta onto a board and cut into thick slices. Brush the polenta slices with melted butter and broil each side for about 4–5 minutes, until golden brown.

5 Meanwhile, heat the olive oil in a frying pan, add the garlic and peppers and stir-fry for 1–2 minutes. Stir in the balsamic vinegar and seasoning.

6 Spoon the pepper mixture onto the polenta slices and garnish with fresh herb sprigs. Serve hot.

Okra Fried Rice

This spicy rich dish is given a creamy consistency by the natural juices of the sliced okra.

Serves 3–4

2 tablespoons vegetable
  oil
1 tablespoon butter or
  margarine
1 garlic clove, crushed
½ red onion, finely
  chopped
4 ounces okra, topped
  and tailed
2 tablespoons diced green
  and red bell peppers
½ teaspoon dried thyme

2 green chilies, finely
  chopped
½ teaspoon five-spice
  powder
1 vegetable stock cube
2 tablespoons soy sauce
1 tablespoon chopped
  fresh cilantro
2½ cups cooked rice
salt and ground black
  pepper
fresh cilantro sprigs, to
  garnish

1 Heat the oil and butter or margarine in a frying pan or wok and cook the garlic and onion over a moderate heat for 5 minutes until soft.

2 Thinly slice the okra, add to the pan or wok and sauté gently for 6–7 minutes.

3 Add the green and red peppers, thyme, chilies and five-spice powder and cook for 3 minutes, then crumble in the stock cube.

4 Add the soy sauce, cilantro and rice and heat through, stirring well. Season to taste with salt and pepper. Serve hot, garnished with cilantro sprigs.

Cook's Tip
Reduce the amount of chopped green chili you include in this dish, if you wish.

Asparagus and Cheese Risotto

Arborio rice is *the* risotto rice and gives this authentic Italian dish a unique creamy texture.

Serves 4

¼ teaspoon saffron
  strands
3⅔ cups hot chicken stock
2 tablespoons butter
2 tablespoons olive oil
1 large onion, finely
  chopped
2 garlic cloves, finely
  chopped
1¼ cups arborio rice
1¼ cups dry white wine

8 ounces asparagus tips
  (or asparagus cut into
  2-inch pieces), cooked
1 cup finely grated
  Parmesan cheese
salt and ground black
  pepper
fresh Parmesan cheese
  shavings and fresh
  basil sprigs, to garnish
ciabatta bread rolls and
  green salad, to serve

1 Sprinkle the saffron over the stock and allow to infuse for 5 minutes. Heat the butter and oil in a frying pan and fry the onion and garlic for about 6 minutes until softened.

2 Add the rice and stir-fry for 1–2 minutes to coat the grains with the butter and oil. Pour on 1¼ cups of the stock and saffron. Cook gently, stirring frequently, until it is absorbed. Repeat with another 1¼ cups stock. When that is absorbed, add the wine and carry on cooking and stirring until the rice has a creamy consistency.

3 Add the asparagus and remaining stock, and stir until the liquid is absorbed and the rice is tender. Stir in the Parmesan cheese and season to taste with salt and pepper.

4 Spoon the risotto onto warmed plates and garnish with the Parmesan cheese shavings and fresh basil. Serve with hot ciabatta rolls and a crisp green salad, if you wish.

Louisiana Rice

Ground pork and chicken livers with mixed vegetables make a tasty dish that is a meal in itself.

Serves 4

4 tablespoons oil
1 small eggplant, diced
8 ounces ground pork
1 green bell pepper,
    seeded and chopped
2 celery stalks, chopped
1 onion, chopped
1 garlic clove, crushed
1 teaspoon cayenne
    pepper
1 teaspoon paprika
1 teaspoon ground black
    pepper

½ teaspoon salt
1 teaspoon dried thyme
½ teaspoon dried oregano
2 cups chicken stock
8 ounces chicken livers,
    very finely chopped
¼ cup long-grain rice
1 bay leaf
3 tablespoons chopped
    fresh parsley
celery leaves, to garnish

1 Heat the oil in a frying pan until really hot, then stir-fry the eggplant for about 5 minutes. Add the pork and cook for about 6–8 minutes, until browned, using a wooden spoon to break up any lumps.

2 Add the pepper, celery, onion, garlic, cayenne pepper, paprika, pepper, salt, thyme and oregano. Cover and cook over high heat for 5–6 minutes, stirring frequently from the bottom to scrape up and distribute the crispy bits of pork.

3 Pour on the chicken stock and stir to clean the bottom of the pan. Cover and cook for 6 minutes over a moderate heat. Stir in the chicken livers, cook for another 2 minutes, then stir in the rice and add the bay leaf.

4 Reduce the heat, cover and simmer for about 6–7 minutes more. Turn off the heat and let stand for 10–15 minutes more until the rice is tender. Remove the bay leaf and stir in the chopped parsley. Serve the rice hot, garnished with the celery leaves.

Indian Pilau Rice

Basmati rice is the most popular choice for Indian dishes, but you could use long-grain rice instead.

Serves 4

1¼ cups basmati rice,
    rinsed well
2 tablespoons oil
1 small onion, finely
    chopped
1 garlic clove, crushed
1 teaspoon fennel seeds
1 tablespoon sesame
    seeds
½ teaspoon ground
    turmeric
1 teaspoon ground cumin

¼ teaspoon salt
2 whole cloves
4 cardamom pods, lightly
    crushed
5 black peppercorns
1¾ cups chicken stock
1 tablespoon ground
    almonds
fresh cilantro sprigs,
    to garnish

1 Soak the rice in water for 30 minutes. Heat the oil in a saucepan, add the onions and garlic, then fry them gently for 5–6 minutes, until softened.

2 Stir in the fennel and sesame seeds, the turmeric, cumin, salt, cloves, cardamom pods and peppercorns and fry for about 1 minute. Drain the rice well, add to the pan and stir-fry for a further 3 minutes.

3 Pour on the chicken stock. Bring to a boil, then cover with a tight-fitting lid, reduce the heat to very low and then simmer gently for 20 minutes, without removing the lid, until all the liquid has been absorbed.

4 Remove from the heat and let stand for 2–3 minutes. Fluff up the rice with a fork and stir in the ground almonds. Garnish with cilantro sprigs.

Chinese Special Fried Rice

This staple of Chinese cuisine consists of a mixture of chicken, shrimp and vegetables with fried rice.

Serves 4

1 cup long-grain white
    rice
3 tablespoons peanut oil
1 garlic clove, crushed
4 scallions, finely
    chopped
1 cup diced cooked
    chicken
1 cup peeled, cooked
    shrimp
½ cup frozen peas

1 egg, beaten with a
    pinch of salt
2 ounces lettuce, finely
    shredded
2 tablespoons light soy
    sauce
pinch of sugar
salt and ground black
    pepper
1 tablespoon chopped,
    roasted cashew nuts,
    to garnish

1 Rinse the rice in warm water to wash away some of the starch. Drain well.

2 Put the rice in a saucepan and add 1 tablespoon of the oil and 1½ cups water. Cover and bring to a boil, stir once, then cover and simmer for 12–15 minutes, until nearly all the water has been absorbed. Turn off the heat and let stand, covered, for 10 minutes. Fluff up with a fork and allow to cool.

3 Heat the remaining oil in a wok or frying pan and stir-fry the garlic and scallions for 30 seconds.

4 Add the chicken, shrimp and peas and stir-fry for about 1–2 minutes, then add the cooked rice and stir-fry for another 2 minutes. Pour in the egg and stir-fry until just set. Stir in the lettuce, soy sauce, sugar and seasoning.

5 Transfer to a warmed serving bowl, sprinkle with the chopped cashew nuts and serve immediately.

Lemon Bulgur Wheat Salad

This Middle-Eastern salad, called *tabbouleh,* is delicious as an accompaniment to broiled meats or fish, or on its own.

Serves 4

1½ cups bulgur
4 scallions, finely
    chopped
5 tablespoons each
    chopped fresh mint
    and parsley
1 tablespoon chopped
    fresh cilantro

2 tomatoes, skinned and
    chopped
juice of 1 lemon
5 tablespoons olive oil
salt and ground black
    pepper
fresh mint sprigs, to
    garnish

1 Place the bulgur in a bowl, pour on enough boiling water to cover and let soak for 20 minutes.

2 After soaking, place the bulgur in a large strainer and drain thoroughly. Transfer to a bowl.

3 Stir in the scallions, herbs, tomatoes, lemon juice, olive oil and seasoning. Mix well and chill in the fridge for about an hour. Garnish with mint.

Cook's Tip
Add some pitted, halved black olives to the salad just before serving, if you wish.

Tanzanian Vegetable Rice

Serve this tasty rice with baked chicken, or a fish dish and a delicious fresh relish – *kachumbali.*

Serves 4

2 cups basmati rice
3 tablespoons oil
1 onion, chopped
3 cups vegetable stock or water
2 garlic cloves, crushed
1 cup corn
½ fresh red or green bell pepper, chopped
1 large carrot, grated

1 Wash the rice in a strainer under cold water, then allow to drain for about 15 minutes.

2 Heat the oil in a large saucepan and fry the onion for a few minutes over moderate heat until just soft.

3 Add the rice and stir-fry for about 10 minutes, taking care to keep stirring all the time so that the rice doesn't stick to the bottom of the pan.

4 Add the stock or water and the garlic and stir well. Bring to a boil and cook over high heat for 5 minutes, then reduce the heat, cover with a tight-fitting lid and cook the rice for 20 minutes.

5 Scatter the corn over the rice, then spread the pepper on top and lastly sprinkle on the grated carrot.

6 Cover tightly and steam over low heat until the rice is cooked, then mix together with a fork and serve immediately.

Rice with Seeds and Spices

A change from plain boiled rice, this spicy dish makes a colorful accompaniment for curries or broiled meats.

Serves 4

1 teaspoon sunflower oil
½ teaspoon ground turmeric
6 cardamom pods, lightly crushed
1 teaspoon coriander seeds, lightly crushed
1 garlic clove, crushed
1 cup basmati rice
1⅔ cups stock
½ cup plain yogurt
1 tablespoon each toasted sunflower seeds and toasted sesame seeds
salt and ground black pepper
fresh cilantro leaves, to garnish

1 Heat the oil in a non-stick frying pan and fry the spices and garlic for about 1 minute, stirring all the time.

2 Add the rice and stock, bring to a boil, then cover and simmer for 15 minutes or until just tender.

3 Stir in the yogurt and the toasted sunflower and sesame seeds. Adjust the seasoning and serve hot, garnished with cilantro leaves.

Cook's Tip
Although basmati rice gives the best texture and flavor, you could substitute ordinary long-grain rice if you prefer.

Lemon and Herb Risotto Cake

This unusual rice dish can be served as a main course with salad, or as a satisfying side dish.

Serves 4
1 small leek, thinly sliced
2½ cups chicken stock
1¼ cups arborio rice
finely grated rind of
    1 lemon
2 tablespoons chopped
    fresh chives

2 tablespoons chopped
    fresh parsley
generous ½ cup grated
    mozzarella cheese
salt and ground black
    pepper
fresh parsley and lemon
    wedges, to garnish

1 Preheat the oven to 400°F. Lightly oil an 8½-inch round springform cake pan.

2 Cook the leek in a large saucepan with 3 tablespoons stock, stirring over moderate heat, to soften. Add the rice and the remaining stock.

3 Bring to a boil. Cover the pan with a tight-fitting lid and simmer gently, stirring occasionally, for about 20 minutes, or until all the liquid is absorbed.

4 Stir in the lemon rind, herbs, cheese and seasoning. Spoon into the pan, cover with foil and bake for 30–35 minutes or until lightly browned. Turn out and serve in slices, garnished with parsley and lemon wedges.

Cook's Tip
This risotto cake is equally delicious served cold, so makes ideal picnic food.

Bulgur and Lentil Pilaf

Bulgur is very easy to cook and can be used in almost any way you would normally use rice, hot or cold.

Serves 4
1 teaspoon olive oil
1 large onion, thinly
    sliced
2 garlic cloves, crushed
1 teaspoon ground
    coriander
1 teaspoon ground cumin
1 teaspoon ground
    turmeric

½ teaspoon ground
    allspice
1¼ cups bulgur
about 3⅔ cups stock or
    water
4 ounces button
    mushrooms, sliced
⅔ cup green lentils
salt, ground black pepper
    and cayenne pepper

1 Heat the oil in a nonstick saucepan and fry the onion, garlic and spices for 1 minute, stirring.

2 Stir in the bulgur and cook, stirring, for about 2 minutes, until lightly browned. Add the stock or water, mushrooms and lentils.

3 Simmer over very gentle heat for about 25–30 minutes, until the bulgur and lentils are tender and all the liquid is absorbed. Add more stock or water, if necessary.

4 Season well with salt, black pepper and cayenne pepper and serve hot.

Cook's Tip
Green lentils can be cooked without presoaking, as they cook quite quickly and keep their shape. However, if you have time, soaking them first will shorten the cooking time slightly.

Minted Couscous Castles

Creole Jambalaya

Couscous, flavored with mint and then molded, makes an unusual accompaniment to a meal.

This version of jambalaya is made with chicken instead of the more traditional ham.

Serves 6

1¼ cups couscous
2 cups boiling stock
1 tablespoon freshly
  squeezed lemon juice
2 tomatoes, diced
2 tablespoon chopped
  fresh mint

oil, for brushing
salt and ground black
  pepper
fresh mint sprigs, to
  garnish

Serves 6

4 chicken thighs, boned,
  skinned and diced
about 1¼ cups chicken
  stock
1 large green bell pepper,
  seeded and sliced
3 celery stalks, sliced
4 scallions, sliced
14-ounce can tomatoes
1 teaspoon ground cumin

1 teaspoon ground
  allspice
½ teaspoon cayenne
  pepper
1 teaspoon dried thyme
1½ cups long-grain rice
scant 2 cups peeled,
  cooked shrimp
salt and ground black
  pepper

1 Place the couscous in a bowl and pour on the boiling stock. Cover the bowl and let stand for 30 minutes, until all the stock is absorbed and the grains are tender.

2 Stir in the lemon juice with the tomatoes and chopped mint. Adjust the seasoning with salt and pepper.

3 Brush the insides of four cups or individual molds with oil. Spoon in the couscous mixture and pack down firmly. Chill in the fridge for several hours.

4 Turn out and serve cold, or alternatively, cover and heat gently in a low oven or microwave, then turn out and serve hot, garnished with mint.

Cook's Tip
Most couscous is sold ready-cooked so can be prepared as above. However, some types require steaming first, so check the instructions on the package.

1 Fry the chicken in a nonstick saucepan without fat, turning occasionally, until golden brown.

2 Add 1 tablespoon stock with the pepper, celery and onions. Cook for a few minutes to soften, then add the tomatoes, spices and thyme.

3 Stir in the rice and remaining stock. Cover closely and cook for about 20 minutes, stirring occasionally, until the rice is tender. Add more stock if necessary.

4 Add the peeled shrimp and heat well. Season to taste and serve with a crisp salad, if you wish.

Red Fried Rice

This vibrant rice dish owes its appeal to the bright colors of red onion, red bell pepper and cherry tomatoes.

Serves 2

¾ cup rice
2 tablespoons peanut oil
1 small red onion, chopped
1 red bell pepper, seeded and chopped
8 ounces cherry tomatoes, halved
2 eggs, beaten
salt and ground black pepper

1 Wash the rice several times under cold running water. Drain well. Bring a large saucepan of water to a boil, add the rice and cook for 10–12 minutes.

2 Meanwhile, heat the oil in a wok until very hot and stir-fry the onion and red pepper for 2–3 minutes. Add the cherry tomatoes and stir-fry for another 2 minutes.

3 Pour in the beaten eggs all at once. Cook for 30 seconds without stirring, then stir to break up the eggs as they set.

4 Drain the cooked rice thoroughly, add to the wok and toss it over the heat with the vegetable and egg mixture for 3 minutes. Season the fried rice with salt and pepper to taste.

Cook's Tip
Use basmati rice for this dish, if possible. Its slightly crunchy texture complements the softness of the egg.

Kedgeree

Popular for breakfast in Victorian England, kedgeree has its origins in *khichri*, an Indian rice and lentil dish.

Serves 4

1¼ pounds smoked haddock
scant ½ cup long-grain rice
2 tablespoons lemon juice
¾ cup single or sour cream
pinch of freshly grated nutmeg
pinch of cayenne pepper
2 hard-boiled eggs, peeled and cut into wedges
4 tablespoons butter, diced
2 tablespoons chopped fresh parsley
salt and ground black pepper
fresh parsley sprigs, to garnish

1 Poach the haddock, just covered by water, for about 10 minutes, until the flesh flakes easily. Lift the fish from the cooking liquid with a draining spoon, then remove any skin and bones. Flake the flesh.

2 Pour the fish cooking liquid into a measuring cup and add water, until it measures 1 cup.

3 Bring the fish cooking liquid to a boil, add the rice, stir, then cover with a tight-fitting lid and simmer for about 15 minutes, until the rice is tender and the liquid absorbed. While the rice is cooking, preheat the oven to 350°F, and butter a baking dish.

4 Remove the rice from the heat and stir in the lemon juice, cream, flaked fish, nutmeg and cayenne. Add the egg wedges to the rice mixture and stir in gently.

5 Turn the rice mixture into the baking dish, dot with butter and bake for about 25 minutes.

6 Stir the chopped parsley into the kedgeree, adjust the seasoning to taste and garnish with fresh parsley sprigs.

Nut Pilaf with Omelet Rolls

This pilaf combines a wonderful mixture of textures – soft fluffy rice with crunchy nuts and omelet rolls.

Serves 2

1 cup basmati rice	2 eggs
1 tablespoon sunflower oil	¼ cup salted peanuts
	1 tablespoon soy sauce
1 small onion, chopped	salt and ground black pepper
1 red bell pepper, finely diced	
1½ cups hot vegetable stock	fresh parsley sprigs, to garnish

1 Wash the rice several times under cold running water. Drain thoroughly. Heat half the oil in a large frying pan and fry the onion and red pepper for 2–3 minutes, then stir in the rice and stock. Bring to a boil and cook for 10 minutes until the rice is tender.

2 Meanwhile, beat the eggs lightly and season to taste with salt and pepper. Heat the remaining oil in a second large frying pan. Pour in the eggs and tilt the pan to cover the bottom thinly. Cook the omelet for 1 minute, then flip it over and cook the other side for 1 minute.

3 Slide the omelet onto a clean board and roll it up tightly. Cut the omelet roll into eight slices.

4 Stir the peanuts and the soy sauce into the pilaf and add pepper to taste. Turn the pilaf into a serving dish, then arrange the omelet rolls on top and garnish with the parsley. Serve immediately.

Cook's Tip
Try salted cashew nuts or toasted flaked almonds in this dish for a change.

Eggplant Pilaf

This hearty dish is made with bulgur, eggplant and pine nuts, subtly flavored with fresh mint.

Serves 2

2 eggplant	1 tablespoon chopped fresh mint
4–6 tablespoons sunflower oil	salt and ground black pepper
1 small onion, finely chopped	
1 cup bulgur	lime and lemon wedges and fresh mint sprigs, to garnish
1¾ cups vegetable stock	
2 tablespoons pine nuts, toasted	

1 Remove the ends of the eggplant. Using a sharp knife, cut the eggplant into neat sticks and then dice into ½-inch pieces.

2 Heat 4 tablespoons of the oil in a large frying pan and sauté the onion for 1 minute.

3 Add the diced eggplant. Cook over high heat, stirring frequently, for about 4 minutes until just tender. Add the remaining oil if needed.

4 Stir in the bulgur, mixing well, then pour in the vegetable stock. Bring to a boil, then lower the heat and simmer for 10 minutes or until all the liquid has evaporated. Season with salt and pepper to taste.

5 Add the pine nuts, stir gently with a wooden spoon, then stir in the mint.

6 Spoon the pilaf onto individual plates and garnish each portion with lime and lemon wedges. Sprinkle with mint sprigs for extra color.

Cabbage with Bacon

In this dish, bacon enhances the flavor of cabbage, making it a delicious vegetable accompaniment.

Serves 2–4
2 tablespoons oil
1 onion, finely chopped
4 ounces bacon, finely chopped

1¼ pounds cabbage, shredded
salt and ground black pepper

1 Heat the oil in a large saucepan and cook the onion and bacon for about 7 minutes, stirring occasionally.

2 Add the cabbage and season with salt and pepper. Stir for a few minutes over moderately high heat until the cabbage begins to shrink in volume.

3 Continue to cook the cabbage, stirring it frequently for 8–10 minutes until tender, but still crisp. (For softer cabbage, cover the pan for part of the cooking.) Serve immediately.

Cook's Tip
This dish is equally delicious if prepared using collard greens instead of cabbage. To make a more substantial dish to serve for lunch or supper, add some chopped button mushrooms and some skinned, seeded and chopped tomatoes.

Braised Red Cabbage

Lightly spiced with a sharp, sweet flavor, this dish goes well with roast pork, duck and game dishes.

Serves 4–6
2 pounds red cabbage
2 onions, chopped
2 tart cooking apples, peeled, cored and grated
1 teaspoon freshly grated nutmeg
¼ teaspoon ground cloves
¼ teaspoon ground cinnamon

1 tablespoon dark brown sugar
3 tablespoons red wine vinegar
2 tablespoons butter or margarine, diced
salt and ground black pepper

1 Preheat the oven to 325°F. Cut off and discard the large white ribs from the outer cabbage leaves using a large sharp knife, then finely shred the cabbage.

2 Layer the shredded cabbage in a large casserole with the onions, apples, spices, sugar and seasoning. Pour on the vinegar and add the diced butter or margarine.

3 Cover the casserole and cook in the oven for about 1½ hours, stirring a couple of times, until the cabbage is very tender. Serve hot.

Cook's Tip
This recipe can be cooked in advance. Bake the cabbage for 1½ hours, then allow to cool. To complete the cooking, bake in the oven at the same temperature for about 30 minutes, stirring occasionally.

Lemon Carrots

The carrots are cooked until just tender in lemon stock which is then thickened to make a light tangy sauce.

Serves 4

2½ cups water
1 pound carrots, thinly
   sliced
bouquet garni
1 tablespoon freshly
   squeezed lemon juice

pinch of freshly grated
   nutmeg
1½ tablespoons butter
1 tablespoon all-purpose
   flour
salt and ground black
   pepper

1 Bring the water to a boil in a large saucepan, then add the carrots, bouquet garni, lemon juice, nutmeg and seasoning and simmer until the carrots are tender. Remove the carrots using a slotted spoon, then keep warm.

2 Boil the cooking liquid hard until it has reduced to about 1¼ cups. Discard the bouquet garni.

3 Mash 1 tablespoon of the butter and all of the flour together, then gradually whisk into the simmering reduced cooking liquid, whisking well after each addition, then simmer for about 3 minutes, until the sauce has thickened.

4 Return the carrots to the pan, heat through in the sauce, then remove from the heat. Stir in the remaining butter and serve immediately.

Ratatouille

Ratatouille may be served hot or cold, as an appetizer, side dish or vegetarian main course.

Serves 4

2 large eggplant, coarsely
   chopped
4 zucchini, coarsely
   chopped
⅔ cup olive oil
2 onions, sliced
2 garlic cloves, chopped
1 large red bell pepper,
   seeded and coarsely
   chopped
2 large yellow bell
   peppers, seeded and
   coarsely chopped

1 fresh rosemary sprig
1 fresh thyme sprig
1 teaspoon coriander
   seeds, crushed
3 plum tomatoes,
   skinned, seeded and
   chopped
8 basil leaves, coarsely
   torn
salt and ground black
   pepper
fresh parsley or basil
   sprigs, to garnish

1 Place the eggplant in a colander, sprinkle with salt and place a plate with a weight on top to extract the bitter juice. Leave for 30 minutes.

2 Heat the olive oil in a large saucepan and gently fry the onions for about 6–7 minutes until just softened. Add the garlic and cook for 2 minutes more.

3 Rinse, drain and pat dry the eggplant with paper towels. Add to the pan with the peppers, increase the heat and sauté until the peppers are just turning brown.

4 Add the herbs and coriander seeds, then cover the pan and cook gently for about 40 minutes.

5 Add the tomatoes and season to taste with salt and pepper. Cook gently for another 10 minutes, until the vegetables are soft but not too mushy. Remove the sprigs of herbs. Stir in the torn basil leaves and check the seasoning. Let cool slightly and serve warm or cold, garnished with sprigs of parsley or basil.

Parsnips with Almonds

Parsnips have an affinity with most nuts, so you could use walnuts or hazelnuts instead of the almonds.

Serves 4
1 pound small parsnips
scant 3 tablespoons
    butter
¼ cup flaked almonds
1 tablespoon light brown
    sugar

pinch of ground mixed
    spice
1 tablespoon lemon juice
salt and ground black
    pepper
chopped fresh chervil or
    parsley, to garnish

1 Cook the parsnips in boiling salted water until almost tender. Drain well. When the parsnips are cool enough to handle, cut each in half across its width, then quarter these halves lengthwise.

2 Heat the butter in a frying pan and cook the parsnips and almonds gently, stirring and turning carefully until they are lightly flecked with brown.

3 Mix together the sugar and mixed spice, sprinkle on the parsnips and stir to mix, then trickle over the lemon juice. Season to taste with salt and pepper and heat for 1 minute. Serve sprinkled with chopped fresh chervil or parsley.

Turnips with Orange

Sprinkle toasted nuts such as flaked almonds or chopped walnuts over the turnips to add contrast.

Serves 4
4 tablespoons butter
1 tablespoon oil
1 small shallot, finely
    chopped
1 pound small turnips,
    quartered

1¼ cups freshly squeezed
    orange juice
salt and ground black
    pepper

1 Heat the butter and oil in a saucepan and cook the shallot gently, stirring occasionally, until soft but not colored.

2 Add the turnips to the shallot and heat. Shake the pan frequently until the turnips start to absorb the butter and oil.

3 Pour the orange juice onto the turnips, then simmer gently for about 30 minutes, until the turnips are tender and the orange juice is reduced to a buttery sauce. Season with salt and pepper, if required, and serve hot.

Red Cabbage with Pears and Nuts

A sweet and sour, spicy red cabbage dish, with the added crunch of pears and walnuts.

Serves 6

1 tablespoon walnut oil
1 onion, sliced
2 whole star anise
1 teaspoon ground cinnamon
pinch of ground cloves
1 pound red cabbage, finely shredded
2 tablespoons dark brown sugar
3 tablespoons red wine vinegar
1¼ cup red wine
scant ¾ cup port
2 pears, cut into ½-inch cubes
½ cup raisins
salt and ground black pepper
½ cup walnut halves

1 Heat the oil in a large pan. Add the onion and cook gently for about 5 minutes until softened.

2 Add the star anise, cinnamon, cloves and cabbage and cook for about 3 minutes more.

3 Stir in the sugar, vinegar, red wine and port. Cover the pan and simmer gently for 10 minutes, stirring occasionally.

4 Stir in the cubed pears and raisins and cook for another 10 minutes or until the cabbage is tender. Season to taste. Mix in the walnut halves and serve.

Swiss Soufflé Potatoes

Baked potatoes are great for cold weather eating, and are both economical and satisfying.

Serves 4

4 baking potatoes
scant 1 cup grated Gruyère cheese
½ cup herb-flavored butter
4 tablespoons heavy cream
2 eggs, separated
salt and ground black pepper

1 Preheat the oven to 425°F. Scrub the potatoes, then prick them all over with a fork. Bake for about 1–1½ hours until tender. Remove them from the oven and reduce the temperature to 350°F.

2 Cut each potato in half and scoop out the insides into a bowl. Return the potato shells to the oven to crisp them while making the filling.

3 Mash the potato using a fork then add the Gruyère, herb-flavored butter, cream and egg yolks, and season to taste with salt and pepper. Beat well until smooth.

4 Whisk the egg whites in a separate bowl until stiff peaks form, then fold into the potato mixture.

5 Pile the mixture back into the potato shells and bake for 20–25 minutes, until risen and golden brown.

Cook's Tip
Choose a floury variety of potato for this dish for the best results.

Thai Vegetables with Noodles

This dish makes a delicious vegetarian supper on its own, or it could be served as an accompaniment.

Serves 4

4 cups egg noodles
1 tablespoon sesame oil
3 tablespoons peanut oil
2 garlic cloves, thinly
   sliced
1-inch piece fresh ginger,
   finely chopped
2 fresh red chilies, seeded
   and sliced
1 cup broccoli florets
4 ounces baby corn

6 ounces shiitake or
   oyster mushrooms,
   sliced
1 bunch scallions, sliced
4 ounces pak choi or
   Chinese cabbage,
   shredded
generous 1 cup bean
   sprouts
1–2 tablespoons dark
   soy sauce
salt and ground black
   pepper

1 Bring a saucepan of salted water to the boil and cook the egg noodles according to the instructions on the packet. Drain well and toss in the sesame oil. Set aside.

2 Heat the peanut oil in a wok or large frying pan and stir-fry the garlic and ginger for 1 minute. Add the chilies, broccoli, baby corn and mushrooms and stir-fry for another 2 minutes.

3 Add the scallions, shredded pak choi or Chinese cabbage and bean sprouts and stir-fry for another 2 minutes.

4 Toss in the drained noodles with the soy sauce and pepper.

5 Continue to cook over high heat, stirring, for 2–3 minutes more, until the ingredients are mixed well and warmed through. Serve immediately.

Cauliflower with Three Cheeses

The mingled flavors of three cheeses give a new twist to cauliflower cheese.

Serves 4

4 baby cauliflowers
1 cup light cream
3 ounces dolcelatte
   cheese, diced
3 ounces mozzarella
   cheese, diced

3 tablespoons freshly
   grated Parmesan
   cheese
pinch of freshly grated
   nutmeg
ground black pepper
toasted bread crumbs, to
   garnish

1 Cook the cauliflowers in a large saucepan of boiling salted water for 8–10 minutes, until just tender.

2 Meanwhile, put the cream into a small pan with the cheeses. Heat gently until the cheeses have melted, stirring occasionally. Season to taste with nutmeg and pepper.

3 When the cauliflowers are cooked, drain them thoroughly and place one on each of four warmed plates.

4 Spoon a little of the cheese sauce over each cauliflower and sprinkle each with a few of the toasted bread crumbs. Serve at once.

Cook's Tip
For a more economical dish or if baby cauliflowers are not available, use one large cauliflower instead. Cut it into quarters with a large sharp knife and remove the central core.

Potato Gnocchi with Sauce

These delicate potato dumplings are dressed with a tasty creamy hazelnut sauce.

Serves 4

1½ pounds large potatoes
1 cup all-purpose flour

For the hazelnut sauce
½ cup hazelnuts, roasted
1 garlic clove, coarsely
 chopped
½ teaspoon grated lemon
 rind

½ teaspoon lemon juice
2 tablespoons sunflower
 oil
¾ cup low-fat ricotta
 cheese
salt and ground black
 pepper

1 Place 2½ ounces of the hazelnuts in a blender with the garlic, grated lemon rind and juice. Blend until coarsely chopped. Gradually add the oil and blend until smooth. Spoon into a bowl and mix in the ricotta. Season.

2 Place the potatoes in a pan of cold water. Bring to a boil and cook for 20–25 minutes. Drain well in a colander. When cool, peel and purée the potatoes while still warm.

3 Add the flour a little at a time (you may not need all of the flour, as potatoes vary in texture). Stop adding flour when the mixture is smooth and slightly sticky. Add salt to taste.

4 Roll the mixture out onto a floured board to form a sausage ½-inch in diameter. Cut into ¾-inch pieces. Take one piece at a time and press it onto a floured fork. Roll each piece while pressing it along the prongs and off the fork. Flip onto a floured plate or tray. Continue with the rest of the mixture.

5 To cook, drop about 20–25 pieces at a time into a large pan of boiling water. They will rise to the surface quickly. Cook for about 10–15 seconds, then lift out with a slotted spoon. Heat the sauce carefully and pour over the gnocchi. Chop the remaining hazelnuts and scatter over the sauce.

Winter Vegetable Hot-pot

Use whatever vegetables you have at hand in this richly flavored and substantial one-pot meal.

Serves 4

2 onions, sliced
4 carrots, sliced
1 small rutabaga, sliced
2 parsnips, sliced
3 small turnips, sliced
½ celery root, cut into
 matchsticks
2 leeks, thinly sliced
2 tablespoons mixed
 chopped fresh herbs
 such as parsley and
 thyme

1 garlic clove, chopped
1 bay leaf, crumbled
1¼ cups vegetable stock
1 tablespoon all-purpose
 flour
1½ pounds red-skinned
 potatoes, scrubbed and
 thinly sliced
4 tablespoons butter
salt and ground black
 pepper

1 Preheat the oven to 375°F. Arrange all the vegetables, except the potatoes, in layers in a large casserole with a tight-fitting lid, seasoning them lightly with salt and pepper and sprinkling them with chopped herbs, garlic and crumbled bay leaf as you go.

2 Blend the vegetable stock into the flour and pour on the vegetables. Arrange the potatoes in overlapping layers on top. Dot with butter and cover tightly.

3 Cook in the oven for 1¼ hours, or until the vegetables are tender. Remove the lid from the casserole and cook for another 15–20 minutes until the top layer of potatoes is golden and crisp at the edges. Serve hot.

Cook's Tip
Make sure the root vegetables are cut into even slices so they cook uniformly.

Beans with Tomatoes

Young green beans are very tender and taste lovely with tomatoes and fresh tarragon.

Serves 4

2 cups young green
  beans
3 tablespoons butter
4 ripe tomatoes, peeled
  and chopped

salt and ground black
  pepper
chopped fresh tarragon,
  to garnish

1 Bring a saucepan of water to a boil, add the beans, return to a boil and cook for 3 minutes. Drain well.

2 Heat the butter in a pan, add the tomatoes and beans and season with salt and pepper. Cover the pan with a tight-fitting lid and simmer gently for about 10–15 minutes, until the beans are tender.

3 Pour the beans and tomatoes into a warm serving dish and sprinkle on the chopped tarragon to garnish. Serve hot as an accompaniment to broiled meats, poultry or fish.

Rosemary Roasties

The potatoes are roasted with their skins on, giving them far more flavor than traditional roast potatoes.

Serves 4

2 pounds small red
  potatoes
2 teaspoons walnut or
  sunflower oil

2 tablespoons fresh
  rosemary leaves
salt and paprika

1 Preheat the oven to 475°F. Leave the potatoes whole with the skins on, or if large, cut in half. Place the potatoes in a large saucepan of cold water and bring to boil, then drain immediately.

2 Return the potatoes to the saucepan and drizzle the walnut or sunflower oil over them. Shake the pan to coat the potatoes evenly in the oil.

3 Transfer the potatoes into a shallow roasting pan. Sprinkle with rosemary, salt and paprika. Roast for 30 minutes or until crisp. Served hot, these potatoes are good with roast lamb.

Vegetable Ribbons

This mixed vegetable side dish looks impressive and will delight dinner party guests.

Serves 4

Using a vegetable peeler or sharp knife, cut 3 medium carrots and 3 medium zucchini into thin ribbons. Bring ½ cup chicken stock to a boil, add the carrots. Return the stock to a boil; add the zucchini. Boil rapidly for 2–3 minutes, or until the vegetable ribbons are just tender. Stir in 2 tablespoons chopped fresh parsley, season lightly with salt and ground black pepper, and serve hot.

Zucchini and Tomato Bake

A *tian* is a heavy earthenware dish in which many French vegetable dishes are cooked. This is one example.

Serves 4

3 tablespoons olive oil
1 onion, chopped
1 garlic clove, crushed
3 slices lean bacon, chopped
4 zucchini, grated
2 tomatoes, skinned, seeded and chopped
scant ¾ cup cooked long-grain rice

2 teaspoons chopped fresh thyme
1 tablespoon chopped fresh parsley
4 tablespoons grated Parmesan cheese
2 eggs, lightly beaten
1 tablespoon sour cream
salt and ground black pepper

1 Preheat the oven to 350°F. Grease a shallow baking dish with a little olive oil.

2 Heat the oil in a frying pan and fry the onion and garlic for 5 minutes until softened.

3 Add the bacon and fry for 2 minutes, then stir in the zucchini and fry for 8 minutes more, stirring from time to time and letting some of the liquid evaporate. Remove the pan from the heat.

4 Add the tomatoes, cooked rice, herbs, 2 tablespoons of the Parmesan cheese, the eggs and sour cream, and season to taste with salt and pepper. Mix together well.

5 Spoon the zucchini mixture into the dish and sprinkle on the remaining Parmesan cheese. Bake for 45 minutes, until set and golden. Serve hot.

Cook's Tip
For a dinner party, divide the mixture among four lightly greased individual gratin dishes and bake for about 25 minutes until set and golden.

Spanish Green Beans with Ham

Judias verdes con jamón are green beans cooked with the Spanish raw-cured Serrano ham.

Serves 4

1 pound green beans
3 tablespoons olive oil
1 onion, thinly sliced
2 garlic cloves, finely chopped

3 ounces Serrano ham, chopped
salt and ground black pepper

1 Cook the beans, left whole, in boiling salted water for about 5–6 minutes, until they are just tender but still with a little bit of bite.

2 Meanwhile, heat the oil in a saucepan and fry the onions for 5 minutes, until softened and translucent. Add the garlic and ham and cook for another 1–2 minutes.

3 Drain the beans, then add them to the pan and cook, stirring occasionally, for 2–3 minutes. Season well with salt and pepper and serve hot.

Cook's Tip
Serrano ham is increasingly available in large supermarkets and has the advantage of being cheaper than prosciutto. However, if you cannot find it, use prosciutto or bacon instead.

Sweet Potatoes with Bacon

This sweet potato dish makes a good Thanksgiving offering with a tart and sweet flavor.

Serves 4

2 large sweet potatoes, 1
   pound each, washed
½ cup light brown sugar
2 tablespoons lemon juice
3 tablespoons butter
4 slices lean bacon, cut
   into thin strips

salt and ground black
   pepper
sprig of Italian parsley,
   to garnish

1 Preheat the oven to 375°F and lightly butter a shallow baking dish. Cut the unpeeled sweet potatoes crosswise into four and place the pieces in a pan of boiling water. Cover with a tight-fitting lid and cook until just tender, about 25 minutes.

2 Drain the potatoes and, when cool enough to handle, peel and slice quite thickly. Arrange in a single layer, overlapping, in the prepared dish.

3 Sprinkle on the sugar and lemon juice and dot with butter. Top with the bacon and season with salt and pepper.

4 Bake uncovered for 35–40 minutes, basting once or twice, until the potatoes are tender.

5 Preheat the broiler to high heat. Broil the potatoes for about 2–3 minutes, until they are browned and the bacon crispy. Serve hot, garnished with parsley.

Potatoes Baked with Tomatoes

This simple hearty dish from the south of Italy is best made with fresh tomatoes but canned plum tomatoes will do.

Serves 6

2 large red or yellow
   onions, thinly sliced
2¼ pounds potatoes,
   peeled and thinly
   sliced
1 pound fresh tomatoes
   (or canned, with their
   juice), sliced
6 tablespoons olive oil

1 cup freshly grated
   Parmesan or mature
   Cheddar cheese
salt and ground black
   pepper
¼ cup water
a few fresh basil leaves, to
   garnish (optional)

1 Preheat the oven to 350°F. Brush a large baking dish generously with oil.

2 Arrange a layer of onions in the dish, followed by layers of potatoes and tomatoes. Pour on a little of the oil, and sprinkle with the cheese. Season with salt and pepper.

3 Repeat until the vegetables are used up, ending with an overlapping layer of potatoes and tomatoes. Tear the basil leaves into pieces, and add them here and there among the vegetables. Sprinkle the top with cheese and a little oil.

4 Pour on the water. Bake for 1 hour, or until tender.

5 If the top begins to brown too much, place a sheet of foil or a flat baking sheet on top of the dish. Serve hot, garnished with basil leaves, if you wish.

Eggplant Baked with Cheeses

This famous dish, with its rich tomato sauce, is a specialty of Italy's southern regions.

Serves 4–6

2 pounds eggplant
flour, for coating
oil, for frying
½ cup freshly grated
    Parmesan cheese
14 ounces mozzarella
    cheese, sliced very
    thinly
salt and ground black
    pepper

For the tomato sauce

4 tablespoons olive oil
1 onion, very finely
    chopped
1 garlic clove, chopped
1 pound fresh tomatoes,
    or canned, chopped,
    with their juice
a few fresh basil leaves or
    parsley sprigs

1   Cut the eggplant into ½-inch slices, sprinkle with salt, and let drain for about 1 hour.

2   To make the tomato sauce, cook the onion in the oil until translucent. Stir in the garlic and the tomatoes (if using fresh tomatoes, add 3 tablespoons water). Season to taste; add the basil or parsley. Cook for 30 minutes. Purée in a vegetable mill.

3   Pat the aubergine slices dry, coat them lightly in flour. Heat a little oil in a large nonstick frying pan. Add one layer of eggplant, and cook over low to moderate heat with the pan covered until they soften. Turn, and cook on the other side. Remove from the pan, repeat with the remaining slices.

4   Preheat the oven to 350°F. Grease a wide shallow baking dish. Spread a little tomato sauce in the base. Cover with a layer of eggplant Sprinkle with a few teaspoons of Parmesan, season to taste with salt and pepper, and cover with a layer of mozzarella. Spoon on some tomato sauce. Repeat until all the ingredients are used up, ending with a layer of the tomato sauce and a sprinkling of Parmesan. Sprinkle with a little olive oil, and bake for about 45 minutes, until golden and bubbling.

Stuffed Onions

These savory onions make a good light lunch or supper. Small onions could be stuffed and served as a side dish.

Serves 6

6 large onions
scant ½ cup ham, cut
    into small dice
1 egg
½ cup dried bread
    crumbs
3 tablespoons finely
    chopped fresh parsley
1 garlic clove, chopped

pinch of freshly grated
    nutmeg
¾ cup freshly grated
    cheese such as
    Parmesan or mature
    Cheddar
6 tablespoons olive oil
salt and ground black
    pepper

1   Peel the onions without cutting through the bases. Cook them in a large pan of boiling water for about 20 minutes. Drain, and refresh in plenty of cold water.

2   Using a small sharp knife, cut around and scoop out each central section. Remove about half the inside (save it for soup). Lightly salt the empty cavities, and let the onions drain upside down.

3   Preheat the oven to 400°F. Beat the ham into the egg in a small bowl. Stir in the bread crumbs, parsley, garlic, nutmeg and all but 3 tablespoons of the grated cheese. Add 3 tablespoons of the oil, and season with salt and pepper.

4   Pat the insides of the onions dry with paper towels. Stuff them using a small spoon. Arrange the onions in one layer in an oiled baking dish.

5   Sprinkle the tops with the remaining cheese and then with oil. Bake for 45 minutes, or until the onions are tender and golden on top.

Baked Fennel with Parmesan Cheese

Fennel is widely eaten in Italy, both raw and cooked. It is delicious married with the sharpness of Parmesan.

Serves 4–6

2 pounds fennel bulbs, washed and cut in half
4 tablespoons butter
½ cup freshly grated Parmesan cheese

1 Cook the fennel bulbs in a large saucepan of boiling water until softened but not mushy. Drain well. Preheat the oven to 400°F.

2 Cut the fennel bulbs lengthwise into four or six pieces. Place them in a buttered baking dish.

3 Dot with butter. Sprinkle with the grated Parmesan. Bake in the hot oven until the cheese is golden brown, about 20 minutes. Serve at once.

Cook's Tip

For a more substantial version of this dish, finely chop 3 ounces ham and scatter it over the fennel before topping with the Parmesan cheese.

Zucchini with Sun-dried Tomatoes

Sun-dried tomatoes have a concentrated sweet flavor that goes well with zucchini.

Serves 6

10 sun-dried tomatoes, dry or preserved in oil and drained
¾ cup warm water
5 tablespoons olive oil
1 large onion, finely sliced
2 garlic cloves, finely chopped
2 pounds zucchini, cut into thin strips
salt and ground black pepper

1 Slice the tomatoes into thin strips. Place in a bowl with the warm water. Allow to stand for 20 minutes.

2 Heat the oil in a large frying pan or saucepan and then cook the onion over low to moderate heat until it softens but does not brown.

3 Stir in the garlic and the zucchini. Cook for about 5 minutes, continuing to stir the mixture.

4 Stir in the tomatoes and their soaking liquid. Season to taste with salt and pepper. Raise the heat slightly and cook until the zucchini is just tender. Serve hot or cold.

Broccoli Cauliflower Gratin

Broccoli and cauliflower combine well, and this dish is much lighter than a classic cauliflower cheese.

Serves 4

1 small cauliflower, about 9 ounces

1 head broccoli, about 9 ounces

½ cup plain low-fat yogurt

¼ cup grated reduced-fat Cheddar cheese

1 teaspoon whole-grain mustard

2 tablespoons whole wheat bread crumbs

salt and ground black pepper

1 Break the cauliflower and broccoli into florets and cook in lightly salted boiling water for 8–10 minutes, until just tender. Drain well and transfer to a flameproof casserole.

2 Mix together the yogurt, grated cheese and mustard, then season the mixture with pepper and spoon over the cauliflower and broccoli.

3 Sprinkle the bread crumbs over the top and place under a moderately hot broiler until golden brown. Serve hot.

Cook's Tip

When preparing the cauliflower and broccoli, discard the tougher parts of the stalks, then break the florets into even-size pieces so they will cook evenly.

Tex-Mex Baked Potatoes with Chili

A spicy chili bean sauce tops baked potatoes and is served with a dollop of sour cream.

Serves 4

2 large potatoes

1 tablespoon oil

1 garlic clove, crushed

1 small onion, chopped

½ small red bell pepper, seeded and chopped

8 ounces lean ground beef

½ small fresh red chili, seeded and chopped

1 teaspoon ground cumin

pinch of cayenne pepper

7-ounce can chopped tomatoes

2 tablespoons tomato paste

½ teaspoon dried oregano

½ teaspoon dried marjoram

7-ounce can red kidney beans, drained and rinsed

1 tablespoon chopped fresh cilantro

salt and ground black pepper

4 tablespoons sour cream

chopped fresh parsley, to garnish

1 Preheat the oven to 425°F. Rub the potatoes with a little oil. Prick with fork or thread onto skewers to speed cooking (or potato baker). Bake them on the top shelf for 30 minutes before beginning to cook the chili.

2 Heat the oil in a pan and fry the garlic, onion and pepper gently for 4–5 minutes, until softened.

3 Add the beef and fry until browned all over, then stir in the chili, cumin, cayenne pepper, tomatoes, tomato paste, 4 tablespoons water and the herbs. Cover with a tight-fitting lid and simmer for about 25 minutes, stirring occasionally.

4 Remove the lid, stir in the kidney beans and cook for 5 minutes. Turn off the heat and stir in the chopped fresh cilantro. Season to taste and set aside.

5 Cut the baked potatoes in half and place them in serving bowls. Top with the chili mixture and a dollop of sour cream,

Bombay Spiced Potatoes

This Indian potato dish uses a delicately aromatic mixture of whole and ground spices.

Serves 4

4 large floury potatoes, diced
4 tablespoons sunflower oil
1 garlic clove, finely chopped
2 teaspoons brown mustard seeds
1 teaspoon black onion seeds (optional)
1 teaspoon ground turmeric
1 teaspoon ground cumin
1 teaspoon ground coriander
1 teaspoon fennel seeds
salt and ground black pepper
generous squeeze of lemon juice
chopped fresh cilantro and lemon wedges, to garnish

1 Bring a saucepan of salted water to a boil, add the potatoes and simmer for about 4 minutes, until just tender. Drain well.

2 Heat the oil in a large frying pan and add the garlic along with all the whole and ground spices. Stir-fry gently for 1–2 minutes, until the mustard seeds start to pop.

3 Add the potatoes and stir-fry over a moderate heat for about 5 minutes, until heated through and well coated with the spicy oil.

4 Season well and sprinkle on the lemon juice. Garnish with chopped fresh cilantro and lemon wedges. Serve as an accompaniment to curries or strongly flavored meat dishes.

Cook's Tip
Look out for black onion seeds – kalonji – in Indian or Pakistani food stores.

Spanish Chili Potatoes

The Spanish name for this dish, *patatas bravas*, means fierce, hot potatoes. Reduce the amount of chili if you wish.

Serves 4

2 pounds new or salad potatoes
4 tablespoons olive oil
1 onion, finely chopped
2 garlic cloves, crushed
1 tablespoon tomato paste
7-ounce can chopped tomatoes
1 tablespoon red wine vinegar
2–3 small dried red chilies, seeded and chopped finely, or 1–2 teaspoons hot chili powder
1 teaspoon paprika
salt and ground black pepper
fresh Italian parsley sprig, to garnish

1 Boil the potatoes in their skins for 10–12 minutes until partly cooked. Drain them well and let cool, then cut in half and set aside.

2 Heat the oil in a large saucepan and fry the onions and garlic for 5–6 minutes, until just softened. Stir in the tomato paste, tomatoes, vinegar, chili and paprika and simmer for about 5 minutes.

3 Add the potatoes and mix into the sauce mixture until well coated. Cover with a tight-fitting lid and simmer gently for about 8–10 minutes, or until the potatoes are tender. Season well and transfer to a warmed serving dish. Serve garnished with a sprig of Italian parsley.

Spicy Jacket Potatoes

These lightly spiced potatoes make a glorious snack, light lunch or accompaniment to a meal.

Serves 2–4

2 large baking potatoes
1 teaspoon sunflower oil
1 small onion, chopped
1-inch piece fresh ginger, grated
1 teaspoon ground cumin
1 teaspoon ground coriander
½ teaspoon ground turmeric
generous pinch of garlic salt
plain yogurt and fresh cilantro sprigs, to serve

1 Preheat the oven to 375°F. Prick the potatoes with a fork. Bake for 40 minutes, or until soft.

2 Cut the potatoes in half and scoop out the insides. Heat the oil in a nonstick frying pan; fry the onion for a few minutes to soften. Stir in the ginger, cumin, coriander and turmeric.

3 Stir over a gentle heat for about 2 minutes, then add the potato, and garlic salt to taste.

4 Cook the potato mixture for another 2 minutes, stirring occasionally. Spoon the mixture back into the potato shells and top each with a spoonful of yogurt and a sprig or two of fresh cilantro. Serve hot.

Beans Provençal

A tasty side dish, these beans would complement a simple main course of broiled meat, poultry or fish.

Serves 4

1 teaspoon olive oil
1 small onion, finely chopped
1 garlic clove, crushed
scant 2 cups green beans
2 tomatoes, skinned and chopped
salt and ground black pepper

1 Heat the oil in a heavy-based or nonstick frying pan and sauté the chopped onion over moderate heat until softened but not browned.

2 Add the garlic, the beans and the tomatoes, then season well and cover tightly.

3 Cook over fairly gentle heat, shaking the pan from time to time, for about 30 minutes, or until the beans are tender. Serve hot.

Cook's Tip

For a dry version of this dish, omit the tomatoes. Simply fry the onion and garlic until softened, boil the beans in lightly salted water until tender, then stir into the rich mixture and combine well.

Chinese Crispy Seaweed

In northern China they use a special kind of seaweed for this dish, but collard greens make a good alternative.

Serves 4

8 ounces collard greens
peanut or sunflower oil,
   for deep-frying
¼ teaspoon salt

2 teaspoons light brown
   sugar
2 – 3 tablespoons toasted,
   flaked almonds

1 Cut out and discard any tough stalks from the collard greens. Place about six leaves on top of each other and roll up into a tight roll.

2 Using a sharp knife, slice across into thin shreds. Lay on a tray and leave to dry for about 2 hours.

3 Heat about 2 – 3 inches of oil in a wok or pan to 375°F. Carefully place a handful of the leaves into the oil – it will bubble and spit for the first 10 seconds and then die down. Deep fry for about 45 seconds, or until a slightly darker green – do not let the leaves burn.

4 Remove with a slotted spoon, drain on paper towels and transfer to a serving dish. Keep warm in the oven while frying the rest.

5 When you have fried all the shredded leaves, sprinkle with the salt and sugar and toss lightly. Garnish with the toasted almonds.

Cook's Tip
Make sure that your deep frying pan is deep enough to allow the oil to bubble up during cooking. The pan should be less than half full.

Leek and Parsnip Purée

Vegetable purées are popular in Britain and France served with meat, chicken or fish dishes.

Serves 4

2 large leeks, sliced
3 parsnips, sliced
pat of butter
3 tablespoons light cream
2 tablespoons plain
   yogurt
generous squeeze of
   lemon juice

salt and ground black
   pepper
large pinch of freshly
   grated nutmeg, to
   garnish

1 Steam or boil the leeks and parsnips together for about 15 minutes, until tender. Drain well, then place in a food processor or blender.

2 Add the remaining ingredients to the processor or blender. Combine them all until really smooth, then check the seasoning. Transfer to a warmed bowl and garnish with a sprinkling of nutmeg.

Middle-Eastern Vegetable Stew

This spiced dish of mixed vegetables can be served as a side dish or as a vegetarian main course.

Serves 4–6

*3 tablespoons vegetable
  or chicken stock*
*1 green bell pepper,
  seeded and sliced*
2 zucchini, sliced
2 carrots, sliced
2 celery stalks, sliced
2 potatoes, diced
*14-ounce can chopped
  tomatoes*
1 teaspoon chili powder

*2 tablespoons chopped
  fresh mint*
*1 tablespoon ground
  cumin*
*14-ounce can
  chick-peas, drained*
*salt and ground black
  pepper*
*fresh mint sprigs,
  to garnish*

1 Heat the vegetable or chicken stock in a large flameproof casserole until boiling, then add the sliced pepper, zucchini, carrot and celery. Stir over a high heat for 2–3 minutes, until the vegetables are just beginning to soften.

2 Add the potatoes, tomatoes, chili powder, mint and cumin. Add the chick-peas and bring to a boil.

3 Reduce the heat, cover the casserole with a tight-fitting lid and simmer for 30 minutes, or until all the vegetables are tender. Season to taste with salt and pepper and serve hot, garnished with mint leaves.

Summer Vegetable Braise

Tender young vegetables are ideal for quick cooking in a minimum of liquid. Use any vegetable mixture you like.

Serves 4

6 ounces baby carrots
*1½ cups sugar snap peas
  or snow peas*
4 ounces baby corn cobs
*6 tablespoons vegetable
  stock*

2 teaspoons lime juice
*salt and ground black
  pepper*
*chopped fresh parsley and
  chopped fresh chives,
  to garnish*

1 Place the carrots, peas and baby corn cobs in a large heavy-based saucepan with the vegetable stock and lime juice. Bring to a boil.

2 Cover the pan and reduce the heat, then simmer for about 6–8 minutes, shaking the pan occasionally, until the vegetables are just tender.

3 Season the vegetables to taste with salt and pepper, then stir in the chopped fresh parsley and chives. Cook the vegetables for a few seconds more, stirring them once or twice until the herbs are well mixed, then serve immediately with broiled lamb chops or roast chicken.

Cook's Tip
You can cook a winter version of this dish using seasonal root vegetables. Cut them into evenly sliced chunks and cook for slightly longer.

Straw Potato Cake

These potatoes are so–called in France because of their resemblance to a woven straw doormat.

Serves 4

1 pound baking potatoes
1½ tablespoons melted
   butter
1–2 tablespoons oil
salt and ground black
   pepper

1 Peel the potatoes and grate them coarsely, then immediately toss them with the melted butter and season with salt and pepper.

2 Heat the oil in a large frying pan. Add the potato mixture and press down to form an even layer that covers the pan. Cook over moderate heat for 7–10 minutes until the base is well browned.

3 Loosen the potato cake by shaking the pan or running a thin spatula under it.

4 To turn it over, invert a large baking sheet over the frying pan and, holding it tightly against the pan, turn them both over together. Lift off the frying pan, return it to the heat and add a little more oil if it looks dry. Slide the potato cake into the frying pan and continue cooking until it is crisp and browned on the second side. Serve hot.

Cook's Tip
Make several small potato cakes instead of one large one, if you prefer. Simply adjust the cooking time.

Sautéed Wild Mushrooms

This is a quick dish to prepare and makes an ideal side dish for all kinds of broiled and roast meats.

Serves 6

2 pounds fresh mixed
   wild and cultivated
   mushrooms such as
   morels, porcini,
   chanterelles, oyster or
   shiitake
2 tablespoons olive oil
2 tablespoons unsalted
   butter
2 garlic cloves, chopped
3 or 4 shallots, finely
   chopped
3–4 tablespoons
   chopped fresh parsley,
   or a mixture of
   different chopped fresh
   herbs
salt and ground black
   pepper

1 Wash and carefully dry the mushrooms. Trim the stems and cut the mushrooms into quarters, or slice if they are very large.

2 Heat the oil in a large frying pan over moderately high heat. Add the butter and swirl to melt, then stir in the prepared mushrooms and cook for 4–5 minutes until beginning to brown.

3 Add the garlic and shallots to the pan and cook for another 4–5 minutes until the mushrooms are tender and any liquid has evaporated. Season to taste with salt and pepper, stir in the parsley or mixed herbs and serve hot.

Cook's Tip
Use as many different varieties of cultivated and wild mushrooms as you can find to create a tasty and attractive dish.

Celery Root Purée

Many chefs add potato to celery root purée, but this recipe highlights the pure flavor of the vegetable.

Serves 4

1 large celery root, about	*pinch of grated nutmeg*
1¾ pounds, peeled	*salt and ground black*
1 tablespoon butter	*pepper*

1 Cut the celery root into large chunks, put in a saucepan with enough cold water to cover and add a little salt. Bring to a boil over moderately high heat and cook gently for about 10–15 minutes until tender.

2 Drain the celery root, reserving a little of the cooking liquid, and place in a food processor fitted with a metal blade or a blender. Process until smooth, adding a little of the cooking liquid if it needs thinning.

3 Stir in the butter and season to taste with salt, pepper and nutmeg. Reheat, if necessary, before serving.

Creamy Spinach Purée

Crème fraîche or béchamel sauce usually gives this dish its creamy richness. Here is a quick light alternative.

Serves 4

4½ cups fresh spinach,	*pinch of freshly grated*
stems removed	*nutmeg*
½ cup cream cheese	*salt and ground black*
milk (if required)	*pepper*

1 Rinse the spinach, shake lightly and place in a deep frying pan or wok. Cook over moderate heat for about 3–4 minutes until wilted. Drain in a colander, pressing with the back of a spoon. The spinach does not need to be completely dry.

2 Purée the spinach and cream cheese in a food processor fitted with a metal blade or a blender until well blended, then transfer to a bowl. If the purée is too thick to fall easily from a spoon, add a little milk, spoonful by spoonful. Season to taste with salt, pepper and nutmeg. Transfer to a heavy-based saucepan and reheat gently before serving.

Navy Bean Purée

This inexpensive dip is a healthy multi-purpose option; use low-fat sour cream to lower its calorie content.

Serves 4

Drain 14-ounce can navy beans, rinse, drain again. Purée in a blender or food processor with 3 tablespoons ricotta, grated zest, rind and juice of 1 large orange and 1 tablespoon finely chopped fresh rosemary. Set aside. Cut 4 heads of Belgian endive in half lengthwise and cut 2 medium radicchio into 8 wedges. Lay them on a baking sheet and brush with 1 tablespoon walnut oil. Broil for 2–3 minutes. Serve with the purée; scatter over the orange rind.

New Potato and Chive Salad

The secret of a good potato salad is to mix the potatoes with the dressing while they are still hot so that they absorb it.

Serves 4– 6

1½ pounds new potatoes
4 scallions
3 tablespoons olive oil
1 tablespoon white wine
   vinegar
¾ teaspoon Dijon mustard

¾ cup good-quality
   mayonnaise
3 tablespoons chopped
   fresh chives
salt and ground black
   pepper

1 Cook the potatoes, unpeeled, in boiling salted water until tender. Meanwhile, finely chop the white parts of the scallions along with a little of the green parts.

2 Whisk together the oil, vinegar and mustard. Drain the potatoes well, then immediately toss lightly with the vinegar mixture and scallions and allow to cool. Stir the mayonnaise and chives into the potatoes and chill in the fridge until ready to serve with broiled pork, lamb chops or roast chicken.

Watercress Potato Salad Bowl

New potatoes are good hot or cold, and this colorful and nutritious salad makes the most of them.

Serves 4

1 pound small new
   potatoes, unpeeled
1 bunch watercress
7 ounces cherry
   tomatoes, halved
2 tablespoons pumpkin
   seeds

3 tablespoons low-fat
   ricotta
1 tablespoon cider
   vinegar
1 teaspoon light brown
   sugar
salt and paprika

1 Cook the potatoes in lightly salted boiling water until just tender, then drain and leave to cool.

2 Toss together the potatoes, watercress, tomatoes and pumpkin seeds. Place the ricotta, vinegar, sugar, salt and paprika in a screw-top jar and shake well to mix. Pour over the salad just before serving.

Frankfurter Salad

A last-minute salad you can throw together quickly using store-cupboard ingredients.

Serves 4

Boil 1½ pounds new potatoes in salted water for 20 minutes. Drain, cover and keep warm. Hard-boil 2 eggs for 12 minutes, peel and quarter. Score the skins of 12 ounces frankfurters cork-screw fashion, cover with boiling water and simmer for 5 minutes. Drain, cover and keep warm. Distribute the leaves of 1 loose-leaf lettuce and 8 ounces young spinach between 4 plates, moisten the potatoes and frankfurters with dressing and scatter on the salad. Finish with the eggs, season and serve.

Niçoise Salad

Serve this rich and filling salad as a main course, simply with crusty bread.

Serves 4

6 tablespoons olive oil
2 tablespoons tarragon vinegar
1 teaspoon tarragon or Dijon mustard
1 small garlic clove, crushed
1 cup green beans
12 small new potatoes
3–4 Bibb lettuces, coarsely chopped
7-ounce can tuna in oil, drained

6 anchovy fillets, halved lengthwise
12 black olives, pitted
4 tomatoes, chopped
4 scallions, finely chopped
2 teaspoons capers
2 tablespoons pine nuts
2 hard-boiled eggs, chopped
salt and ground black pepper
crusty bread, to serve

1 Mix the oil, vinegar, mustard, garlic and seasoning with a wooden spoon in the bottom of a large salad bowl.

2 Cook the green beans and potatoes in separate saucepans of boiling salted water until just tender. Drain and add to the bowl with the lettuce, tuna, anchovies, olives, tomatoes, scallions and capers.

3 Just before serving, toast the pine nuts in a small frying pan until lightly browned.

4 Sprinkle on the salad while still hot, add the eggs and toss all the ingredients together well. Serve with chunks of hot crusty bread.

Cook's Tip
Look out for salad potatoes, such as Charlotte, Belle de Fontenay or Pink Fir Apple, to use in this recipe.

Caesar Salad

Any crisp lettuce will do in this delicious salad, which was created by Caesar Cardini in the 1920s.

Serves 4

1 large Romaine lettuce
4 thick slices white or whole wheat bread, without crusts
3 tablespoons olive oil
1 garlic clove, crushed

For the dressing
1 egg
1 garlic clove, chopped

2 tablespoons lemon juice
dash of Worcestershire sauce
3 anchovy fillets, chopped
½ cup olive oil
5 tablespoons grated Parmesan cheese
salt and ground black pepper

1 Preheat the oven to 425°F. Separate, rinse and dry the lettuce leaves. Tear the outer leaves coarsely and chop the heart. Arrange the lettuce in a large salad bowl.

2 Dice the bread and mix with the olive oil and garlic in a separate bowl until the bread has soaked up the oil. Lay the bread chunks on a baking sheet and place in the oven for about 6–8 minutes (keeping an eye on them) until golden. Remove and allow to cool.

3 To make the dressing, break the egg into the bowl of a food processor or blender and add the garlic, lemon juice, Worcestershire sauce and one of the anchovy fillets. Process until smooth.

4 With the motor running, pour in the olive oil in a thin stream until the dressing has the consistency of light cream. Season to taste with salt and pepper, if needed.

5 Pour the dressing over the salad greens and toss well, then toss in the garlic croûtons, Parmesan cheese and finally the remaining anchovies and serve immediately.

197

Tuna and Bean Salad

This substantial salad makes a good light meal, and can be very quickly assembled from canned ingredients.

Serves 4–6

2 x 14-ounce cans navy or kidney beans
2 x 7-ounce cans tuna fish, drained
4 tablespoons extra virgin olive oil
2 tablespoons lemon juice
salt and ground black pepper
1 tablespoon chopped fresh parsley
3 scallions, thinly sliced

1 Pour the beans into a large strainer and rinse under cold water. Drain well. Place in a serving dish.

2 Break the tuna into fairly large flakes with a fork and arrange over the beans.

3 Make the dressing by combining the oil with the lemon juice in a small bowl. Season with salt and pepper, and stir in the parsley. Mix well. Pour over the beans and tuna.

4 Sprinkle the scallions over the salad and toss well before serving.

Cook's Tip
If you prefer a milder onion flavor, gently sauté the scallions in a little oil until softened, but not browned, before adding them to the salad.

Grilled Pepper Salad

This colorful salad is a southern Italian creation; all the ingredients thrive in the Mediterranean sun.

Serves 6

4 large bell peppers, red or yellow or a combination of both
2 tablespoons capers in salt, vinegar or brine, rinsed
18–20 black or green olives

For the dressing
6 tablespoons extra-virgin olive oil
2 garlic cloves, chopped
2 tablespoons balsamic or wine vinegar
salt and ground black pepper

1 Place the peppers under a hot broiler and turn occasionally until they are black and blistered on all sides. Remove from the heat and place in a paper bag. Leave for 5 minutes.

2 Peel the peppers, then cut them into quarters. Remove the stems and seeds.

3 Cut the peppers into strips, and arrange them in a serving dish. Distribute the capers and olives evenly over them.

4 To make the dressing, mix the oil and garlic together in a small bowl, crushing the garlic with a spoon to release as much flavor as possible. Mix in the vinegar, and season to taste with salt and pepper. Pour on the salad, mix well, and allow to stand for at least 30 minutes before serving.

Cook's Tip
Skinning the peppers brings out their delicious sweet flavor and is well worth the extra effort.

Chicken Liver and Tomato Salad

Warm salads are especially welcome during the autumn months when the evenings are growing shorter and cooler.

Serves 4

8 ounces young spinach, stems removed
1 frisée lettuce
7 tablespoons peanut or sunflower oil
6 ounces bacon, cut into strips
3 slices day-old bread, without crusts, cut into short slices
1 pound chicken livers
4 ounces cherry tomatoes
salt and ground black pepper

1 Wash and spin the salad greens. Put in a salad bowl. Heat 4 tablespoons of the oil in a large frying pan and cook the bacon for 3–4 minutes until crisp and brown. Remove the bacon with a slotted spoon and let drain on a piece of paper towel.

2 To make the croûtons, fry the bread in the bacon-flavored oil, tossing until crisp and golden. Drain on paper towels.

3 Heat the remaining 3 tablespoons of oil in the frying pan and fry the chicken livers briskly for 2–3 minutes. Transfer the livers to the salad greens, add the bacon, croûtons and tomatoes. Season with salt and pepper, toss, and serve.

Cook's Tip
Although fresh chicken livers are preferable, frozen ones could be used in this salad. It is important to make sure they are completely thawed before cooking.

Maryland Salad

Chicken, corn, bacon, banana and watercress are combined here in a sensational main-course salad.

Serves 4

4 free-range chicken breasts, boned
8 ounces bacon
4 baby corn
3 tablespoons soft butter, softened
4 ripe bananas, peeled and halved
4 firm tomatoes, halved
4 escarole lettuces
1 bunch watercress, about 4 ounces
salt and ground black pepper

For the dressing
5 tablespoons peanut oil
1 tablespoon white wine vinegar
1 teaspoon maple syrup
2 teaspoons mild mustard

1 Season the chicken breasts, brush with oil and barbecue or broil for 15 minutes, turning once. Barbecue or broil the bacon for 8–10 minutes or until crisp.

2 Bring a large saucepan of salted water to the boil. Trim the baby corn or leave the husks on if you prefer. Boil for 20 minutes. For extra flavor, brush with butter and brown over the barbecue or under the broiler. Barbecue or broil the bananas and tomatoes for 6–8 minutes. You can brush these with butter too if you wish.

3 To make the dressing, combine the oil, vinegar, maple syrup and mustard with 1 tablespoon water in a screw-top jar and shake well.

4 Wash, spin thoroughly and dress the escarole lettuce and the watercress.

5 Distribute the salad greens among four large plates. Slice the chicken and arrange on the leaves with the bacon, banana, corn and tomatoes.

Leeks with Mustard Dressing

Pour the dressing over the leeks while they are still warm so that they absorb the mustardy flavors.

Serves 4

8 slim leeks, each about 5 inches long

1–2 teaspoons Dijon mustard

2 teaspoons white wine vinegar

1 hard-boiled egg, halved lengthwise

5 tablespoons light olive oil

2 teaspoons chopped fresh parsley

salt and ground black

1 Steam the leeks over a saucepan of boiling water until they are just tender.

2 Meanwhile, stir together the mustard and vinegar in a bowl. Scoop the egg yolk into the bowl and mash thoroughly into the vinegar mixture using a fork.

3 Gradually work in the oil to make a smooth sauce, then season to taste with salt and pepper.

4 Lift the leeks out of the steamer and place on several layers of paper towels, then cover the leeks with several more layers of paper towels and pat dry.

5 Transfer the leeks to a serving dish while still warm, spoon the dressing over them and let cool. Finely chop the egg white using a large sharp knife, then mix with the chopped fresh parsley and scatter on the leeks. Chill in the fridge until ready to serve.

Cook's Tip
Pencil-slim baby leeks are increasingly available nowadays, and are beautifully tender. Use three or four of these smaller leeks per serving.

Lettuce and Herb Salad

For a really quick salad, look out for prepared bags of mixed baby lettuce leaves in the supermarket.

Serves 4

½ cucumber

mixed lettuce leaves

1 bunch watercress, about 4 ounces

1 Belgian endive head, sliced

3 tablespoons mixed chopped fresh herbs such as parsley, thyme, tarragon, chives and chervil

For the dressing

1 tablespoon white wine vinegar

1 teaspoon prepared mustard

5 tablespoons olive oil

salt and ground black pepper

1 To make the dressing, mix the vinegar and mustard together, then whisk in the oil and seasoning.

2 Peel the cucumber, if you wish, then cut it in half lengthwise and scoop out the seeds. Thinly slice the inside. Tear the lettuce leaves into bite-size pieces.

3 Toss the cucumber, lettuce, watercress, Belgian endive and herbs together in a bowl, or arrange them in the bowl in layers, if you prefer.

4 Stir the dressing, then pour over the salad, toss lightly to coat the salad vegetables and leaves. Serve at once.

Cook's Tip
Do not dress the salad until just before serving, otherwise the lettuce leaves will wilt.

Goat Cheese Salad

The robust flavors of the cheese and buckwheat combine especially well with figs and walnuts in this salad.

Serves 4

1 cup couscous
2 tablespoons toasted buckwheat groats
1 hard-boiled egg
2 tablespoons chopped fresh parsley
4 tablespoons olive oil, preferably Sicilian
3 tablespoons walnut oil
4 ounces arugula

½ frisée lettuce
6 ounces crumbly white goat cheese
½ cup broken walnuts, toasted
4 ripe figs, trimmed and almost cut into four (leaving the pieces joined at the base)

1 Place the couscous and buckwheat groats in a bowl, cover with boiling water and let soak for 15 minutes. Place in a strainer if necessary to drain off any remaining water, then spread out on a metal tray and allow to cool.

2 Peel the hard-boiled egg and grate finely.

3 Toss the egg, parsley and couscous in a bowl. Combine the two oils and use half to moisten the couscous mixture.

4 Wash and spin the salad leaves, dress with the remaining oil and distribute among four large plates.

5 Pile the couscous in the center of the leaves, crumble on the goat cheese, scatter with toasted walnuts, and add the trimmed figs.

Cook's Tip
Serve this strongly flavored salad with a gutsy red wine from the Rhône or South of France.

Waldorf Ham Salad

Waldorf salad originally consisted of apples, celery and mayonnaise. This ham version is a meal in itself.

Serves 4

3 apples, peeled
1 tablespoon lemon juice
2 slices cooked ham, about 6 ounces each
3 celery stalks
⅔ cup mayonnaise
1 escarole or Batavia lettuce

1 small radicchio, finely shredded
½ bunch watercress
3 tablespoons walnut oil or olive oil
½ cup walnut pieces, toasted
salt and ground black pepper

1 Core, slice and shred the apples finely. Moisten with lemon juice to keep them white. Cut the cooked ham into 2-inch strips, then cut the celery into similar-size pieces, and combine in a bowl.

2 Add the mayonnaise to the apples, ham and celery and stir to combine well.

3 Wash and spin the salad greens. Shred the leaves finely, then toss with the walnut or olive oil. Distribute the greens between four plates. Pile the mayonnaise mixture in the center, scatter with toasted walnuts, season to taste with salt and pepper, and serve at once.

Baby Leaf Salad with Croutons

Crispy ciabatta croutons give a lovely crunch to this mixed leaf and avocado salad.

Serves 4

1 tablespoon olive oil
1 garlic clove, crushed
1 tablespoon freshly
    grated Parmesan
    cheese
1 tablespoon chopped
    fresh parsley
4 slices ciabatta bread,
    crusts removed, diced
1 large bunch watercress
large handful of arugula

1 bag mixed baby salad
    greens, including red
    leaf and Romaine
    lettuce
1 ripe avocado

For the dressing
3 tablespoons olive oil
1 tablespoon walnut oil
juice of ½ lemon
½ teaspoon Dijon
    mustard
salt and ground black
    pepper

1 Preheat the oven to 375°F. Put the oil, garlic, Parmesan, parsley and bread in a bowl and toss to coat well. Spread out the diced bread on a baking sheet and bake for about 8 minutes until crisp. Let cool.

2 Remove any coarse or discolored stalks or leaves from the watercress and place in a serving bowl with the arugula and baby salad greens.

3 Halve the avocado and remove the pit. Peel and cut into chunks, then add it to the salad bowl.

4 To make the dressing, mix together the oils, lemon juice, mustard and seasoning in a small bowl or screw-top jar until evenly blended. Pour over the salad and toss well. Sprinkle over the croûtons and serve immediately.

Wild Rice with Broiled Vegetables

Broiling brings out the delicious and varied flavor of these summer vegetables.

Serves 4

1¼ cups wild and long-
    grain rice mixture
1 large eggplant, thickly
    sliced
1 red, 1 yellow and 1
    green bell pepper,
    seeded and cut into
    quarters
2 red onions, sliced
8 ounces brown cap or
    shiitake mushrooms
2 small zucchini, cut in
    half lengthwise

olive oil, for brushing
2 tablespoons chopped
    fresh thyme

For the dressing
6 tablespoons extra-
    virgin olive oil
2 tablespoons balsamic
    vinegar
2 garlic cloves, crushed
salt and ground black
    pepper

1 Put the rice mixture in a saucepan of cold salted water. Bring to a boil, reduce the heat, cover with a tight-fitting lid and cook gently for 30–40 minutes or according to the package instructions, until all the grains are tender.

2 To make the dressing, mix together the olive oil, vinegar, garlic and seasoning in a small bowl or screw-topped jar until well blended. Set aside while you broil the vegetables.

3 Arrange the vegetables on a broiler rack. Brush with olive oil and broil for 8–10 minutes, until tender and well browned, turning them occasionally and brushing again with oil.

4 Drain the rice and toss in half the dressing. Turn into a serving dish and arrange the broiled vegetables on top. Pour over the remaining dressing and scatter over the chopped fresh thyme.

Russian Salad

Russian salad became fashionable in the hotel dining rooms of Europe in the 1920s and 1930s.

Serves 4

4 ounces large button mushrooms
½ cup mayonnaise
1 tablespoon freshly squeezed lemon juice
12 ounces peeled, cooked shrimp
1 large dill pickle, finely chopped, or 2 tablespoons capers
4 ounces fava beans
4 ounces small new potatoes, scrubbed or scraped

4 ounces young carrots, trimmed and peeled
4 ounces baby corn
4 ounces baby turnips, trimmed
1 tablespoon olive oil, preferably French or Italian
4 eggs, hard-boiled and shelled
pinch of salt, pepper and paprika
1 ounce canned anchovies, cut into fine strips, to garnish

1 Slice the mushrooms thinly, then cut into matchsticks. Combine the mayonnaise and lemon juice. Fold half of the mayonnaise into the mushrooms and shrimp, add the dill pickle or capers, then season to taste with salt and pepper.

2 Bring a large saucepan of salted water to a boil, add the fava beans, and cook for 3 minutes. Drain and cool under running water, then pinch the beans between thumb and forefinger to release them from their tough skins. Boil the potatoes for 20 minutes and the remaining vegetables for 6 minutes. Drain and cool under running water.

3 Toss the vegetables with the oil and divide among four shallow bowls. Spoon on the dressed shrimp and place a hard-boiled egg in the center. Garnish the egg with strips of anchovy and sprinkle with paprika.

Crunchy Coleslaw

Homemade coleslaw is quick and easy to make – and it tastes fresh, crunchy and wonderful.

Serves 4–6

¼ firm white cabbage
1 small onion, finely chopped
2 celery stalks, thinly sliced
2 carrots, coarsely grated
1–2 teaspoons caraway seeds (optional)
1 eating apple, cored and chopped (optional)

½ cup walnuts, chopped (optional)
salt and ground black pepper

For the dressing

3 tablespoons mayonnaise
2 tablespoons light cream or natural yogurt
1 teaspoon grated lemon rind

1 Cut and discard the core from the cabbage quarter, then shred the leaves finely. Place them in a large bowl.

2 Toss the onion, celery and carrot into the cabbage, plus the caraway seeds, apple and walnuts, if using. Season well with salt and pepper.

3 Mix the dressing ingredients together in a small bowl, then stir into the vegetables. Cover the salad with plastic wrap and allow to stand for 2 hours, stirring occasionally, then chill lightly in the fridge before serving.

Pear and Roquefort Salad

Choose ripe but firm Comice or Bartlett pears for this attractive and deeply flavorful salad.

Serves 4

3 ripe pears
lemon juice
about 6 ounces mixed
    fresh salad greens
6 ounces Roquefort
    cheese
½ cup hazelnuts, toasted
    and chopped

For the dressing

2 tablespoons hazelnut
    oil
3 tablespoons olive oil
1 tablespoon cider vinegar
1 teaspoon Dijon mustard
salt and ground black
    pepper

1 To make the dressing, mix together the oils, vinegar and mustard in a bowl or screw-top jar. Season to taste with salt and pepper.

2 Peel, core and slice the pears and toss them in lemon juice.

3 Divide the salad greens among four serving plates, then place the pears on top. Crumble the cheese and scatter over the salad along with the toasted hazelnuts. Spoon over the dressing and serve at once.

Mediterranean Mixed Pepper Salad

Serve this colorful salad either as a tasty appetizer or as an accompaniment to cold meats for lunch or supper.

Serves 4

2 red bell peppers, halved
    and seeded
2 yellow bell peppers,
    halved and seeded
⅔ cup olive oil
1 onion, thinly sliced

2 garlic cloves, crushed
generous squeeze of
    lemon juice
chopped fresh parsley, to
    garnish

1 Broil the pepper halves for about 5 minutes, until the skin has blistered and blackened. Pop them into a plastic bag, seal and leave for 5 minutes.

2 Meanwhile, heat 2 tablespoons of the olive oil in a frying pan and fry the onion for about 5–6 minutes, until softened and translucent. Remove from the heat and reserve.

3 Take the peppers out of the bag and peel off the skins. Discard the pepper skins and slice each pepper half into fairly thin strips.

4 Place the peppers, cooked onions and any oil from the pan in a bowl. Add the crushed garlic, pour in the remaining olive oil, add a generous squeeze of lemon juice and season to taste. Mix well, cover and marinate for 2–3 hours, stirring the mixture once or twice.

5 Just before serving, garnish the pepper salad with chopped fresh parsley.

Californian Salad

Full of vitality and vitamins, this is a lovely light and healthy salad for sunny summer days.

Serves 4

1 small crisp lettuce, torn into pieces
2 cups young spinach leaves
2 carrots, coarsely grated
4 ounces cherry tomatoes, halved
2 celery stalks, thinly sliced
½ cup raisins
½ cup blanched almonds or unsalted cashew nuts, halved

2 tablespoons sunflower seeds
2 tablespoons sesame seeds, lightly toasted

For the dressing
3 tablespoons extra-virgin olive oil
2 tablespoons cider vinegar
2 teaspoons honey
juice of 1 small orange
salt and ground black pepper

1 Put the salad vegetables, raisins, almonds or cashew nuts and seeds into a large bowl.

2 Put all the dressing ingredients into a screw-top jar, shake them up well and pour over the salad.

3 Toss the salad thoroughly and divide it among four small salad bowls. Serve chilled, sprinkled with salt and pepper.

Cucumber and Dill Salad

This Scandinavian salad is particularly complementary to hot and spicy food.

Serves 4

2 cucumbers
2 tablespoons chopped fresh chives
2 tablespoons chopped fresh dill

⅔ cup sour cream
salt and ground black pepper

1 Slice the cucumbers as thinly as possible, preferably in a food processor or with a slicer.

2 Place the slices in layers in a colander set over a plate to catch the juice. Sprinkle each layer evenly, but not too heavily, with salt.

3 Allow the cucumber to drain for up to 2 hours, then lay the slices on a clean dish towel and pat them dry.

4 Mix the cucumber with the herbs, cream and plenty of pepper. Serve as soon as possible.

Cook's Tip
The juice in this salad continues forming after salting, so only dress it when you are ready to serve.

Chicory, Fruit and Nut Salad

Mildly bitter chicory is wonderful with sweet fruit, and is delicious when complemented by a creamy curry sauce.

Serves 4

3 tablespoons
  mayonnaise
1 tablespoon strained
  plain yogurt
1 tablespoon mild curry
  paste
6 tablespoons light cream

½ iceberg lettuce
2 heads of chicory
1 cup flaked coconut
½ cup cashew nuts
2 red eating apples
½ cup currants

1 Mix together the mayonnaise, yogurt, curry paste and light cream in a small bowl. Cover and chill in the fridge until required.

2 Tear the iceberg lettuce into even-size pieces and put into a salad bowl.

3 Cut the root end off each head of chicory and discard. Slice the chicory and add it to the salad bowl. Preheat the broiler.

4 Spread out the coconut flakes on a baking sheet. Broil for 1 minute until golden. Turn into a bowl and set aside. Toast the cashew nuts for 2 minutes until golden.

5 Quarter the apples and cut out the cores. Slice the apple quarters and add to the lettuce with the toasted coconut, cashew nuts and currants.

6 Spoon the dressing over the salad, toss lightly and serve.

Cook's Tip
Choose a sweet, well-flavored variety of red apple for this salad, such as Braeburn or Royal Gala.

Tzatziki

This Greek salad is typically served with broiled lamb and chicken, but is also good with salmon and trout.

Serves 4

1 cucumber
1 teaspoon salt
3 tablespoons finely
  chopped fresh mint,
  plus a few sprigs to
  garnish

1 clove garlic, crushed
1 teaspoon sugar
scant 1 cup strained
  plain yogurt
paprika, to garnish
  (optional)

1 Peel the cucumber. Reserve a little to use as a garnish if you wish and cut the rest in half lengthwise. Remove the seeds with a teaspoon and discard. Slice the cucumber thinly and combine with salt. Let stand for about 15-20 minutes. Salt will soften the cucumber and draw out any bitter juice.

2 Combine the mint, garlic, sugar and yogurt in a bowl, reserving a few sprigs of mint as decoration.

3 Rinse the cucumber in a colander under cold running water to drain away the salt. Combine with the yogurt. Decorate with cucumber and mint. Serve cold, garnished with paprika if you wish.

Cook's Tip
If preparing tzatziki in a hurry, leave out the method for salting the cucumber at the end of step 1. The cucumber will have a more crunchy texture, and will be slightly less sweet.

Tomato and Bread Salad

This salad is a traditional peasant dish from Tuscany which was created to use up bread that was several days old.

Serves 4

14 ounces stale white or
    brown bread or rolls
4 large tomatoes
1 large red onion, or
    6 scallions
a few fresh basil leaves,
    to garnish

For the dressing
4 tablespoons extra-
    virgin olive oil
2 tablespoons white wine
    vinegar
salt and ground black
    pepper

1   Cut the bread or rolls into thick slices. Place in a shallow bowl and soak with cold water. Leave for at least 30 minutes.

2   Cut the tomatoes into chunks. Place in a serving bowl. Finely slice the onion or scallions, and add them to the tomatoes. Squeeze as much water out of the bread as possible, and add it to the vegetables.

3   Mix together the dressing ingredients. Season to taste with salt and pepper. Pour it on the salad and mix well. Decorate with the basil leaves. Allow to stand in a cool place for at least 2 hours before serving.

Fennel and Orange Salad

This salad originated in Sicily, following the seventeenth-century custom of serving fennel at a meal's end.

Serves 4

2 large fennel bulbs,
    about 1½ pounds total
2 sweet oranges
2 scallions, to garnish

For the dressing
4 tablespoons extra-
    virgin olive oil
2 tablespoons fresh lemon
    juice
salt and ground black
    pepper

1   Wash the fennel bulbs and remove any brown or stringy outer leaves. Slice the bulbs and stems into thin pieces. Place in a shallow serving bowl.

2   Peel the oranges with a sharp knife, cutting away the white pith. Slice thinly. Cut each slice into thirds. Arrange over the fennel, adding any juice from the oranges.

3   To make the dressing, mix the oil and lemon juice together. Season with salt and pepper. Pour the dressing on the salad and mix well.

4   Slice the white and green sections of the scallions thinly. Sprinkle on the salad.

Parmesan and Poached Egg Salad

Soft poached eggs, hot garlic croûtons and cool crisp salad greens make an unforgettable combination.

Serves 2

½ small loaf white bread
5 tablespoons extra-
virgin olive oil
2 eggs
4 ounces mixed salad
greens

2 garlic cloves, crushed
½ tablespoon white wine
vinegar
2 tablespoons freshly
shaved Parmesan
cheese
black pepper

1 Remove the crust from the bread. Cut the bread into 1-inch cubes.

2 Heat 2 tablespoons of the oil in a frying pan and cook the bread for about 5 minutes, tossing the cubes occasionally, until they are golden brown.

3 Meanwhile, bring a saucepan of water to a boil. Slide in the eggs carefully, one at a time. Gently poach the eggs for 4 minutes until lightly cooked.

4 Divide the salad greens between two plates. Remove the croûtons from the pan and arrange them on the leaves. Wipe the pan clean with paper towels.

5 Heat the remaining oil in the pan and cook the garlic and vinegar over high heat for about 1 minute. Pour the warm dressing over the salad greens and croûtons.

6 Place a poached egg on each salad. Scatter with shavings of Parmesan cheese and a little freshly ground black pepper.

Cook's Tip
Add a dash of vinegar to the water before poaching the eggs. This helps to keep the whites together. To make sure that a poached egg has a good shape, swirl the water with a spoon before sliding in the egg.

Classic Greek Salad

If you have ever visited Greece you'll know that a Greek salad with a chunk of bread makes a delicious filling meal.

Serves 4

1 Romaine lettuce
½ cucumber, halved
lengthwise
4 tomatoes
8 scallions
3 ounces Greek black
olives

4 ounces feta cheese
6 tablespoons white wine
vinegar
⅔ cup extra-virgin olive
oil
salt and ground black
pepper

1 Tear the lettuce leaves into pieces and place them in a large serving bowl. Slice the cucumber and add to the bowl.

2 Cut the tomatoes into wedges and put them into the bowl.

3 Slice the scallions. Add them to the bowl along with the olives and toss well.

4 Dice the feta cheese and add to the salad.

5 Put the vinegar and olive oil into a small bowl and season to taste with salt and pepper. Whisk well. Pour the dressing over the salad and toss to combine. Serve at once with extra olives and chunks of bread, if you wish.

Cook's Tip
This salad can be assembled in advance, but should only be dressed just before serving. Keep the dressing at room temperature as chilling deadens its flavors.

Potato Salad with Egg and Lemon

Potato salads are a popular addition to any salad spread and are enjoyed with an assortment of cold meats and fish.

Serves 4

2 pounds new potatoes,
  scrubbed or scraped
1 onion, finely chopped
1 hard-boiled egg
1¼ cups mayonnaise
1 garlic clove, crushed

finely grated juice and
  zest of 1 lemon
4 tablespoons chopped
  fresh parsley
salt and ground black
  pepper

1 Bring the potatoes to a boil in a saucepan of salted water. Simmer for 20 minutes. Drain and allow to cool. Cut the potatoes into large cubes, season with salt and pepper to taste, and combine with the onion.

2 Peel the hard-boiled egg and grate into a mixing bowl, then add the mayonnaise. Combine the garlic and lemon rind and juice in a small bowl and stir into the mayonnaise. Stir gently into the potatoes.

Cook's Tip
Use an early season variety of potato for this salad or look out for baby salad potatoes. They will not disintegrate when boiled and have a sweet flavor.

Sweet Turnip Salad

The robustly flavored turnip partners well with the taste of horseradish and caraway seeds in this delicious salad.

Serves 4

12 ounces turnips
2 scallions, white part
  only, chopped
1 tablespoon sugar
pinch of salt

2 tablespoons creamed
  horseradish
2 teaspoons caraway
  seeds

1 Peel, slice and shred the turnips – or you could grate them if you wish.

2 Add the scallions, sugar and salt, then rub together with your hands to soften the turnip.

3 Fold in the creamed horseradish and caraway seeds and serve the salad immediately.

Queen of Puddings

This pudding was developed from a seventeenth-century recipe by Queen Victoria's chefs at Buckingham Palace.

Serves 4

1½ cups fresh bread
   crumbs
4 tablespoons sugar, plus
   1 teaspoon
grated rind of 1 lemon

2½ cups milk
4 eggs
3 tablespoons raspberry
   jam, warmed

1 Stir the bread crumbs, 2 tablespoons of the sugar and the lemon rind together in a heat proof bowl. Bring the milk to a boil in a saucepan, then stir into the bread crumbs.

2 Separate three of the eggs and beat the yolks with the whole egg. Stir into the bread crumb mixture, pour into a buttered baking dish and let stand for 30 minutes. Meanwhile, preheat the oven to 325°F. Bake the pudding for 50–60 minutes, until set.

3 Whisk the egg whites in a large clean bowl until stiff but not dry, then gradually whisk in just under 2 tablespoons sugar until the mixture is thick and glossy, taking care not to overwhip.

4 Spread the jam over the pudding, then spoon on the meringue to cover the top completely. Evenly sprinkle about 1 teaspoon sugar over the meringue, then bake for another 15 minutes, until the meringue is beginning to turn a light golden color.

Pear and Blackberry Brown Betty

All this delicious fruity pudding needs to go with it is some hot homemade custard, light cream or ice cream.

Serves 4–6

6 tablespoons butter,
   diced
3 cups bread crumbs
1 pound ripe pears
1 pound blackberries

grated rind and juice of
   1 small orange
½ cup brown sugar
extra brown sugar, for
   sprinkling

1 Preheat the oven to 350°F. Heat the butter in a heavy-based frying pan over moderate heat and add the bread crumbs. Stir until golden.

2 Peel and core the pears, then cut them into thick slices and mix with the blackberries, orange rind and juice.

3 Mix the brown sugar with the bread crumbs, then layer with the fruit in a 3-cup buttered baking dish, beginning and ending with a layer of sugared bread crumbs.

4 Sprinkle the extra brown sugar over the top. Cover the baking dish, then bake the dessert for 20 minutes. Uncover the dish, then bake for a further 30–35 minutes, until the fruit is cooked and the top is brown and crisp.

Baked Stuffed Apples

When apples are plentiful, this traditional dessert is a popular and easy choice.

Serves 4

scant 1 cup ground
  almonds
2 tablespoons butter,
  softened
1 teaspoon honey

1 egg yolk
2 ounces dried apricots,
  chopped
4 cooking apples

1 Preheat the oven to 400°F. Beat together the almonds, butter, honey, egg yolk and apricots.

2 Remove the cores from the cooking apples using a large apple corer, then cut a line with the point of a sharp knife around the circumference of each apple.

3 Lightly grease a shallow baking dish, then arrange the cooking apples in the dish.

4 Divide the apricot mixture among the cavities in the apples, then bake in the oven for 45–60 minutes, until the apples are fluffy.

Kentish Cherry Batter Pudding

Kent, known as the "Garden of England", is particularly well known for cherries and the dishes made from them.

Serves 4

3 tablespoons Kirsch
  (optional)
1 pound dark cherries,
  pitted
½ cup all-purpose flour
4 tablespoons sugar

2 eggs, separated
¼ cup milk
6 tablespoons butter,
  melted
sugar, for sprinkling

1 Sprinkle the Kirsch, if using, over the cherries in a small bowl and let them to soak for about 30 minutes.

2 Mix the flour and sugar together, then slowly stir in the egg yolks and milk to make a smooth batter. Stir in half the butter and set aside for 30 minutes.

3 Preheat the oven to 425°F, then pour the remaining butter into a 2½-cup baking dish and put in the oven to heat.

4 Whisk the egg whites until stiff peaks form, then fold into the batter with the cherries. Pour into the dish and bake for 15 minutes.

5 Reduce the oven temperature to 350°F and bake for 20 minutes, or until golden and set in the center. Serve sprinkled with sugar.

Sticky Toffee Pudding

If you prefer, use pecan nuts instead of walnuts in this delightfully gooey pudding.

Serves 6

1 cup toasted walnuts, chopped
¾ cup butter
1½ cups brown sugar
4 tablespoons heavy cream
2 tablespoons lemon juice
2 eggs, beaten
1 cup self-rising flour

1 Grease a 3¾-cup ovenproof bowl and add half the nuts.

2 Heat 4 tablespoons of the butter with 4 tablespoons of the sugar, the cream and 1 tablespoon of the lemon juice in a small saucepan, stirring until smooth. Pour half into the bowl, then swirl to coat it a little way up the sides.

3 Beat the remaining butter and sugar until light and fluffy, then gradually beat in the eggs. Fold in the flour and the remaining nuts and lemon juice and spoon into the bowl.

4 Cover the bowl with baking parchment with a pleat folded in the center, then tie securely with string.

5 Steam the pudding for 1¼ hours, or until it is completely set in the center.

6 Just before serving, gently warm the remaining sauce. Unmold the pudding onto a warm plate and pour on the warm sauce.

Easy Chocolate and Orange Soufflé

The base in this soufflé is a simple semolina mixture, rather than the thick white sauce of most soufflés.

Serve 4

scant ½ cup semolina
scant ½ cup brown sugar
2½ cups milk
grated rind of 1 orange
6 tablespoons fresh orange juice
3 eggs, separated
2½ ounces plain chocolate, grated
confectioner's sugar, for sprinkling

1 Preheat the oven to 400°F. Butter a shallow 7½-cup baking dish.

2 Pour the milk into a heavy-based saucepan, sprinkle on the semolina and brown sugar, then heat, stirring the mixture all the time, until boiling and thickened.

3 Remove the pan from the heat; beat in the orange rind and juice, egg yolks and all but 1 tablespoon of the chocolate.

4 Whisk the egg whites until stiff but not dry, then lightly fold into the semolina mixture in three batches. Spoon the mixture into the dish and bake for about 30 minutes until just set in the center and risen. Sprinkle the top with the reserved chocolate and the confectioner's sugar, then serve immediately.

Plum and Walnut Crisp

Walnuts add a lovely crunch to the fruit layer in this rich dessert – almonds would be just as good.

Serves 4–6

¾ cup walnut pieces
2 pounds plums
1½ cups brown sugar

6 tablespoons butter or
* hard margarine, diced*
1½ cups all-purpose flour

1 Preheat the oven to 350°F. Spread the nuts on a baking sheet and place in the oven for 8–10 minutes, until evenly colored.

2 Butter a 5-cup baking dish. Halve and pit the plums, then put them into the dish and stir in the nuts and half of the brown sugar.

3 Rub the butter or margarine into the flour until the mixture resembles coarse crumbs. (Alternatively, use a food processor.) Stir in the remaining sugar and continue to rub in until fine crumbs are formed.

4 Cover the fruit with the crumb mixture and press it down lightly. Bake the crisp for about 45 minutes, until the top is golden brown and the fruit tender.

Cook's Tip
To make an oat and cinnamon crisp, substitute rolled oats for half the flour in the crisp mixture and add ½ –1 teaspoon ground cinnamon, to taste.

Baked Rice Pudding

Canned rice pudding simply cannot compare with this creamy homemade version, especially if you like the skin.

Serves 4

¼ cup short-grain rice
2 tablespoons light
* brown sugar*
4 tablespoons butter
3¾ cups milk

small strip of lemon rind
pinch of freshly grated
* nutmeg*
fresh mint sprigs, to
* decorate*
raspberries, to serve

1 Preheat the oven to 300°F, then butter a 5-cup shallow baking dish.

2 Put the rice, sugar and butter into the dish, stir in the milk and lemon rind and sprinkle a little nutmeg over the surface.

3 Bake the rice pudding in the oven for about 2½ hours, stirring after 30 minutes and another couple of times during the next 2 hours until the rice is tender and the pudding has a thick and creamy consistency.

4 If you like skin on top, leave the rice pudding undisturbed for the last 30 minutes of cooking (otherwise, stir it again). Serve hot, decorated with fresh mint sprigs and raspberries.

Cook's Tip
Baked rice pudding is even more delicious with fruit. Add some golden raisins, raisins or chopped ready-to-eat dried apricots to the pudding, or serve it alongside sliced fresh peaches or nectarines, fresh raspberries or fresh strawberries.

Floating Islands in Plum Sauce

This unusual, low-fat dessert is simpler to make than it looks, and is quite delicious.

Serves 4
1 pound red plums
1¼ cups apple juice
2 egg whites

2 tablespoons concentrated
 apple juice syrup
pinch of freshly grated
 nutmeg

1 Halve the plums and remove the pits. Place them in a wide saucepan with the apple juice.

2 Bring to a boil, then cover with a tight-fitting lid and allow to simmer gently until the plums are tender.

3 Meanwhile, place the egg whites in a clean, dry bowl and whisk until stiff peaks form.

4 Gradually whisk in the apple juice syrup, whisking until the meringue holds fairly firm peaks.

5 Using a tablespoon, scoop the meringue mixture into the gently simmering plum sauce. (You may need to cook the "islands" in two batches.)

6 Cover again and allow to simmer gently for 2–3 minutes, until the meringues are just set. Serve immediately, sprinkled with a little freshly grated nutmeg.

Cook's Tip
For ease of preparation when you are entertaining, the plum sauce can be made in advance and reheated just before you cook the meringues.

Souffléd Rice Pudding

The inclusion of fluffy egg whites in this rice pudding makes it unusually light.

Serves 4
¼ cup short-grain rice
3 tablespoons honey
3⅔ cups low-fat milk
1 vanilla pod or ½
 teaspoon vanilla
 extract

2 egg whites
1 teaspoon finely grated
 nutmeg

1 Place the rice, honey and the milk in a heavy-based or nonstick saucepan and bring to a boil. Add the vanilla pod, if using.

2 Reduce the heat and cover with a tight-fitting lid. Leave to simmer gently for about 1–1¼ hours, stirring occasionally to prevent sticking, until most of the liquid has been absorbed.

3 Remove the vanilla pod from the saucepan, or if using vanilla extract, add this to the rice mixture now. Preheat the oven to 425°F.

4 Place the egg whites in a clean dry bowl and whisk until stiff peaks form.

5 Using a metal spoon or spatula, fold the egg whites evenly into the rice mixture and turn into a 4-cup buttered baking dish.

6 Sprinkle with grated nutmeg and bake for 15–20 minutes, until the pudding has risen well and is golden brown. Serve hot.

Cabinet Pudding

Dried and candied fruit, sponge cake and macaroons, spiked with brandy if you wish, make a rich pudding.

Serves 4

2½ teaspoons raisins, chopped
2 tablespoons brandy (optional)
1 ounce candied cherries, halved
1 ounce angelica, chopped
2 slices sponge cakes
2 ounces ratafias
2 eggs
2 egg yolks
2 tablespoons sugar
1¾ cups light cream or milk
few drops of vanilla extract

1 Soak the raisins in the brandy, if using, for several hours.

2 Butter a 3⅔ cup charlotte mold and arrange some of the cherries and angelica in the bottom.

3 Dice the sponge cake and crush the macaroons. Mix with the remaining cherries and angelica, add the raisins and spoon into the mold.

4 Lightly whisk together the eggs, egg yolks and sugar. Bring the cream or milk just to a boil, then stir into the egg mixture with the vanilla extract.

5 Strain the egg mixture into the mold, then set aside for 15–30 minutes.

6 Preheat the oven to 325°F. Place the mould in a roasting pan, cover with baking parchment and pour in enough boiling water to half-fill the pan. Bake for 1 hour, or until set. Let sit for 2–3 minutes, then turn out onto a warm plate.

Eve's Pudding

The tempting apples beneath the sponge topping are the reason for this pudding's name.

Serves 4–6

½ cup butter, softened
½ cup sugar
2 eggs, beaten
grated rind and juice of 1 lemon
scant 1 cup self-rising flour
generous ¼ cup ground almonds
½ cup brown sugar
1½ pounds cooking apples, cored and thinly sliced
¼ cup flaked almonds

1 Preheat the oven to 375°F. Beat together the butter and sugar in a large mixing bowl until the mixture is very light and fluffy.

2 Gradually beat the eggs into the butter mixture, beating well after each addition, then fold in the lemon rind, flour and ground almonds.

3 Mix the brown sugar, apples and lemon juice, turn into an ovenproof dish, add the sponge mixture, then the almonds. Bake for 40–45 minutes, until golden.

Surprise Lemon Pudding

The surprise is a delicious tangy lemon sauce that forms beneath the light topping in this pudding.

Serves 4

6 tablespoons butter,
  softened
1½ cups light brown
  sugar

4 eggs, separated
grated rind and juice of 4
  lemons
½ cup self-rising flour

1   Preheat the oven to 350°F, then butter a 7-inch soufflé dish or cake pan and stand it in a roasting pan.

2   Beat the butter and sugar together in a large bowl until pale and very fluffy. Beat in one egg yolk at a time, beating well after each addition and gradually beating in the lemon rind and juice until blended; do not worry if the mixture curdles a little at this stage.

3   Sift the flour and stir into the lemon mixture until blended, then gradually stir in the milk.

4   Whisk the egg whites in a separate bowl until stiff peaks form but the whites are not dry, then lightly, but thoroughly, fold into the lemon mixture in three batches. Carefully pour the mixture into the soufflé dish or cake pan, then pour boiling water into the roasting pan to come halfway up the sides.

5   Bake the pudding in the center of the oven for about 45 minutes, or until risen, just firm to the touch and golden brown on top. Serve immediately.

Castle Puddings with Custard

These attractive puddings may be baked in ramekin dishes if you do not have dariole molds.

Serves 4

3 tablespoons
  blackcurrant,
  strawberry or
  raspberry jam
½ cup butter, softened
½ cup sugar
2 eggs, beaten
few drops of vanilla
  extract

generous 1 cup self-
  rising flour

For the custard
1 scant cup milk
4 eggs
1–2 tablespoons sugar
few drops of vanilla
  extract

1   Preheat the oven to 350°F. Butter eight dariole molds. Put about 2 teaspoons of your chosen jam in the base of each mold.

2   Beat the butter and sugar together until light and fluffy, then gradually beat in the eggs, beating well after each addition, and add the vanilla extract towards the end. Lightly fold in the flour, then divide the mixture among the molds. Bake the puddings for about 20 minutes until well risen and a light golden color.

3   To make the custard, whisk the eggs and sugar together. Bring the milk to a boil in a heavy, preferably nonstick, saucepan, then slowly pour onto the sweetened egg mixture, stirring constantly.

4   Return the milk to the pan and heat very gently, stirring, until the mixture thickens enough to coat the back of a spoon; do not allow to boil. Cover the pan and remove from the heat.

5   Remove the molds from the oven, let stand for a few minutes, then turn the puddings onto warmed plates and serve with the custard.

Bread and Butter Pudding

An unusual version of a classic recipe, this pudding is made with French bread and mixed dried fruit.

Serves 4–6

4 ready-to-eat dried
   apricots, finely
   chopped
1 tablespoon raisins
2 tablespoons golden
   raisins
1 tablespoon chopped
   mixed peel
1 French bread, about 7
   ounces, thinly sliced
4 tablespoons butter,
   melted
1¾ cups milk

⅔ cup heavy cream
½ cup caster sugar
3 eggs
½ teaspoon vanilla
   extract
2 tablespoons whiskey

For the cream
⅔ cup heavy cream
2 tablespoons plain
   strained yogurt
1–2 tablespoons whiskey
1 tablespoon sugar

1 Preheat the oven to 350°F. Butter a deep 6¼-cup baking dish. Mix together the dried fruits. Brush the bread on both sides with butter. Fill the dish with alternate layers of bread and dried fruit starting with fruit and finishing with bread. Heat the milk and cream in a saucepan until just boiling. Whisk together the sugar, eggs and vanilla extract.

2 Whisk the milk mixture into the eggs, then strain into the dish. Sprinkle the whiskey over the top. Press the bread down, cover with foil and allow to stand for 20 minutes.

3 Place the dish in a roasting pan half filled with water and bake for 1 hour, or until the custard is just set. Remove the foil and cook for 10 minutes more, until golden. Just before serving, heat all the cream ingredients in a small pan, stirring. Serve with the hot pudding.

Chocolate Amaretti Peaches

This dessert is quick and easy to prepare, yet sophisticated enough to serve at the most elegant dinner party.

Serves 4

4 ounces amaretti
   cookies, crushed
2 ounces semi-sweet
   chocolate, chopped
grated rind of ½ orange
1 tablespoon honey
¼ teaspoon ground
   cinnamon

1 egg white, lightly
   beaten
4 firm ripe peaches
⅔ cup white wine
1 tablespoon sugar
whipped cream, to serve

1 Preheat the oven to 375°F. Mix together the crushed amaretti cookies, chocolate, orange rind, honey and cinnamon in a bowl. Add the beaten egg white and mix to bind the mixture together.

2 Halve and pit the peaches and fill the cavities with the chocolate mixture, shaping it upwards slightly.

3 Arrange the stuffed peaches in a lightly buttered shallow baking dish which will just hold the fruit comfortably. Pour the wine into a measuring cup and stir in the sugar.

4 Pour the wine mixture around the peaches. Bake for 30–40 minutes, until the peaches are tender. Serve immediately with a little of the cooking juice spooned over and the whipped cream.

Cook's Tip
Prepare this dessert using fresh nectarines or apricots instead of peaches, if you wish.

Warm Autumn Compôte

This is a simple yet quite sophisticated dessert featuring succulent ripe autumnal fruits.

Serves 4

generous ¼ cup sugar
1 bottle red wine
1 vanilla pod, split
1 strip pared lemon rind

4 pears
2 fresh figs, quartered
2 cups raspberries
lemon juice, to taste

1 Put the sugar and red wine in a large saucepan and heat gently until the sugar has completely dissolved. Add the vanilla pod and lemon rind and bring to a boil. Reduce the heat and simmer for 5 minutes.

2 Peel and halve the pears, then scoop out the cores, using a melon baller or teaspoon. Add the pears to the syrup and poach for about 15 minutes, turning them several times so they color evenly.

3 Add the quartered figs and poach for another 5 minutes, until the fruits are tender.

4 Transfer the poached pears and figs to a serving bowl using a slotted spoon, then scatter on the raspberries.

5 Return the syrup to the heat and boil rapidly to reduce slightly and concentrate the flavor. Add a little lemon juice to taste. Strain the syrup over the fruits and serve warm.

Apple Soufflé Omelet

Apples sautéed until they are slightly caramelized make a delicious autumn filling for this sweet omelet.

Serves 2

4 eggs, separated
2 tablespoons light cream
1 tablespoon sugar
1 tablespoon butter
sifted confectioner's
   sugar, for dredging

For the filling
1 eating apple, peeled,
   cored and sliced
2 tablespoons butter
2 tablespoons soft light
   brown sugar
3 tablespoons light cream

1 To make the filling, sauté the apple slices in the butter and sugar until just tender. Stir in the cream and keep warm, while making the omelet.

2 Place the egg yolks in a bowl with the cream and sugar and beat well. Whisk the egg whites until stiff peaks form, then fold into the yolk mixture.

3 Melt the butter in a large heavy-based frying pan, pour in the soufflé mixture and spread evenly. Cook for 1 minute until golden underneath, then place under a hot grill to brown the top.

4 Slide the omelet onto a plate, spoon the apple mixture on to one side, then fold over. Dredge the icing sugar over thickly, then quickly mark in a criss-cross pattern with a hot metal skewer. Serve the omelet immediately.

Cook's Tip
In the summer months, make the filling for the omelet using fresh raspberries or strawberries.

Warm Lemon and Syrup Cake

This simple cake is made special by the lemon syrup which is poured over it when baked.

Serves 8

3 eggs
¾ cup butter, softened
¾ cup sugar
1½ cups self-rising flour
½ cup ground almonds
¼ teaspoon freshly grated nutmeg
2 ounces candied lemon peel, finely chopped

grated rind of 1 lemon
2 tablespoons freshly squeezed lemon juice
poached pears, to serve

For the syrup
¼ cup sugar
juice of 3 lemons

1 Preheat the oven to 350°F. Lightly grease and base-line a deep round 8-inch cake pan.

2 Place all the cake ingredients in a large bowl and beat well for 2–3 minutes, until light and fluffy.

3 Turn the mixture into the prepared pan, spread evenly and bake for 1 hour, or until golden and firm to the touch.

4 To make the syrup, put the sugar, lemon juice and 5 tablespoons water in a saucepan. Heat gently, stirring until the sugar has completely dissolved, then boil, without stirring, for 1–2 minutes.

5 Turn out the cake onto a plate with a rim. Prick the surface of the cake all over with a fork, then pour on the hot syrup. Allow to soak for about 30 minutes. Serve the cake warm with thin wedges of poached pears.

Papaya and Pineapple Crisp

Crisps are always popular with children and adults, but you can make a change with this exotic variation.

Serves 4–6

For the topping
1½ cups all-purpose flour
6 tablespoons butter, diced
generous ¼ cup sugar
½ cup mixed chopped nuts

For the filling
1 medium-ripe pineapple
1 large ripe papaya
1 tablespoon sugar
1 teaspoon mixed spice
grated rind of 1 lime
plain yogurt, to serve

1 Preheat the oven to 350°F. To make the topping, sift the flour into a bowl and rub in the butter until the mixture resembles bread crumbs. Stir in the sugar and mixed chopped nuts.

2 Peel the pineapple, remove the eyes, then cut in half. Cut away the core and cut the flesh into bite-size chunks. Halve the papaya and scoop out the seeds using a spoon. Peel, then cut the fruit into similar-size pieces.

3 Put the pineapple and papaya chunks into a large pie pan. Sprinkle over the sugar, mixed spice and lime rind and toss gently to mix.

4 Spoon the crisp topping over the fruit and spread out evenly with a fork, but don't press it down. Bake in the oven for 45–50 minutes, until golden brown. Serve the crisp hot or warm with plain yogurt.

Zabaglione

A much-loved simple Italian dessert traditionally made with Marsala, an Italian fortified wine.

Serves 4

4 egg yolks
4 tablespoons sugar
4 tablespoons Marsala
amaretti cookies, to serve

1 Place the egg yolks and sugar in a large heat-proof bowl and beat with an electric hand mixer until the mixture is pale and thick.

2 Gradually add the Marsala, about 1 tablespoon at a time, beating well after each addition (at this stage the mixture will be quite runny).

3 Place the bowl over a saucepan of gently simmering water and continue to beat for at least 5–7 minutes, until the mixture becomes thick and mousse-like; when the beaters are lifted they should leave a thick trail on the surface of the mixture. (If you don't beat the mixture for long enough, the zabaglione will be too runny and will probably separate.)

4 Pour into four warmed stemmed glasses and serve immediately with the amaretti cookies for dipping.

Cook's Tip

If you don't have any Marsala, substitute Madeira, a medium-sweet sherry or a dessert wine.

Thai-fried Bananas

This is a very simple and quick Thai dessert – bananas are simply fried in butter, brown sugar and lime juice.

Serves 4

3 tablespoons unsalted
  butter
4 large slightly under-
  ripe bananas
1 tablespoon dried
  coconut
4 tablespoons ight brown
  sugar
4 tablespoons lime juice
2 lime slices, to decorate
thick and creamy plain
  yogurt, to serve

1 Heat the butter in a large frying pan or wok and fry the bananas for 1–2 minutes on each side, or until they are lightly golden in color.

2 Meanwhile, dry fry the coconut in a small frying pan until lightly browned and reserve.

3 Sprinkle the sugar into the pan with the bananas, add the lime juice and cook, stirring, until dissolved. Sprinkle the coconut over the bananas, decorate with lime slices and serve with the thick and creamy yogurt.

Crêpes Suzette

This dish is a classic of French cuisine and still enjoys worldwide popularity as a dessert or a daytime treat.

Makes 8

1 cup all-purpose flour
pinch of salt
1 egg
1 egg yolk
1¼ cups low-fat milk
1 tablespoon butter, melted, plus extra, for shallow frying

For the sauce
2 large oranges
4 tablespoons butter
½ cup soft light brown sugar
1 tablespoon Grand Marnier
1 tablespoon brandy

1 Sift the flour and salt into a bowl and make a well in the center. Crack the egg and extra yolk into the well. Stir the eggs to incorporate all the flour. When the mixture thickens, gradually pour in the milk, beating well after each addition, until a smooth batter is formed. Stir in the butter, transfer to a measuring cup, cover and chill for 30 minutes.

2 Heat a shallow frying pan, add a little butter and heat until sizzling. Pour in a little batter, tilting the pan to cover the base. Cook over moderate heat for 1–2 minutes until lightly browned underneath, then flip and cook for minute more. Make eight crêpes and stack them on a plate.

3 Pare the rind from one of the oranges and reserve about 1 teaspoon. Squeeze the juice from both oranges.

4 To make the sauce, melt the butter in a large frying pan and heat the sugar with the rind and juice until dissolved and gently bubbling. Fold each crêpe in quarters. Add to the pan one at a time, coat in the sauce and fold in half again. Move to the side of the pan to make room for the others.

5 Pour on the Grand Marnier and brandy and cook gently for 2–3 minutes, until the sauce has slightly caramelized. Sprinkle with the reserved orange rind and serve immediately.

Bananas with Rum and Raisins

Choose almost-ripe bananas with evenly colored skins, all yellow or just green at the tips for this dessert.

Serves 4

scant ¼ cup seedless raisins
5 tablespoons dark rum
4 tablespoons unsalted butter
½ cup light brown sugar
4 bananas, peeled and halved lengthwise
¼ teaspoon grated nutmeg

¼ teaspoon ground cinnamon
2 tablespoons slivered almonds, toasted
chilled cream or vanilla ice cream, to serve (optional)

1 Put the raisins in a bowl with the rum. Allow them to soak for about 30 minutes to plump up.

2 Melt the butter in a frying pan, add the sugar and stir until completely dissolved. Add the bananas and cook for a few minutes until tender.

3 Sprinkle the spices over the bananas, then pour on the rum and raisins. Carefully ignite using a long taper and stir gently to mix.

4 Scatter over the slivered almonds and serve immediately with chilled cream or vanilla ice cream, if you wish.

Cook's Tip
Stand a way back when you ignite the rum and shake the pan gently until the flames subside.

Orange Rice Pudding

In Spain, Greece, Italy and Morocco rice puddings are a favorite dish, especially when sweetened with honey.

Serves 4

¼ cup short-grain rice
2½ cups milk
2–3 tablespoons honey, to taste
finely grated rind of ½ small orange
⅔ cup heavy cream
1 tablespoon chopped pistachios, toasted

1 Mix the rice with the milk, honey and orange rind in a saucepan and bring to a boil, then reduce the heat, cover with a tight-fitting lid and simmer very gently for about 1¼ hours, stirring regularly.

2 Remove the lid and continue cooking and stirring for about 15–20 minutes, until the rice is creamy.

3 Pour in the cream and simmer for 5–8 minutes longer. Serve the rice sprinkled with the chopped toasted pistachios in individual warmed bowls.

Apple and Blackberry Nut Crisp

This much-loved dish of tart apples and blackberries is topped with a golden, sweet topping.

Serves 4

2 pounds tart apples, peeled, cored and sliced
½ cup butter
½ cup light brown sugar
1½ cups blackberries
¾ cup whole wheat flour
¾ cup all-purpose flour
½ teaspoon ground cinnamon
3 tablespoons chopped mixed nuts, toasted
custard, cream or ice cream, to serve

1 Preheat the oven to 350°F. Lightly butter a 5-cup baking dish.

2 Place the apples in a saucepan with 2 tablespoons of the butter, 2 tablespoons of the sugar and 1 tablespoon water. Cover with a tight-fitting lid and cook gently for about 10 minutes, until just tender but still holding their shape.

3 Remove from the heat and gently stir in the blackberries. Spoon the mixture into the baking dish and set aside while you make the topping.

4 To make the crisp topping, sift the flours and cinnamon into a bowl (add in any of the bran left in the sifter). Add the remaining 6 tablespoons butter and rub into the flour with your fingertips until the mixture resembles fine bread crumbs (or you can use a food processor).

5 Stir in the remaining generous ¼ cup sugar and the nuts and mix well. Sprinkle the crisp topping on the fruit. Bake for 35–40 minutes, until the top is golden brown. Serve hot with custard, cream or ice cream.

Apple Strudel

This Austrian dessert, traditionally made with strudel pastry, is just as good prepared with phyllo pastry.

Serves 4–6

¾ cup hazelnuts, chopped and roasted
2 tablespoons nibbed almonds, roasted
4 tablespoons brown sugar
½ teaspoon ground cinnamon
grated rind and juice of ½ lemon

2 large cooking apples, peeled, cored and chopped
⅓ cup golden raisins
4 large sheets phyllo pastry
4 tablespoons unsalted butter, melted
sifted confectioner's sugar, for dusting
cream, custard or yogurt, to serve

1 Preheat the oven to 375°F. In a bowl mix together the hazelnuts, almonds, sugar, cinnamon, lemon rind and juice, apples and raisins. Set aside.

2 Lay one sheet of phyllo pastry on a clean dish towel and brush with melted butter. Lay a second sheet on top and brush again with melted butter. Repeat with the remaining two sheets.

3 Spread the fruit and nut mixture over the pastry, leaving a 3-inch border at each of the shorter ends. Fold the pastry ends in over the filling. Roll up from one long edge to the other, using the dish towel to help.

4 Carefully transfer the strudel to a greased baking sheet, placing it join-side down. Brush all over with butter and bake for 30–35 minutes, until golden and crisp. Dust the strudel generously with confectioner's sugar and serve while still hot with cream, custard or yogurt.

Banana, Maple and Lime Crêpes

Crêpes are a treat any day of the week, and they can be made in advance and stored in the freezer for convenience.

Serves 4

1 cup all-purpose flour
1 egg white
1 cup skim milk
¼ cup cold water
sunflower oil, for frying

For the filling
4 bananas, sliced
3 tablespoons maple or golden syrup
2 tablespoons freshly squeezed lime juice
strips of lime rind, to decorate

1 Beat together the flour, egg white, milk and water until smooth and bubbly. Chill in the fridge until needed.

2 Heat a small amount of oil in a nonstick frying pan and pour in enough batter just to coat the bottom. Swirl it around the pan to coat evenly.

3 Cook until golden, then toss or turn and cook the other side. Place on a plate, cover with foil and keep hot while making the remaining pancakes.

4 To make the filling, place the bananas, syrup and lime juice in a saucepan and simmer gently for 1 minute. Spoon into the pancakes and fold into quarters. Sprinkle with shreds of lime rind to decorate. Serve hot, with yogurt or sour cream, if you wish.

Cook's Tip
To freeze the crêpes, separate them with nonstick baking parchment and seal in a plastic bag. They should be used within 3 months.

Spiced Pears in Cider

Any variety of pear can be used for cooking, but choose a firm variety such as Conference for this recipe.

Serves 4

4 medium-firm pears
1 cup hard cider
thinly pared strip of
    lemon rind
1 cinnamon stick

2 tablespoons light
    brown sugar
1 teaspoon arrowroot
ground cinnamon, to
    sprinkle

1 Peel the pears thinly, leaving them whole with the stalks on. Place in a saucepan with the cider, lemon rind and cinnamon. Cover and simmer gently, turning the pears occasionally, for 15–20 minutes or until tender.

2 Lift out the pears. Boil the syrup, uncovered, to reduce by about half. Remove the lemon rind and cinnamon stick, then stir in the sugar.

3 Mix the arrowroot with 1 tablespoon cold water in a small bowl until smooth, then stir into the syrup. Bring to a boil and stir over the heat until thickened and clear.

4 Pour the sauce over the pears and sprinkle with ground cinnamon. Let cool slightly, then serve warm with yogurt, if you wish.

Cook's Tip
Whole pears look impressive but if you prefer they can be halved and cored before cooking. This will shorten the cooking time slightly.

Fruity Bread Pudding

A delicious old-fashioned family favorite is given a lighter, healthier touch in this version.

Serves 4

⅔ cup mixed dried fruit
⅔ cup apple juice
4 ounces stale brown or
    white bread, diced
1 teaspoon mixed spice

1 large banana, sliced
⅔ cup skim milk
1 tablespoon brown
    sugar
plain yogurt, to serve

1 Preheat the oven to 400°F. Place the mixed dried fruit in a small saucepan with the apple juice and bring to a boil.

2 Remove the pan from the heat and stir in the diced bread, mixed spice and banana. Spoon the mixture into a shallow 5-cup baking dish; pour over the milk.

3 Sprinkle with brown sugar and bake for about 25–30 minutes, until firm and golden brown. Serve hot or cold with plain yogurt.

Cook's Tip
Different types of bread will absorb varying amounts of liquid, so you may need to adjust the amount of milk used to allow for this.

Crunchy Gooseberry Crisp

Gooseberries are perfect for traditional family desserts such as this extra-special crisp.

Serves 4

4¼ cups gooseberries
4 tablespoons sugar
1 cup rolled oats
¼ cup whole wheat flour
4 tablespoons sunflower
   oil

4 tablespoons brown
   sugar
2 tablespoons chopped
   walnuts
plain yogurt or vanilla
   custard, to serve

1 Preheat the oven to 400°F. Place the gooseberries in a saucepan with the sugar. Cover the pan and cook over a low heat for 10 minutes, until the gooseberries are just tender. Pour into a baking dish.

2 To make the crisp, place the oats, flour and oil in a bowl and stir with a fork until evenly mixed.

3 Stir in the brown sugar and walnuts, then spread evenly over the gooseberries. Bake for 25–30 minutes, or until golden and bubbling. Serve hot with yogurt or custard.

Cook's Tip
When gooseberries are out of season substitute other fruits, such as apples, plums or rhubarb.

Gingerbread Upside-down Pudding

A proper pudding goes down well on a cold winter's day. This one is quite quick to make and looks very impressive.

Serves 4–6

sunflower oil, for
   brushing
1 tablespoon brown
   sugar
4 peaches, halved and
   pitted, or canned
   peach halves, drained
8 walnut halves

For the base
½ cup whole wheat flour
½ teaspoon baking soda
1½ teaspoons ground
   ginger
1 teaspoon ground
   cinnamon
½ cup dark brown sugar
1 egg
½ cup skim milk
¼ cup sunflower oil

1 Preheat the oven to 350°. Brush the bottom and sides of a 9-inch round springform cake pan with oil. Sprinkle the brown sugar evenly over the base.

2 Arrange the peaches, cut-side down, in the pan with a walnut half in each.

3 To make the base, sift together the flour, baking soda, ginger and cinnamon, then stir in the sugar. Beat together the egg, milk and oil, then mix into the dry ingredients until smooth.

4 Pour the mixture evenly over the peaches and bake for 35–40 minutes, until firm to the touch. Turn out onto a serving plate. Serve hot with yogurt or custard, if liked.

Cook's Tip
The brown sugar caramelizes during baking, creating a delightfully sticky topping.

Lemon Meringue Pie

In this popular dish, light meringue topping crowns the delicious citrus-filled pie.

Makes an 7½-inch pie

1 cup all-purpose flour
4 tablespoons butter, cubed
3 tablespoons ground almonds
2 tablespoons sugar
1 egg yolk

finely grated rind of 2 lemons
3 tablespoons cornstarch
generous ¼ cup sugar
2 egg yolks
1 tablespoon butter

For the filling
juice of 3 lemons

For the meringue
2 egg whites
½ cup sugar

1 Rub the butter into the flour until the mixture resembles bread crumbs. Stir in the almonds and sugar, add the egg yolk and 2 tablespoons cold water. Mix until the pastry comes together. Knead on a lightly floured surface, then wrap and chill in the fridge for about 30 minutes.

2 Preheat a baking sheet at 400°F. Roll out the pastry and use to line a 7½-inch fluted loose-based tart pan. Prick the base. Line with greaseproof paper and fill with baking beans. Place the pan on the baking sheet and bake blind for 12 minutes. Remove the paper and beans and bake for 5 minutes more. Allow to cool. Reduce the temperature to 300°F.

3 For the filling, blend the lemon juice, rind and cornflour. Pour into a saucepan and add ⅔ cup water. Bring to a boil, stirring until smooth and thickened. Remove and beat in the sugar and egg yolks, then add the butter. Spoon into the pastry case. For the meringue, whisk the egg whites until stiff, then gradually whisk in the sugar until thick and glossy. Pile on top of the filling. Bake for 30–35 minutes, or until golden.

Apple and Orange Pie

A simple but tasty two-fruit pie: make sure you choose really juicy oranges or even blood oranges.

Serves 4

14 ounces ready-made shortcrust pastry
3 oranges, peeled
2 pounds cooking apples, cored and thickly sliced

2 tablespoons brown sugar
beaten egg, to glaze
sugar, for sprinkling

1 Roll out the pastry on a lightly floured surface to about ¾ inches larger than the top of a 5-cup pie pan. Cut off a narrow strip around the edge of the pastry and fit on the rim of the pie pan.

2 Preheat the oven to 375°F. Hold one orange at a time over a bowl to catch the juice; cut down between the membranes to remove the segments.

3 Mix the segments and juice, the apples and sugar in the pie dish. Place a pie funnel in the center of the dish.

4 Moisten the pastry strip. Cover the dish with the rolled out pastry and press the edges to the pastry strip. Brush the top with beaten egg, then bake for 35–40 minutes, until lightly browned. Sprinkle with sugar before serving.

Bakewell Tart

A classic English dessert, this tart is moist with a delicious almond flavor.

Serves 4

8 ounces ready-made puff
  pastry
2 tablespoons raspberry
  or apricot jam
2 eggs
2 egg yolks
½ cup sugar

½ cup butter, melted
⅔ cup ground almonds
few drops of almond
  extract
sifted confectioner's
  sugar, for dredging

1 Preheat the oven to 400°F. Roll out the pastry on a lightly floured surface and use it to line a 7-inch pie pan or fluted loose-based tart pan. Spread the jam over the base of the pastry case.

2 Whisk the eggs, egg yolks and sugar together in a large bowl until thick and pale.

3 Gently stir the butter, ground almonds and almond extract into the mixture.

4 Pour the mixture into the pie shell and bake for about 30 minutes, until the filling is just set and browned. Dredge with confectioner's sugar before eating hot, warm or cold.

Cook's Tip
Since the pastry case isn't baked blind first, place a baking sheet in the oven while it preheats, then place the pie pan or tart pan on the hot sheet. This will make sure that the base of the pastry shell cooks through.

Yorkshire Curd Tart

The distinguishing characteristic of this tart is the allspice, or "clove pepper" as it was once known in Yorkshire, England

Serves 8

2 cups all-purpose flour
½ cup butter, cubed
1 egg yolk

For the filling
large pinch of allspice
1 scant cup light brown
  sugar

3 eggs, beaten
grated rind and juice of
  1 lemon
3 tablespoons butter,
  melted
2 cups ricotta cheese
½ cup raisins or golden
  raisins

1 Place the flour in a bowl. Add the butter and rub it into the flour with your fingertips until the mixture resembles bread crumbs. (Alternatively, you can use a food processor.) Stir the egg yolk into the flour mixture with a little water to bind the dough together.

2 Turn the dough onto a lightly floured surface, knead lightly and briefly, then form into a ball. Roll out the pastry thinly and use to line an 8-inch fluted loose-based tart pan. Chill for 15 minutes in the fridge.

3 Preheat the oven to 375°F. To make the filling, mix the allspice with the sugar, then stir in the eggs, lemon rind and juice, melted butter, ricotta cheese and the raisins or golden raisins.

4 Pour the filling into the pie shell, then bake for about 40 minutes until the pastry is cooked and the filling is lightly set and golden brown. Serve still slightly warm, cut into wedges, with cream, if you wish.

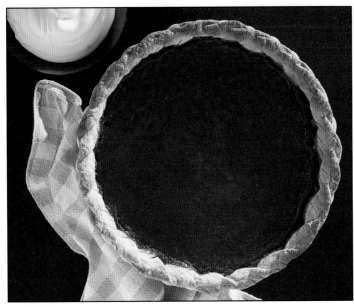

American Spiced Pumpkin Pie

This is a rich, delicately-spiced pie that deservedly goes with Thanksgiving.

Serves 4–6

1½ cups all-purpose flour
pinch of salt
6 tablespoons unsalted
 butter
1 tablespoon caster sugar
3 cups peeled fresh diced
 pumpkin, or 14
 ounces canned
 pumpkin, drained
1 cup light brown sugar

¼ teaspoon salt
¼ teaspoon ground
 allspice
½ teaspoon ground
 cinnamon
½ teaspoon ground
 ginger
2 eggs, lightly beaten
½ cup heavy cream
whipped cream, to serve

1 Place the flour in a bowl with a pinch of salt. Rub in the butter until the mixture resembles bread crumbs. Add the sugar and 2–3 tablespoons water. Mix to a soft dough. Knead briefly, shape into a ball, wrap and chill for 1 hour.

2 Preheat the oven to 400°F with a baking sheet inside. If using fresh pumpkin, steam for 15 minutes, then cool. Purée in a food processor or blender until smooth.

3 Line a 9½-inch x 1-inch deep pie pan with the pastry. Prick the bottom. Cut out leaf shapes from the excess pastry and mark veins with the back of a knife. Brush the edges with water and stick on the leaves. Chill.

4 Mix together the pumpkin purée, sugar, salt, spices, eggs and cream and pour into the pie shell. Place on the preheated baking sheet and bake for 15 minutes. Then reduce the temperature to 350°F and cook for another 30 minutes, or until the filling is set and the pastry golden. Serve warm with whipped cream.

Pear and Blueberry Pie

A variation on plain blueberry pie, this dessert is just as delicious served cold as it is warm.

Serves 4

2 cups all-purpose flour
pinch of salt
4 tablespoons lard, diced
4 tablespoons butter,
 diced
4½ cups blueberries
2 tablespoons sugar
1 tablespoon arrowroot

2 ripe but firm pears,
 peeled, cored and
 sliced
½ teaspoon ground
 cinnamon
grated rind of ½ lemon
beaten egg, to glaze
sugar, for sprinkling

1 Sift the flour and salt into a bowl. Rub in the fats until the mixture resembles fine bread crumbs. Mix to a dough with 3 tablespoons cold water. Chill for 30 minutes.

2 Place 2 cups of the blueberries in a saucepan with the sugar. Cover with a lid and cook gently until the blueberries have softened. Press through a nylon strainer. Blend the arrowroot with 2 tablespoons cold water and add to the blueberries. Bring to a boil, stirring until thickened. Allow to cool slightly.

3 Preheat the oven to 375°F with a baking sheet inside. Roll out just over half the pastry on a lightly floured surface and use to line an 8-inch shallow pie pan.

4 Mix together the remaining blueberries, the pears, ground cinnamon and lemon rind and spoon into the dish. Pour over the blueberry purée.

5 Use the remaining pastry to cover the pie. Make a slit in the center. Brush with egg and sprinkle with sugar. Bake on the baking sheet for 40–45 minutes, until golden. Serve warm, with crème fraîche, if you wish.

Mississippi Pecan Pie

Serve this gooey pie with a bowl of fluffy whipped cream or ice cream.

Serves 4–6
For the pastry
1 cup all-purpose flour
4 tablespoons butter
2 tablespoons caster sugar
1 egg yolk

For the filling
5 tablespoons maple or corn syrup
⅓ cup dark brown sugar
4 tablespoons butter
3 eggs, lightly beaten
½ teaspoon vanilla extract
1¼ cups pecan nuts
fresh cream, whipped, if liked or ice cream, to serve

1 Place the flour in a bowl. Dice the butter, then rub it into the flour with your fingertips until the mixture resembles bread crumbs. (Alternatively use a food processor.) Stir in the sugar, egg yolk and about 2 tablespoons cold water. Mix to a dough and knead on a lightly floured surface until smooth.

2 Roll out the pastry and use it to line an 8-inch fluted loose-based tart pan. Prick the bottom, then line with greaseproof paper and fill with baking beans. Chill for 30 minutes in the fridge. Preheat the oven to 400°F.

3 Bake the pie shell blind for 10 minutes. Remove the paper and beans and continue to bake for 5 more minutes. Reduce the oven temperature to 350°F.

4 To make the filling, heat the syrup, sugar and butter in a saucepan until the sugar dissolves. Remove from the heat and cool slightly. Whisk in the eggs and vanilla extract and stir in the pecan nuts.

5 Pour into the pastry case and bake for 35–40 minutes until the filling is set. Serve with cream or ice cream.

Upside-down Apple Tart

Use tart apples in this delicious dessert with a lovely caramel layer.

Serves 4
For the pastry
4 tablespoons butter, softened
3 tablespoons sugar
1 egg
1 cup all-purpose flour
pinch of salt

For the apple layer
generous ¼ cup butter, softened
scant ½ cup light brown sugar
10 Granny Smith's apples, peeled, cored and thickly sliced
whipped cream, to serve

1 For the pastry, cream the butter and sugar until pale and creamy. Beat in the egg, sift in the flour and salt and mix to a soft dough. Knead, wrap and chill for 1 hour.

2 For the apple layer, grease a 9-inch cake pan, then add 4 tablespoons of the butter. Place on the stove and melt the butter. Remove from the heat and sprinkle over 4 tablespoons of the sugar. Arrange the apple slices on top, sprinkle with the remaining sugar and dot with the remaining butter.

3 Preheat the oven to 450°F. Place the cake tin on the stove again over low to moderate heat for about 15 minutes, until a light golden caramel forms on the bottom.

4 Roll out the pastry on a lightly floured surface to around the same size as the pan and lay it on top of the apples. Tuck the pastry edges down around the sides of the apples.

5 Bake for about 20–25 minutes, until the pastry is golden. Remove from the oven and let stand for 5 minutes.

6 Place an upturned plate on top of the pan and, holding the two together with a dish towel, turn the apple tart out onto the plate. Serve while still warm with whipped cream.

Gooseberry and Elderflower Cream

When elderflowers are in season, instead of using the cordial, cook two to three elderflower heads with the gooseberries.

Serves 4

4¼ cups gooseberries
1¼ cups heavy cream
about 1 cup sifted
   confectioner's sugar,
   to taste

2 tablespoons elderflower
   cordial or orange-
   flower water
   (optional)
fresh mint sprigs, to
   decorate
almond cookies, to serve

1 Place the gooseberries in a heavy saucepan, cover and cook over low heat, shaking the pan occasionally, until the gooseberries are tender. Transfer the gooseberries to a bowl, crush them, then leave to cool completely.

2 Beat the cream until soft peaks form, then fold in half of the crushed gooseberries. Sweeten with confectioner's sugar and add the elderflower cordial, or orange-flower water to taste, if using. Sweeten the remaining gooseberries.

3 Layer the cream mixture and the crushed gooseberries in four dessert dishes or tall glasses, then cover and chill. Decorate the dessert with the fresh mint sprigs and serve with almond cookies.

Cook's Tip
If preferred, the cooked gooseberries can be puréed and strained instead of crushed.

Eton Mess

This dish forms part of the picnic meals enjoyed by parents and pupils at Eton, a prestigious English private school.

Serves 4

4¼ cups strawberries,
   coarsely chopped
3–4 tablespoons Kirsch
1¼ cups heavy cream

6 small white meringues
fresh mint sprigs, to
   decorate

1 Put the strawberries in a bowl, sprinkle on the Kirsch, then cover and chill in the fridge for 2–3 hours.

2 Whip the cream until soft peaks form, then gently fold in the strawberries with their juice.

3 Crush the meringues into coarse chunks, then scatter on the strawberry mixture and fold in gently.

4 Spoon the strawberry mixture into a glass serving bowl, decorate with the fresh mint sprigs and serve immediately.

Cook's Tip
If you would prefer to make a less rich version of this dessert, use strained plain or thick and creamy yogurt instead of part or all of the cream. Simply beat the yogurt gently before adding the strawberries.

Atholl Brose

Crunchy toasted oatmeal and soft raspberries combine to give this dessert a lovely texture.

Serves 4

4 tablespoons honey
3 tablespoons whiskey
¾ cup medium oatmeal
1¼ cups heavy cream

3 cups raspberries
fresh mint sprigs, to
*   decorate*

1 Gently warm the honey in the whiskey, then leave to cool.

2 Preheat the broiler. Spread the oatmeal in a very shallow layer in the broiler pan and toast, stirring occasionally, until browned. Allow to cool.

3 Whip the cream in a large bowl until soft peaks form, then gently stir in the oats, honey and whiskey until well combined.

4 Reserve a few raspberries for decoration, then layer the remainder with the oat mixture in four tall glasses. Cover and chill in the fridge for 2 hours.

5 About 30 minutes before serving, transfer the glasses to room temperature. Decorate with the reserved raspberries and mint sprigs.

Old English Trifle

If you are making this pudding for children, replace the sherry and brandy with orange juice.

Serves 6

2 cups day-old sponge
*   cake, broken into*
*   bite-size pieces*
1 cup macaroon crumbs
⅓ cup medium sherry
2 tablespoons brandy
3 cups prepared fruit
*   such as raspberries,*
*   peaches or*
*   strawberries*
1¼ cups heavy cream

scant ½ cup toasted
*   flaked almonds, to*
*   decorate*
strawberries, to decorate

For the custard
4 egg yolks
2 tablespoons sugar
1¾ cups light or
*   whipping cream*
few drops of vanilla
*   extract*

1 Put the sponge cake and macaroon crumbs in a glass serving dish, then sprinkle on the sherry and brandy and let sit until they have been absorbed.

2 To make the custard, whisk the egg yolks and sugar together. Bring the cream to a boil in a heavy saucepan, then pour onto the egg yolk mixture, stirring constantly.

3 Return the mixture to the pan and heat very gently, stirring all the time with a wooden spoon, until the custard thickens enough to coat the back of the spoon; do not allow to boil. Allow to cool, stirring occasionally.

4 Put the fruit in an even layer over the sponge cake and macaroon crumbs in the serving dish, then strain the custard over the fruit and allow to set. Lightly whip the cream, spread it over the custard, then chill the trifle well. Decorate with flaked almonds and strawberries just before serving.

Cherry Syllabub

This recipe follows the style of the earliest syllabubs and produces a frothy creamy layer over a liquid one.

Serves 4
2 cups ripe dark cherries, pitted and chopped
2 tablespoons Kirsch
2 egg whites
2 tablespoons lemon juice
¾ cup sweet white wine
generous ¼ cup sugar
1¼ cups heavy cream

1 Divide the chopped cherries among six tall dessert glasses and sprinkle over the Kirsch.

2 In a clean bowl, whisk the egg whites until stiff peaks form. Gently fold in the lemon juice, wine and sugar.

3 In a separate bowl (but using the same whisk), lightly beat the cream, then fold into the egg white mixture. Spoon the cream mixture over the cherries, then chill overnight in the fridge.

Damask Cream

It is important not to move this simple, light, yet elegant dessert while it is setting, otherwise it will separate.

Serves 4
2½ cups milk
3 tablespoons sugar
several drops of triple-strength rose water
2 teaspoons rennet
4 tablespoons heavy cream
sugared rose petals, to decorate (optional)

1 Gently heat the milk and 2 tablespoons of the sugar, stirring, until the sugar has melted and the temperature reaches 98.4°F, or the milk feels neither hot nor cold. Stir rose water to taste into the milk, then remove the saucepan from the heat and stir in the rennet.

2 Pour the milk into a serving dish and leave undisturbed for 2–3 hours, until set. Stir the remaining sugar into the cream, then carefully spoon on the top. Decorate with sugared rose petals, if you wish.

Mandarins in Orange-flower Syrup

Mandarins, tangerines, clementines, mineolas: any of these lovely citrus fruits are suitable to use in this recipe.

Serves 4
Pare some rind from one mandarin and cut it into fine shreds for decoration. Squeeze the juice from two mandarins and reserve it. Peel eight more mandarins, removing the white pith. Arrange the whole fruit in a wide dish. Mix the reserved juice, 1 tablespoon confectioner's sugar and 2 teaspoons orange-flower water and pour it over the fruit. Cover and chill. Blanch the rind in boiling water for 30 seconds. Drain, cool and sprinkle on the mandarins, with pistachio nuts, to serve.

Chocolate Blancmange

For a special dinner party, flavor the blancmange with peppermint extract, crème de menthe or orange liqueur.

Serves 4

4 tablespoons cornstarch
2½ cups milk
3 tablespoons sugar

2–4oz semisweet
   chocolate, chopped
vanilla extract, to taste
chocolate curls, to
   decorate

1 Rinse a 3⅔-cup fluted mold with cold water and leave it upside down to drain. Blend the cornstarch to a smooth paste with a little of the milk.

2 Bring the remaining milk to a boil, preferably in a non-stick saucepan, then pour onto the blended mixture, stirring all the time.

3 Pour all the milk back into the saucepan and bring slowly to a boil over a low heat, stirring all the time until the mixture boils and thickens. Remove the pan from the heat, then add the sugar, chopped chocolate and a few drops of vanilla extract. Stir until the chocolate has melted.

4 Pour the chocolate mixture into the mold and leave in a cool place for several hours to set.

5 To unmold the blancmange, place on a large serving plate, then holding the plate and mold firmly together, invert them. Give both plate and mold a gentle but firm shake to loosen the blancmange, then lift off the mold. Scatter white and plain chocolate curls on the top of the blancmange to decorate and serve immediately.

Cook's Tip
If you prefer, set the blancmange in four or six individual molds.

Honeycomb Mold

These honeycomb molds have a fresh lemon flavor. The layered mixture looks most attractive.

Serves 4

2 tablespoons cold water
½ ounce gelatin
2 eggs, separated
generous ¼ cup sugar

2 cups milk
grated rind of 1 small
   lemon
4 tablespoons lemon juice

1 Chill four individual molds or, if you prefer, use a 5-cup fluted mold. Mix together the water and the gelatin and let soften for 5 minutes. Place the bowl over a small saucepan of hot water and stir occasionally until dissolved.

2 Meanwhile, whisk the egg yolks and sugar together until pale, thick and fluffy.

3 Bring the milk to a boil in a heavy, preferably nonstick, saucepan, then slowly pour onto the egg yolk mixture, stirring all the time.

4 Return the milk mixture to the pan, then heat gently, stirring continuously until thickened. Do not allow to boil or it will curdle. Remove from the heat and stir in the grated lemon rind and juice.

5 Stir 2 or 3 spoonfuls of the lemon mixture into the gelatin, and then stir this back into the saucepan. In a clean dry bowl, whisk the egg whites until they are stiff but not too dry, then gently fold into the mixture in the saucepan in three batches, being careful to retain the air.

6 Rinse the molds or mold with cold water and drain well, then pour in the lemon mixture. Allow to cool, then cover and chill in the fridge until set. To serve, invert on to four individual or one serving plate.

Peach Melba

The original dish created for the opera singer Dame Nelli Melba had peaches and ice cream served upon an ice swan.

Serves 4

scant 2 cups raspberries
squeeze of lemon juice
confectioner's sugar, to
   taste

2 large ripe peaches or
   15-ounce can sliced
   peaches
8 scoops vanilla ice cream

1 Press the raspberries through a non-metallic strainer.

2 Add a little lemon juice to the raspberry purée and sweeten to taste with confectioner's sugar.

3 Dip fresh peaches in boiling water for 4–5 seconds, then slip off the skins, halve along the indented line, then slice; or put canned peaches into a strainer and drain them.

4 Place two scoops of ice cream in each individual glass dish, top with peach slices, then pour over the raspberry purée. Serve immediately.

Summer Pudding

You may use any seasonal berries you wish in this unique and ever-popular English dessert.

Serves 4

about 8 thin slices day-
   old white bread, crusts
   removed

4½ cups mixed summer
   fruits
2 tablespoons sugar

1 Cut a circle from one slice of bread to fit in the bottom of a 5-cup ovenproof bowl, then cut strips of bread about 2inches wide to line the bowl, overlapping the strips.

2 Gently heat the fruit, sugar and 2 tablespoons water in a large heavy-based saucepan, shaking the pan occasionally, until the juice begins to run.

3 Reserve about 3 tablespoons fruit juice, then spoon the fruit and remaining juice into the basin, taking care not to dislodge the bread.

4 Cut the remaining bread to fit entirely over the fruit. Stand the bowl on a plate and cover with a saucer or small plate that will just fit inside the top of the basin. Place a heavy weight on top. Chill the pudding and the reserved fruit juice overnight in the fridge.

5 Run a knife carefully around the inside of the bowl rim, then invert the pudding onto a cold serving plate. Pour over the reserved juice and serve.

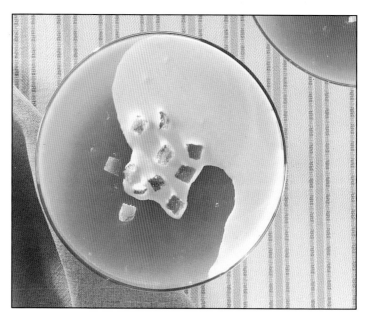

Boodles' Orange Fool

This fruit fool has become the specialty of Boodles Club, a gentlemen's club in London's St James's area.

Serves 4

1¼ cup sponge cake, cubed
1¼ cups heavy cream
2–4 tablespoons sugar
grated rind and juice of 2 oranges
grated rind and juice of 1 lemon
orange and lemon slices and rind, to decorate

1 Line the bottom and halfway up the sides of a large glass serving bowl or china dish with the cubed sponge cake.

2 Whip the cream with the sugar until it starts to thicken, then gradually whip in the fruit juices, adding the fruit rinds towards the end.

3 Carefully pour the cream mixture into the bowl or dish, taking care not to dislodge the sponge. Cover and chill for about 3–4 hours. Serve the fool decorated with orange and lemon slices and rind.

Apricot and Orange Jelly

You could also make this light dessert using nectarines or peaches instead of apricots.

Serves 4

12 ounces well-flavored fresh ripe apricots, pitted
about ⅓ cup sugar
1¼ cups freshly squeezed orange juice
1 tablespoon gelatin
light cream, to serve
finely chopped candied orange peel, to decorate

1 Heat the apricots, sugar and ½ cup of the orange juice, stirring until the sugar has dissolved. Simmer gently until the apricots are tender.

2 Press the apricot mixture through a nylon strainer into a small measuring cup with a spout.

3 Pour 3 tablespoons orange juice into a small heatproof bowl, sprinkle on the gelatin and leave for about 5 minutes, until softened.

4 Place the bowl over a saucepan of hot water and heat until the gelatin has dissolved. Pour into the apricot mixture slowly, stirring all the time. Add orange juice until it measures 2½ cups.

5 Pour the apricot mixture into four individual dishes and chill in the fridge until set. Pour a thin layer of cream over the surface of the desserts before serving, decorated with candied orange peel.

Summer Berry Medley

Make the most of seasonal fruits in this refreshing dessert. The sauce is also good swirled into plain yogurt.

Serves 4–6

1½ cups red currants, stripped from their stalks
1½ cups raspberries
¼ cup sugar
2–3 tablespoons crème de framboise

4½ cups fresh mixed soft summer fruits such as strawberries, raspberries, blueberries, red currants and blackcurrants
vanilla ice cream, to serve

1 Place the red currants in a bowl with the raspberries, sugar and crème de framboise. Cover and allow to macerate for 1–2 hours.

2 Put the macerated fruit with its juices in a saucepan and cook gently for 5–6 minutes, stirring occasionally, until the fruit is just tender.

3 Pour the fruit into a blender or food processor and process until smooth. Press through a nylon strainer to remove any seeds. Let cool, then chill in the fridge.

4 Divide the mixed soft fruit among four individual glass serving dishes and pour on the sauce. Serve with scoops of vanilla ice cream.

Brown Bread Ice Cream

This delicious textured ice cream is best served with a blackcurrant sauce spiked with crème de cassis.

Serves 6

½ cup roasted and chopped hazelnuts, ground
1½ cups whole wheat bread crumbs
½ cup brown sugar
3 egg whites
½ cup sugar
1¼ cups heavy cream
few drops of vanilla extract

For the sauce
2 cups blackcurrants
generous ¼ cup sugar
1 tablespoon crème de cassis
fresh mint sprigs, to decorate

1 Combine the hazelnuts and bread crumbs on a baking sheet, then sprinkle on the brown sugar. Place under a moderate broiler and cook until crisp and browned.

2 Whisk the egg whites in a bowl until stiff, then gradually whisk in the sugar until thick and glossy. Whip the cream until soft peaks form and fold into the meringue with the bread crumb mixture and vanilla extract.

3 Spoon the mixture into a 5-cup loaf pan. Smooth the top even, then cover and freeze until firm.

4 To make the sauce, put the blackcurrants in a small bowl with the sugar. Toss gently to mix and let sit for about 30 minutes. Purée the blackcurrants in a food processor or blender, then press through a nylon strainer until smooth. Add the crème de cassis and chill in the fridge.

5 To serve, arrange a slice of ice cream on a plate, spoon on a little sauce and decorate with fresh mint sprigs.

Raspberry Meringue Cake

This rich hazelnut meringue is filled with raspberries and cream and served with a raspberry sauce.

Serves 6

4 egg whites
1 cup sugar
*few drops of vanilla
    extract*
1 teaspoon malt vinegar
*1 cup roasted and
    chopped hazelnuts,
    ground*
1¼ cups heavy cream
3 cups raspberries
*sifted confectioner's
    sugar, for dusting*

*raspberries and fresh
    mint sprigs, to
    decorate*

For the sauce

2 cups raspberries
*3–4 tablespoons
    confectioner's sugar,
    sifted*
*1 tablespoon orange
    liqueur*

1 Preheat the oven to 350°F. Grease and bottom-line two 8-inch cake pans.

2 Whisk the egg whites until stiff peaks form, then gradually whisk in the sugar a tablespoon at a time. Continue whisking for a minute or two until very stiff, then fold in the vanilla extract, vinegar and hazelnuts. Transfer the mixture to the cake pans. Bake for 50–60 minutes, until crisp. Remove from the pans and cool.

3 Meanwhile, make the sauce. Purée the raspberries with the confectioner's sugar and orange liqueur in a food processor or blender, then press through a fine nylon strainer to remove any seeds. Chill the sauce in the fridge until ready to serve.

4 Whip the cream until soft peaks form, then fold in the raspberries. Use to sandwich the meringue rounds together.

5 Dust the top of the gâteau with confectioner's sugar. Decorate with raspberries and mint sprigs and serve with the sauce.

Iced Chocolate and Nut Cake

Autumn hazelnuts add crunchiness to this popular frozen dinner-party dessert.

Serves 6–8

¾ cup shelled hazelnuts
*32 ladyfingers or slices of
    sponge cake*
*⅔ cup cold strong black
    coffee*
*2 tablespoons Cognac or
    other brandy*
1¾ cups heavy cream

*scant 1 cup
    confectioner's sugar,
    sifted*
*5 ounces semisweet
    chocolate*
*confectioner's sugar and
    cocoa powder, for
    dusting*

1 Preheat the oven to 400°F. Spread out the hazelnuts on a baking sheet and toast them in the oven for 5 minutes until golden. Transfer the nuts to a clean dish towel and rub off the skins. Cool, then chop finely.

2 Line a 5-cup loaf pan with plastic wrap and cut the cake slices to fit the base and sides, or select sufficient ladyfingers. Reserve the remaining cake or ladyfingers.

3 Mix the coffee with the Cognac or other brandy in a shallow dish. Dip the sponge cake or ladyfingers briefly into the coffee mixture and put in the pan, coffee-side up.

4 Whip the cream with the confectioner's sugar until it holds soft peaks. Coarsely chop 3 ounces of the chocolate, and fold into the cream with the hazelnuts.

5 Melt the remaining chocolate in a heat proof bowl set over a saucepan of barely simmering water. Cool, then fold into the cream mixture. Spoon into the pan.

6 Moisten the remaining cake or ladyfingers in the coffee mixture and lay over the filling. Wrap and freeze until firm.

7 Remove the cake from the freezer 30 minutes before serving. Turn out onto a serving plate and dust with confectioner's sugar and cocoa powder.

Blackberry Brown Sugar Meringue

A rich dessert which is elegant enough in presentation to be served at an autumnal dinner party.

Serves 6

For the meringue	**For the filling**
1½ cups light brown sugar	3–4 cups blackberries
3 egg whites	2 tablespoons crème de cassis
1 teaspoon malt vinegar	1¼ cups heavy cream
½ teaspoon vanilla extract	1 tablespoon confectioner's sugar, sifted
	small blackberry leaves, to decorate (optional)

1 Preheat the oven to 325°F. Draw an 8-inch circle on a sheet of nonstick baking parchment, turn over and place on a baking sheet. Spread the brown sugar out on a baking sheet, dry in the oven for 8–10 minutes, then sift.

2 Whisk the egg whites in a bowl until stiff. Add half the dried brown sugar, 1 tablespoon at a time, whisking well after each addition. Add the vinegar and vanilla extract, then fold in the remaining sugar.

3 Spoon the meringue onto the drawn circle on the paper, making a hollow in the center. Bake for 45 minutes, then turn off the oven and leave the meringue in the oven with the door slightly open, until cold. Meanwhile, place the blackberries in a bowl, sprinkle over the crème de cassis and leave to macerate for 30 minutes.

4 When the meringue is cold, carefully peel off the nonstick baking parchment and transfer the meringue to a serving plate. Lightly whip the cream with the confectioner's sugar and spoon into the center. Top with the blackberries and decorate with small blackberry leaves, if liked. Serve at once.

Clementines in Cinnamon Caramel

The combination of sweet, yet sharp clementines and caramel sauce with a hint of spice is divine.

Serves 4–6

8–12 clementines	2 tablespoons orange-flavored liqueur
1 cup sugar	
1½ cups hand-hot water	¼ cup shelled pistachio nuts
2 cinnamon sticks	

1 Pare the rind from two clementines using a vegetable peeler and cut it into fine strips. Set aside.

2 Peel the clementines, removing all the pith but keeping them intact. Put the fruits in a serving bowl.

3 Gently heat the sugar in a pan until it dissolves and turns a rich golden brown. Turn off the heat immediately.

4 Pour the water into the pan, protecting your hand with a dish towel (the mixture will bubble and splutter). Bring slowly to a boil, stirring until the caramel dissolves. Add the shredded peel and cinnamon sticks, then simmer for 5 minutes. Stir in the liqueur.

5 Allow the syrup to cool for about 10 minutes, then pour over the clementines. Cover the bowl and chill for several hours or overnight.

6 Blanch the pistachio nuts in boiling water. Drain, cool and remove the dark outer skins. Scatter over the clementines and serve at once.

Chocolate Chestnut Roulade

Don't worry if this moist sponge cracks as you roll it – this is the sign of a good roulade.

Serves 8

6 ounces semisweet
    chocolate
2 tablespoons strong
    black coffee
5 eggs, separated
1 cup sugar
1 cup heavy cream

8 ounces unsweetened
    chestnut purée
3 – 4 tablespoons
    confectioner's sugar,
    plus extra for dusting
light cream, to serve

1 Preheat the oven to 350°F, then line and oil a 13 x 9-inch jelly roll pan; use wax paper. Melt the chocolate in a bowl, then stir in the coffee. Allow to cool slightly.

2 Whisk the egg yolks and sugar together until thick and light, then stir in the cooled chocolate mixture. Whisk the egg whites in another bowl until stiff. Stir a spoonful into the chocolate mixture to lighten it, then gently fold in the rest.

3 Pour the mixture into the prepared pan, and spread evenly. Bake for 20 minutes. Remove from the oven, cover with a dish towel and let cool in the pan for several hours.

4 Whip the cream until soft peaks form. Mix together the chestnut purée and confectioner's sugar; fold into the whipped cream.

5 Dust a sheet of greaseproof paper with confectioner's sugar. Turn out the roulade onto this paper and peel off the lining paper. Trim the sides. Gently spread the chestnut cream evenly over the roulade to within 1 inch of the edges. Using the wax paper to help you, carefully roll up the roulade as tightly and evenly as possible. Chill the roulade for about 2 hours, then dust liberally with confectioner's sugar. Cut into thick slices. Serve with a little light cream on each slice.

Pasta Timbales with Apricot Sauce

If orzo cannot be found, other small soup pastas can be used for this dessert, which is made like a rice pudding.

Serves 4

1 cup orzo
⅓ cup sugar
pinch of salt
2 tablespoons butter
1 vanilla pod, split
3⅔ cups milk
1¼ cups ready-made
    custard
3 tablespoons Kirsch

1 tablespoon powdered
    gelatin
oil, for greasing
14 ounces canned
    apricots in juice
lemon juice
fresh flowers, to decorate
    (optional)

1 Place the pasta, sugar, pinch of salt, butter, vanilla pod and milk in a heavy saucepan and bring to a boil. Turn down the heat and simmer for 25 minutes until the pasta is tender and most of the liquid is absorbed. Stir frequently to prevent it from sticking.

2 Remove the vanilla pod and transfer the pasta to a bowl to cool. Stir in the custard and add 2 tablespoons of the Kirsch.

3 Sprinkle the gelatin over 2 tablespoons water in a small bowl set in a pan of barely simmering water. Allow to become spongy and heat gently to dissolve. Stir into the pasta.

4 Lightly oil 4 timbale molds and spoon in the pasta. Chill for 2 hours until set.

5 Meanwhile, blend the apricots, pass through a seive and add lemon juice and Kirsch to taste. Dilute with a little water if too thick. Loosen the timbales from their molds and turn out onto individual plates. Serve with apricot sauce, decorated with fresh flowers if you wish.

Coffee Jellies with Amaretti Cream

This impressive dessert is very easy to prepare. For the best results, use a high–roasted Arabica bean for the coffee.

Serves 4

generous ¼ cup sugar
1¾ cups hot strong coffee
2 – 3 tablespoons dark
 rum or coffee liqueur
4 teaspoons gelatin

2 – 3 teaspoons instant
 coffee granules
 dissolved in 4
 tablespoons hot water
6 large amaretti cookies,
 crushed

For the amaretti cream

⅔ cup heavy cream
1 tablespoon
 confectioner's sugar,
 sifted

1 Put the sugar in a saucepan with 5 tablespoons water and stir over a gentle heat until dissolved. Increase the heat and allow the syrup to boil steadily, without stirring, for about 3 – 4 minutes.

2 Stir the hot coffee and rum or coffee liqueur into the syrup, then sprinkle the gelatin over the top and stir the mixture until it is completely dissolved.

3 Carefully pour the coffee gelatin mixture into four moistened ⅔-cup molds, allow to cool and then leave in the fridge for several hours until set.

4 To make the amaretti cream, lightly whip the cream with the confectioner's sugar until the mixture holds stiff peaks. Stir in the coffee, then gently fold in all but 2 tablespoons of the crushed amaretti cookies.

5 Unmold the jellies onto four individual serving plates and spoon a little of the amaretti cream to one side. Dust over the reserved amaretti crumbs and serve immediately.

Chocolate Date Torte

A stunning cake that tastes wonderful. Rich and gooey – it's a chocoholic's delight!

Serves 8

4 egg whites
½ cup sugar
7 ounces semisweet
 chocolate
6 ounces Medjool dates,
 pitted and chopped
1½ cups walnuts or
 pecan nuts, chopped

2 teaspoons vanilla
 extract, plus a few
 extra drops

For the frosting

scant 1 cup plain yogurt
scant 1 cup mascarpone
confectioner's sugar, to
 taste

1 Preheat the oven to 350°F. Lightly grease and bottom-line an 8-inch springform cake pan.

2 To make the frosting, mix together the plain yogurt and mascarpone, add a few drops of vanilla extract and confectioner's sugar to taste, then set aside.

3 Whisk the egg whites in a bowl until stiff peaks form. Whisk in 2 tablespoons of the sugar until the meringue is thick and glossy, then fold in the remainder.

4 Chop 6 ounces of the chocolate. Carefully fold into the meringue with the dates, nuts and 1 teaspoon of the vanilla extract. Pour into the prepared pan, smooth the top evenly and bake for about 45 minutes, until risen around the edges.

5 Allow to cool in the tin for about 10 minutes, then turn out onto a wire rack. Peel off the lining paper and let stand until completely cold. When cool, swirl the frosting over the top of the torte.

6 Melt the remaining chocolate in a bowl over hot water. Spoon into a small paper icing bag, snip off the top and drizzle the chocolate over the torte. Chill in the fridge before serving, cut into wedges.

Crème Caramel

This creamy, caramel-flavored custard from France enjoys worldwide popularity.

Serves 4–6
½ cup sugar
1¼ cups milk
1¼ cups light cream
6 eggs

generous ¼ cup sugar
½ teaspoon vanilla
  extract

1 Preheat the oven to 300°F and half-fill a large roasting pan with water. Place the sugar in a saucepan with 4 tablespoons water and heat gently, swirling the pan occasionally, until the sugar has dissolved. Increase the heat and boil for a good caramel color. Immediately pour the caramel into an ovenproof soufflé dish. Place in the roasting pan and set aside.

2 To make the egg custard, heat the milk and cream together in a pan until almost boiling. Meanwhile, beat the eggs, sugar and vanilla extract together in a bowl using a large balloon whisk.

3 Whisk the hot milk into the eggs and sugar, then strain the liquid through a strainer into the soufflé dish, on top of the cooled caramel base.

4 Transfer the pan to the center of the oven and bake for about 1½–2 hours (topping up the water level after 1 hour), or until the custard has set in the center. Lift the dish carefully out of the water and let cool, then cover and chill overnight in the fridge.

5 Loosen the sides of the chilled custard with a knife and then place an inverted plate (large enough to hold the caramel sauce that will flow out as well) on top of the dish. Holding the dish and plate together, turn upside down and give the whole thing a quick shake to release the crème caramel.

Australian Hazelnut Pavlova

A hazelnut meringue base is topped with orange cream, nectarines and raspberries in this famous dessert.

Serves 4–6
3 egg whites
1 cup sugar
1 teaspoon cornstarch
1 teaspoon white wine
  vinegar
generous ¼ cup chopped
  roasted hazelnuts
1 cup heavy cream
1 tablespoon orange juice

2 tablespoons plain thick
  and creamy yogurt
2 ripe nectarines, pitted
  and sliced
2 cups raspberries,
  halved
1–2 tablespoons
  redcurrant jelly,
  warmed

1 Preheat the oven to 275°F. Lightly grease a baking sheet. Draw an 8-inch circle on a sheet of baking parchment. Place pencil-side down on the baking sheet.

2 Place the egg whites in a clean, dry, grease-free bowl and beat with an electric mixer until stiff peaks form. Beat in the sugar 1 tablespoon at a time, beating well after each addition.

3 Add the cornstarch, vinegar and hazelnuts and fold in carefully with a large metal spoon.

4 Spoon the meringue onto the marked circle and spread out to the edges, making a dip in the center.

5 Bake for about 1¼–1½ hours, until crisp. Allow to cool completely and transfer to a serving platter.

6 Whip the heavy cream and orange juice until the mixture is just thick, stir in the yogurt and spoon onto the meringue. Top with the prepared fruit and drizzle over the warmed redcurrant jelly. Serve immediately.

Chinese Fruit Salad

Apricot and Almond Jalousie

For an unusual fruit salad with an oriental flavor, try this mixture of fruits in a tangy lime and lychee syrup.

Jalousie means "shutter", and the slatted pastry topping of this pie looks exactly like French window shutters.

Serves 4

½ cup sugar
thinly pared rind and
    juice of 1 lime
14-ounce can lychees in
    syrup
1 ripe mango, pitted and
    sliced

1 eating apple, cored and
    sliced
2 bananas, chopped
1 star fruit, sliced
    (optional)
1 teaspoon sesame seeds,
    toasted

Serves 4

8 ounces ready-made puff
    pastry
a little beaten egg
6 tablespoons apricot
    conserve

2 tablespoons sugar
2 tablespoons flaked
    almonds
cream or plain yogurt, to
    serve

1 Place the sugar in a small saucepan with the lime rind and 1¼ cups water. Heat gently until the sugar dissolves completely, then increase the heat and boil gently for about 7–8 minutes. Remove the saucepan from the heat and allow the syrup to cool.

2 Drain the lychees into a pitcher and pour the juice into the cooled lime syrup with the lime juice. Place all the prepared fruit in a bowl and pour over the lime and lychee syrup. Chill in the fridge for about 1 hour. Just before serving, sprinkle with toasted sesame seeds.

Cook's Tip
Try different combinations of fruit in this salad. You might like to include pawpaw, kiwi fruit or pineapple for a change.

1 Preheat the oven to 425°F. Roll out the pastry on a lightly floured surface and cut into a square measuring 12 inches. Cut in half to make two rectangles.

2 Place one piece of pastry on a moistened baking sheet and brush all round the edges with beaten egg. Spread on the apricot conserve.

3 Fold the remaining rectangle in half lengthwise and cut about eight diagonal slits from the center fold to within about ½-inch from the edge all the way along.

4 Unfold the cut pastry and lay it on top of the pastry on the baking sheet. Press the pastry edges together well, and seal using the back of a knife.

5 Brush the slashed pastry with water and sprinkle over the sugar and flaked almonds.

6 Bake in the oven for 25–30 minutes, until well risen and golden brown. Remove the jalousie from the oven and allow to cool. Serve sliced, with cream or plain yogurt.

Cook's Tip
Make smaller individual jalousies and serve them with morning coffee, if you like. Use other flavors of fruit conserve for a change.

Baked Cheesecake

The lemon-flavored cream cheese provides a subtle filling for this classic dessert.

Makes 9 squares
For the base
1½ cups crushed graham crackers
3 tablespoons butter, melted

For the topping
2½ cups ricotta cheese or cream cheese
½ cup sugar
3 eggs
finely grated rind of 1 lemon
1 tablespoon lemon juice
½ teaspoon vanilla extract
1 tablespoon cornstarch
2 tablespoons sour cream
⅔ cup sour cream and ¼ teaspoon ground cinnamon, to decorate

1 Preheat the oven to 325°F. Lightly grease and line a 7-inch springform pan.

2 Place the crumbs and butter in a bowl and mix well. Pat into the bottom of the prepared pan and press down firmly .

3 Place the cheese in a bowl, add the sugar and beat well until smooth. Add the eggs one at a time, beating well after each addition and then stir in the lemon rind and juice, the vanilla extract, cornstarch and sour cream. Beat until the mixture is completely smooth.

4 Pour the mixture onto the base and smooth the top evenly. Bake for 1¼ hours, or until the cheesecake has set in the center. Turn off the oven but leave the cheesecake inside until completely cold.

5 Remove the cheesecake from the pan, top with the soured cream and swirl with the back of a spoon. Sprinkle with cinnamon and cut into squares.

Mango Ice Cream

Canned mangoes are used to make this deliciously rich and creamy ice cream, which has an oriental flavor.

Serves 4–6
2 x 15-ounce cans sliced mango, drained
¼ cup sugar
2 tablespoons lime juice
1 tablespoon gelatin
1½ cups heavy cream, lightly whipped
fresh mint sprigs, to decorate

1 Reserve four slices of mango for decoration and chop the remainder. Place the mango pieces in a bowl with the sugar and lime juice.

2 Put 3 tablespoons hot water in a small heatproof bowl and sprinkle over the gelatin. Place over a saucepan of gently simmering water and stir until dissolved. Pour onto the mango mixture and mix well.

3 Add the lightly whipped cream and fold into the mango mixture. Pour the mixture into a plastic freezer container and freeze until half frozen.

4 Place the half-frozen ice cream in a food processor or blender and process until smooth. Spoon back into the container and return to the freezer to freeze completely.

5 Remove from the freezer 10 minutes before serving and place in the fridge. Serve scoops of ice cream decorated with pieces of the reserved sliced mango and fresh mint sprigs.

Rippled Chocolate Ice Cream

Rich, smooth and packed with chocolate, this heavenly ice cream is an all-round-the-world chocoholics' favorite.

Serves 4

*4 tablespoons chocolate
    and hazelnut spread
1¾ cups heavy cream
1 tablespoon
    confectioner's sugar*

*2 ounces semisweet
    chocolate, chopped
semisweet chocolate
    curls, to decorate*

1 Mix together the chocolate and hazelnut spread and 5 tablespoons of the heavy cream in a bowl.

2 Place the remaining cream in a second bowl, sift in the confectioner's sugar and beat until softly whipped.

3 Lightly fold in the chocolate and hazelnut mixture with the chopped chocolate until the mixture is rippled. Transfer to a plastic freezer container and freeze for 3–4 hours, until firm.

4 Remove the ice cream from the freezer about 10 minutes before serving to allow it to soften slightly. Spoon or scoop into dessert dishes or glasses and top each serving with a few semisweet chocolate curls.

Fruited Rice Ring

This pudding ring looks beautiful but you could stir the fruit in and serve it in individual dishes instead.

Serves 4

*¼ cup short-grain rice
3¾ cups low-fat milk
1 cinnamon stick
6 ounces dried mixed
    fruit
¾ cup orange juice*

*3 tablespoons sugar
finely grated rind of
    1 small orange*

1 Place the rice, milk and cinnamon stick in a large saucepan and bring to a boil. Cover and simmer, stirring occasionally, for about 1½ hours, until all the liquid is absorbed.

2 Meanwhile, place the fruit and orange juice in a pan and bring to a boil. Cover and simmer very gently for about 1 hour, until the fruit is tender and all the liquid is absorbed.

3 Remove the cinnamon stick from the rice and discard. Stir in the sugar and orange rind.

4 Place the cooked fruit salad on the bottom of a lightly oiled 6-cup ring mold. Spoon the rice on, smoothing it down firmly. Chill in the fridge.

5 Run a knife around the edge of the mold and turn out the rice carefully onto a serving plate.

Apricot Mousse

This light fluffy dessert can be made with any dried fruits instead of apricots – try dried peaches, prunes or apples.

Serves 4

10 ounces ready-to-eat
   dried apricots
1¼ cups fresh orange
   juice

¾ cup plain yogurt
2 egg whites
fresh mint, to decorate

1   Place the apricots in a saucepan with the orange juice and heat gently until boiling. Cover the pan and simmer gently for 3 minutes.

2   Cool slightly, then place in a food processor or blender and process until smooth. Stir in the yogurt.

3   Whisk the egg whites until stiff enough to hold soft peaks, then fold gently into the apricot mixture.

4   Spoon the mousse into four stemmed glasses or one large serving dish. Chill in the fridge before serving. Decorate with sprigs of fresh mint.

Cook's Tip
To make a speedier, fool-type dessert, omit the egg whites and simply swirl together the apricot mixture and the yogurt.

Apple Foam with Blackberries

Any seasonal soft fruit can be used for this lovely dessert if blackberries are not available.

Serves 4

2 cups blackberries
generous ½ cup apple
   juice

1 teaspoon powdered
   gelatin
1 tablespoon honey
2 egg whites

1   Place the blackberries in a saucepan with 4 tablespoons of the apple juice and heat gently until the fruit is soft. Remove from the heat, cool then chill in the fridge.

2   Sprinkle the gelatin over the remaining apple juice in a small pan and stir over a gentle heat until dissolved. Stir in the honey.

3   Whisk the egg whites until stiff peaks form. Continue whisking hard and gradually pour in the hot gelatin mixture until well mixed.

4   Quickly spoon the foam into mounds on individual plates. Chill. To serve, spoon the blackberries and juice around the foam rounds.

Cook's Tip
Make sure you dissolve the gelatin over a very low heat. It must not boil, or it will lose its setting ability.

Raspberry Passionfruit Swirls

If passionfruit is not available, this simple dessert can be made with raspberries alone.

Serves 4
generous 2½ cups
    raspberries
2 passionfruit
1⅔ cups low-fat ricotta
    cheese

2 tablespoons sugar
raspberries and sprigs of
    fresh mint, to decorate

1 Mash the raspberries in a small bowl with a fork until the juice runs. Scoop out the passionfruit pulp into a separate bowl with the ricotta and sugar and mix well.

2 Spoon alternate spoonfuls of the raspberry pulp and the ricotta mixture into stemmed glasses or one large serving dish, stirring lightly to create a swirled effect.

3 Decorate the desserts with whole raspberries and sprigs of fresh mint. Serve chilled.

Creamy Mango Cheesecake

This low-fat cheesecake is as creamy as any other, but makes a healthier dessert option.

Serves 4
1¼ cups rolled oats
3 tablespoons sunflower
    margarine
2 tablespoons honey
1 large ripe mango
1¼ cups light cream
    cheese

⅔ cup low-fat plain
    yogurt
finely grated rind of
    1 small lime
3 tablespoons apple juice
4 teaspoons gelatin
fresh mango and lime
    slices, to decorate

1 Preheat the oven to 400°F. Mix together the oats, margarine and honey; press into the bottom of an 8-inch loose-bottomed cake pan. Bake for 12–15 minutes. Cool.

2 Peel, pit and coarsely chop the mango. Process with the cheese, yogurt and lime rind until smooth. Heat the apple juice until boiling, sprinkle the gelatin over it, stir to dissolve, then stir into the cheese mixture. Pour into the pan and chill until set. Turn out and decorate with mango and lime slices.

Frudités with Honey Dip

This dish is shared and would be ideal to serve at an informal lunch or supper party.

Serves 4
Place 1 cup plain strained yogurt in a dish, beat until smooth, then stir in 3 tablespoons honey, leaving a marbled effect. Cut a selection of fruits into wedges or bite-size pieces or leave whole, depending on your choice. Arrange on a platter with the bowl of dip in the center. Serve chilled.

Boston Banoffee Pie

This dessert's rich, creamy, toffee-style filling just can't be resisted – but who cares!

Serves 4–6
1¼ cups all-purpose flour
1 cup butter
¼ cup sugar
14-ounce can skim,
   sweetened condensed
   milk
⅔ cup light brown sugar

2 tablespoons corn syrup
2 small bananas, sliced
a little lemon juice
whipped cream and
   grated semisweet
   chocolate, to decorate

1 Preheat the oven to 325°F. Place the flour and ½ cup of the butter in a bowl, then stir in the sugar. Squeeze the mixture together with your hands until it forms a dough. Press into the bottom of an 8-inch loose-bottom fluted tart pan. Bake blind for 25–30 minutes, until the pastry is lightly browned.

2 Place the remaining butter with the condensed milk, brown sugar and corn syrup into a nonstick saucepan and heat gently, stirring, until the butter has melted and the sugar has completely dissolved.

3 Bring to a gentle boil and cook for 7 minutes, stirring all the time (to prevent burning), until the mixture thickens and turns a light caramel color. Pour into the cooked pie shell and leave until cold.

4 Sprinkle the bananas with lemon juice and arrange in overlapping circles on top of the caramel filling, leaving a gap in the center. Pipe a swirl of whipped cream in the center and sprinkle with the grated chocolate.

Cook's Tip
Do not peel and slice the bananas until you are ready to serve or they will become slimy.

Strawberry and Blueberry Tart

This tart works equally well using either autumn or winter fruits as long as there is a riot of color.

Serves 6–8
2 cups all-purpose flour
pinch of salt
scant ¾ cup
   confectioner's sugar
generous ½ cup unsalted
   butter
1 egg yolk

few drops of vanilla
   extract
finely grated rind of
   1 orange
4½ cups fresh mixed
   strawberries and
   blueberries
6 tablespoons redcurrant
   jelly
2 tablespoons orange
   juice

For the filling
1¾ cups mascarpone
2 tablespoons
   confectioner's sugar

1 Sift the flour, salt and sugar into a bowl. Dice the butter and rub it in until the mixture resembles coarse bread crumbs. Mix in the egg yolk and 2 teaspoons cold water. Gather the dough together, knead lightly, wrap and chill for 1 hour.

2 Preheat the oven to 375°F. Roll out the pastry and use to line a 10-inch fluted tart pan. Prick the bottom and chill for 15 minutes in the fridge.

3 Line the chilled pie shell with wax paper and baking beans, then bake blind for 15 minutes. Remove the paper and beans and bake for a further 15 minutes, until crisp and golden. Let cool in the tin.

4 Beat together the mascarpone, sugar, vanilla extract and orange rind in a mixing bowl until smooth.

5 Remove the pie shell from the pan, then spoon in the filling and pile the fruits on top. Heat the redcurrant jelly with the orange juice until runny, strain, then brush over the fruit to form a glaze.

Strawberries in Spiced Grape Jelly

This light dessert would be ideal to serve after a rich and filling main course.

Serves 4

1¾ cups red grape juice
1 cinnamon stick
1 small orange
1 tablespoon gelatin

2 cups strawberries, chopped
strawberries and shredded orange rind, to decorate

1 Place the grape juice in a saucepan with the cinnamon and thinly pared orange rind. Infuse over a gentle heat for 10 minutes, then remove the cinnamon and orange rind. Sprinkle the squeezed orange juice over the gelatin. Stir into the grape juice to dissolve. Allow to cool until just beginning to set.

2 Stir in the strawberries and then quickly turn the mixture into a 4-cup mold or serving dish. Chill in the fridge until it has set. Dip the mold quickly into hot water and invert onto a serving plate. Decorate with fresh strawberries and shreds of orange rind.

Plum and Port Sherbet

Rather a grown-up sherbet this one, but you could use fresh red grape juice in place of the port or wine.

Serves 4

2 pounds ripe red plums, pitted and halved
generous ¼ cup sugar
3 tablespoons water

3 tablespoons ruby port or red wine
crisp sweet cookies, to serve

1 Place the plums in a saucepan with the sugar and water. Stir over a gentle heat until the sugar is melted, then cover and simmer gently for about 5 minutes, until the fruit is soft.

2 Turn into a food processor or blender and purée until smooth, then stir in the port or red wine. Cool completely, then turn into a plastic freezer container and freeze until the sherbet is firm around the edges. Process until smooth. Spoon back into the freezer container and freeze until solid.

3 Allow to soften slightly at room temperature for about 15–20 minutes before serving in scoops, with sweet cookies.

Quick Apricot Blender Whip

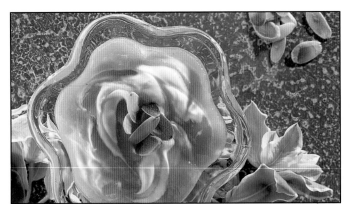

This is one of the quickest desserts you could make – and also one of the prettiest.

Serves 4

Drain the juice from 14-ounce can apricot halves in juice and place the fruit in a blender or food processor with 1 tablespoon Grand Marnier or brandy. Process until smooth. Spoon the fruit purée and ¾ cup plain strained yogurt in alternate spoonfuls into four tall glasses or glass dishes, swirling them together slightly to give a marbled effect. Lightly toast 2 tablespoons slivered almonds until they are golden. Let them cool slightly and then sprinkle them on top.

Bean Curd Berry Brulée

This is a lighter variation of a classic dessert. Use any soft fruits that are in season.

Serves 4

2 cups red berry fruits
  such as strawberries,
  raspberries and
  redcurrants
11-ounce package silken
  bean curd

3 tablespoons
  confectioner's sugar
¼ cup brown sugar

1 Halve or quarter any large strawberries, but leave the smaller ones whole. Mix with the other chosen berries.

2 Place the bean curd and confectioner's sugar in a food processor or blender and process until smooth.

3 Stir in the fruits and spoon into a flameproof dish with a 3¾-cup capacity. Sprinkle the top with enough brown sugar to cover evenly.

4 Place under a very hot broiler until the sugar melts and caramelizes. Chill in the fridge before serving.

Cook's Tip
Choose silken bean curd rather than firm bean curd as it gives a smoother texture in this type of dish. Firm bean curd is better for cooking in chunks.

Emerald Fruit Salad

This vibrant green fruit salad contains a hint of lime and is sweetened with honey.

Serves 4

2 tablespoons lime juice
2 tablespoons honey
2 green eating apples,
  cored and sliced
1 ripe honeydew melon,
  diced

2 kiwi fruit, sliced
1 star fruit, sliced
fresh mint sprigs, to
  decorate
plain yogurt, to serve

1 Mix together the lime juice and honey in a large bowl, then toss in the apple slices.

2 Stir in the melon, kiwi fruit and star fruit. Place in a glass serving dish and chill in the fridge before serving.

3 Decorate with mint sprigs and serve with yogurt, if you wish.

Cook's Tip
Color-themed fruit salads are fun to create and easy, given the wide availability of exotic fruits. You could try an orange-colored salad using cantaloupe melon, apricots, peaches or nectarines, oranges or clementines, and mango or pawpaw.

Peach and Ginger Pashka

This simpler adaptation of a Russian Easter favorite is made with lighter ingredients than the traditional version.

Serves 4–6

1½ cups low-fat cottage cheese
2 ripe peaches
½ cup low-fat plain yogurt
2 pieces preserved ginger in syrup, drained and chopped
2 tablespoons preserved ginger syrup
½ teaspoon vanilla extract
peach slices and toasted flaked almonds, to decorate

1 Drain the cottage cheese and rub through a strainer into a bowl. Pit, and coarsely chop the peaches.

2 Mix together the chopped peaches, cottage cheese, yogurt, ginger, syrup and vanilla extract.

3 Line a new clean flowerpot or a strainer with a piece of clean fine cloth such as cheesecloth.

4 Put in the cheese mixture, then wrap with the cloth and place a weight on top. Leave above a bowl in a cool place to drain overnight. To serve, unwrap the cloth and invert the pashka onto a plate. Decorate with peach slices and almonds.

Chilled Chocolate Slice

This is a very rich family dessert, but it is also designed to use up the occasional leftover.

Serves 6–8

½ cup butter, melted
8 ounces ginger cookies, finely crushed
2 ounces stale sponge cake crumbs
4–5 tablepoons orange juice
4 ounces pitted dates
¼ cup finely chopped nuts
6 ounces unsweetened chocolate
1¼ cups whipping cream
grated chocolate and confectioner's sugar, to decorate

1 Mix together the butter and ginger cookie crumbs, then pack around the sides and bottom of a 7-inch loose-bottom tart pan. Chill in the fridge while making the filling.

2 Put the cake crumbs into a large bowl with the orange juice and allow to soak. Warm the dates thoroughly, then mash and blend into the cake crumbs along with the nuts.

3 Melt the chocolate with 3–4 tablespoons of the cream. Softly whip the rest of the cream, then fold in the melted chocolate mixture.

4 Stir the cream and chocolate mixture into the crumbs and mix well. Pour into the cookie crust, mark into portions and let set. Scatter on the grated chocolate and dust with confectioner's sugar. Serve cut in wedges.

Tangerine Trifle

An unusual variation on a traditional trifle – of course, you can add a little alcohol if you wish.

Serves 4

5 ladyfingers or slices of
   sponge cake, halved
   lengthwise
2 tablespoons apricot
   conserve
1 cup macaroon crumbs
¾ ounce package
   tangerine gelatin
11-ounce can mandarin
   oranges, drained,
   reserving juice

2½ cups ready-made
   (or homemade)
   custard
whipped cream and
   shreds of orange rind,
   to decorate
sugar, for sprinkling

1 Spread the ladyfingers or sponge cake with apricot conserve and arrange in the bottom of a deep serving bowl or glass dish. Sprinkle the macaroon crumbs over the top.

2 Break up the jelly into a heat proof measuring cup, add the juice from the canned mandarins and dissolve in a saucepan of hot water or in the microwave. Stir until the liquid clears.

3 Add ice cold water until it measures 2½ cups, stir well and set aside to cool for up to 30 minutes. Scatter the mandarin orange segments on the cake and macaroon crumbs.

4 Pour the jelly over the mandarin oranges, cake and ratafias and chill in the fridge for 1 hour, or more.

5 When the jelly has set, pour the custard on the top and chill again in the fridge.

6 When ready to serve, pipe the whipped cream over the custard. Wash the orange rind shreds, sprinkle them with sugar and use to decorate the trifle.

Blackberry and Apple Romanoff

Rich yet fruity, this dessert is popular with most people and very quick and easy to make.

Serves 6–8

12 ounces tart eating
   apples, peeled, cored
   and chopped
3 tablespoons sugar
1 cup whipping cream
1 teaspoon grated lemon
   rind
6 tablespoons strained
   plain yogurt

2 ounces (about 4–6)
   crisp meringues,
   coarsely crumbled
2 cups blackberries (fresh
   or frozen)
whipped cream, a few
   blackberries and
   fresh mint leaves,
   to decorate

1 Line a 4–5 cup ovenproof bowl with plastic wrap. Toss the chopped apples into a saucepan with 2 tablespoons sugar and cook for 2–3 minutes, or until softening. Mash with a fork and allow to cool.

2 Whip the cream and fold in the lemon rind, yogurt, the remaining sugar, apples and meringues.

3 Gently stir in the blackberries, then turn the mixture into the ovenproof bowl and freeze for 1–3 hours.

4 Turn out onto a plate and remove the plastic wrap. Decorate with whirls of whipped cream, blackberries and mint leaves.

Apple and Hazelnut Shortcake

This is a variation on the classic strawberry shortcake and is equally delicious.

Serves 8–10

*generous 1 cup whole
   wheat flour*
½ cup ground hazelnuts
*6 tablespoons
   confectioner's sugar,
   sifted*
*generous 1 cup unsalted
   butter*
3 tart eating apples
1 teaspoon lemon juice

1–2 tablespoons sugar
*1 tablespoon chopped
   fresh mint, or 1
   teaspoon dried mint*
1 cup whipping cream
*a few drops of vanilla
   extract*
*a few fresh mint leaves
   and whole hazelnuts,
   to decorate*

1   Process the flour, ground hazelnuts and confectioner's sugar with the butter in a food processor in short bursts, until they come together. Bring the dough together, adding a little ice water if needed. Knead briefly, wrap and chill for 30 minutes.

2   Preheat the oven to 325°F. Cut the dough in half and roll out each half to a 7-inch round. Place on wax paper on baking sheets. Bake for 40 minutes, or until crisp. Allow to cool.

3   Peel, core and chop the apples into a saucepan with the lemon juice. Add sugar to taste; cook for 2–3 minutes, until just soft. Mash the apple gently with the mint; set aside.

4   Whip the cream with the vanilla extract. Place one shortcake round on a serving plate. Spread half the apple and half the cream on top.

5   Place the second shortcake round on top, then spread on the remaining apple and cream, swirling the top layer of cream gently. Decorate the top with mint leaves and a few whole hazelnuts, then serve immediately.

Lemon Cheesecake

A lovely light cream cheese filling is sandwiched between brandy snaps in this tasty dessert.

Serves 8

*4¾ -ouncs package lemon
   gelatin*
2 cups light cream cheese
*2 teaspoons grated lemon
   rind*
about ½ cup sugar
*a few drops of vanilla
   extract*

*½ cup strained plain
   yogurt*
8 brandy snaps
*a few fresh mint leaves
   and confectioner's
   sugar, to decorate*

1   Dissolve the jelly in 3–4 tablespoons boiling water in a heat proof measuring cup and, when clear, add sufficient cold water to measure up to ⅔ cup. Chill in the fridge until beginning to thicken. Meanwhile, line a 1-pound loaf pan with plastic wrap.

2   Cream the cheese with the lemon rind, sugar and vanilla and beat until light and smooth. Then fold in the thickening lemon jelly and the yogurt. Spoon into the prepared pan and chill until set. Preheat the oven to 325°F.

3   Place two or three brandy snaps at a time on a baking sheet. Put in the oven for no more than 1 minute, until soft enough to unroll and flatten out completely. Leave on a cold plate or tray to harden again. Repeat with the remaining brandy snaps.

4   To serve, turn the cheesecake out onto a board with the help of the plastic wrap. Cut into eight slices and place one slice on each brandy snap base. Decorate with mint leaves and dust with confectioner's sugar.

Frozen Strawberry Mousse Cake

Children love this cake because it is pink and pretty, and it is just like an ice cream treat.

Serves 4–6

15-ounce can
strawberries in syrup
1 tablespoon powdered
gelatin
6 ladyfingers or slices of
sponge cake

3 tablespoons strawberry
conserve
scant 1 cup crème fraîche
scant 1 cup whipped
cream, to decorate

1 Strain the syrup from the strawberries into a large heatproof pitcher. Sprinkle on the gelatin and stir well. Stand the pitcher in a saucepan of hot water and stir until the gelatin has dissolved.

2 Set aside to cool, then chill in the fridge for just under 1 hour, until beginning to set. Meanwhile, cut the sponge cake in half lengthwise, if using, and then spread the cut surfaces or the ladyfingers evenly with the strawberry conserve.

3 Slowly whisk the crème fraîche into the strawberry jelly, then whisk in the canned strawberries. Line a deep 8-inch loose-bottom tart pan with nonstick baking parchment.

4 Pour half the strawberry mousse mixture into the pan, arrange the sponge cake or ladyfingers over the surface and then spoon on the remaining mousse mixture, pushing down any sponge cake which rises up.

5 Freeze for 1–2 hours until firm. Unmold the cake and carefully remove the lining paper. Transfer to a serving plate. Decorate with whirls of cream, plus a few strawberry leaves and a fresh strawberry, if you have them.

Lemon and Blackberry Soufflé

This tangy dessert is complemented wonderfully by a rich blackberry sauce.

Serves 6

grated rind of 1 lemon
and juice of 2 lemons
1 tablespoon powdered
gelatin
5 small eggs, separated
1¼ cups sugar
a few drops of vanilla
extract
1⅔ cups whipping cream

For the sauce
1½ cups blackberries
(fresh or frozen)
2–3 tablespoons sugar
a few fresh blackberries
and blackberry leaves,
to decorate

1 Place the lemon juice in a small saucepan and heat through. Sprinkle on the gelatin and allow to dissolve, or heat further until clear. Allow to cool. Put the lemon rind, egg yolks, sugar and vanilla into a large bowl and whisk until the mixture is very thick, pale and really creamy.

2 Whisk the egg whites until almost stiff. Whip the cream until stiff. Stir the gelatin mixture into the yolks, then fold in the whipped cream and finally the egg whites. When lightly but thoroughly blended, turn into a 6-cup soufflé dish and freeze for about 2 hours.

3 To make the sauce, place the blackberries in a pan with the sugar and cook for 4–6 minutes until the juice begins to run and all the sugar has dissolved. Strain to remove the seeds, then chill until ready to serve.

4 When the soufflé is almost frozen, scoop or spoon out onto individual plates and serve with the blackberry sauce.

Index

Alfredo's Noodles, 157
Apples: apple and blackberry nut
    crisp, 222
  apple and hazelnut
    shortcake, 252
  apple and orange pie, 226
  apple foam with
    blackberries, 245
  apple soufflé omelette, 218
  apple strudel, 223
  baked stuffed apples, 211
  Eve's pudding, 215
  upside-down apple tart, 229
Apricots: apricot and almond
    jalousie, 242
  apricot and orange jelly, 235
  apricot mousse, 245
  quick apricot blender whip, 248
Asparagus: asparagus and cheese
    risotto, 170
  asparagus rolls with herb
    sauce, 131
  asparagus with tarragon
    butter, 25
Atholl Brose, 231
Avocados: Mexican dip with
    chips, 31
  with tangy topping, 33

Bacon: bacon and sausage
    sauerkraut, 115
  bacon koftas, 123
  ruby bacon chops, 106
  spinach, bacon and shrimp
    salad, 24
Baked beans: cowboy hot-pot, 139
Bakewell tart, 227
Bananas: banana, maple and lime
    crêpes, 223
  Boston banoffee pie, 247
  with rum and raisins, 221
  Thai fried bananas, 220
Barley and vegetable soup, 19
Bean curd: bean curd and crunchy
    vegetables, 133
  bean curd berry brulée, 249
  with ginger, chili and leeks, 140
Beans: bean purée with grilled
    vegetables, 130
  beans with tomatoes, 184
  Spanish green beans with
    ham, 185
  Provençal, 191
Beef: beef and mushroom
    burgers, 106
  beef casserole and
    dumplings, 111
  beef in Guinness, 100
  beef olives, 98
  beef paprika with roasted
    peppers, 99
  beef stew with red wine, 125
  beef strips with orange and
    ginger, 106
  beef Wellington, 102
  best-ever American burgers, 115
  Burgundy Beef, 122

cheesy pasta bolognese, 114
chili beef pizza, 163
cottage pie, 100
Hungarian beef goulash, 118
Peking beef and pepper
    stir-fry, 124
peppered steaks with
    Madeira, 108
rich beef casserole, 110
roast with Yorkshire pudding, 98
sizzling beef with celery root
    straw, 119
steak, kidney and mushroom
    pie, 107
Stilton burgers, 111
sukiyaki-style beef, 117
Beet and apricot swirl, 15
Black bean and vegetable
    stir-fry, 143
Blackberries: blackberry and apple
    Romanoff, 251
  blackberry brown sugar
    meringue, 238
Blancmange, chocolate, 233
Blinis, smoked salmon and dill, 29
Bread: bread and butter
    pudding, 217
  brown bread ice cream, 236
  fruity bread pudding, 224
Broccoli: broccoli and chestnut
    terrine, 130
  broccoli and ricotta
    cannelloni, 146
  broccoli and Stilton soup, 11
  broccoli cauliflower gratin, 189
  penne with chili and, 149
Bruschetta with goat cheese, 33
Bubble and squeak, 127
Bulgur: bulgur and lentil pilaf, 174
  lemon bulgur salad, 172

Cabbage: cabbage with bacon, 200
  bubble and squeak, 127
  crunchy coleslaw, 203
  green lentil and cabbage
    salad, 138
Cabinet pudding, 215
Carrots: carrot and cilantro
    soup, 8
  lemon carrots, 179
Castle puddings with custard, 216
Cauliflower with three cheeses, 182
Celery root: purée, 195
  fritters with mustard dip, 29
Cheese: bruschetta with goat
    cheese, 33
  bubble and squeak, 127
  English ploughman's pâté, 36
  feta and roasted garlic pizza, 158
  four cheese, 161
  goat cheese salad, 201
  golden cheese puffs, 36
  nutty cheese balls, 129
  Parmesan and poached egg
    salad, 208
  pears and Stilton, 27
  ricotta and pinto bean pâté, 32

Stilton burgers, 111
Cheesecakes: baked, 243
  creamy mango, 246
  lemon, 252
Cherries: cherry syllabub, 232
  Kentish cherry batter
    pudding, 211
Chick-pea stew, 142
Chicken: Cajun chicken
    jambalaya, 75
  Caribbean chicken kebabs, 90
  chicken and ham pie, 95
  chicken biryani, 93
  chicken charter pie, 95
  chicken in creamy orange
    sauce, 85
  chicken in green sauce, 72
  chicken, leek and parsley pie, 94
  chicken parcels, 82
  chicken Stroganov, 91
  chicken tikka, 92
  chicken with lemon and
    herbs, 70
  chicken with peppers, 71
  chicken with red cabbage, 73
  chili chicken couscous, 88
  Chinese chicken with cashew
    nuts, 78
  Chinese-style chicken salad, 79
  cock-a-leekie soup, 14
  coq au vin, 87
  coronation chicken, 77
  Creole jambalaya, 175
  golden Parmesan chicken, 71
  Hampshire farmhouse quiche, 94
  honey and orange glazed, 74
  Italian chicken, 74
  Maryland salad, 199
  minty yogurt chicken, 84
  Moroccan chicken couscous, 75
  Normandy roast chicken, 86
  oat-crusted chicken with sage, 85
  roast chicken with celery root, 70
  simple chicken curry, 92
  sticky ginger chicken, 84
  stoved chicken, 73
  tandoori chicken kebabs, 78
  Thai-style chicken soup, 16
  Tuscan chicken, 81
Chili beans with basmati rice, 136
Chinese crispy seaweed, 192
Chocolate: chilled chocolate
    slice, 250
  chocolate blancmange, 233
  chocolate chestnut roulade, 239
  chocolate date torte, 240
  easy chocolate and orange
    soufflés, 212
  iced chocolate and nut
    cake, 237
  rippled chocolate ice cream, 244
Clementines in cinnamon
    caramel, 238
Cock-a-leekie soup, 14
Cod: baked fish Creole-style, 61
  Cajun spiced fish, 63
  cod Creole, 51

cod with spiced red lentils, 57
crunchy-topped cod, 50
fish and chips, 41
Coffee jellies, 240
Collard greens: Chinese crispy
    seaweed, 192
Coq au vin, 87
Corn and shellfish chowder, 9
Corn: corn and shellfish chowder, 9
  corn and bean tamale
    pie, 141
  Kansas City fritters, 37
  Thai-style corn soup, 14
Corned beef and egg hash, 114
Cornish hens: Moroccan spiced
    roast, 88
  pot-roast Cornish hen, 87
  spatchcocked deviled Cornish
    hens, 72
  spatchcock of Cornish hen, 93
  with grapes in vermouth, 82
Cottage pie, 100
Country cider hot-pot, 80
Couscous: minted castles, 175
  root vegetable couscous, 168
Crab: crab and Parmesan
    calzonelli, 166
  egg and tomato salad with
    crab, 26
Cranachan, 231
Crème caramel, 241
Creole jambalaya, 175
Crêpes: banana, maple and
    lime, 223
  crêpes Suzette, 221
Cucumber and dill,
    Scandinavian, 205
Curries: chicken tikka, 92
  curried eggs, 134
  curried lamb and lentils, 120
  curried parsnip soup, 13
  Indian curried lamb
    samosas, 112
  Kashmir coconut fish curry, 62
  simple chicken curry, 92

Damask cream, 232
Dim sum, 35
Dip, Mexican, with chips, 31
Duck: duck, avocado and berry
    salad, 79
  duck breasts with orange
    sauce, 86
  duck with chestnut sauce, 89
  duck with Cumberland sauce, 77
  mandarin sesame duck, 84

Eggplant: eggplant and red pepper
    pâté, 128
  eggplant and shallot
    calzone, 167
  eggplant baked with
    cheeses, 187
  eggplant pilaf, 177
Eggs: curried eggs, 134
  egg and tomato salad with
    crab, 26

Eve's pudding, 215

Fennel: baked fennel with
    Parmesan cheese, 188
    fennel and orange salad, 207
Fish and seafood, 40-69
    Cajun spiced fish, 63
    fish and chips, 41
    fish balls in tomato sauce, 50
    fish goujons, 54
    fish soup, 18
    golden fish pie, 64
    Mediterranean fish stew, 58
    spicy fish Rösti, 46
Fish cakes, 65
    tuna and corn fish cakes, 50
    tuna fishcake bites, 61
    beans Provençal, 191
Fritters, Kansas City style, 37
Fruit: Chinese fruit salad, 242
    emerald fruit salad, 249
    bean curd berry brulée, 249
    frudités with honey dip, 246
    summer berry medley, 236
    summer pudding, 234
    warm autumn compôte, 218

Gingerbread upside-down
    pudding, 225
Gooseberries: crunchy crumble, 225
    gooseberry and elderflower
    cream, 230

Haddock: Kashmir coconut fish
    curry, 62
    and broccoli chowder, 14
    special fish pie, 64
    with parsley sauce, 40
    see also Smoked haddock
Hake, Spanish-style, 54
Ham: ham and mozzarella
    calzone, 167
    ham, pepper and mozzarella
    pizzas, 160
    pasta carbonara, 147
    Waldorf ham salad, 201
Hampshire farmhouse flan, 94
Herrings: with mustard sauce, 41
    pickled, 40
Hoki: fish balls in tomato sauce, 50
Honeycomb mould, 233

Ice cream: brown bread, 236
    mango, 243
    rippled chocolate, 244
Irish stew, 101

Jerusalem artichoke soup, 11

Kedgeree, 176
    mixed smoked fish, 53
Kidneys, deviled, 25

Lamb: butterflied cumin and garlic
    lamb, 102
    curried lamb and lentils, 120
    five-spice lamb, 109
    Greek lamb pie, 113
    Greek pasta bake, 123
    Indian curried lamb
    samosas, 112

Irish stew, 101
    lamb and spring vegetable
    stew, 99
    lamb pie with mustard
    thatch, 107
    lamb with mint sauce, 103
    Lancashire hot-pot, 104
    Mexican spiced roast leg, 121
    Middle-Eastern lamb
    kebabs, 121
    oatmeal and herb rack of
    lamb, 101
    pan-fried Mediterranean
    lamb, 113
    Scotch broth, 21
    skewers of lamb with mint, 125
    spiced lamb bake, 122
    spiced lamb with apricots, 105
    Turkish lamb and apricot
    stew, 120
Lasagne, spinach and hazelnut, 148
Leeks: leek and parsnip purée, 192
    leek and potato soup, 21
    leek, potato and arugula soup, 8
    leek terrine with deli meats, 28
    leeks with mustard dressing, 178
Lemon: lemon and blackberry
    soufflé, 253
    lemon cheesecake, 252
    lemon meringue pie, 226
    surprise lemon pudding, 216
    warm lemon and syrup
    cake, 219
Lentils: green lentil and cabbage
    salad, 138
    lentil stir-fry, 136
Linguine with pesto sauce, 149
Liver: chicken liver and tomato
    salad, 199
    chicken liver pâté, 30

Macaroni and cheese with
    mushrooms, 151
Mackerel: kebabs with parsley, 66
    with gooseberry sauce, 40
    with mustard and lemon, 45
    with tomatoes and pesto, 44
Mandarins in orange-flower
    syrup, 232
Mangoes: creamy mango
    cheesecake, 246
    mango ice cream, 243
Mediterranean fish stew, 58
Mediterranean plaice rolls, 47
Mediterranean tomato soup, 17
Mediterranean turkey skewers, 89
Melon salad, minted, 38
Meringues: Austrian hazelnut
    pavlova, 241
    blackberry brown sugar
    meringue, 238
    floating islands in plum
    sauce, 214
    lemon meringue pie, 226
    Queen of puddings, 210
    raspberry meringue gâteau, 237
Minestrone with pesto, 12
Monkfish with Mexican
    salsa, 52
Moroccan fish tagine, 43
Mulligatawny soup, 23

Mushrooms: Chinese garlic
    mushrooms, 32
    garlic mushrooms, 39
    multi-mushroom Stroganoff, 132
    mushroom and pancetta
    pizzas, 165
    risotto with mushrooms, 168
    sautéed wild mushrooms, 194
    stuffed mushrooms, 26
    wild mushroom pizzettes, 159
Mussels: grilled garlic mussels, 34
    mussel and leek pizzettes, 159
    mussels with wine and
    garlic, 62
    tagliatelle with saffron
    mussels, 150
Navy beans: navy or white bean
    purée, 130, 195
    white bean soup, 18
Navy beans: broccoli and
    ricotta, 146
Nut patties with mango relish, 34
Oats: cranachan, 231
Okra fried rice, 170
Omelets: apple soufflé, 218
    soufflé, 127
    tomato omelet envelopes, 134
Onions: French onion soup, 12
    onion and Gorgonzola
    pizzettes, 158
    onion and Gruyère tart, 145
    stuffed onions, 187
Orange fool, Boodles, 235

Paella: Spanish seafood, 59
Pancakes, seafood, 52
Papaya and pineapple crisp, 219
Parsnips: curried parsnip soup, 13
    parsnips with almonds, 180
    spiced parsnip soup, 10
Pasta: cannelloni al forno, 157
    Greek pasta bake, 123
    pasta and chick-pea soup, 20
    pasta and dried bean soup, 19
    pasta and lentil soup, 20
    pasta bolognese, 114
    pasta bows with smoked
    salmon, 155
    pasta carbonara, 147
    pasta rapido with parsley
    pesto, 151
    pasta spirals with pepperoni, 154
    pasta timbales with apricot
    sauce, 239
    penne with broccoli and
    chili, 149
    salmon pasta with parsley
    sauce, 51
    with roasted pepper sauce, 152
    with shrimp and feta cheese, 156
    with spring vegetables, 147
    with tomatoes and arugula, 154
    with tuna and capers, 155
    see also Lasagne; Spaghetti etc
    chicken liver with Marsala, 30
Pâtés: eggplant and red
    pepper, 128
    English ploughman's, 36
    ricotta and pinto bean, 32
    smoked haddock, 24
Pavlova, Austrian hazelnut, 241

Peaches: chocolate amaretti
    peaches, 217
    peach and ginger pashka, 250
    peach Melba, 234
Peanuts: nut pilaf, 177
Pears: pear and blackberry brown
    Betty, 210
    pear and blueberry pie, 228
    pear and Roquefort salad, 204
    pears and Stilton, 27
    spiced pears in cider, 224
Peas: green pea and mint soup, 15
Pecan pie, Mississippi, 229
Peking beef and pepper stir-fry, 124
Pepperoni: pasta spirals with, 154
    pepperoni pizza, 165
Peppers: grilled mixed peppers, 126
    grilled pepper salad, 198
    grilled polenta with peppers, 169
    Mediterranean mixed pepper
    salad, 204
    pasta with roasted pepper
    sauce, 152
    pepper and potato tortilla, 141
    red pepper soup with lime, 13
    red pepper watercress
    parcels, 128
    stuffed peppers, 146
Pheasant: autumn pheasant, 91
    Normandy pheasant, 97
    pheasant with mushrooms, 83
Pilaf: eggplant, 177
    bulgur and lentil, 174
    nut, 177
    seafood, 67
    smoked trout, 57
Pita bread, salad-filled, 206
Pizzas, 158-67
Plaice: herb plaice croquettes, 53
    Mediterranean plaice rolls, 47
    stuffed plaice rolls, 66
Plums: plum and port sherbert, 248
    floating islands in plum
    sauce, 214
    plum and walnut crisp, 213
Polenta, grilled with peppers, 169
Pork: Breton pork and bean
    casserole, 112
    ginger pork with black bean
    sauce, 116
    golden pork and apricot
    casserole, 116
    pork loin with celery, 105
    pork satay with peanut
    sauce, 118
    pork steaks with gremolata, 110
    pork with mozzarella and
    sage, 109
    pork with plums, 104
    Ruby chops, 106
    Somerset pork with apples, 103
    stir-fried pork with lychees, 119
    stir-fried pork with mustard, 117
    Texan barbecued ribs, 124
Potatoes: Bombay spiced, 190
    bubble and squeak, 127
    Chinese potatoes, 140
    new potato and chive salad, 196
    potato and broccoli stir-fry, 142
    potato and spinach gratin, 145
    potato gnocci with sauce, 183

potatoes baked with tomatoes, 186
potatoes with blue cheese, 135
rosemary roasties, 184
salad with egg and lemon, 209
Spanish chili potatoes, 190
spicy fish rösti, 46
spicy jacket potatoes, 191
straw potato cake, 194
Swiss soufflé potatoes, 181
Tex-Mex baked potatoes, 189
watercress potato salad bowl, 196
Prosciutto, tagliatelle with, 156
Pumpkin: American spiced pumpkin pie, 228
New England pumpkin soup, 16
pumpkin soup, 10

Queen of puddings, 210

Rabbit: country cider hot-pot, 80
rabbit with mustard, 76
Raspberries: cranachan, 231
raspberry meringue cake, 237
raspberry passion fruit swirls, 246
Ratatouille, 179
with cheese croutons, 132
Red cabbage: braised, 178
with pears and nuts, 181
Red kidney beans: chili beans with basmati rice, 136
Red mullet: with fennel, 48
with tomatoes, 68
Rice: asparagus and cheese risotto, 170
baked rice pudding, 213
chicken biryani, 93
Chinese special fried rice, 172
Creole jambalaya, 175
fruited rice ring, 244
Indian pilau rice, 171
kedgeree, 176
lemon and herb risotto cake, 174
Louisiana rice, 171
mixed smoked fish kedgeree, 53
okra fried rice, 170
orange rice pudding, 222
red fried rice, 176
rice with seeds and spices, 173
risotto with mushrooms, 168
souffléed rice pudding, 214
Tanzanian vegetable rice, 173
tomato risotto, 169
Rigatoni with garlic crumbs, 153
Root vegetable couscous, 168
Runner beans: beans with tomatoes, 184

Salads: baby leaf, 202
Caesar, 197
Californian, 205
chicken liver and tomato, 199
chicory, fruit and nut, 206
Chinese-style chicken, 79
classic Greek, 208
crunchy coleslaw, 203
duck, avocado and berry, 79
egg and tomato with crab, 26

fennel and orange, 207
Frankfurter, 196
French goat's cheese, 31
goat's cheese, 201
green lentil and cabbage, 138
grilled pepper, 198
hot tomato and mozzarella, 25
lemony bulgur wheat, 172
lettuce and herb, 200
Maryland, 199
Mediterranean mixed pepper, 204
minted melon, 38
new potato and chive, 196
Parmesan and poached egg, 208
pear and Roquefort, 204
potato and Frankfurter, 196
potato with egg and lemon, 209
Russian, 203
salad-filled pita bread, 206
salad Niçoise, 197
Scandinavian cucumber and dill, 205
shrimp and mint, 44
smoked trout, 43
spinach, bacon and shrimp, 24
sweet turnip, 209
Thai shrimp, 63
tomato and bread, 207
tricolor, 38
tuna and bean, 198
Waldorf ham, 201
warm salmon, 48
watercress potato salad bowl, 196
Salmon: grilled salmon steaks with fennel, 67
salmon and avocado pizza, 164
salmon pasta with parsley sauce, 51
salmon rillettes, 30
salmon with herb butter, 58
salmon with spicy pesto, 69
salmon with watercress sauce, 47
sautéed salmon with cucumber, 49
spicy fish rösti, 46
warm salmon salad, 48
see also Smoked salmon
Sardines: grilled fresh sardines, 68
pan-fried garlic sardines, 55
Sauerkraut, bacon and sausage, 115
Sausage and bean ragout, 108
Scallops with ginger, 56
Scotch broth, 21
Sea bass en papillote, 55
Sea bream, Middle Eastern, 69
Seafood and fish, 40-69
seafood pancakes, 52
seafood pilaf, 67
spaghetti with seafood sauce, 59
Spanish seafood paella, 59
Sesame shrimp toasts, 35
Shrimp: chili shrimp, 56
garlic chili shrimp, 60
garlic shrimp in phyllo tartlets, 28
pasta with feta cheese and, 156
sesame shrimp toasts, 35
shrimp and mint salad, 44
Thai shrimp salad, 63

Shrimps, potted, 27
Smelt: deep-fried spicy, 60
with herb sandwiches, 45
Smoked fish kedgeree, 53
Smoked haddock: haddock and broccoli chowder, 14
kedgeree, 176
smoked haddock and potato soup, 23
smoked haddock pâté, 24
Smoked salmon: pasta bows with, 155
smoked salmon and dill blinis, 29
Smoked trout: pilaf, 57
smoked trout salad, 43
smoked trout with cucumber, 65
Sole: fish goujons, 54
goujons with lime mayonnaise, 46
Sorbet, plum and port, 248
Soufflé omelet, 127
Soufflés: easy chocolate and orange, 212
lemon and blackberry, 253
Spaghetti: with herb sauce, 150
with seafood sauce, 59
with tuna sauce, 148
Spinach: Arabian spinach, 137
creamy spinach purée, 195
Fiorentina pizza, 163
Greek spinach and cheese pies, 135
spinach and cheese dumplings, 37
spinach and hazelnut lasagne, 148
spinach and potato galette, 139
spinach, bacon and shrimp salad, 24
Split pea and bacon soup, 22
Split pea and zucchini soup, 17
Sprouting beans and pak choi, 133
Squash, baked with Parmesan, 131
Steak, kidney and mushroom pie, 107
Sticky toffee pudding, 212
Strawberries: Eton mess, 230
frozen strawberry mousse cake, 253
strawberries in spiced grape jelly, 248
strawberry and blueberry tart, 247
Sukiyaki-style beef, 117
Summer pudding, 234
Sweet potatoes with bacon, 186
Syllabub, cherry, 232

Tagliatelle: with Gorgonzola sauce, 153
with hazelnut pesto, 148
with prosciutto, 156
with saffron mussels, 150
Tandoori chicken kebabs, 78
Tangerine trifle, 251
Thai-style chicken soup, 16
Thai-style corn soup, 14

Tomatoes: fried tomatoes with polenta crust, 129

hot tomato and mozzarella salad, 25
Mediterranean tomato soup, 17
pasta with arugula and, 154
tomato and basil soup, 9
tomato and basil tart, 138
tomato and bread salad, 207
tomato and okra stew, 144
tomato cheese tarts, 32
tomato omelet envelopes, 134
tomato risotto, 169
Trifles: old English, 231
tangerine, 251
Trout: trout with hazelnuts, 42
trout wrapped in a blanket, 42
see also Smoked trout
Tuna: pasta with capers and, 155
salad Niçoise, 197
spaghetti with tuna sauce, 148
tuna, anchovy and caper pizza, 164
tuna and bean salad, 198
tuna and corn fish cakes, 50
tuna fishcake bites, 61
tuna with pan-fried tomatoes, 49
Turkey: crumbed turkey steaks, 80
Mediterranean turkey skewers, 89
turkey and snow pea stir-fry, 96
turkey hot-pot, 76
turkey pastitsio, 81
turkey spirals, 90
Turnips: sweet turnip salad, 209
turnips with orange, 180
Tzatziki, 206

Vegetables: chunky paella, 144
country vegetable soup, 22
Middle-Eastern vegetable stew, 193
pasta with spring vegetables, 147
pizza with fresh vegetables, 162
root vegetable couscous, 168
stir-fried with pasta, 152
summer vegetable braise, 193
Thai vegetables with noodles, 182
vegetable and bean curd kebabs, 126
vegetable ribbons, 184
winter vegetable hot-pot, 183
with lentil bolognese, 143
with tahini, 39
Venison: farmhouse venison pie, 97
pot-roast of venison, 83
venison with cranberry sauce, 96

White bean soup, 18
Wild rice with broiled vegetables, 202

Yorkshire curd tart, 227

Zabaglione, 220
Zucchini: zucchini and tomato bake, 185
zucchini en papillote, 137
with sun-dried tomatoes, 188

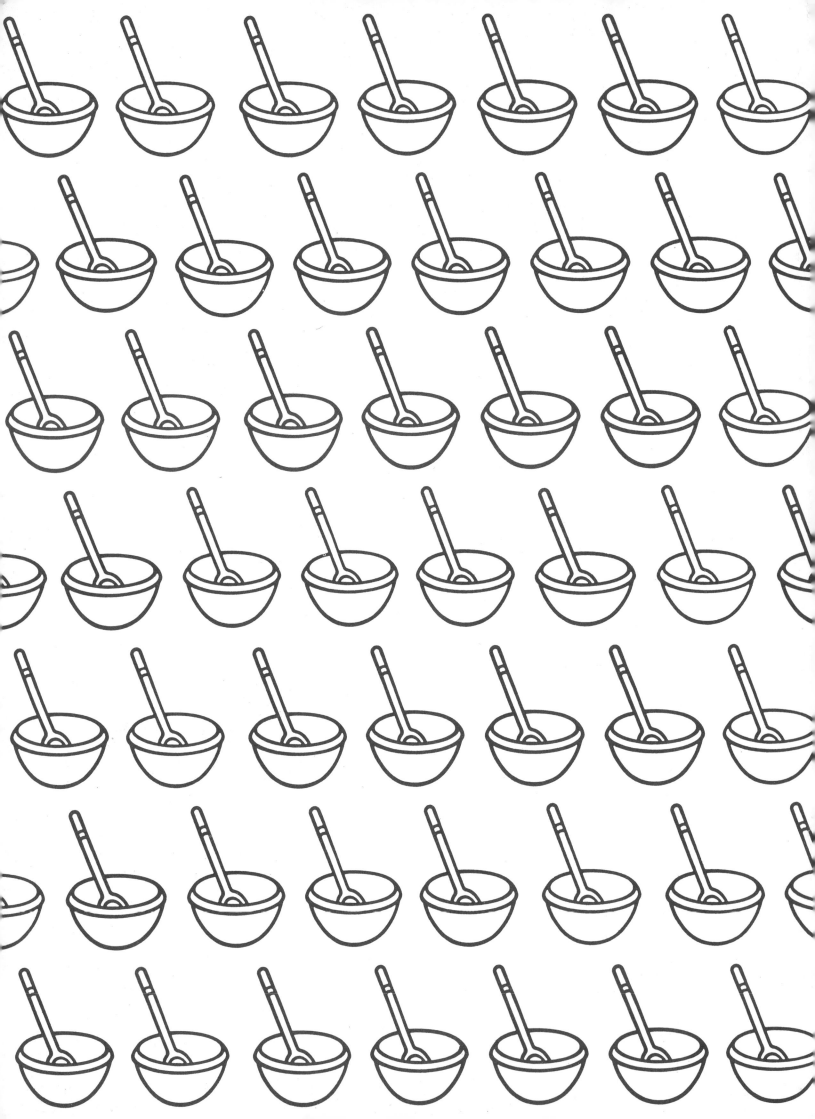